D0882420

REASON REVISITED

Reason Revisited

The Philosophy of Karl Jaspers

Sebastian Samay, O.S.B., Ph. D.

University of Notre Dame Press

American edition, 1971

UNIVERSITY OF NOTRE DAME PRESS
Notre Dame, Indiana 46556

FIRST PUBLISHED 1971 BY
GILL AND MACMILLAN LTD
2 BELVEDERE PLACE
DUBLIN I

and in London through association with the
MACMILLAN
Group of Publishing Companies

Jacket design by Alex Scott

Library of Congress Catalog Card Number: 72-160423

PRINTED AND BOUND IN THE REPUBLIC OF IRELAND BY THE
BOOK PRINTING DIVISION OF SMURFIT PRINT AND PACKAGING,
LIMITED, DUBLIN

Acknowledgements

The publishers wish to thank Insel Verlag
(Frankfurt am Main) for permission
to quote Rainer Maria Rilke's sonnet
'Römische Fontäne' from Volume III
of the poet's *Gesammelte Werke*,
published in 1930.

Contents

PART II: REASON AND SCIENCE

PART III: REASON AND PHILOSOPHY

Key to Jaspers' Quoted Works

AllgemPsych   *Allgemeine Psychopathologie* (Berlin, Heidelberg: Springer-Verlag, 1948), 5th ed., xvi–748 pp.

PsychWeltansch   *Psychologie der Weltanschauungen* (Berlin, Göttingen, Heidelberg: Springer–Verlag, 1954) 4th ed., xiii–486 pp.

Ph I   *Philosophie* (Berlin, Göttingen, Heidelberg: Springer–Verlag, 1956), 3rd ed., volume I, 'Philosophische Weltorientierung', lv–340 pp;

Ph II   volume II, 'Existenzerhellung', 440 pp;

Ph III   volume III, 'Metaphysik', 276 pp.

Weber   *Max Weber, Politiker-Forscher-Philosoph* (München: Piper-Verlag, 1958), 2nd ed., 89 pp.

VuEx   *Vernunft und Existenz* (München: Piper-Verlag, 1960), 4th ed., 156 pp.

Desc   *Descartes und die Philosophie* (Berlin: Verlag Walter de Gruyter & Co., 1956), 3rd ed., 104 pp.

ExP   *Existenzphilosophie* (Berlin: Verlag Walter de Gruyter & Co., 1956), 2nd ed., 90 pp.

VdW   *Von der Wahrheit. Philosophische Logik,* volume I (München: Piper–Verlag, 1947), xxiii–1103 pp.

PGl   *Der philosophische Glaube* (München: Piper–Verlag, 1955), 4th ed., 131 pp.

EiP   *Einfuhrung in die Philosophie* (Zürich: Artemis–Verlag, 1950), 159 pp.

WiderV   *Vernunft und Widervernunft in unserer Zeit* (München: Piper–Verlag, 1952), 2nd ed., 71 pp.

RuAusbl   *Rechenschaft und Ausblick* (München: Piper–Verlag, 1958), 2nd ed., 432 pp.

Entmytholog   *Die Frage der Entmythologisierung* [Jaspers–Bultmann] (München: Piper–Verlag, 1954), 118 pp.

PuW   *Philosophie und Welt* (München: Piper–Verlag, 1958), 404 pp.

PGlangOff   *Der philosophische Glaube angesichts der Offenbarung* (München: Piper–Verlag, 1962), 536 pp.

Biographical Note

'In einem solchen Augenblick mag nichts so fern liegen wie die Vorstellung, dass das Leben, das sie führen, und das sie führt, die Menschen nicht viel, nicht innerlich angeht. . . . Doch war ganz deutlich in diesem siedenden Begehren eine quälende Ahnung des Gefangenwerdens, ein beunruhigendes Gefühl, eine nagende Vermutung, dass in dieser Welt die unwahren, achtlosen und persönlich unwichtigen Äusserungen kräftiger widerhallen werden als die eigensten und eigentlichen'.

ROBERT MUSIL, *Der Mann ohne Eigenschaften*

KARL JASPERS was born on 23 February 1883, in Oldenburg in north-western Germany, close to the coast of the North Sea. His father was the high constable of the district and director of a bank. Between 1893 and 1901, young Jaspers attended his native city's *Gymnasium* where the emphasis was on the humanities. After matriculation, he spent three semesters studying jurisprudence in Heidelberg and Munich, and later studied medicine in Berlin, Göttingen, and Heidelberg. He passed his state medical examination in 1908, and received his M.D. degree in 1909. He then started work as a voluntary assistant at the psychiatric clinic of the University Hospital of Heidelberg. In 1913 he became *Privatdozent* of psychology on the Philosophy Faculty under the professorship of Windelband, and in 1922 full professor of philosophy under the chairmanship of Rickert. Besides a few critical reports and some short articles on psychiatry and psychology, two important publications mark this period: *Allgemeine Psychopathologie* (1913), and *Psychologie der Weltanschauungen* (1919).

According to Jasper's own admission, the latter work marked the turn of his interests towards philosophy. Nevertheless, it was only after his appointment to full professorship on 1 April 1922, that he really began to assemble the methodological bases of his future philosophy.

This appointment found him, as he himself admits, 'philosophically unready'. His previous philosophical training was anything but formal. He never thought very highly of philosophy as taught by professional academicians. As universally valid doctrines, he found their teaching objectively indefensible, and as guidance in life, disappointingly indifferent. Whatever formation Jaspers possessed consisted rather in his own private readings of great philosophers: Plato, Plotinus, Spinoza, Kant, Hegel, Kierkegaard, Nietzsche. How extensive and intensive these readings were, would be difficult to judge. All through his career he professed to be a student of the history of philosophy, but he never cared much for a factual interpretation of historical texts. He regarded them as a 'heap of dead conceptual shells' if they were not accompanied by a 'living appropriation' of their underlying intention. His text-studies of other philosophers usually served to spark off his own trend of thought rather than to acquaint him with the objective thought of these thinkers.

With his 1922 appointment, he decided that his scientific publications should stop for the time being and except for a study on *Strindberg und Van Gogh* in 1922 and *Die Idee der Universität* in 1923 (both revisions of earlier manuscripts), he published nothing for ten years. He spent these years in studying, lecturing, and slowly preparing his first great philosophical statement. His classroom lectures met with mixed reactions. Some of his hearers found them 'uninformed and frivolous'; others found them 'fascinating'. His own department chairman, Rickert, often ridiculed him publicly.

Jaspers bided his time. His situation changed with the publication of his first major work. The three-volume *Philosophie,* which appeared in 1931 (copyrighted for 1932), earned him considerable critical acclaim. He was immediately recognised as an original thinker in his own right, and classified among the exponents of existentialism. All the explicit repudiations of this label on Jaspers' part, all his later publications which have tried to soften the heavy emphasis on Existence that characterised this first work, were insufficient to modify the public impression that he was a typical existentialist. His *Vernunft und Existenz* (1935), *Von der Wahrheit* (1947), *Vernunft und Widervernunft in unserer Zeit* (1950) were not enough to convince the public that Jaspers' insistence on the importance of personal authenticity was by no means to imply that philosophy should be arbitrary or subjectivistic. It has never been sufficiently recognised that beside the personalist note there is another, more communicative effort in his philosophy. Although this effort may not run along strictly logical lines, it is still an attempt to reconcile the existential and rational elements of thought.

Until his dismissal by the Nazi regime in 1937, Jaspers kept his chair of philosophy in Heidelberg, declining offers from Greifwald, Kiel, and Bonn. Forbidden to teach and to publish, he spent the war years in silence, but not in inactivity. He read a lot of Shakespeare and composed the manuscript of his monumental *Von der Wahrheit*. Immediately after the war, he was reinstated into his old office by the authorities of the occupying American Forces. Before accepting a call to the University of Basle in 1948, where he taught until his retirement in 1961, he had time to help Alfred Weber to re-open and re-organise the University of Heidelberg. Because of his generally poor and precarious health (due to a chronic cardiac condition), he was seldom willing to give guest lectures or to participate in philosophical congresses. But neither ill health nor advancing old age ever impaired his writing activities. Since the Second World War alone, there are close to a hundred different works, some of them books of considerable length, to his credit. I mention only a few important ones: *Nietzsche und das Christentum* (1946); *Unsere Zunkunft und Goethe* (1947); *Der philosophische Glaube* (1948); *Vom Ursprung und Ziel der Geschichte* (1949); *Einführung in die Philosophie* (1950); *Rechenschaft und Ausblick* (1951); *Lionardo als Philosoph* (1953); *Die Frage der Entmythologisierung* (1954); *Schelling: Grösse und Verhängnis* (1955); *Die grossen Philosophen* vol. I (1957); *Die Atombombe und die Zukunft des Menschen* (1958); *Vernunft und Freiheit* (1959); *Wahrheit und Wissenschaft* (1960); *Der philosophische Glaube angesichts der Offerbarung* (1962); *Nikolaus Cusanus* (1964); *Kleine Schule des philosophischen Denkens* (1965).

Jaspers' external bearing gave the impression of aloofness and distance. He knew that and regretted it. He blamed it partly on his physical debility, partly on his natural diffidence, a heritage of his native region. But those who had personal dealings of any length with him testified unanimously to a gentle inner warmth, and, above all, to a rare quality of complete genuineness about him. He never seemed to look for effect: he never charmed, but never frightened either. He listened with great attention to the people who consulted him, thought for a minute, and then spoke. What he said was always intensely Jasperian. He died in Basle of a stroke, on 26 February 1969.

A Way of Posing the Problem

EVERY philosophy is by nature also a philosophy of philosophy, or at least it ought to be. The moment a philosophy takes itself for granted, it gives the lie to its proudest claim of being a work of reason and repudiates its own nature as a rational inquiry. In short, philosophy must accept its critical burden. It must be accompanied by a constant awareness of what philosophy is. In order to attain this awareness of itself, philosophy must call itself into question, it must institute a self-trial, a self-examination.

This self-examination must be carried out by every philosophy in regard to itself. It must always be of the present time, contemporary. There are some philosophers who would like to cut corners and dispense with such an examination by pointing out that somewhere in the past philosophy has already examined itself, so that we already have the answers to the question of what philosophy is. One wonders. Is it possible to settle the question once and for all? Has not the image of the world, the cultural context, in which past philosophies examined themselves and found their answers, undergone some profound changes, so that the question should or could be stated differently today?

Today's cultural climate in which philosophy and philosophical reason have to examine themselves is profoundly marked by the development and resounding success of the positive sciences. There is hardly a day that passes without a new scientific discovery. With great refinement of method, scientists penetrate deeper and deeper into the nature of the infinitely small and the infinitely large. They explore the space around this planet; lay open the secret workings of life; gather information about man's psychic processes; plan, predict, and alter the economic and political development of large areas of the earth. There is no doubt that man knows more and better than ever before and has every reason to expect that his knowledge will increase as time goes on. It is entirely just, therefore, that the self-examination of philosophy, which is as obligatory today as it was in the past, should take into account this scientific atmosphere. As Professor Jean Ladrière aptly points out, 'we must wonder whether in such a universe there is still a place for philosophy, whether science is not today the only possible expression of the ideal of rationality, whether it has not taken over for its own purposes, and according to its own methods, all that was actually rational in traditional philosophy,'[1] Much depends on the answers to these questions. Our whole outlook and our very concept of rationality is at stake. 'If science is the only field of activity, if the scientific method is identified with rationality, everything which does not depend upon this method becomes necessarily irrelevant for reason.'[2]

The current prestige of science and scientific rationality necessitates another radical rethinking of the status of science and, in relation to it, the status of philosophy. This is not happening for the first time in history. The presence of science has acted before now as a catalyst in provoking a new effort at self-clarification on the part of philosophy.

Mutatis mutandis, the same sort of examination took place in the philosophical self-awareness of the late twelfth and early thirteenth centuries. Historians of this period do not fail to call attention to the tremendous upheaval caused at that time in Western thought by the momentous arrival of Aristotle's writings about physical reality, the so-called *libri naturales,* that reached the Western scene mostly in Latin translations from Arabic sources. Philosophy, which up to that time consisted in a loose theologico-philosophic synthesis, where elements of revealed faith freely mingled with bits of Neoplatonic theories, now had to experience the impact of a coherent 'science' which could furnish a nearly complete rational world picture without involving the authority of supernatural revelation. This impact was to elicit a concerted effort on the part of thinkers to reflect seriously on the possibilities of 'unaided reason', and to see in what relation it stood to revealed truth, and how it could or could not be reconciled with faith. The towering representative of this appraisal was, of course, Saint Thomas Aquinas. Apart from a few dissenting voices, historians of Thomism generally agree that there is a genuinely philosophical synthesis in the works of Thomas, and that he tried the best he could to distinguish methodologically between particular sciences, philosophy, and the 'sacred science' of theology. His teachings in this regard became classics in Western thought.

Another important example of this philosophical *prise de conscience* provoked by the impact of science is the work of

Immanuel Kant. It is commonly accepted that one of the mainsprings of his reflections was his encounter with the classical
mechanics of Newton. He wanted to know the ultimate conditions that made this science possible. It was in order to discover
these conditions that he embarked upon his famous *Critique of
Pure Reason,* which in fact comprises three successive levels: the
critique of sensibility, the critique of understanding, and finally
the critique of reason. Together they form an extended answer to
the question: 'What can we know?' In the first two sections of
his *Critique,* Kant believed that he demonstrated that objective
science is limited to the knowledge of spatio-temporal phenomena. Objective knowledge, in other words, is restricted to the
synthetic elaboration by the intellect of the data furnished by
sense experience, according to the *a priori* forms of the intellect
itself. By contrast, the third part of the *Critique* set out to show
that metaphysics as a science is impossible because it claims to
treat of objects which cannot in any way be given in sense
experience. Such objects are merely ideas of reason, objects in
idea only, which we can *think of* perhaps, but cannot really *know.*
The task of critical reflection is to unmask this 'natural illusion'
of reason and to restrict the legitimate use of reason to the investigation of spatio-temporal objects. These findings have
haunted the consciousness of Western thinking ever since.

Closer still, we have the example of phenomenology, especially
that of Edmund Husserl. His work can also be regarded as an
attempt to determine the nature of reason in relation to science.
Philosophy, he insisted, must be strictly scientific and not merely
a string of opinions which may or may not be true. In fact,
philosophy must be the universal science that lays the foundations
and justifies all the other sciences and at the same time also carries
its own immanent justification. As Quentin Lauer, S.J., tells us,
this concept of philosophy combines the double ideal of a
Cartesian universal science and a Kantian sort of idealism. 'The
synthesis of these two ideals', says Lauer, 'requires that Husserl
admit nothing which cannot be the object of science and that
he accept no other source for the necessity which belongs to
scientific knowledge than consciousness itself. With Kant . . . he
will designate the subjective "faculty" in which necessity resides
by the name of reason. Thus, the ultimate source of science in
the strict sense must be reason; and if phenomenology is to be

an investigation of consciousness, then phenomenology which is to be a universal science must be an investigation of reason, in the sense that it determines how and when reason is operative.'³ Reason signifies the necessary constitution of consciousness, and *rational* means *scientific,* because 'to be scientific and to be constituted in reason are synonymous.'⁴ Husserl's originality consisted, however, in the fact that he sought to determine this rationality not apart from lived experience, but on the contrary, in the internal structure of experience itself, for he considered that the rational activity was only the explication of what was contained already in the experience of a *Lebenswelt*. In the words of Lauer, 'Husserl wanted to regulate the relationship of reason and experience according to a law which is intrinsic to both.'⁵ Of course, to discover such a law is not a simple affair, since a law like that should, by definition, combine certain qualities of reason and experience that are not easily reconcilable. 'Husserl will, on one hand, credit experience with an *immediate* contact with reality, but he will seek to suppress the contingency commonly assumed to be involved in immediacy. On the other hand, he will credit reason with *necessity* in its grasp of reality, but he will accept no mediation in reason's operation. The result, then, is a necessary experience and an immediate reason—which is but another way of saying a "rational experience" and an "experimental reason".'⁶ Whether this complete penetration of experience by reason is possible or not, whether Husserl suceeded in showing anything more than the formal necessity of structuring experience rationally: these are questions for discussion. What is clear is that he sought to determine the nature of reason and rationality in the context of science and scientific necessity. It is scarcely relevant to the point I am making here that he also thought that by determining the essence of science he automatically defined the essence of philosophy. My intention is simply to indicate by these examples that very often the philosophical self-examination of reason takes place in connection with a critical examination of what science is.

The philosophy of Karl Jaspers could also be considered according to this pattern. He too instituted a radical investigation into the nature of science and, in connection with it, into the nature of reason. In a certain sense, his thought could be looked upon as an immense contemporary critique of the sciences. This is not to imply, of course, that his philosophy is exausted by this theme, or even that this theme necessarily held the centre of his attention. His critique merely provided him with an occasion to rouse philosophy to a new degree of self-awareness. We may note that this intention was sufficiently indicated by the very plan of some of his writings. In *Existenzphilosophie* (1937), for instance, he introduced his treatment of truth by posing the problem of science and philosophy, and terminated it by a description of reason. The three conferences of Heidelberg (1950), comprised in *Vernunft und Widervernunft in unserer Zeit,* were even clearer in this regard. Under three successive headings he discussed the nature of science, the nature of reason, and then their possible distortions. In the introductory lines of this work he wrote: 'In the short hours before me . . . I would like to indicate that which is essential and all-embracing to philosophising, that which may once more provide a common meeting ground: reason. An indispensable aspect of reason is science. Today I will speak of that, tomorrow of reason itself, and the day after tomorrow of reason in conflict.' For him, the essential thing was to see in what relationship reason stood to science. He wanted to discover whether the operations of reason were really exhausted by science, whether or not scientific validity was a completely synonymous term for rationality.

Needless to say, he posed his questions differently from Kant and Husserl. Notably, he did not agree that it was sufficient to investigate 'pure' reason, or to see the necessary constitution of an impersonal consciousness in order to decide what man can or cannot think rationally. He insisted that one must also investigate the personal sources of man's thinking: his individual Existence.

Part I
Key Concepts

Introduction

The surprises in which Jaspers' works abound, and for which his readers must always be prepared, begin in fact with the very first sentence of his philosophy: 'What is Being?'[1] It is not the question as such that one finds surprising, for that is as old as philosophy itself. The unusual thing about it is rather the place it occupies in the thought of Jaspers. Placing it at the very outset of his reflection, Jaspers seems to suggest that the question of Being is not only basic but also first in the order of philosophical inquiry. Other philosophers, those few who still bother to ask it at all, usually put it towards the end as the crowning theme of their reflection. In other words, Jaspers seems to begin with metaphysics, whereas others gradually lead up to it through a series of lesser considerations.

However, this unnatural order in Jaspers is only apparent. His concern with the metaphysical problem of Being takes a more personal and existential turn in the next few opening questions: 'What am I?' 'What is my authentic purpose?' This indicates that the consciousness of Being is inseparably bound up with the consciousness we have of our own existence in the world. Jaspers is interested in the problem of Being from the beginning, but he implies that any possible treatment of it must constantly keep in mind the situation of the questioner. In other words, he indicates that the basic question about Being is at the source of our philosophical inquiry, but not at the beginning of it.[2] The beginning is in man's situation from which he poses the question about Being. Consequently, a profitable meditation on the question of Being must at least have its start in the situation of the questioner, and a philosophy of Being must be accompanied by an analysis of this situation.[3] These two are inseparable in such a way that one cannot be treated adequately without the other. Indeed, 'whenever the question about the situation of man is posed, it always indicates an effort to know the human "plus" . . . Man is somehow ordained to something which belongs to him as his complement, perfection, transcendence, or whatever we may call it. In other words, *the question of human situation is always a metaphysical question*. It is a question about the position of his reality in the hierarchy of Being. Therefore, to know what he

3

truly is, he should be acquainted with Being as such, in order that he be able to determine his own place in the variety of beings.'[4] In short, man's being is such that it raises the whole question of Being.

But if it is true that the problem of the human situation is always a metaphysical question, it is equally true in reverse; that is, that *the metaphysical problem of Being is an existential question.*[5] As a rule, man philosophises not merely in order to glean a few ideas about the supposedly basic feature of everything that is, but to achieve a more authentic existence in himself. He is interested not only in the theoretical aspects of knowing but also in its edifying, ethical value. He is animated by a secret passion for more truth and more being. He is aware of the fact that in his actual situation he is not all that he could be. He realises that existence is more or less a possibility for him, rather than a possession with which he is endowed by nature.[6] He is aware of some possibilities of selfhood offered to him by the plentitude of Being. 'The central point of philosophising is first reached in the awareness of potential existence.'[7] The thinker undertakes a systematic inspection of Being not merely because he wants to *know* more, but because he hopes that in the limitless horizons of being revealed by his reflections he can *be* more. He seeks to understand his condition expressly for the purpose of expanding beyond it. In short, Jaspers holds that the ethos of metaphysics is not purely contemplative but is coloured by existential interests. This means that in posing the question concerning Being we are also directed towards the being that is ours, and that in striving for a greater awareness of reality in general we must also strive for a greater clarity about our own reality.

This complementarity of metaphysics and philosophical anthropology implies, therefore, that the original question, 'What is Being?' really asks about the meaning of Being for us, *Sinn des Seins-für-uns.* What is the significance of reality as a whole for us who live in finite situations? Can we possibly rise out of these situations and attain to Being which is not limited or ephemeral? Can our particular acts of awareness encompass the totality of Being, so that our lives are securely anchored in it? These questions form a part of what Jaspers calls 'the basic philosophical operation'.[8] The aim of this operation is gradually to free our minds from the fascination with particular beings and to sharpen our awareness of the contrast between the finitude of our condition and the magnitude of Being for which we are searching. Attempts to answer these questions slowly bring home to us the realisation that whatever we meet in our particular acts of knowledge is always only this or that being but never Being itself, Being 'in the sense of *goal* and *origin,* in which our whole life and all our thinking efforts could find rest.'[9] Gradually a desperate clarity spreads over our awareness that perhaps there are no comprehensive answers to the question of Being, no global theories of reality. Our vision moves in limited horizons and can never catch sight of Being as such, of Being in itself. We cannot rise to ultramundane heights from which to inspect the total panorama of reality. Jaspers firmly believes that 'we can secure no standpoint from which the closed totality of Being would be surveyable, nor any sequence of standpoints through whose completeness Being could present itself, even indirectly, as a whole.'[10] What precludes such direct encounters and total visions is precisely our being humanly situated, or, as Paul Ricoeur would say, 'the violent contrast between the immensity of the question and the narrowness of situation of the one questioning.'[11]

All in all, the original question about Being has a very definite existential dimension for Jaspers. But by the same token it also has a criteriological dimension. One can notice all along that the unrest which affects existence in the face of Being is identical with the unrest of reason. The same human finitude which deflects the problem of Being towards the problems of existence also deflects it towards the problems of knowledge, and raises questions about the scope of human reason. At one point, Jaspers immediately seconds his original metaphysical question with a question about knowledge. 'The question is: what is Being? The question to this question is: how can I and how must I think of Being?'[12]

Thus, for Jaspers the existential and the rational are two aspects of one and the same metaphysical concern for Being. These two aspects are sometimes so closely intertwined as to be almost indistinguishable. Though at different times he may emphasise one or the other of these aspects, his philosophy as a whole is marked by a consistent refusal to opt for the primacy of either.[13] He is neither an existentialist nor a rationalist, or rather, he tries to be both at the same time. As Jean Paumen points out (see note 13), Jaspers tries to harmonise the plenitude and intensity of existence with the transparence and lucidity of reason. The measure in which he succeeds in doing so is directly attributable to his efforts to ground both aspects in a metaphysical awareness of Being.

This effort places Jaspers' thought in the tradition of perennial philosophy. 'What is Being and how can I know it?' is a classical question of philosophy all through the ages. Indeed, 'what the history of thought reveals to be the primeval and perennial problems is that of the relation between mind and reality, between knowing and being. In contemporary language Jaspers speaks of it as the question of reason and existence; of the reason which Kant undertook to criticise, and the existence to which Kierkegaard bore witness.'[14] Perhaps it would be more correct to say that Jaspers poses the same problem of Being and reason as traditional philosophy, but that he poses it in the context of existence. As we shall see later, at one point in his career Jaspers explicitly affirmed that the philosophy of existence is merely the contemporary approach to perennial philosophy, which is essentially a philosophy of reason. The question of the relationship between reason and reality which past philosophies have asked in a more abstract fashion is now situated by him among the concrete issues of existence. In its broadest characterisation, philosophy is always somehow the quest for, and clarification of, Being through reason, but Jaspers makes us aware of the fact that this quest is undertaken by and for the sake of human existence, which wants to clarify itself in the light of Being.

The principal aim of this book is to investigate the concept of reason in Jaspers' philosophy. In order to give this problem its true place in the ensemble of his thought, we must, therefore, constantly keep in mind that the question of reason is essentially relative to the quest of Being; that it presents itself as a *Seinsfrage,* in both the metaphysical and the existential sense of the word. Contrary to Kant and even to Husserl, Jaspers does not believe that one can determine the nature, function, and scope of reason by a reductive analysis of the constitution of pure, transcendental subjectivity alone. One must also examine the personal source and soil of reason: man's historical existence. This existence may be affected with certain fundamental limitations that would alter radically the whole problematics of reason.

In order to enter into this problematics, it seems necessary first to clarify a few of Jaspers' key concepts, and to see if we can discover some of his central intuitions that govern the internal logic of his philosophy. I believe that the concept of *situation* or *situatedness* of existence is one such concept. The chapters of this Part I will, therefore, investigate this concept precisely in so far as it influences Jaspers' ideas on reason. This means that the interest of these chapters will bear primarily on the epistemological implications of human situatedness. In other words, we shall try to discover the fundamental *cognitive situation* of man, and to examine what consequences this situation has for our possible knowledge of Being. Our investigations will range far and wide over the field of Jaspers' theory of knowledge. In a certain sense, the whole of Part I could be regarded as a preliminary survey of Jaspers' thought, from which the dominant *Stimmung* and the basic trend of his philosophy should become apparent. Our survey will include some tentative analyses of the nature and genesis of consciousness, certain summary reflections on Jaspers' thought on objectivity and subjectivity, some notes on his ideas of immanence and transcendence, and finally a few indications of his idea of Being. I believe that the best method of getting acclimatised to the highly personal atmosphere of Jaspers' thought is to work ourselves into his basic terminology not by abrupt definitions and transpositions, which would hopelessly simplify the elusive character of his thought, but by a certain convergence of repeated considerations. Needless to add, this survey can in no way claim to be complete; and the clarification of much of what will be asserted here will have to be postponed for later parts of this book.

I The Subject - Object Dichotomy

As we have had occasion to remark, Jaspers usually begins his philosophising with the formal question, what is Being, but eventually he retraces his steps in order to show us how he came to pose the question in the first place. Although this question is 'original' and 'basic' to philosophy, it is not man's first question because philosophy itself is not man's first activity. Philosophy is rather at the term of a gradual (but not necessarily continuous) formation of man's awareness of reality. Long before asking philosophical questions, man goes through a series of pre-philosophical stages in his formative process. In other words, man does not start out as a metaphysician, but he can gradually become one through a series of changes that take place in his consciousness. Through this formative process he moves from the state of an almost unconscious physical event in the world, which is scarcely more than a process of impersonal natural forces, through various degrees of consciousness to a pitch of self-awareness, which includes the awareness of Being as such.

Although Jaspers is miserly with explanations of his ideas about the original emergence of consciousness in man, he manages to imply that the pre-philosophical stages of this emergence are decisive for philosophy. His reticence may be due to his belief that consciousness is an absolutely primitive fact that cannot be reduced to anything else. It is especially impossible to observe directly how the unconscious turns into consciousness in man, because the moment we advert to it, we are already on this side of the line that divides them: 'the unconscious exists for us the way it becomes conscious.'[1] Nevertheless, Jaspers is eager to throw as much indirect light on this *Urphänomen* as possible, for he considers that the kind of consciousness man has will largely set the limits of what he will or will not be able to do in philosophy.[2]

POSTIVITY

First, as a living corporeal being, man is a part of the psycho-physical totality which we generally designate with the term,

8

Nature. Jaspers calls it *Dasein*.[3] Stressing the etymological side of the word, he means to indicate that Dasein is the factual mode of existence of something that is situated in space and time. In a general sense, Dasein or Nature is the empirical domain of what is already given, already 'there', well-rounded and positive. Comprehensively, we could term it the realm of facticity or positivity. Inasmuch as man belongs to this domain, in so far as he is a child of Nature and a homogeneous part of the positive world, his being is characterised by a striking absence of questioning. On this level, man is more like an 'event' (*das Geschehende, das Vorkommende*), than the actor or engineer of his own destiny.[4] He can afford to live at ease in the sheltered security of familiar evidences and to repose in soft somnolence because benevolent mother Nature lends perfection to his vital processes and carries him on the crest of infallible natural laws and life-cycles. To be sure, the very fact of living implies for man a certain number of tensions, drives, desires, that seek resolution and fulfilment in spontaneous exchange with the external world; but their satisfaction does not call for anything that is not in some way accessible in the world, in Nature itself. Things we need for our bodily welfare are there in palpable presence and obedient plasticity to be fashioned and assimilated by us; people are there with whom we can share our vital interests and secure a common future; even laws, customs, institutions, which we inherit, into which we are recieved, which become a 'second nature' to us, are there. Given the happy balance of these commodities, man's empirical being can know the happiness and perfection of occasional satisfaction.[5] During these moments of fulfilment, Dasein is overflowing with the innocent joy of 'just being here'. Pure and positive Dasein is the image of triumphant and jubilant life without obstacles. Pure and positive Dasein is perfectly 'at home' in the world and in no way looks beyond it; it is entirely mundane even in its orientation.

THE RISE OF CONSCIOUSNESS

But Jaspers shows immediately that this seemingly blissful situation is fraught with unrest and inarticulate questioning. He points out that Dasein is charged with ambiguities from both the existential and the cognitive points of view. Both of these am-

biguities can be crystallised around two expressions frequently
used by Jaspers: *Daseinsbewusstsein* and *Zeitdasein*. As Dasein,
man is 'there' as an unbroken part of the great 'there is'. But the
point is that this Dasein also conceals a privileged centre, a point
of consciousness, in virtue of which man can become *aware of
his being there,* and in fact of his *being there in time.* In other words,
the moment of awakening from positivity brings for Dasein the
awareness of its situatedness and transiency.[6] This is the moment
when consciousness breaks the harmony of the immediate and
interrupts life's contentment and charm with phantom forecasts
of the future. Man is shocked into realising that what he would
like to be his lasting presence is only a temporary being-there,
a process, the beginning and end of which disappear in the
obscurity of an irrecoverable past, an uncertain future, and a
certain death. Finding himself between beginning and end, man
begins to ask about the beginning and the end.[7] Anguished by
the fugitive nature of his own being, he would like to anchor it
in permanent reality, in 'Being that does not simply disappear'.[8]
He begins to search for something that would account for and
lend purpose to his temporal life.

All this amounts to saying that, when all is said and done,
pure empirical Dasein does not really exist as such. It means that
the state of perfect harmony and continuity between man and
Nature, with no rupture or distinction between them, is only a
supposition, an imagined lower limit of human existence, a sort
of paradisiacal myth of man's original union with the world. It
is a myth because in point of fact this union is never so entirely
innocent and questionless (*fraglos*) as to be altogether unconscious.
There is an unrest in man's Dasein that is like an *implicit* or lived
consciousness. In other words, man's mode of existence, even in
its supposedly empirical dimensions, is already more than a
factual being-there[9] since it can and does erupt in sudden acts
of awareness of being-there. Manifestly, then, even man's original
presence in the world is different from the simple presence of a
thing among things. It is rather a restless and unstable presence,
because it cannot find itself in what is already given and positive.
Its intent points beyond its purely factual existence. What at a
later stage will become a question, is already inscribed in man's
being-there as an unrest and an impulse.[10] It is this unrest that
ruins his repose in thing-likeness.[11]

When this inarticulate inner unrest erupts into *explicit* awareness, the situation of man in the world changes. There is a difference between actually being in the world and realising that one is in the world. In the words of Merleau-Ponty, 'would I know that I am caught up and situated in the world, if I were truly caught up and situated in it? I should then merely *be* where I was, as a thing, and since I know where I am and see myself among things, it is because I am a consciousness, a strange creature which resides nowhere and is present everywhere in intention.'[12] This does not mean, of course, that through consciousness man can escape his situatedness altogether, but it does mean that he can confront it and question it from an infinite number of other situations. Consciousness gives him the flexibility to do so, and this flexibility already sets him apart from mere Dasein.

Although man sometimes tends to identify himself with Nature's course of events and to forget himself in this process, he has, nevertheless, the power of recognising that, while he is largely carried by events, he is also above them, that he is more than an inert particle of Nature; he is a conscious subject. For man to recognise that he is more than Nature, that he does not totally fade into his environment, means above all *the power to question,* the power to contest. Being a conscious subject signifies man's capacity for negating his complete kinship and complicity with Nature, his ability for detaching himself from his environment and for confronting it. Consciousness is like an awakening from the organic torpor of merely enduring one's being to the awareness of possessing it.

THE INTENTIONAL SPLIT OF BEING

With the emergence of consciousness the situation of man is altered without, however, losing its fundamental character of situation. The kind of undifferentiated symbiosis with his surroundings that characterises his pre-conscious, pre-interrogative condition is now changed into a *situation of confrontation.* Man's unstable alliance with things, which we globally refer to when we say that he is a subject, always tends to lift him out of and oppose him to his ambiance. Being thus directed upon a portion of the whole of which it was itself originally a precarious part, is an important aspect of man's subjectivity. Through this unique directional mode of being, man is irrevocably set apart from the being of things which are incapable of such directionality. However, this new mode of being is still one of situation. Because the tendency to split off from Nature (first manifesting itself as a mere unrest, later as a full-blown question) is *given to man,* or more accurately *given with man,* the resulting state of confrontation in which man finds himself at the emergence of his consciousness is truly a fundamental situation, and not a particular point of view that could have been assumed or left behind at will. Situations may change, but the situation of being in *some* situation remains.

In properly cognitive terms, this situation of confrontation is generally called *intentionality.* Intentionality designates the peculiar structure of conscious subjectivity which differs from simple Dasein in that it is essentially a *Gerichtetsein,* a relational being, which immediately implies a duality of terms and points to its correlate, the object. This is why Jaspers chooses to call this situation of confrontation the subject-object-dichotomy, *die Subjekt-Objekt-Spaltung.* He considers this split or dichotomy to be the basic condition of man's conscious existence which defines his most fundamental cognitive situation.[13] This dichotomy is verified in every act of consciousness and underlies all further acts of knowledge.

Reflection on this basic situation will prove decisive for the philosophical undertaking of Jaspers in many ways. Notably it will be decisive for the quest of authentic reality which, as has already been intimated, is sought by him as the 'Being which holds everything together, lies at the base of everything, as the Being from which everything issues.'[14] As a primordial situation from the cognitive point of view, the subject-object-dichotomy will predetermine the basic formal concepts, the general logical structure, and the main divisions of Jaspers' reflection. In a certain sense it will also forecast the task that reason will have to perform in this philosophical programme.

In order to indicate, at least in part, the nature and amplitude of this subject-object-dichotomy, the reader is asked to bear with the long direct quotations which follow, where Jaspers treats of this question explicitly:

That which we think, of which we talk, is always other than our-selves; it is that towards which we, subjects, are orientated as towards an object in front of us. When we make ourselves the object of our thought, we become 'other' for ourselves, yet, the same time, we are also present as the 'I-who-thinks' who accomplishes this act of thinking of itself. . . . We call this fundamental trait of our conscious life the subject-object-dichotomy. . . . We are always confronted outwardly or inwardly by objects, which occupy our consciousness. To use Schopenhauer's phrase: there is neither object without a subject, nor subject without an object.[15]

Everything I know, stands in the subject-object-dichotomy, is object for me, is a phenomenon and not in itself. . . . There is no object without a subject, nor a subject without an object. Whatever I experience, therefore, as being, is always situated in the whole of the subject-object-dichotomy, and not on the one side of it alone.[16]

The fact that I (the subject) am directed upon a thing (the object), considering it (intentionally), constitutes the prime phenomenon of conscious existence. 'Intentional' consciousness has something before itself to which it is mentally related in a manner incomparable to any other relationship in the world. The fact that it is absolutely common-place does not make this irreducible prime phenomenon any less puzzling. It cannot be clarified through anything else, rather itself is the medium of all clarification in the world.

It is a most encompassing medium, for nothing that is being for us can exempt itself from objectivity. Whenever we would like to force our way through it by 'intending' something beyond it, straightway we drag in what is outside, and in so far as we intend it, we make it somehow an object. We can designate nothing exterior to knowledge without thereby transforming it into an object of knowledge, and thus into an object among other objects. . . . Hence, everything that be-comes being for us has its side of objectivity: the thinkable and the unthinkable; the real and the unreal; the true and the false; the per-ceptual and the imaginary; the possible and the impossible. Whatever we think of is in some ways an object: numbers and figures; $\sqrt{-1}$ and the sum of all sums; atoms and electrons; formulae and equations; angels and centaurs; virtue and law.

Nor am I aware of myself, even for an instant, without having an object. . . . Hence comes the validity of the dictum: no self without an object, no object without a self. In the subject-object-dichotomy neither side exists without the other.[17]

When we ask what Being is, we have several answers to choose from: empirical reality in space and time; animate or inanimate matter; things and persons; tools and materials; thoughts that apply

to the real; cogent constructions of ideal objects, as in mathematics;
phantasms of the imagination—in a word, objectivity in general.
Whatever being I find in my situation is an *object* to me.[18]

Whenever knowledge gets hold of something, it turns out that the
thing I know is not Being in itself, and not being that I am myself.
There is no rest for knowledge in any determinate being. Rather, it
is as if Being drew back from our eager will-to-know, and only left
remnants and traces of itself in our hand in guise of objects. No known
being is Being *as such* ('Kein gewusstes Sein is das Sein').[19]

These passages constitute a rich source of interpretation. In one
form or another they contain nearly all the principles necessary
for the understanding of Jaspers' philosophy as a whole. For this
reason, one must return to them time and again, but for the
moment our consideration has to limit itself to underlining a few
important general points that can be gathered from these quotations. Some of these points will receive fuller treatment in later
chapters, while others will merely be touched upon when the
handling of particular questions requires it.

In the first place, it can be asserted without fear of contradiction
that the phenomenon of subject-object-dichotomy constitutes
the point of departure for Jaspers' reflection. The general task
that Jaspers sets himself is to find out all the implications of the
fact that our consciousness is intentional, i.e. it manifests the
fundamental duality of subject and object, of noesis and noema.
This duality makes him reflect over and over again on the limits
and possibilities of philosophy itself. Is philosophy possible as a
science of Being *qua* Being, since from the very first moment of
explicit consciousness we can only intend this or that particular
being, which becomes an object *for us* by the very fact that we
intend it? Is the grasp of Being as one and whole within the
competence of our knowing ability, since our acts of intending
split reality into at least two great areas: the subject and the object?

Our intentional acts of knowing are always limited, specific,
and partial. What such acts encounter is never Being as such,
never Being as a whole, but only multiple aspects and appearances
of Being. We know Being only as it manifests itself in object-
beings. It seems that, in order to grasp the Whole, consciousness
should somehow overcome its own definiteness and envelop the
scissions which itself creates. It will be for further philosophical
thought to judge whether and in what sense this might be possible.

For the moment, the subject-object-dichotomy only indicates an irreparable rupture in Being. Short of lapsing into total unconsciousness, there seems to be no way of eliminating the opposition between subject-being (*Subjektsein*) and object-being (*Objektsein*), or of uniting them under some sort of being-in-itself (*Ansichsein*). These are three inseparable and yet irreducible poles of Being. If I were to reduce everything to being-in-itself, I would thereby transform it into an object-being. If I were to reduce everything to object-being, I would be doing something contradictory, since objects exist only for a subject. Nor can I reduce everything to subject-being, since a subject is by nature relative to something other than itself.

Thus the awareness of the subject-object-dichotomy mediates for us the first great experience of what Jaspers calls the 'torn state of Being for us', *die Zerrissenheit des Seins für uns*.[20] Whatever we light upon in our cognitive situation are only multiple phenomena of Being, only objects for us. It is as if through our consciousness we had fallen out of reality.[21] We are searching for the ground of reality, for absolute Being, which is the source and end of all, but we find only remnants and vestiges of Being which are doubly relative. 'Every object, every thought content stands in a twofold dichotomy, first in reference to me, the thinking subject, and secondly in reference to other objects.'[22] Moreover, *qua* phenomena, objects are also relative to Being-in-itself. One must get accustomed to the fact that from the beginning 'object' and 'phenomenon' will be used by Jaspers almost synonymously. He means the same relative thing by both terms: in the one case as opposed to the subject, in the other as opposed to Being-in-itself.

THE THREE BASIC AREAS OF PHILOSOPHY

As a good Kantian, however, Jaspers immediately declares that the notion of Being-in-itself is an inaccessible limit-concept, an abortive attempt to think of something as it would be independently of its appearance to a subject. Abortive, because the very act of intending it immediately turns Being-in-itself into an object and thus into an appearance for us.[23] This amounts to saying that we can have no concept of Being as such; we can only have concepts of objects. Just like Kant, Jaspers finds it

3

necessary to postulate the *existence* of Ansichsein but at the same
time to deny its *knowability*. It remains a source of an unresolved,
and perhaps unresolvable, paradox in the thought of both men
that with one hand they take away the self-consistency of objects[24]
and relegate them to the rank of mere appearances, while with
the other they cross out the conceivability of Being-in-itself
which appears in objects. Thus, for them, the relative that can
be known is unsubstantial, while the absolute that exists in
itself is unknowable. The only cognitive value Jaspers admits
for the concept of Ansichsein is that through it we are able to
contest the absoluteness of objects or whatever can be known
objectively.[25]

This unresolved paradox, however, does not prevent Jaspers
from exploring methodically, as much as possible, the domain
of phenomena or object-beings which constitute the positive
world, the same world that positive science investigates. The
fruit of this exploration is the first volume of his *Philosophie*,
which Jaspers entitles *Weltorientierung*, world-orientation. The
work is not an object theory of the physical universe, not even
a unitary cosmology, but an effort to think philosophically about
the whole of object-being, the world, which in itself, however,
is not an object. To philosophical reflection it is not even a
compact whole. Jaspers distinguishes at least four irreducible
spheres or areas in it: matter, vegetative life, sensitive life, and
spirit.[26] He considers those four areas to be discontinuous with
each other. Kurt Hoffman rightly points out that 'Jaspers' primary
concern is to resist the tendency of making one of the spheres
absolute and to subject the others to its logic and laws. Philosophy
must avoid the pitfalls of materialism and biologism as well as
those of pan-psychism and radical existentialism. Physics, biology,
psychology, and the humanities have no common criterion and
cannot be ordered to any one standard. Each order fails if it
pretends to be the one true order. The totality of the universe is
neither a possible object of a universal science, nor can it become
unified by systematic philosophy.'[27] Thus, the essential task of
world-orientation is not to form unitary theories about the
world, but to seek out the definite limits of objective science in
order to designate those points where philosophical rationality
must take over from scientific rationality and transcend it in the
exploration of reality.

Since to intentional consciousness Being must necessarily appear under the guise of objectivity, at each moment the two domains of intentionality and objectivity coincide with each other. Any effort to transcend the field of objectivity by 'intending' something beside or beyond it only enlarges the scope of object-being encompassed by intentional consciousness. This hold of objectivity on our knowledge is so universal that it extends even over the grasp of subjectivity or the self. In order to grasp the 'self' as being, we must make it into an 'other'; that is, we must grasp it in object-categories as an *object for* itself. That this object-bound knowledge is ultimately doomed to failure, is a favourite point with Jaspers. The subject, apprehended in object-categories, is not a subject as such but only its objectified appearance. For this reason Jaspers proceeds to construct a whole series of non-objective 'categories' which he thinks would be more suitable for the description of subjectivity. The second volume of his *Philosophie* is, in fact, the result of this endeavour. However, significantly enough, he does not call it rational psychology or philosophical anthropology but *Existenzerhellung*; for what he wants is not to provide an objective doctrine on selfhood but to point out with the aid of his subjective categories the definitive limitations of the objective approach to selfhood, and thereby to shed some indirect light on its original mode of existence.[28]

With Objektsein and Subjektsein we have the first two relative modes of Being and the first two formal concepts of a possible philosophical reflection. Ansichsein, as we saw, is cognitively inaccessible and stands for that absolute and transcendental unity of reality which both precedes and follows the break-up of subject and object. According to Jaspers, it is to this unity that man seeks to return from his basic situation of subject-object-dichotomy by way of thinking. Although this dichotomy will remain the permanent situation of man's thinking existence, the *aim* of his knowing efforts is to transcend this rupture and to return to the unity of reality.[29] The description of these transcending efforts constitute the subject matter of the third volume of Jaspers' *Philosophie*. The title is symptomatic: *Metaphysik*—not ontology, for Jaspers does not pretend to fix the structure of reality in general in a universally cogent science of Being,[30] but wants, with the aid of methodical thinking, to initiate a personal experience of the unconditioned unity and inseity of Being in Transcendence.

The Kantian inspiration of this démarche is unmistakable. It was the transcendental philosophy of Kant that first exposed in a systematic way that, contrary to Descartes, neither the subject nor any 'thing-in-itself' can ever become the adequate object of knowledge. The subject, because as such it is the one *who* thinks, cannot be the object thought *of*; and if it is thought of, it no longer is the subject as such but its objective appearance. Similarly, anything else that is to exist for us must appear to us as an object. The 'in-itself' is inaccessible to intentional thinking. The limits of this thinking coincide with the limits of the realm of objective appearances. Paradoxically, this concept of limitation triggered a larger and more inward consciousness of Being, and opened the way for new modes of thinking. Having become aware of the phenomenal nature of object-beings, philosophical consciousness turned to investigating the transcendental forms of appearances which reside in the knowing faculties of the subject. Kant thus stands at the onset of a powerful current of *subject-consciousness*, which continues to gain prestige down to our own days. Nevertheless, Kant's philosophy still remained a possible science; and his doctrines concerning the structure of the knowing subject still make the claim of objective, scientific exactitude. It was not until the scorching critiques of Kierkegaard, who blasted the pretensions of scientific rationality, that this subject-consciousness achieved its present-day level. His concept of 'existence' was to reveal the frightening depth and exceptionality of the individual subject which resists all determinate knowledge and all placid structuration of selfhood. Tracing thought out of its objectification back to this dark, inward origin which is existence, Kierkegaard has accomplished the 'Copernican revolution' in the manner of our consciousness of Being, which Kant had started. Jaspers himself operates in the shadow of these two thinkers. Keeping them in mind, he nevertheless tries to surpass both by overcoming the latent objectivism of the one as well as the irrational subjectivism of the other.

REMARKS

At this point several pertinent questions could be posed in regard to the possibility, nature, or simply the meaningfulness of philosophical reflection thus conceived. One can see, for instance, that for Jaspers philosophy issues from the experience of a basic split between man's consciousness and reality, and from there it proceeds with a single impulse in three different directions: the self, the world, and transcendence. But what we would like to see more clearly is where these directions will take us in the end. Do they converge on some unseen point so that by degrees the original cleavage will tend to repair itself; or do they, on the contrary, run farther and farther apart until the last hope of ever seeing them rejoined must appear illusory? Is there for Jaspers a privileged point in consciousness or in reflection where subject and object are one, in spite of their dichotomy, so as to constitute the image of Being in itself and for itself; or must such a point necessarily lie outside of consciousness which by definition seems to be the creation of cleavages? These are serious questions that must be answered eventually. Any attempt to do so at this early stage of our exposition, however, would be premature since we are not yet in possession of all the elements of an adequate answer. Notably our understanding of the Jaspersian use [31] of the terms 'object', 'subject', 'consciousness', 'selfhood', and so on, is still rudimentary. A greater precision for each of these terms is therefore indispensable.

Nevertheless, it is not difficult to guess how far-reachingly philosophy will be compromised by such a starting point as the subject-object-dichotomy and how many obstacles it will put in the way of further reflection. To say nothing of lesser problems, it will cause some grave difficulties in regard to the experience of unity. Somewhere along the line we will have to invoke this experience of unity, whose subject and object are thought to coincide, or to account for our transcendental awareness of Being (*Seinsbewusstsein*), the idea of which is again supposed to embrace both subjective and objective being. If, however, the prime fact of consciousness is the recognition of a fundamental duality or, more correctly, if consciousness *is* this very duality of subject and object, then where and how do we experience unity? If consciousness only comes about when duality is introduced, then should we not conclude that our experience of unity is fatally an unconscious or at least pre-conscious experience? Unconscious or even pre-conscious experience, however, is meaningful only for certain schools of psychoanalysis but very hard to conceive philosophically. Perhaps more basically than an experience of duality, consciousness is primarily an experience of unity. If that is true, Jaspers would have been better advised to take that as a prime factor of consciousness and a starting point of philosophy. He could have spared himself a lot of agonising problems, which perhaps are no problems at all.

II   Objects and Objectivity

THE quest for Being through reason which defines the ultimate task of philosophy suffers a first and major setback from the narrowness of the situation from which this quest must take its start. In properly cognitive terms, Jaspers calls this situation the subject-object-dichotomy. This dichotomy signifies that from the first moment of our conscious existence Being appears to us split into subject and object, and as soon as we try to grasp Being, it turns into an object-being.

The present chapter is intended as a further elucidation of this polarity between subject and object, considered here from the noematic side. We want to find out further what an object is. What sort of status does Jaspers ascribe to object-beings? What is there common between such diverse objects as 'instruments' and '$\sqrt{-1}$'? How does Jaspers characterise objects in general? What is objectivity for him? The manner of our presentation will by synthetic and summary in the sense that we shall try to establish the necessary features of *objectivity in general,* rather than to give detailed account of all the various modes and meanings of object-being that could be gathered from Jaspers' writings. Although an adequate phenomenology of his object-concept should describe such things as the sense-object, empirical object, object-construct, pragmatic object, etc.,[1] our treatment will pass over these distinctions in silence. For, different as these various modes of objectivity may be, they all have this in common that they can all become partially or fully constituted counterparts of an objective intention; in other words, they satisfy the requirements of objectivity in general and thus fit into the basic cognitive frame of the subject-object polarity.

Dufrenne and Ricoeur begin their commentary on this issue by distinguishing the meaning of *Gegenstand* and *Objekt,* two terms which Jaspers uses in treating the problems of objectivity. '*Gegenstand* is the object for a subject, the correlative of the activity of a consciousness, in the sense (both precise and enlarged) in which a *cogitatum* is always correlative to a *cogito*. . . . The *Objekt* is the object of an objective knowledge, that is, one that lays claim to rigorousness and universality. The first poses the very general problem of relationship between consciousness and being, or at least between consciousness and its object; the second poses the problem of the validity of knowledge, and particularly that of scientific knowledge.'[2] Unfortunately, the indiscriminate use Jaspers makes of these two terms scarcely substantiates this very neat distinction. There is very little or no regularity in his use that would permit us to think of *Gegenstand* as object for a subject rather than an object of objective knowledge, or to take *Objekt* for the object of scientific knowledge rather than the correlate of consciousness.[3] Apart from a few isolated instances, the two terms are synonymous for Jaspers. The only noticeable difference is in the frequency of their use in the two major works, *Philosophie* and *Von der Wahrheit*. In the former Jaspers writes more in terms of *Objekt,* in the latter more in terms of *Gegenstand* Nevertheless, this distinction is not entirely without interest. Although is is largely factitious in so far as it is attached to the use of these terms which Jaspers himself does not distinguish, it is nevertheless real in so far as it calls attention to the fact that the question of objectivity poses two different though not unrelated problems. As we shall see a little later on, scientific validity will be accorded to objects only after they have proved themselves objective as correlates of consciousness. Between object-being as a *cogitatum* and object-being as a matter of scientific knowledge there is no real break, but only an interval of added determinations. Consequently, the problem of object-being can temporarily be dissociated from that of the objectivity of knowledge by simply leaving aside these added determinations. For the sake of clarity, we too will try to separate these two problems though aware that this rather distorts the unity and continuity of Jaspers' thought, where these two themes intimately combine.

The following three sections will treat successively of *opposition, unity,* and *generality,* as the three basic features of object-being according to Jaspers. In each of these sections we shall first state the meaning of the feature in question in reference to object-being; then in a few remarks we shall indicate its consequences for the objectivity of knowledge, leaving the full epistemological implications to other chapters.

OPPOSITION

The chief characteristic of object-being is opposition. This first feature simply redefines the subject-object polarity which, as we know, is the basic condition of man's conscious existence according to Jaspers. An object is whatever enters into this polarity as the 'other', and 'stands opposite' the subject.[4] The subject in this case, of course, is man's consciousness because it is only in virtue of this consciousness that the polarity arises in the first place. On the pre-conscious level (as it is conjecturally reconstructed in retrospect from the state of consciousness) where man is thought to have existed in a state of thing-likeness, so to speak, there was no 'otherness' (*Anderssein*) since there was no rift in the homogeneousness and continuity of man with things. It was only by conscious thematisation that the other became other. With man's thematising consciousness something original has happened in the world; a new mode of being has been introduced which is no longer caught up in the tissue of mutual action-reaction relationships of like substances, but is able to represent to itself its own *vis-à-vis*.[5] Following a time-honoured usage, Jaspers calls this new mode of being intentionally,

Intentional consciousness is by nature the consciousness of an object, of an opposite. Therefore, it is necessary for the promotion of this consciousness that its counterpart, the object, be in some way or other affected by alterity, that it be exterior to the subjective act. Alterity and exteriority are secondary dimensions of the object's opposition. There is a passage of Jaspers in which both these dimensions are assumed and united in the aspect of objectivity in the sense of oppositeness. I quote it here in the original in order to show the sequence of ideas, suggested by the sequence of the German expressions themselves, which link objectivity with alterity and exteriority: 'Objektiv ist erstens das *Gegenständliche, das einem Ich als dem Subjektiven gegenüber-*steht. Das Gegenständliche ist das *Äussere* im Unterschied vom Inneren des Subjekts. Das Äussere ist das *Andere* und Fremde.'[6]

Opposition then is the first determination of object-being, and defines the very condition of possibility of intentional consciousness. 'I exist consciously only in so far as, aimed at something other, I come to be conscious of myself in opposition to it.'[7] Though one cannot agree with Maximilian Beck, who charges

that for Jaspers 'object-being *is exhausted* by the mere opposition
of subject and object' or that 'this very opposition *alone* constitutes
the characteristic of objectivity',[8] it can be granted that opposition,
alterity, or exteriority is fundamental in this regard; that there is
a primary accent on *gegen* in *Gegenstand*. The feature of opposition
is fundamental for Jaspers precisely because it will also have far-
reaching implications for objectivity in the other sense, the
objectivity of knowledge.

In every intentional act of knowledge, no matter what kind,
consciousness must be directed on something 'other than' its own
self. This is the meaning of the sentence quoted in the first
chapter: 'That which we think, of which we talk, is always other
than ourselves.' Opposition of subject and object and not their
coincidence, their tension rather than their reduction, will be
the basic and permanent condition of every objective grasp. Any
act of knowledge will be objective that will establish and maintain
this tension of subject and object. It is not difficult to see that
Jaspers is already moving away from the traditional conception
according to which in a fully constituted act of knowledge the
knower and the object known become identified. For him the
distance between subject and object, called into existence by
intentional consciousness itself, can never be bridged by any of
the acts of this same intentional consciousness. If for any reason
the opposition between subject and object were not established,
or if, once established, this opposition were somehow suppressed,
we would have either a blind and dull and indefinite sentiment
or else a mystical union, but never an act of objective knowledge.

As a last remark, we must briefly touch upon the question of
self-awareness and self-knowledge. The phenomenon of self-
awareness and the possibility of self-knowledge seem to contradict
the statement that consciousness must necessarily be object-bound.
While it is true that consciousness is basically intentional, it is no
less true that consciousness is also *reflexive*. It does not seem
impossible that the flow of intentionality should bend back and
discharge itself on the subject from which it issued. Consequently,
it should seem false to say that in every intentional act the subject
has to focus on something other than its own self.

Jaspers does not hesitate to endorse the possibility of reflexive
self-awareness, but he is careful to point out its limitations. First
of all he indicates that reflexivity is only a secondary phenomenon,

in the sense that it is consequent upon the direct awareness of
objects. He insists that there can be no self-awareness without the
awareness of some object.[9] Only by returning fron the object
can the subject become aware of itself. Moreover, far from contradicting intentionality, reflexivity prolongs it. Instead of
eliminating the characteristic duality of intentionality, reflexivity
transports it into the very subject itself. Now even the subject
is divided into two, inasmuch as it is an object for itself. The
'self', as the object of self-reflection, is 'other' than the subject
from which this reflection proceeds; it 'stands against' this subject
and, as such, is no longer the *source* of the conscious activity but
the *term* of it. In short, the alterity of the object is attenuated here
but not eliminated.[10] Reflexivity can never be complete, it can
never undo the polarity of intentionality, so that the intentional
distance between subject and object remains even in self-reflection.
All the same, here we are closer to the unity of subject and object
than in pure external reflection.

UNITY

The second basic feature comprises several cognate aspects of
objectivity which Jaspers sums up under the common term
'unity'. In view of what the term is supposed to signify, we might
question its aptness. In the passive sense the term is intended to
signify 'determinateness' or 'stability', while in the active sense
it is to stand for 'synthesis'.

In reference to object-being, unity designates the *qualitative
oneness* that a thing must display in order to become an object
for us. An object must be something determinate, and it is in this
qualitative oneness that the determination of an object is ultimately grounded. Jaspers considers this form of unity to be at
the root of all other forms of unity and determinateness.[11] We
distinguish 'one' object from 'another' by a certain break of this
unity either in perception or in thought. Thus, for instance, two
things that imperceptibly 'fade' into each other will appear to
us as one object; whereas two objects that were heterogeneous
on every point could not constitute the object of one intention.

However, Jaspers indicates immediately that this unity belongs
to the objects only derivatively. He goes along with Kant in
affirming that unity lies primarily in the subject, from which it is

then spontaneously communicated to the objects. This subjective unity is in fact twofold: categorical and transcendental. Categories are *a priori* forms of subjectivity, whereby the manifold of sense perception is actively synthesised into a unity, the object. Strictly speaking, therefore, objects *are* not one, rather they *become* one through this active synthesis performed by the subject. Many of Jaspers' expressions imply this becoming, this genesis of the objects' unity. 'Whatever does not become a unity, cannot be an object for us. That which becomes an object for us is gathered into one, as something intended in the unity of the intending act of thought.'[12] As a synthetic unity, the derivative unity of objects is not without multiplicity. An object in fact is a multiplicity of elements tied together into a unity by the subject.[13] Pure unity, which never becomes but always is, and which founds even the unity of the categories, is the transcendental unity of apperception whereby the pure subject is conscious of its own identity and invariance amidst the flux of its manifold representations. Jaspers agrees with Kant that the primary source from which all unity flows is this unity of apperception.[14]

Metaphorically speaking, it is as if the subject awakening to consciousness, thanks to the presence of objects, and returning upon itself in self-reflection, now reclaimed something of the unmitigated alterity of its objects. It is as if it realised that something in the constitution of the objects depends on itself, notably that the unity required for the appearance of an object is for the most part conditioned by its own subjective unity. We have noted already that with the rise of intentional representations a new mode of being has been introduced into the world. Without these conscious representations the world would be only an aggregate of casually interacting things. But that these representations be really more than a shower of disconnected impressions, 'less than the stuff of dreams',[15] they must first of all be gathered into categorical unity in which these manifold impressions coalesce into an organised whole, the object, and secondly they must be accompanied by an invariable apperception of an invariable subject to which all the objects are related. Jaspers calls this subject variously the subject as such, the general subject, consciousness in general, the point-like intellect, the I in general.[16] To be related to this unvarying point of reference in consciousness is what provides objects with objective unity and cohesion.

With this new determination, object-beings now appear less exterior to the subject, but none the less solid for all that. The intelligible unity, which they receive from the general subject, renders them more intimate, more immanent we could say, but also more stable. They stand invested with the stability proper to thought-objects. They are no longer just a part of the blind turbulence of exterior Dasein, but they participate in the ideality of being thought of.[17] By taking cognisance of them, consciousness carries them over into its own sphere, aggregates them to itself, and makes them fit to be valid objects for knowledge. Validity (*Gültigkeit*) then is the first benefit that objects draw from the unity conferred upon them by general consciousness. This validity is, moreover, universal in extent because it originates in a universal, impersonal, unvarying subject. From the point of view of thought and knowledge, objective signifies that which is universally valid.[18]

Thought-objects manifest a peculiar stability, we have noted. Objective thought is valid because it is not a fluid state of consciousness but an invariant grasp of something firm and determined. This characteristic trait of objectivity is called by Jaspers *Bestehen* or *Bestand,* which now displaces the emphasis from *gegen* to *stand.* That which guarantees the objectivity of an act of knowledge is this stability of its object. More precisely, a fully objective act of knowledge is the intentional rapport between a 'steady' subject and an equally steady object. Their correlation, once established, remains 'stable' and unaffected by time and changing circumstances, and can be repeated indefinitely in the identically same sense: *es besteht, dass....* Through stability in this sense, objects and objective thoughts are lifted out of the changing temporal flux and are invested with firm and durable identity. An act of knowledge is, therefore, fully objective whenever its tendency can come to a full stop, whenever its movement can terminate in an object that is perfectly defined and immobile and one. As Bernard Welte quite correctly remarks on this point, 'That is objective which in its own determination *stands* opposite to thought, and in which thought, on its part, is brought to *halt.*'[19]

The faculty par excellence of this objective thought is the intellect (*Verstand*); and its chief instrument, the concept (*Begriff*). The intellect is the power of objective understanding which through concepts fixes and immobilises whatever it encounters. In it the odd, the fleeting, the fickle, the unmatched, the changing, the diverse are left aside or reduced to what is timeless, homogeneous, stable.[20] Out of the coupling of stability and unity the intellect constructs an image of positive being, of being which *is* and *is what it is*—a univocally determinable object for knowledge.

GENERALITY

The complex nature of the subject-object polarity is further illustrated by the third principal feature of object-beings; namely, generality. Jaspers asserts that objects must somehow be affected by generality. An object, as we know, results from a synthesis whereby a multiplicity of components is tied together into a unity. This unity comprises a multiplicity of *particular elements* under a *general form*. In other words, an object is the combination of 'this' which is grasped by sense-intuition, and 'something' which, as has been pointed out, is universally represented by the intellect. An object is never just one or the other, purely particular or simply general, but always both in one. This implies that in the grasp of an object both the intellect and the senses cooperate.

In fact, Jaspers insists that the objects of sense-perception already contain this generality which is a feature of all intentional objects. When we deliberately look at something and not just vacuously stare ahead, we see the object of our vision as an instance of a general kind.[21] The absolute particularity of a non-thematic intuition, in which we would become aware only of a 'this' is a mere limit-concept that is useful only in a psychological description of some semi-conscious experiences.[22]

A thing, then, becomes an object when it is thematised, that is, inserted into a general object-form or category as a concrete example of the latter. This insertion is the process of objectification. Objectification, according to the great lessons of Kant whom Jaspers echoes, is the work of the active subject. It underscores the original spontaneity of the subject. Without this objectifying activity of the subject, no objectivity can come into existence.[23]

But Jaspers warns that this is not all. He does not want us to infer now that the production of the general object-form by the subject accounts for the whole phenomenon of objectification.

The spontaneous activity of the subject must bear on data passively received through sense-intuition. It is this intuition that puts us into contact with the particular. For the constitution of an object, the general category produced by the subject must find a 'filling' (*Erfüllung*) in the opaque stuff of the particular, and the senses must cooperate with the intellect.

The affirmation of the subject's creativity becomes even more untenable if it is made the sole explanation of the object's genesis, for the activity of the subject is productive only of the general *appearance* of the object, not of its *existence*.[24] In other words, subjectivity in general is the condition of the experience of things, not of the fact of their being-there. Through this precision Jaspers avoids absolute phenomenism but is able to maintain the phenomenality of object-beings in so far as he credits the general form of their appearance to the categories which proceed from the understanding of the general subject. It is in this sense, and in this sense alone, that Jaspers feels himself justified in calling objects 'phenomena' and in speaking of the 'phenomenality of the world',[25] which is the sum of objects.

Jaspers lingers on this correlativity of the universal and the particular in order to distinguish his position both from idealism and from positivism. In both philosophies there is a natural proneness to stop either at the conceivable universal or at the sensible particular, and to prefer one or the other as *the* true reality. When we consider that the individuals receive their validity from the general form, that they are *what* they are in virtue of their participation in this form, we are overawed by the prestige of the universal and are likely to regard the particular as incidental and negligible. When we reflect, on the other hand, that everything that exists is a particular, we are seized by the pathos of the individual and tend to relegate the universal to the status of mere names, useful perhaps for the classification of individuals but nothing real. In the first case, we must then be confronted with the problem of individuation; and in the second, with that of abstraction. For Jaspers both problems are insoluble pseudo-problems because 'both have their origin in a one-sided fixation of reality'[26] which, he charges, is the pernicious practice of both positivistic and idealistic ontologies. There lies at the bottom of both problems an unnoticed assumption that either the universal of the particular is less really real than the other; and therefore, one should be able to be deduced from and explained by the other. But Jaspers declares that the real for us is neither the concretely palpable individual as such, nor the universal as such, but that which is both in one. Consequently, neither can be deduced from the other.[27]

He then formulates the same relationship of the particular and the universal in terms of *matter and form*. 'Being becomes accessible to us in object-being only through the split of the universal and the particular, which in the object are linked into one. If we call the universal "form" and the concrete individual "matter", we can say that an object is two-in-one: form and matter.'[28] It should be noted with special care that Jaspers is talking about objects for us, not about things in themselves. He is concerned with the making of a phenomenon of knowledge and not with the ontological structure of things in themselves. Calling a concrete individual 'matter' would certainly be a nonsense in ontology. He is trying to describe the noema whose matter, according to him, is furnished by sense-intuition and whose form is constructed in thought.[29] Matter and form are separated and then brought together in a mysterious unity of the object. This division and composition becomes apparent when we talk of objects in a judicative act of knowledge, where we perform an 'original partition' (*Urteil*) into subject and predicate.[30]

Jaspers is quick to remind himself of the doubly symbolic nature of this terminology. In the first place, he recalls that the terms 'matter' and 'form' refer primarily to the ontological principles of things, and have their origin in plastic art. From there their meaning has been extended to symbolise the characteristic duality of all thought-objects.[31] But neither in the parent-image nor in its secondary application may we hypostatise matter and form as if they were two independently representable principles.[32] Matter as such and form as such are unthinkable. By 'matter' we merely try to designate the furthermost 'stuff' of reality, precisely inasmuch as in its indetermination it escapes all designation. As pure indetermination, possibility, apeiron, matter is just beyond the limit of objective thought. For lack of determination, intional thought expires in it. Nor can 'form' as such be represented. Without any particular material support, any realisation, any content, a form is entirely empty. In itself it is as indefinite as pure matter. Both matter and form can be represented only in so far as they have already determined each other in an object.[33] In the second place, neither matter nor form can be determined once and for all, because in the matter-form relationship which constitutes a noema nothing is just matter or just form once and for all. The form can in another configuration become the matter. All depends on the intention with which one approaches the object.[34]

From another point of view, the synthesis of unity and plurality in the universal is also called totality; and the knowledge which integrates a multitude of individuals into such totalities is always a kind of totalisation, an act of rescuing the individuals from the narrowness of their isolation and inserting them into a larger context. In the unity of the universal, the particular becomes a part of a whole. The decisive question is whether or not the whole should be conceived statically or dynamically, whether we should think of totalisation as the progressive disclosure of a pre-existing structure or as a dialectical process in which each point is also a moment of transformation for the whole. Is the relationship which links the part to the whole univocal or analogical? The answer cannot be in doubt. Objective knowledge (which is the same as thematic conceptual knowledge), because it proceeds from an invariable and timeless intention of consciousness in general, completely encloses the individual and transports it into a tissue of abiding relationships. In objective knowledge each individual item serves only to illustrate again and again the whole of the universal; and in so far as an individual shows itself recalcitrant to fill this role, it is declared unknowable. Just as in general consciousness deviations from the common norm are attributed to failure of attention, fault, untruth,[35] the object in its material individuality is taxed with irrationality. Objective knowledge must presuppose totality; and each new item of knowledge becomes objective only to the degree in which it reveals some new aspect of the same stable structure of the whole, already known in part through other items.

Totalisation explains both the immense success and the failure of objective knowledge, both its strength and its weakness. Objective knowledge succeeds because, by transporting the individual into the universal, it supplies what the individual reality lacks in itself: stable identity, sameness, universal validity; in one word, *perfection*, *Vollständingkeit*. But this perfection is already

4

too much. Individual reality is always less perfect, less achieved, than its ideal image and, as such, is incapable of 'filling out' the thematic intention. But this grasp is also less than adequate because in each individual there is a margin, a remnant, that is unattainable to knowledge.[36] Hence the peculiar avidity in the march of this knowledge. It tries to fill the inadequacy by an unending series of general aspects or by encasing the individual in successively vaster and vaster totalities. In both cases it is driven by a vague impulse of reaching a super-object that would completely fill its anticipative intention, which is too large for ordinary objects.

SUMMARY REMARKS

To conclude this short sketch of the principal characteristics of objectivity according to Jaspers I should like to summarise its main points. Objectivity, as we had occasion to note, involves two related problems: that of the correlation between consciousness and its object, and that of objective knowledge. As to the first problem, I have simply listed three main features which more or less define the correlate of consciousness. As to the second, I have tried to indicate some of the epistemological implications of Jaspers' conception. Now in retrospect I believe myself justified in drawing the following conclusions and making the following remarks:

(*a*) An object must display all three features of opposition, unity, and generality in order to be an adequate object; and a fully objective act of knowledge must exhibit validity, stability, and universality. Of course, objectivity will admit different degrees. There can be partial objects and more or less objective disciplines, but in that case knowledge has to be on its guard to keep track of its own limits and not to stray into domains where its claims are no longer valid. In other words, a critique of knowledge must accompany both science and philosophy. It is one thing to say, for instance, that 'everything that becomes being for us has to have its side of objectivity', as Jaspers asserted; and it may be quite another thing to say that Being is objective. The first affirmation states the universal condition of the knowledge of Being; the second seems to assert something about Being itself, or at least it can make that claim. It may surreptitiously identify Being in all its aspects with object-being and assume that there is nothing that is not given in stable objects and registered in public consciousness.

(*b*) All this is quite easily recognisable as the Kantian distinction between the phenomenal and the noumenal orders. When all is said and done, one can see that Jaspers contributes very little to what Kant has already taught concerning these matters of objectivity. It is not surprising to find, therefore, that Jaspers designates the same entities as Kant as being unknowable objectively: the world, the soul, and God. Only he calls them the World, Existence, and Transcendence. Nor is it difficult to guess the basic reasons for which each of them is declared non-objective.[37] They are non-objective because they manifest definite shortcomings in one or other aspect needed for objectivity. Existence, for instance, will be considered objectively unknowable precisely because it lacks all generality. The World, on the other hand, will resist all our efforts of totalisation, of bringing its elements to a common denominator, because its major spheres lack the required unity or qualitative oneness. There are recognisable levels of unity and totality within the World, but the World itself is not a unity.[38] As soon as we try to think of the World, it splinters into at least four irreducible regions: inorganic matter with its mechanical laws, life with its biological laws, psyche with its laws of experiencing, and spirit with its laws of ideation. How these four worlds are encompassed by the one World is not accessible to objective thought. We can think unity only in analogies which, when subjected to closer scrutiny, must again be dissolved.[39] Jaspers is unmistakable on the point that 'there are no cognitively (*erkenntnismässig*) fruitful global theories of the World.'[40] Such apparently comprehensive world views are serviceable for one of the spheres but harmful when transferred to the others.

(*c*) It should be sufficiently clear that what Jaspers means by objective knowledge in the full sense is equivalent to *univocal knowledge*. The organ of this kind of knowledge is the intellect and its instrument the concept. For Jaspers' concepts exist only as constant meanings which are univocally determined. The clarity and incontestable validity of objective knowledge is due precisely to this determination. Where this determination is lost from view, thought is exposed to the danger of lapsing into fantasy and sophistry. 'The object "demands" to be thought of in a definite way.'[41] This may explain why Jaspers does not consider analogy and analogous concepts fully objective, if objective at all. Analogy blurs the clear borderlines of conceptual determination. It takes away the univocal determination of a concept, which made it objectively valid for everybody everywhere. This suggests already that for Jaspers objectivity and analogy will be opposites. They represent for him two directions of one and the same dialectical thought process, two dimensions of rationality. Like the ever-widening swing of a pendulum along the same arc, *the movement of rationality creates greater and greater clarity in the direction of objectivity, and wider unity in the direction of analogy.* Clarity and unity are in fact the two principal demands of Reason as a whole. In living and dynamic thought, in thought that is more than just a calm contemplation, both unity and clarity are only provisional; they are made and unmade at each moment by this double movement of rationality.[42]

(d) There is a whole series of identifications and implications among certain important ideas that play a part in the question of objectivity. Some of these are explicitly stated by Jaspers, while some are only implied by his arguments. We have already seen that 'object' and 'phenomenon', 'objectivity' and 'phenomenality', are used almost synonymously by him. I think the following pretty nearly summarises his views in this regard:

The basic phenomenon of the subject-object-dichotomy consists in the intentional rapport between the subject and an object. 'Intentionality' implies the 'determination' of the object because something indeterminate could not *stand* opposite the subject and, consequently, the subject's intentional flow could not come to *halt* in it. In turn, 'determination' spells 'finitude' for the object since determination opposes the object not only to the subject but to other objects as well. 'Whenever we think, we think of something and, indeed, something definite,' notes Gerhard Knauss in this connection.[43] Every intentional act has its definite intended object; consequently, an intentional or object-directed act of thought is always a finite act of thought in the sense of being the thought of something finite. Negatively put, the infinite cannot be thought of intentionally; that is, it cannot become the correlate of an act of intending except in an indirect, analogical way *as if* the infinite too were an object. The point to remark is that, while traditional philosophy maintains that by means of analogical thinking we are capable of intending the infinite in such a way that only opposition and finitude are excluded from it but not its determinateness and objectivity, the concepts of determination and finitude are so inseparably linked by Jaspers that for him the elimination of finitude *eo ipso* signifies the destruction of determinateness and objectivity also. The infinite is at best a 'vanishing object' for him.

(e) I believe, however, that there is a way of valorising objective intentionality (which Jaspers seems to belittle) from within its very weakness and shortcoming, although this could not be done according to the spirit of Jaspers himself. Jaspers has presented intentionality mostly in its acts, which by definition are particular and finite. Each one of these acts aims at a definite and limited object, some one thing and one thing only. Thanks to this limitation set by intentionality itself, the desire to know, to grasp, comes to rest and intellectual possession is achieved. But this is not the complete image of intentionality. For the fact remains that after each particular grasp comes a new one, that those particular possessions leave the soul unencumbered for more knowledge. In other words, essentially finite in its acts, intentionality is endless in its dynamism. This is precisely the paradox of our knowledge: it is both objective and intentional at the same time. In so far as it is objective, it must 'come to halt' in a definite object, but as intentional, it must go on. In it each end becomes a means, each satisfaction a new pang of hunger, each union a distance.

Thus, within intentionality a far-away *finality* begins to outline itself; a goal to which objects, like so many signposts, stake out the road, even though they never take us there. From within the essential limitation of objectivity, a demand springs up for infinite openess. At the heart of the provisional satisfaction procured by clear and objective understanding (*Verstand*) the interior unrest of reason (*Vernunft*) makes its appearance. Reason is precisely that 'unrest which permits acquiescence in nothing'.[44] Reason is the constant impetus behind the intellect, but its driving force does not consist merely in directing the intellect from one definite object to another; its impetus is also nourished by the secret hope of apprehending Being itself, the hidden goal of all our efforts which alone promises final rest.

III Subjectivity

IN the second chapter I have tried to cast some light on the subject-object polarity from the point of view of object-being. Now I would like to carry out briefly the same clarification from the point of view of subject-being. This new perspective will bring to light certain articulations of the subject-object-dichotomy and even show up certain new aspects of object-being itself, which hitherto have remained in the background. The treatment will be very brief and straightforward, summing up without much comment the different aspects of subjectivity that Jaspers believes he discerns within the subject-object polarity. For the interesting point is that Jaspers refuses the rationalistic prejudice which simply identifies subjectivity with consciousness in general, the disincarnate and anonymous subject of the *cogito*. His analyses are designed to show us that general consciousness is only one in a series of aspects (although an important one) that are comprised in concrete subjectivity. In the different portions of his work, Jaspers proposed at least four different articulations of subjectivity: twice in terms of selfhood (*Ich*),[1] once in terms of consciousness (*Bewusstsein*),[2] and finally in terms of subject (*Subjekt*).[3] Because the elements of these considerations partly or wholly overlap, I will take them synthetically and speak of subjectivity now in terms of selfhood, now in terms of consciousness, without attending to the slightly different perspectives.

EMPIRICAL SUBJECT

The analysis of subjectivity has its limits. Backwards it is arrested at the point where subject and object seperate, where in a sudden intentionality conscious subjectivity emerges from the obscurity of pre-reflective indifferentiation with things; and in the forward direction it can never reach the point where subject and object would fuse in a perfect identity and transparence, where the subject would completely penetrate its object. Neither the absolute begining nor the final achievement of subjectivity is accessible to analysis. We can follow it neither to its original darkness nor to its perfect luminosity. Our research must remain penumbral. Ar the very first moment of awakening to the fact of the subject-object-dichotomy, we have a vague initial intuition about the originality of our subjectivity; but by asking what it is, we take one step outside of it. We no longer merely exercise it but also confront it as an object.[4] Yet this confrontation is not perfect because it too happens by virtue of an exercise of subjectivity. Therefore, our original subjectivity can only be hinted at by approximations.

Things and animals *are*. They *are there* without knowing it. I am there too, but I can also know that I am there.[5] This fact alone is enough to set me apart from the rest. But more than that, 'my being is radically different from the being of things, because I can *say* "I am".'[6] By the power of the word, I take possession of my being. I *exist*. Instead of simply enduring my being there, I can identify it as mine. I can discern my being. One of the fundamental aspects of what is meant by subjectivity is this power to say 'I'. The subject is an *ichsagendes Sein,* as Jaspers would say.

But before the advent of the word, before saying 'I', we first *live* our awareness of being there. It is this *Daseinsbewusstsein,* to which reference has already been made in the first chapter, that constitutes the first aspect of empirical subjectivity. This awareness is mostly implicit; it is exercised unreflectingly. But be it as dim and as lateral as it may, 'from the viewpoint of things subsisting outwardly, it is already a kind of inwardness ... which is distinguished from an objective, thing-like process by the fact that a certain "I" can remember and retrospectively see this lived experience as existing at a time when I was not yet fully awakened.'[7] Empirical subjectivity in this sense signifies functional subjectivity, and is scarcely more than an echo of events in the world, a mirror that reflects its environment.

But empirical subjectivity also has a second related meaning in Jaspers. In this second sense it no longer designates the semi-conscious functioning of lived subjectivity, but rather the concrete subject, as it is given to manifold empirical observation and presented either to external or to introspective study. What this second usage underlines is the givenness, positivity, the untranslatable *Gewordensein* of the subject. Empirical subject is the subject that is already there, has already become what it is, and we have failed to surprise it in its originality, at the point of its emergence. This positive subject reveals itself in piecemeal objectivities. Every one of these objective aspects is partially identifiable with my I-ness or selfhood; yet none of them, or even all of them together, will make up my total or even fundamental subjectivity.[8]

Jaspers describes several of these aspects in great phenomenological detail. But a brief summary of them will suffice us here:

My body. I am intimately one with my body. Whatever I do, I do through my body; whatever happens to it, happens to me. 'Yet this oneness is not identity. I am not my body.'[9] I can lose certain single parts of my body, yet I remain the same. 'My body renews its stuff continuously; its material is replaced, but I remain myself.'[10] I do not receive my self-identity from my body, but rather the other way round. Whatever portion of the universal matter at any given moment belongs to me receives its identity through me as my body. I freely decide about my body. My corporeity is in my power. I can deny even its legitimate demands on me, and in an extreme case I can destroy it. In short, I am neither different from nor identical with my body.

Social identity. What I am and what I am worth is largely measurable by what I am with and for others. I am a part of societies and institutions that stamp my identity, so that, once detached from them, I seem to lose something of my selfhood. Both in primitive and in rationalised modern society, the substance of the individual tends to be absorbed by the collectivity, where it becomes a socially useful cell, defined and evaluated by what it contributes to the good of the whole. 'But as a social subject, I am not myself.'[11] The proof of this is that even when I am torn out of my social milieu, uprooted and tossed about, I can survive the catastrophe and preserve something of my inalienable and singular selfhood. Moreover, I can always defend myself, at least interiorly, against the social pressures that threaten to crush me into a bleak uniformity. I feel entitled to certain rights and a certain respect, even when I am not yet or no longer a useful member of society. Finally, if I accept the role appointed me by society, it is *I* who accept it, which proves that I am more than this role; I am not identical with it.

Productivity. Jaspers speaks of *Leistungsich*. It is another aspect of my empirically observable subjectivity. There is a tendency to identify me with my productivity, to see me through my works. I am often co-equated with the *homo faber*. 'Yet, what I produce in no way exhausts my possibilities.'[12] My work, when it is finished, can be detached from me and I can even disown it later because my whole self did not enter into it. 'What I am and what I do are now and forever one, but not identical.'[13] I can perform actions into which I myself hardly enter at all.

My past. 'Finally, I know what I am by examining my past. What I have lived through, what I have seen, what I have done or thought, what people have done to me or the way they have helped me, all this determines my present self-awareness either unconsciously or in conscious remembering. . . . The past becomes my looking-glass: I am what I have become.'[14] My past is determined. I can wish it had been otherwise, but I cannot change it. Nevertheless, I do not have to identify myself totally with my past, 'for I am also present and have a future.'[15] My past may be determined, but it does not entirely determine me. And if I were to construct my present and future possibilities entirely on the model of my past, I would thereby lose something of my authentic self and injure the possibilities proper to my present and future.[16] I am most genuinely myself, I show forth my originality, not when I simply perpetuate my past, carrying it over into my future, but when by free decisions I create my future out of past material.

My character. My positive subjectivity which is thus composed of biological, social, economic, and psychological factors can be summed up under the general term 'character'. More precisely my character is not what I thus know of myself directly in all these factors, but what I can conclude from them as underlying them.[17] These factors are thought to be manifestations and sedimentations of my character. My character is then the qualitative facticity (*Sosein*) of my being, which discovers itself in its existential positivity (*Dasein*). Through it I appear to myself as an objective substance, relatively stable. This stability is a valuable asset, a solid prop, for both selfhood and self-knowledge.[18] However, as really myself, I transcend even my character; I 'stand above it' as Jaspers says. I can assume and modify my character by controlling the motivations that rise out of its positivity.[19] In other words, I am *free* whereas my character is determined. Jaspers is strong on the point that in my real selfhood the blind determinism and facticity of my being is dissolved and becomes freedom. *Vis-à-vis* my positive subjectivity I remain a self, a possibility of autonomy.[20]

Jaspers' main purpose in all these considerations is clear. He wants to show that empirical subjectivity, accessible to objective knowledge, is not the whole of my selfhood or even its most fundamental aspect. In the depths of subjectivity there lies something utterly undomesticated which escapes all our attempts at objectification. This something is like a free spontaneity which in all objectivities (and sometimes against them) *decides* about itself, is *origin* to itself.[21] By making myself an empirical object, I miss precisely this originality and see myself only as I have already become.

As a last point, let us note that the basic impulses of empirical subjectivity are self-centred and pragmatic. Empirical subjectivity is individual subjectivity, whose most insistent urge is self-affirmation (*Selbstbehauptung*) over against, and sometimes at the expense of, other selves. Jaspers characterises it as an essentially pragmatic process in the service of the expansion of individual life. As such, it is also a temporal process which varies, grows and diminishes, according to the fluctuation of individual vitality. Empirical subjects are diverse and manifold.

GENERAL SUBJECT

The second level of subjectivity is general subjectivity. In contrast to the diversity of empirical subjects, on this second level I am aware of 'being essentially identical with all other subjects.'[22] When I act and reflect without relating the content and validity of my reflection to *me*, to this particular subject, and when I endeavour to suspend my individuality and try to find what must be universally valid for everyone, then I become interchangeably one with all other conscious subjects 'who are numerically distinct from me, but the same in kind.'[23] In the German tradition, this universal dimension of subjectivity, to which reference has already been made, is called consciousness in general, *Bewusstsein überhaupt*. Jaspers emphasises that the interchangeability of general consciousness is not to be understood 'as the sameness of average qualities among empirical individuals, but as selfhood in general, subjectivity that is the condition of all object-being.'[24] In virtue of it, we not only think and feel and act in similar ways, but in an *identical* way.

It goes without saying that selfhood is almost entirely absent in this general subjectivity. In fact, in order to partake in it, in order to assent to its 'truths which stand without me, are universally valid, unhistorical, and timeless,'[25] I must abdicate my concrete individuality almost completely. I must become in a way not I but 'a subject in general which is substitutable by any other subject.'[26] In playing proxy for the general subject, I must efface myself and let the timeless truth *be spoken* through me impersonally, anonymously by the general subject, which speaks in nobody's name. Indeed, from the point of view of general subjectivity, our personality and selfhood constitute a negative value, a non-coincidence with complete truth and a lack of it. Our individual personalities come from our imperfect participation in the impersonal; our private selves are deviations from the public ego; our concrete subjectivity is a defective realisation of ideal subjectivity.

Concrete empirical subjectivity, as has been mentioned, is an object for psychological observation. It is essentially a temporal process which begins, develops, regresses, is now clear, now obscure. We have distinguished different elements, degrees, aspects in it. Naturally, these distinctions were made in the light of general consciousness, anticipating it, as it were, because it is only by general consciousness that distinctions are apprehended and through it every clear and distinct idea must pass. In contrast to empirical subjectivity, general consciousness 'does not constitute an object of observation, for what is observable of it is its temporal appearance in empirical subjectivity. It is, by definition, alien to time (*zeitfremd*); has no gaps, does not begin and does not change. To the degree that I participate in it, my subjectivity loses that which is psychologically characteristic of it, that which is particular and observable about it.'[27]

But this loss of particularity is not necessarily a pure and simple loss; it also represents a gain and an advantage. Impersonality can lend a specific dignity to subjectivity.[28] The repression of individual perspectives, private views, and self-interests permits the appearance of disinterested, universal truth and allows the creation of general norms according to which the rational ordering of common thought and action becomes possible. Though subjectivity loses its character of reality when transformed into general subjectivity, it also gains by being lifted out of its isolation and installed in a community that is ruled by universally valid truth.[29]

It must be noted in passing that this depersonalised subject is also the general subject of all scientific knowledge properly so-called. It is the invariable intention issuing from this subject which makes scientific grasp universally and impersonally valid.

Between the empirical subject and the subject in general, between their respective modes of being, there can be no continuity. Jaspers is clear on the point that from one to the other there can only be a leap, *Sprung*. The general subject exists on a different level of being from the empirical subject and cannot be deduced from any other source, any other *Ursprung*, than itself.[30] This discontinuousness is another manifestation of the more general diremption of Being, to which allusion was made in the first chapter. Because of this separateness of sources, Jaspers believes that the activity of general consciousness is in a certain sense independent of empirical subjectivity.[31] This independence does not mean, of course, that the activity of general consciousness does not need to be embodied in individual subjects, but that 'individual vital motives (*Daseinsmotive*) need not have a decisive influence over the content and orientation of general consciousness.'[32] In fact, general consciousness is characterised by its capacity for abstention from such motives.

In short, there seems to be no pure harmony between these two forms of subjectivity. For instance, 'it can be shown that thought (general consciousness) has beneficial results for the empirical individual; . . . that thought, in itself independent of the empirical subject, can serve individuality. Nevertheless, it can also be shown how thought disturbs Dasein, confuses its instincts, exposes it to illusions, and especially when false, causes senseless havoc. Even true insight not only supports life, it also makes it vacillating and unhappy.'[33] The allusion is not very clear, but Jaspers is probably thinking of the tension that usually exists between action and thought, between practical and theoretical intentions which are always a little inimical to each other. Thought tends to suspend action, and action tends to cloud thought.

But Jaspers calls attention to this discrepancy because he thinks that 'this discrepancy is a new indication of the separateness of sources from which empirical and general subjectivity flow.'[34] For the moment at least, these two seem irreducibly separate for him, separate not only as two different intentionalities of one and the same subject bearing upon two different objects but as two intentions proceeding from two different subjects and attaining two different objects. Once the intention changes, so it seems, everything in the subject-object relation changes: the subject, the relation, and the object.[35] Schematically:

empirical subject————practical intention——> empirical object

general subject————theoretical intention——> theoretical object

and not

subject $\left\{\begin{array}{c}\text{————————practical intention————————>}\\\text{————————theoretical intention————————>}\end{array}\right\}$ object

SPIRIT

Spirit is the third figure of subjectivity for Jaspers. He notes that, besides our private preoccupation with our empirico-temporal life and our theoretical concern with immutable truths, we also live by historically changing ideals and ideal ensembles, which provide the context of understanding for a whole historical epoch or community. The subjective and creative source of these ideals is called spirit, *Geist,* in the German philosophic tradition.

Jaspers takes great pains to render intelligible just what exactly he understands by this term.[36] His formulations are often hesitant, but it soon becomes clear that he considers the spirit as one of the figures of subject-being. Subjectivity, spirit, means for him the creative impulse of comprehensive thought, action, and feeling, which articulates and orientates these activities towards a certain *totality of purpose and meaning.*[37] The spirit is that active presence and guidance of the subject in his activities which lends these activities measure and well-roundedness according to certain self-constructed norms. Spirit is the continual process of fusing

and reshaping the ideals of an age. As such, the spirit strives for
a totality that is intelligible and, to some extent, practicable by
a given historico-cultural community as well as by the individual
within that community. For this reason, the spirit endeavours to
preserve and heighten the meaning of everything it encounters,
by relating everything to the rest, by assigning each thing to its
place and limit, 'by admitting that which belongs to its wholeness
and excluding that which it cannot assimilate.'[38]

The spirit investigates reality by means of its guiding ideas,
which it constructs more or less imaginatively, so that they are
symbols rather than concepts. Hence, the language of the spirit
is not objective in the same sense as that of general consciousness.
The latter speaks the language of impersonal *explanation,* the
former that of more personal *comprehension.* For comprehension,
one must transcend the language of explanation and allow oneself
to be moved personally by the values expressed in the symbols
of the spirit. The difference between explanation and comprehension is precisely the difference expressed by the Weberian
terms of *Zweckrationalität* and *Sinngebung.*[39] The former consists
in an anonymous grasp of objective relationships between certain
means and a given end, whereas the latter always refers to a
meaning constructed by and for a community of personal
subjects. This is why Jaspers notes that 'the actor of the spirit is
not the "I think" of general consciousness, but always an irreplaceable individual, who in his personal being feels himself summoned
by something impersonally objective.'[40]

In order to underline the originality of the spirit, Jaspers
contrasts it still further to the other modes of subject-being. 'In
contrast to the abstraction of timeless consciousness in general,
spirit is once more a temporal process and, as such, comparable
to empirical subjectivity. But it is distinguished from this latter
in that it moves by a reflexivity of knowledge instead of by some
merely biologico-psychological process.'[41] The similarity
between empirical subjectivity and the spirit consists in their
realness and historicity, while the similarity between general
consciousness and the spirit consists in their communicability
and validity, But whereas general consciousness is a timeless gaze
that creates nothing, the spirit is 'in a constant travail of self-
realisation'.[42] The roots of empirical subjectivity are sunk into
the impenetrable obscurity of matter, life, and nature; spirit, on

the contrary, seems to spring from a source of transparency. As to their respective possibility of being objectified: 'empirical subjectivity is objectifiable as a biological and psychological event; spirit is objectified as a configuration of meaning and purpose (*Sinngebilde*) by moral and historical sciences;'[43] general consciousness, itself unobjectifiable, 'is the medium in which the spirit transforms itself and the world into comprehensibility.'[44] Empirical subjectivity lends itself to positive observation in categories of casuality and its temporality is qualitative and non-homogenous.[45]

By such contrasts and comparisons Jaspers wants to preclude the suggestion that the spirit is nothing else than lived subjectivity and general consciousness put together, a kind of 'addition' of the two. He leaves no doubt of the irreducible originality of the spirit. 'Spirit is real like the empirical subject and inward like thought (general consciousness), but it flows from another source and is more than both of them.'[46] And this 'more' that constitutes the originality of the spirit is precisely a *special kind of inwardness* that promotes the subjectivity of the spirit to the threshold of absolute subjectivity which is genuine Existence. 'In thought, and hence also in spirit, we are focused upon objects. There exists a pervading opposition between the thinking subject and the object thought of. . . . Now, in general consciousness this split is absolute: the thought of general consciousness aims at the object as the absolutely other. The spirit, on the contrary, finds itself in the object it intends. For the spirit the split serves as a passage to self-discovery in the other. . . . In short: the spirit is concerned with itself, general consciousness always with the other.'[47]

It is, therefore, with good reason that Dufrenne and Ricoeur remark that for Jaspers 'the idea of the spirit constitutes an intermediary form which preludes absolute consciousness and serves as a transition between empirical selfhood and Existence.'[48] Thus, the spirit is a privileged form of subjectivity. 'Privileged, because the other which the spirit intends is nevertheless kin to me: the spiritual universe is not as irreducibly alien to me as the material universe. It is alien only in so far as it exceeds my individual consciousness in which it is none the less incessantly embodied.'[49] The self-discovery in the representation of the other, which makes the activity of the spirit a privileged form of subjectivity, does not yet make it an absolute form of subjectivity, however. Absolute subjectivity should coincide much too closely with itself to be able to turn back upon itself, and to appear to itself in ideal representations. Absolute subjectivity, subjectivity without distance, escapes intentional consciousness, and can be experienced only in the immediacy of an act or decision.

What is meant by absolute subjectivity will, we hope, become clearer as our exposition continues. For the time being, it should suffice to note that absolute subjectivity signifies that transcendent ground of selfhood or personal existence in which all other degrees of subjectivity are rooted. Jaspers generally refers to it simply as *Existence*. The whole of Part III will concern itself with this concept.

SOME NOTES ON THE TRANSCENDENCE AND IMMANENCE OF CONSCIOUSNESS

Here we must pause a little in order to recall the original guiding ideas of the reflection we began together with Jaspers. We must remember that for Jaspers the philosophical quest is essentially a quest for the Absolute, a quest for Being that does not simply disappear. Thus far, however, we have met only beings which, in the all-pervading duality of subject and object, are relative. The intentionality of consciousness together with the phenomenality of the objects constitute what Jaspers surprisingly calls the domain of *immanence*.

It is a surprising and at the same time disturbing feature of Jaspers' thought that he includes in immanence a great deal of what others would certainly consider transcendent. There is, first of all, the transcendence of the noema in relation to the noetic act. Even though the noema is intended in a noetic act, it is not an inner constituent of the act but its exterior correlate. Secondly, there is the real transcendence of the extra-mental thing which is independent of the intentional activity of the subject. Jaspers is, of course, aware of these forms of transcendence, but he is not impressed by them to the point of honouring them with the name of transcendence. He simply calls them *transsubjective* and ranges them in immanence. He reasons that, as correlates of consciousness, they too must be *present* in consciousness, independently of the ontological status they might have in themselves.[50]

Immanence, thus understood, does not signify merely the immanence of the subjective act but also, above all, the objective term of that act. That is why there is no line of demarcation between consciousness and the world, because for Jaspers the world is equally immanent, once it is made into an object of an act of consciousness. Likewise, immanence is not the world, as opposed to things outside the world, because as soon as we think of the outside, 'straightway we drag in what is outside, and thus make it an object in the world.' It is not difficult to see where such a curious idea of immanence is leading. It is leading to the thesis that 'only immanence can be known, or inversely, all knowledge only encounters immanence.'[51]

What are we to think of such a view? It would be useless to point out to Jaspers that the kind of immanence he is positing is proper only to a special class of ideal objects, such as some of the constructs of pure mathematics, but not to objects in general. Only these ideal objects exist entirely in and for consciousness, so that outside of this relationship they have no reality at all. As for the class of real objects, consciousness is only the condition of their being known but not, as in the case of ideal objects, of their being *tout court*. Consequently, to the extent that these objects are independent of consciousness, they could be called transcendent. It would be useless to argue these issues, because Jaspers' point is precisely that even real objects are not independent of consciousness, but that as noemata they too must pass into consciousness and, as such, they are as immanent as consciousness itself. A thing that is in no way represented in consciousness is as good as non-existent for us; or inversely, a thing is an object for us only in so far as it is represented in consciousness.

The real difficulty is rather with the alleged immanence of the objective term of an act of consciousness. Apparently, the noema cannot be immanent *au même titre* as the noesis; otherwise the distinction of subject-object could not be established between them, so that there would be actually no act of consciousness at all. But if within the immanence of consciousness there is a distinction between noesis and noema, the distinction can only be that the noema is intended precisely as transcendent to the subjective act.

In short, Jaspers should have distinguished between *what* we know in an act of consciousness and *how* we know it. What

5

exactly is immanent and what is transcendent in an act of
knowledge, and to what degree? What is the relationship between
the noema and the real object on one hand, and between the
noema and the intentional act on the other? Which is the real
problem of consciousness: to show how an immanent act can
take hold of something transsubjective, or to describe how something transsubjective becomes immanent to the subject? Or if
both questions are badly put, what is the right way to pose them?
These problems are dismissed rather than clarified by Jaspers.

It is regrettable that Jaspers finds it so easy to shrug off both
the real and the logical transcendence of objects, so that he is able
to lump everything knowable into immanence. There is very
little gained by such gestures, except an alibi to elaborate a new
and highly problematic theory of transcendence.

One can see that Jaspers emphasises the immanence of
intentional consciousness, in fact he identifies the principle of
consciousness with the principle of immanence,[52] in order to go
beyond it to what he calls 'authentic transcending'. He regards
intentional consciousness as an inventory of Being in terms of
objects, a stock-taking that measures out Being in piecemeal
determinations. As such, of course, it can never encounter Being
in itself. In order to become the organ of genuine transcending,
in order to grasp Being that transcends the particular ontic
limitations of objects, consciousness must wreck its own object-
bound determinations. Somehow it must surpass itself by thinking
what can no longer be thought of because it is nothing determinate. Indeed, for Jaspers, *'authentic transcending means going out
beyond objectiveness into the non-objective.'*[53] In order to become
aware of the overflowing character of Being which envelops
every particular object, the objective thought of intentional
consciousness must somehow judge its own poverty, and must
deny that it is itself the immanent measure of Being.

In the beginning we were called upon to perform a 'basic
philosophical operation' which was to liberate our awareness of
Being from all specific knowledge, that is, from all particular
objectivity. Now we can see that fundamentally that operation
is a movement of transcending the determinations of consciousness in general by means of an *absolute consciousness*,[54] in which
objective knowledge must expire. Transcending, therefore, is at
once the highest achievement and the ruin of consciousness.

What emerges from this ruin, however, is a sovereign image of *Being as spontaneity and liberty*. In spontaneity and liberty we reach the deepest source of Being as self-deciding,[55] which, as such, has no reference to any cause or antecedent: it is absolute. Absolute Being is grasped by absolute consciousness. But, as has been indicated earlier, spontaneity and liberty is also the unrepresentable image of the deep-down selfhood that Jaspers calls *Existenz*, or Existence.[56] Existence too is absolute; that is why Jaspers defines it, if such be the word, as 'that which is in rapport with itself'.[57]

The meeting of sovereign Being and genuine selfhood in the unconditionality of freedom and spontaneity is a sign that we have touched on what we had set out to find as the 'source and aim' of our meditation on Being. The circle is now complete. Perhaps it is a little more evident now why our search has revolved around these two focal points, Being and Existence, all along; why the question about Being had to be at the same time a question about the questioner; why our eventual answer had to indicate what Being was inseparably from what we are ourselves. Now we can at least suspect that the whole enterprise was an initiative of Existence. It was Existence that wanted to clarify and ultimately to find itself in the light of Being. Existence was searching for Being, because from the beginning it was animated by a then hidden faith that it would find there both its foundation and its final end. 'The search for Being led us back to the question of the one who searches. The searcher is not a mere Dasein, for Dasein does not search for Being, since it derives its satisfaction from itself. The being of the searcher as such is potential Existence, and his search, philosophy. Only when Existence experiences the impact of its Dasein and the urge to reach Being by way of thought drives it to philosophise, then, and not before, does Being become a question.'[58]

IV   The Enveloping

At long last we are in a position to sum up the full ontological significance of the subject-object-dichotomy, which is the initial and fundamental situation of our interrogative quest for reality.

What is then the meaning of this mystery which is implied at each moment by the subject-object-dichotomy? It can only mean that Being as a whole is neither subject nor object but must be the *Enveloping,* which reveals itself in this dichotomy.

Clearly then, Being as such cannot be an object. Everything that becomes an object for me breaks away from the Enveloping in confronting me, while I myself emerge from it as a subject. An object is a definite kind of being for the subject, whereas the Enveloping remains obscure for my consciousness. It is brought to light only through objects, and takes on greater and greater clarity to the extent that the objects become more sharply present to consciousness. The Enveloping itself does not become an object, but it appears in the cleavage of the subject and the object. It is a *background* which is incessantly illuminated through the appearance of objects, while remaining forever the Enveloping.[1]

Some points are clear from this text itself. Jaspers clearly affirms that Being as a whole does not fall on either side of the subject-object distinction, rather it presents itself as a background against which this distinction is inscribed and made possible. Furthermore, Being is presented as something which envelops the subject-object distinction; in fact, the proper name given to it by Jaspers is the Enveloping, *das Umgreifende.*

Some other points, however, need greater clarification. The following is intended as such a clarification of the origins of the Jaspersian concept of the Enveloping.

AN APPROACH

The problem of the Enveloping in the philosophy of Jaspers could constitute a complete study by itself. And if it is taken into account that Jaspers interprets all philosophy as a philosophy of the Enveloping, a study of this nature could grow into formidable proportions. For the purpose at hand, however, a short sketch of the more salient points of the origins of this concept of the Enveloping (both in history and in the mind of Jaspers) will suffice.

For the sake of brevity, one can do no better than summarise the essential points of the admirable article by Gerhard Knauss, 'The Concept of the "Encompassing" in Jaspers' Philosophy', *The Library of Living Philosophers*, vol. 9, pp. 141–75.

Mr Knauss starts out by stating that the ruling idea of all philosophy is the idea of totality. 'Philosophising is a thinking from out of totality. We speak of philosophy only when there is an intent to penetrate unity and totality' (p. 141). Truly philosophical reflection begins with this operation of locating things in a totality. Mr Knauss argues that even historically philosophy must have taken its start from the act of encompassing everything in a whole. Before the first Greek philosophers thought of everything in terms of fire, water, air, and so on, they must have thought of it under the concept of 'everything', the whole reality, of which particular beings are only more detailed qualifications. As an example he cites the *apeiron* of Anaximander. 'Notwithstanding the difficulty of whether the *apeiron* is to be understood as infinite or as undetermined, this much seems certain: Anaximander thought of it in the manner of an Encompassing of all the elemental materials contained in it; and not, indeed, as a mere summation of all things, but as something that penetrates, rules and regulates everything. Being, therefore, is really thought of as Being and not as a mere heap of all existing things' (p. 142).

When, under the disintegrating influence of the Sophists, philosophical thinking began to fall apart, Plato united it again under the unity of the *Idea*. Unlike the unity posited by the pre-Socratic cosmologists, this unity was no longer physical but logico-ideal. With Plato, thinking in Ideas was ordered once again under an enveloping unity, the highest Idea of the One and the Good. This fact is shown by the frequent use of the verb *periechein*, in terms of which the rapport between the Idea and its inferiors was described in Platonic philosophy. This verb 'signifies not only an encompassing but also a superiority of the encompassing over the encompassed. The concept, therefore, implies not only a quantitative encompassing, but also a qualitative gradation, which finally binds the Ideas hierarchically into a Highest' (p. 143).

Plato's valorisation of the Idea as the Enveloping left its mark upon the whole history of Western philosophy. Ever since his time, our thinking stands under the sign of, and is held together by, this unity of the Idea. 'The history of the Idea in Western thought is, at the same time, a history of the idea of the Enveloping, which accompanies it' (*ibid.*).

From this long varied history, Mr Knauss singles out two major philosophies, both of which had a direct influence on Jaspers' own notion of the Enveloping.

The first of these is the philosophy of Kant. Contrary to the run-of-the-mill interpretations of Kantian philosophy which emphasise the categorical aspects of it, Jaspers saw the basic relevance of Kant in his theory of Ideas. In a separate study, which constitutes the Appendix of the *Psychologie der Weltanschauungen* (1st ed. 1919, 6th ed. 1963), Jaspers discussed the ruling principle of the formation of Ideas according to Kant. This principle is to make the unconditioned, the unlimited, or the totality the guiding ideal of philosophical reflection. Wholeness, unconditionality, and non-limitation are the essential notes of the Idea. The Idea is the unconditioned among a set of given conditions and, as such, it encompasses within its scope the totality of these conditions. As such an embracing totality, Mr Knauss comments, the Idea is both subjective and objective at the same time. 'The subject-object-dichotomy, which forms the essence of the intellect, has no absolute significance for the Idea. Ideas go beyond the intellect by embracing its boundaries together with the intellect itself. . . . The idea, therefore, is the final Enveloping of subject and object' (*ibid.*). In other words, through the unconditionality of the Idea, philosophical reflection is able to transcend the split of subject and object, which is the usual condition of knowledge. Mr Knauss then remarks that such an interpretation, namely placing the theory of Ideas at the summit of Kantian philosophy, was at the time of its first publication very much contrary to the current views of Kant. It was usual at that time to regard the transcendental deduction and the problems of the categories as the very essence of Kantian philosophy. 'Over against this, Jaspers pointed out—to be sure without finding much resonance at the time—that the distinctive feature of Kantian thought consists in the union and unity of all the faculties of man's nature. He found in Kant's theory of Ideas the representative achievement of this basic intention' (p. 144). The sympathies of Mr Knauss clearly lie with Jaspers, in that he considers Jaspers' interpretation 'the natural development of Kantian thought under contemporary conditions,' a development which 'reverses all the deviations from and misrepresentations of Kant' (*ibid.*). Nevertheless, there is a very important difference between the Idea in the Kantian sense and the concept of the Enveloping in the Jaspersian sense. This difference is precisely between the scientific and objective claim of the former, and the merely synbolic and non-objective intention of the latter. 'For Kant philosophy has the character of a possible science, and its concepts (therefore also the Ideas) lay claim to scientific exactitude' (*ibid.*).

The radical break with the scientific pretensions of philosophy was the work of Kierkegaard. It was he who delivered the most severe blow to the view of philosophy as a science. This, in the estimation of Mr Knauss, was not merely an act of destruction, but also a definite enrichment for philosophy. 'What Plato had accomplished for objective consciousness with the concept of the Idea, Kierkegaard did for subjectivity with his concept of *Existence*' (p. 145). Kierkegaard's great merit in this connection consisted in having traced thought from its initial Platonic objectification back to its birth place, i.e., to the subjectivity of the thinking person. This emphasis on the subject has since then changed the whole philosophical outlook on the Enveloping also. Henceforward the Enveloping could no longer be regarded merely from the objective side, accomplished once and for all and binding for everybody, but had to be reconquered through a subjective adoption by each individual person. Mr Knauss notes that this new awareness that 'the truth of our subjective existence also determines the truth of our objective thinking, has necessarily forced a new and more original understanding of truth. Just as the naïve truths of the physiologists became untrue when the spirit qua *logos* was discovered, so can objective truth become untrue as soon as thinking is brought face to face with its own existing. There are truths which can be untrue for me' (*ibid.*).

Under the influence, then, of this conception of truth as something which is thus conditioned by our individual selves, Jaspers has tried to rethink the idea of Being, the total conditioning background of philosophical truth, in a way which would keep account both of the objective Idea and of the subjective Self, without submerging either one in the other.

This new conception has prompted Jaspers to think of Being in terms of the Enveloping which, as such, is neither objective nor subjective but encompasses both the subject and the object. In one sense, therefore, the Enveloping is the totality of reality not as a mere sum of beings but rather as the ground and source of all beings. Needless to say, the effort to think of this encompassing ground presents some insurmountable problems. 'If Being is more than object, and if, in philosophising, we always keep Being as a totality in mind, then the thought of the Enveloping of subject and object can no longer be the thought of a definite object. . . . The way in which we think of the Enveloping can no longer be the way in which we think of specific objects as objects. Thinking must acquire a new dimension, it must become movement, become dialectic. It must rise up against itself and contradict itself, and thereby suppress itself in its definiteness' (pp. 148-9). This new mode of thinking the Enveloping in a dialectical movement is what Jaspers generally designates by *transcending thinking,* which, since it is no longer object-bound, requires an important change on the part of the thinker. 'Transcending from the objective to the Enveloping demands from the thinker a corresponding *transcending of his intentionality*' (p. 149). The efforts of such a transcending together with all the ramifications that result from it constitute Jaspers' philosophy of the Enveloping.

These are in a nutshell the absolutely essential points of Mr Knauss' article. They outline an approach to the idea of the Enveloping and intimate the origins of it in history. They also spotlight some stages of its development and indicate briefly what it signifies in Jaspers' use. For the time being, two essential points should be kept in mind: first that the Enveloping is for Jaspers the symbolical image of total reality which encompasses and conditions both subject and object; and secondly that thinking of the Enveloping requires a new mode of thinking which transcends the ordinary intentional mode of thinking.

For my part I would like to prolong these considerations by asking to what extent such an idea of Being and such a new mode of thinking permit, or do not permit, the charting of the general course of a philosophical programme.

ONTOLOGY OR METAPHYSICS?

Accepting the thesis that the aim of philosophical reflection is always to find an ultimate and all-embracing explanation of Being as a totality, let us take stock of what we have accomplished so far in this regard.

The immediate picture is highly discouraging. Our intention to master the total meaning of Being is frustrated on all sides by the inevitable subject-object-dichotomy. In this dichotomy, which defines our basic cognitive situation, we can only meet with phenomena, i.e., with objects that are at best only delegates of Being for us but not Being itself.[2]

The first cleavage of Being into subject and object is aggravated by a second one, in so far as each object in addition to its polarity with the subject also opposes itself to all other objects. As a result, every being that we encounter as an object is limited, partial, determined, particular, and not Being in its encompassing reality.[3] In the direction of objectivity we meet Being precisely in so far as it escapes us. To intend it as an object is already 'to make it fall outside of the Enveloping'.[4] Being as the enveloping totality is, therefore, something which only announces itself. 'We never encounter *it*, but everything we encounter we encounter *in* it.'[5]

We are equally unsuccessful in regard to subjectivity. Jaspers does not believe that any of the known or analysable forms of consciousness can yield an answer to the encompassing nature of reality. 'Philosophy', our nostalgic search for the absolute, 'cannot be consummated by self-observation of an empirical consciousness, nor in the constructions of the ever-present general consciousness, nor in a historical knowledge.'[6] In other words, neither empirical psychology, nor a structural analysis of consciousness in general, nor yet a genetic study of any sort of *Zeitbewusstsein* will reveal the basic mystery of Being.

In a last attempt to bridge the split between subject and object, the mind can try to construct the concept of Being as such, of which the concepts of subject and object would merely be two correlative modes. We feel justified in calling Being that aspect which is common to both subject and object, namely, the fact that they both *are*, both exist. It would seem that the concept of *that which is*, or simply the idea of *is*, abstracting from the possible determinations of subjectivity or objectivity, is inclusive enough to permit us to transcend the scission and to intend Being as such. In other words, we should be able to represent for ourselves an objective system of reality in an ontology which would account for the general structure of everything that is.

From what we have learned thus far, we can easily suspect that such an orientation would be inacceptable to Jaspers. He would find it mistaken on several counts. First of all, he would point out that in order to abstract the concept of being from the concepts of subject and object, or inversely to combine the concepts of subject and object in the concept of being as such, subject and object should be comparable and compatible on some point. But they are not: they are incomparable and mutually exclusive, because free spontaneity, which constitutes the essence of subjectivity, and substantiality, *Bestand*, which constitutes the essence of objectivity, are incomparable and exclusive.[7] Jaspers would, of course, not deny that an ultimate abstraction of *is* or *exists*, and a last concept of *that which is* is possible. But let us not imagine that that is an abstraction from both subject and object, and that the resulting concept really applies to Being as a whole. Apart from being a banal 'watering down of Being',[8] an indefinite subject of an indifferent predication, the concept of being thus obtained applies only to the sum of objects, to the whole of positive being, because it was abstracted only from objects in the first place, and not, as one would imagine, from subjectivity as well. One cannot abstract anything from subjectivity, because subjectivity as such does not consist in a set of determinations to be abstracted from. Subjectivity is rather a possibility or a negativity. Finally and similarly, Jaspers would dispute that the concept of Being in itself—another attempt to conceive of the enveloping reality—is a genuine concept at all, in the sense of having a direct meaning in itself. He insists that the concept of Being in itself is only a limit-concept. Although this concept is necessary for thought, it has no determinable content. Its sole function is negative; to contest the absoluteness of representable being and to relativise, by pointing up its phenomenality, the claims of object-being to be taken for Being in the absolute sense.[9]

For all these reasons, Jaspers thinks we should give up trying to think of Being in ontologies. 'Ontologies must fall away . . . ontologies must be dissolved', he says.[10] Their place should be taken by transcendental metaphysics which, instead of claiming to be an objective science of Being, consists in progressive illumination of the open horizon of the Enveloping within which the subject-object-dichotomy arises and our knowledge takes place.[11] Metaphysics is not knowledge, but an illumination by means of knowledge.

Jaspers thus distinguishes between *metaphysics* and *ontology*. His distinction, for what it is worth, is commanded by the now currently accepted difference between Being-in-itself and that-which-is.[12] By its very nature as an object-directed study, ontology cannot be anything else than a science of beings (*ta onta*), a study of that-which-is, although in its pretensions it also claims to be a science of Being-in-itself. In Jaspers' view, ontology is a science that studies the beingness of beings, but not the Being of beings. In other words, ontology does not recognise, or after an initial recognition forgets, the said difference between Being and beings. It treats of Being as if Being were merely the sum of objects, or as if the totality of Being were synonymous with the totality of positive beings. Ontologising, therefore, involves some measure of naïvety or a certain amount of bad faith. This naïvety or insincerity also shows itself in the refusal to see the basic fragmentation of Being for us. Ontologies try to veil the irreducible oppositions between the different modes of reality which prevent us from extending our knowledge, except after some radical changes, beyond the domain of object-beings. Ontologies have a tendency to cover up the basic discrepancies (*Grundunstimmigkeiten*) in the knowledge that we can possibly have of Being. Instead of recognising that 'our force is in separation, for we have lost our naïvety,'[13] ontologies seek a deceptive reconciliation in a compact science of Being.

But if Jaspers repudiates ontology as a science of Being, he takes it back as a theory of categories, *Kategorienlehre*, which he considers as an indispensable part of philosophical logic. Ontology, thus considered, is no longer a 'knowledge of Being itself, but a knowing of the modes and forms in which Being becomes objectively thinkable for us.'[14]

Transcendental metaphysics, which Jaspers proposes in place of

ontology, is quite another matter. This metaphysics will preserve
the original awareness of the fragmented character of reality and
will not try to discourse about Being as if Being too were
structured in a thoroughly objective system. It will recognise
that objects are not the only forms of Being, and that Being as a
whole is, therefore, not justifiable by objective knowledge; that
is, it cannot become the correlate of an intentional grasp. Paradoxically, however, it is the awareness of this limitation that will
permit us to go beyond the boundaries of objective knowledge
and to obtain an indirect insight into the overflowing and
encompassing nature of Being. For the fact remains that, as soon
as we think, we think by means of objects, but if we keep in
mind that objects are only one side of total Being, we may
succeed in touching upon the non-objective reality of the
Enveloping.

The critical point of Jaspersian thought lies here. His insistence
on the unknowable and non-objective character of Being could
easily be construed to mean that in regard to Being thought must
cease and lapse into a vague feeling or mysticism, without any
rational relationship to Being at all. Transcending thinking looks
much more like a mystical intuition than a philosophical act.
Indeed, how can we think of the Enveloping, if it does not
become an object for us? What sort of thinking is that which has
no object in mind? Is transcending a mystical leap into the
irrational where nothing is objective?

Jaspers' intent is different. He is not a mock mystic. He simply
wants to mobilise thought into a kind of thinking that no longer
clings absolutely to the fixity of objective knowledge. Between
a direct intuition of Being, which would be a kind of mystical
experience, and an objective grasp of it, which would not be the
grasp of Being at all, he believes in an indirect intuition of Being
by means of objects. He calls this indirect intuition *Innewerden*.
He knows that 'to philosophise directly about the Enveloping
would mean to penetrate into Being itself. But this cannot be
done except indirectly, because as soon as we think, we think in
terms of objects. What we must accomplish by our objective
thought, however, is to designate the non-objective reality of the
Enveloping.'[15] His point is that objective thought is not an end
in itself but that it points beyond itself. There is no question of
leaving behind or of bypassing objectivity, rather we must

assume and traverse it, to use it as a 'possible springboard towards Transcendence'.[16] Indeed, objects are necessary for transcending because, by revealing their own phenomenality, they may point to authentic reality.[17] Therefore, *the aim of the proposed basic philosophical operation or transcending is not to sink into the ineffable, but to exceed all fixed thought content precisely by means of thinking*.[18] According to the metaphor of Jaspers, in this act of transcending we are somewhat in the position of Baron Münchhausen, who lifted himself from the bog by pulling on his own pigtail.[19]

The philosophy of the Enveloping is not an esoteric discipline that provides a direct access to Being and can afford to dispense with clear and objective thought; rather, it is a constant act of awareness of that which objective knowledge points to: Being.

This awareness is invaluable for philosophy. It reminds us that the philosophical value of thought does not lie in its objective content as fixed by the intellect, but in its mobility and infinite openness that shows the way for reason. Consequently, this awareness puts us on our guard and compels us to metamorphose constantly the objective content of our thought from within. 'It is only with this reserve that we will be capable of the inward experience of the Enveloping, which is never the formulable result of a positive research but an attitude of consciousness. It is not my knowledge that is changed but the awareness I have of myself and of Being.'[20] We could say, therefore, that in general the Enveloping is that transobjective sense we have of ourselves and of Being, that surplus in both, which we experience whenever we try to think beyond the objective.[21]

With the new attitude of consciousness concerning the nature, possibilities, and limitations of thought, we now begin to see the essentially symbolic function of all objectively enunciable knowledge in philosophy. Objective knowledge merely points to, implies, conjures up. announces that which philosophy intends. One might say, objective knowledge is only a catalyst of philosophical awarness.[22] Being, which philosophy intends, remains obstinately beyond the grasp of objective knowledge, which clings to the appearances of Being. But the point is that objective knowledge can become a cipher for Being. Borrowing the striking image of Dufrenne and Ricoeur, objective knowledge is 'the finger which points to Being like the index finger of John the Baptist in the "Crucifixion" by Grünewald'.[23] And just as the

Precursor had to diminish in order that the presence of Christ be revealed more and more, objects too must slowly vanish before the advent of Being.

The impulse of Existence towards Being can transform objective knowledge into a sign-language of the Enveloping, and it is in metaphysics that we attend to and try to decode this sign-language. In fact, Jaspers likens the whole metaphysical enterprise to the reading and decoding of a cryptogram, *Lesen und Deuten der Chiffreschrift*.[24] Needless to say, however, this decoding is not the work of the intellect but of reason. The symbols of Being are essentially indecipherable for the understanding which can never translate them into final, univocal meanings; they can only be translated by reason into other symbols.[25]

There is an irreconcilable ambiguity in all this. On the one hand, we are fastened to the subject-object-dichotomy so irrevocably that even Being, the univerasl and absolute foundation of everything, must take on a determined and objective form in this cleavage; while on the other hand, we are commanded by the overflowing character of Being to demolish this objective form in order that from its ruin the pure presence of the Enveloping may shine forth.[26] For clarity, we must think objectively, but for transcendence, we must think non-objectively. These two demands of thought, clarity and transcendence, are in a never-ending conflict with each other. But perhaps it is the polemic tension of these two demands that creates those open spaces in which thought can move freely, and from which authentic Being is able to speak to us. It may be the ability to float (*Schwebenkönnen*) between these two demands of thought that guarantees the fruitfulness and measure of every truly philosophical research, and prevents it from falling into either a rigid intellectualism or a thoughtless enthusiasm.

Our new attitude also prepares the way for philosophical faith By recognising the limits of knowledge and of the knowable, 'so that through these limits we become aware of the phenomenality of empirical being and hence the encompassing nature of Being, we enter into the area of faith.'[27] Indeed, the conviction that 'it is thinkable that there be things inexpressible in thought'[28] must be an act of faith. The ability to believe that reality extends 'above us' constitutes both the sacred and the metaphysical dimension of human existence.

MODES OF THE ENVELOPING

The Enveloping has been presented thus far in terms of totality. But if we consider that the basic structure of the Enveloping is the simultaneity of subject-being and object-being, it could also be proposed as the fundamental image of the unity of Being. Through the idea of the Enveloping we endeavour to transcend not only the duality of subject and object but also all possible distinction and multiplicity of objects. Through it we touch upon unity which makes distinction and multiplicity possible. It is, therefore, very surprising to hear Jaspers speak of several modes of the Enveloping.

If in transcending the subject-object-dichotomy our intention is precisely to suspend all variation and separation, then how can there be various modes of the Enveloping? Does not the very idea of the Enveloping signify the exclusion of multiplicity? There is no doubt that in itself the Enveolping is only one. However, as Mr Knauss rightly points out, 'from the manner of our transcending movement there arise *for us* various manners of the Enveloping.'[29] In other words, multiplicity and variation are not properties of the Enveloping in itself but the expression of our finite approach to it. From the way we transcend to it, the unique Enveloping assumes various perspectives.

The idea of the Enveloping has been present in Jaspers' writings, at least implicitly,[30] ever since the publication of *Philosophie* (1933), but its articulation into distinct modes did not appear until *Vernunft und Existenz* (1935), and still more methodically in *Von der Wahrheit* (1947). A complete account of these articulations, the reasons and methodical steps that lead to them, would take us too far afield from our present purpose which is quite adequately served by a simple enumeration of the different modes and figures of the Enveloping.[31]

As we have seen, the modes of the Enveloping arise from the different manners of approaching it. Fundamentally, our approach can take two opposite directions: our transcending efforts may go either towards Being itself or towards ourselves. In other words, we can try to plumb the depths of Being as it presents itself either from without or from within.[32] That is why Jaspers distinguishes two principal modes of the Enveloping: the Enveloping that is Being itself, and the Enveloping that we are ourselves. In a general way, one could call them the objective and the subjective dimensions of the Enveloping. In the first direction Being presents itself as the *World* and as *Transcendence,* which is sometimes called God; in the second direction Being appears as *Empirical Being, General Consciousness,* and *Spirit.*[33] To these Jaspers adds two other modalities which he identifies as the ground and bond of all the other modes. These are *Existence* and *Reason.* The division can be presented schematically as follows:

The Enveloping that is *Being* itself:	The Enveloping that *we* are ourselves:	*Ground* and *bond* of the modes:
World Transcendence	Empirical Being General Consciousness Spirit	Existence Reason

Next, in order to show the dynamic character of philosophy, which he conceives as 'an unslackening exploration of the Enveloping in all its modalities',[34] Jaspers superimposes a second division on the first one in terms of movement from immanence to transcendence. The two divisions together give the following compound schema:

	The Enveloping that *we* are ourselves:	The Enveloping that is *Being* itself:
Immanent:	Empirical Being General Consciousness Spirit	World
Transcendent:	Existence	Transcendence

Reason,
the bond of all the modes of Enveloping in us

For the moment let us simply note for future reference that Reason, the principal subject of this book, figures as one of the encompassing modes. Its peculiar position in both schemas, somewhat apart from the rest of the modes, will prove of some importance later on when the time comes to treat of it explicitly.

It is much more important at this point to prevent a possible misunderstanding that is readily suggested by the foregoing schematic presentation. These schemas can mislead us into thinking that we are dealing with the different fundamental ways in which the whole of Being can originally be present to us, and that their common denominator, 'enveloping', is a common denominator in the objective sense of the word.[35] Enveloping is not a common denominator, because each mode envelops, so to speak, in an essentially different way. Similarly, these schemas do not represent the division of Being in itself, as if the seven of them together would constitute the whole of Being. The point is precisely that, in different ways, each of them envelops all the rest; each of them *is* the whole of Being in a certain sense. They are the images of how total Being appears as Being-for-us at different times and from different perspectives. Although by an act of philosophical faith we believe that in the ground of Being itself these modes of the Enveloping are somehow united, we cannot determine what this ground is and how these modes form a unity in it. The best we can do is to cast some light on the systematic ambiguity of these modes and of their relationship to each other. These relationships constitute a complex and mobile network, in which the meaning of each mode is constantly varied according to its momentary position in relation to the others. Somewhat like the individual notes of a melody, which do not reveal their full import except as carriers of a larger movement that realises itself in them, the meaning of each Enveloping only comes to light when we consider it as a moment of a complex stream of sense. Unfortunately, the limitations of this essay make it impossible to indicate even the great outlines of this network. Jaspers' detailed treatment of it covers two chapters of *Von der Wahrheit,* and is nearly a hundred pages long.[36] However, we shall have occasion to come back briefly to this question in Part III, where we shall treat explicitly of the role of reason in philosophy. Here a few observations as general conclusions to Part I should suffice.

Conclusions to Part I

THE modes of the Enveloping are the various transcendental figures in which Being shows itself as Being-for-us, and according to which the total image of Being has been constructed ever since the first days of Western philosophy. Jaspers maintains that they form a part of our cultural heritage; our ancestors lived and thought in them.[1] The names and even the number of these different figures have changed during history. They have been variously called matter, life, logos, apeiron, spirit, will, God, nature, idea, cosmos, existence, and so on. Jaspers calls them by other names and thinks that the seven he usually lists cover all of them.[2] Though he maintains that each individual mode is an Enveloping by itself, he also insists that they should not be isolated from one another under pain of falling into lopsided isms which are the curse of our whole history of philosophy: materialism, idealism, vitalism, intellectualism, acosmism, and the rest. Such isolations are always the work of the intellect, which is basically a reductionist faculty. On the contrary, the truth of each Enveloping is promoted only when Reason grasps them in their relatedness and interpenetration. That is why Reason is called the bond of the other figures. In an unceasing work of mediation, Reason searches out all the other modes and creates unity among them; not the unity of a harmoniously coalescing whole, but the unity of a dialectical movement.

Jaspers' philosophy as a whole has been diversely characterised as a 'negative ontology',[3] a 'philosophy of shipwreck',[4] the 'destruction of the philosophical illusion',[5] a 'contemporary Kant-interpretation',[6] and so on. All these characterisations are no doubt justified by the patient investigations and sometimes brilliant insights that preceded their formulation, yet somehow all of them have a curious un-Jaspersian ring about them. So, if there must be labelling at all, I should prefer to borrow a tag from Jaspers' own terminology and call his philosophy a 'philosophy of the Enveloping'. In fact this appellation in a certain sense includes all the others. Since the modes of the Enveloping are the conditions under which authentic Being presents itself to us, a philosophy of the Enveloping could be compared to the Kantian search for the transcendental conditions of possibility. Similarly, the philosophy of the Enveloping could be regarded as a kind of negative ontology which, instead of investigating positive beings, studies their background. Jaspers sometimes calls it *periechontology*. For the same reason, it is also a critique of the ingrained illusion that philosophy has to do with objects. The philosophy of the Enveloping is an awareness of the subjective conditions of having objects rather than a science of objects themselves. All these aspects belong to the philosophy of the Enveloping by virtue of a transcending impulse which is Reason. That is why at one point in his career Jaspers preferred to change the label of his own thought from Existence-philosophy to philosophy of Reason.[7]

In measuring out the limitations of intentional consciousness, Jaspers has tried to evoke for us certain topics whose consideration exceeds the competence of this consciousness. He wanted thus to indicate that our human plus, our metaphysical dimension, consists in the fact that we are open not only to objects (through intentional consciousness) but also to the condition of objects (through Reason). By showing that intentionality extends only as far as the domain of object-beings, he invited our thought to transcend itself towards the regions which envelop and render object-beings possible. These encompassing regions can no longer be intended in particular and detached acts of knowledge, but can only be affirmed in acts of philosophical faith and commitment.

The apparent circle involved in this process of affirmations is vital. In order to affirm Being, two things are simultaneously required. On the one hand, we must have an experience of Being not only as of an object that is correlative to a subject, but also in its act of profound self-identity. Such an experience is available to us only in the intuition of our own incommensurable selfhood or Existence. What it means 'to be in itself' for anything or anybody else outside me can only be grasped in analogy to this act of self-identity within me. In this regard, selfhood is the absolute primary analogate of Being, the origin and condition of all further affirmation and attribution of Being. Jaspers calls the awareness of this identity with oneself the absolute consciousness. On the other hand, experience is not enough. In philosophy we must account for the condition of its possibility; we must say how it can be. This accounting for is precisely the activity whereby philosophy prolongs the grasp of experience, or more

accurately, whereby metaphysics continues the movement of
phenomenological description. Even though we experience that
Existence is *in itself,* we are also aware of the fact that it is not
by itself. Consequently, our selfhood must be brought into relation
with the Being that is by itself, with Being that is absolutely
absolute and eternal, with the All-Other of Existence: God. To
account for our selfhood, we must refer it to the Absolute and
discover it as a gift of the Absolute, because 'Existence exists only
in relation to Transcendence, or not at all.'[8] Here the condition
for our affirmation is the consciousness of the Absolute. *Absolute
consciousness and consciousness of the Absolute are the 'primum quoad
nos' and the 'primum quoad se' conditions for our affirmation of Being.*

The ultimate aim of insisting on the subject–object–dichotomy
as the fundamental situation of our knowledge was not to
demonstrate that we are condemned perpetually to go round
and round the phenomenal and the relative; on the contrary, it
was to invite us to look for Being beyond the cleavage of subject
and object in the Enveloping. Jaspers wanted to remind us that
the objects which we encounter in the dichotomy should be
treated as mediative of the revelation of Being, as symbols and
ciphers of authentic reality. In order to become truly mediative,
these objects must efface themselves, must become empty and
transparent ciphers, so as to permit our gaze to penetrate beyond
their appearance. As Dufrenne and Ricoeur remark, it is 'the
philosophy of ciphers which completes the Metaphysics of
Jaspers that lends true meaning to the theory of objectivity which
inaugurated it.'[9] However, going beyond the phenomenal does
not mean avoiding it. On the contrary, it means discovering at
the heart of the phenomenal that which leads beyond it. Transcending consists in exploring well the domain of phenomenal
objects and discovering their transparence, their openness, which
point to Being. We should not be content with analysing the
different levels of penomena, but we should account for them
somehow, designating both the origin (*Ursprung*) from which
they emerge and the goal (*Ziel*) towards which they tend.

As we can already surmise, *the power that surpasses intentionality
by deflecting its movement from going towards objects themselves to
going towards their founding first principle and comprehensive final end,
is the power of Reason. Reason is the 'intentio obliqua' of the intellect,
or as Jaspers likes to put it, repeating Hegel's phrase, 'Mystik für den*

Verstand'.[10] It is oblique because the direct intention of the intellect aims each time at some determined object in which it comes to rest, whereas the aim of Reason is to reflect in its movement the transobjective and unlimited One.[11] In other words, the efforts of Reason do not consist in drafting a blueprint of Being in terms of objects, in gaining possession of it in knowledge, but in mediating a methodical intuition of Being by means of the movement of knowledge.[12]

'By means of' indicates that Reason inserts objective knowledge into the flow of its own dynamism, or more accurately, subordinates it to the teleology of selfhood. For as we saw, the search for Being through Reason is the enterprise of Existence. 'Reason has substance through Existence alone',[13] Jaspers says. This finalisation or relativation (= relating to an end) of knowledge through Reason could be likened to an act of demythologisation. It is essentially an act of piety in the sense that it sorts out the means from the end, the image from the reality, the idol from the deity. The Heideggerian phrase, *Das Fragen ist die Frömmigkeit des Denkens*, could be converted into a Jaspersian phrase: *Vernunft ist die Frömmigkeit des Denkens*. Reason liberates thought from its fascination with appearances and directs its flow to Being that is hidden under the shell of objects. That is why at one point Jaspers can boast that his philosophy of Reason is a liberating demythologisation of thought.[14]

Part II
Reason and Science

Introduction

THE chapters of Part I were intended for highlighting some of the fundamental concepts of Jaspers' philosophy. I say 'some' of them, because there are certainly others, such as the concepts of 'communication', 'limit-situation', 'historicity', 'law of day and passion of the night', which have not been touched upon at all, even though they are equally basic to Jaspers' thought as a whole. The ones discussed were selected in the hope that they might prove more immediately useful for leading up to the concepts of reason and rationality which are, after all, the final objectives of this book.

Thus, for instance, Jaspers' theory on objectivity and the issues connected with it indicated that he understood philosophy to be a methodical transcending which, in order to attain Being, must go beyond the domain of that which is logically graspable, systematic, consistent, universally and univocally valid for consciousness as such, in short, beyond the domain of objectivity. On the other hand, his doctrine on the subject-object-dichotomy left no doubt that he held objectivity to be insurmountable. Whenever we know anything, we know it as an object. It is the very structure of consciousness to be occupied with objects. Thus transcending does not seem possible at first, unless somehow the direct intention of consciousness can be deflected from its habitual objects and directed towards the encompassing ground of object-beings. This indirect intention calls for a change in the noetic stance of the subject from intentional consciousness, which is the ordinary attitude involved in objective knowledge, to absolute consciousness, which is the awareness of Being. In fact, transcending seems to demand a running counter to ordinary objective knowledge and exercising a sort of non-knowledge, *Nichtwissen*. But lest one should think that philosophy is, therefore, a kind of irrationalism which in the end sinks into the amorphousness of feeling or mysticism, Jaspers points out that this transcending is still the work of reason. As a rational activity, philosophy cannot afford to discard objective knowledge purely and simply. The transcendence of philosophy over objective knowledge is not a simple suppression of objectivity, it is rather a sublimation of it. Indeed, the movement of thought which is called upon to surpass objectivity is often presented by Jaspers in the Hegelian term as an *Aufhebung* or *Aufheben* which signifies suppression through sublimation.[1]

Now the organised body of objective knowledge goes by the name of science. Science is thus the sum total of what philosophy must transcend. But if this transcendence is to be a genuine sublation or sublimation and not an arbitrary suppression of science, philosophy must first be clear about the nature of science and scientific rationality. For if philosophy is rational, science is much more evidently so. While there exists a relatively unanimous agreement on the point that science is a rational inquiry, the rational character of philosophy is contested by many. In the end it may turn out that philosophical reason is in fact superior to scientific reason, but this superiority must first be shown by the fact that philosophy is able to discern the nature and limits of science and thus situate science in its own larger scope. Whatever its true status may be, philosophy cannot assume an attitude of sovereign scorn towards objective science, and philosophical rationality cannot be a simple supplanting of objectivity; it must rather be a repossession, a new reading, a new application of it.[2]

Of all the existentialists, Jaspers is the most alive to the relevance of science for philosophy. He considers science an indispensable part in the development of thought whose first stage consists in being oriented in the world. This world-orientation, *Weltorientierung*, unfolds on two distinct levels: the one scientific, the other philosophical. Scientific world-orientation consists in the empirical search by the intellect for objectively verifiable facts about the world.[3] Moreover, this search is methodical. It flows from certain principles which are either explicitly postulated or tacitly presupposed from the beginning, and is guided by certain standards and methods whose application results in a logically coherent and unitary body of information, a *Weltbild* or world-image. Philosophical world-orientation, on the other hand, is essentially a critique which evaluates the principles and presuppositions of science, determines the limits of scientific methods, and passes judgement on the validity of unitary world-pictures constructed by empirical world-orientation.[4] The measure in which this critique is successful shows that it is possible to think beyond objective knowledge; that scientific world-orientation has its limits and cannot claim to make the complete tour of

Being; and that, consequently, there is a place for philosophy. In other words, the sense and purpose of science can be grasped only from a point of view that is outside of science. The clarification of science is a philosophical task.[5] Nevertheless, Jaspers insists that this philosophical task can be performed only by those who have previously been schooled in factual scientific research, or have at least reflected on the actual workings of science.[6]

It is instructive to see the amount of effort Jaspers spends on trying to clarify the relationship between science and philosophy. There is hardly a work of his which does not contain long chapters about this problem. Difficult and incomplete as these passages may be when taken individually, they all converge on several important issues, and from this convergence one can reconstruct the main lines of Jaspers' position with a fair amount of accuracy. The following four chapters are intended as such an attempt at reconstruction.

Views Rejected by Jaspers (Chapter V) will indicate the negative side of Jaspers' position and will set the general tone of subsequent considerations. Next follows a more or less factual

Description of Science (Chapter VI). This chapter will treat of the domains and methods of science and discuss the definitive limits of scientific knowledge as Jaspers sees them. It will also situate science in the teleology of thought in general.

Relationship of Science and Philosophy (Chapter VII) will make some fundamental distinctions between these two disciplines. It will also enable us to see better the place science occupies in man's global relation to reality as a whole, a relation which Jaspers alternately calls Reason and Existence. Finally,

Reason in Science (Chapter VIII) will deal with the first principles of reason as it is operative in the sciences.

V   Views Rejected by Jaspers

THE relationship between science and philosophy presents more problems today than it did traditionally. These problems are more complex and more acute, because today science has a new and specific meaning that it did not have before. This new meaning is the result of a historical evolution of some three hundred years, during which period modern sciences came of age, so to speak. They not only freed themselves from the tutelage of philosophy, they also acquired a degree of prestige that traditionally belonged to philosophic wisdom alone. Orginally, it was only philosophy that bore the name of science.

Jaspers notes that 'philosophy has from its very beginnings looked upon itself as science, indeed as science *par excellence*. To achieve the highest and most certain knowledge is the goal that has always animated its devotees.'[1] In other words, philosophy was regarded as the ultimate achievement of humanly possible knowledge, the final, most fundamental explanation of reality as a whole. As such, it stood in contrast to mere conjecture, skill, or simple opinion whereby man could only guess or suspect the real natures of things but could not really account for them. To truly understand and to explain why and how things were what they were, or why they were other than what they seemed to be, one had to possess the knowledge of the proper causes of each thing in question. The wise man was he who understood the causes, and the wisest, most fortunate of them all, the philosopher, who could penetrate to the deepest causes of all reality. *Felix, qui potuit rerum cognoscere causas.*

Traditionally, then, philosophy was looked upon as a universal and total science. It occupied the most respected place among the other disciplines as the ultimate in cognition. In each period the philosopher-thinker was convinced that he stood on the summit of the thereto acquired knowledge.[2] He thought himself to be in possession of a finished and closed science. The fact that for some time it has become questionable whether philosophy is a science

74

at all, and if so, in what sense, must be understood in the light of the development of a specifically modern scientific outlook.

Jaspers believed that this new outlook was born out of the intermingling of three component motives or attitudes. He calls the first one scientificity, W*issenschaftlichkeit.* Scientificity represents the secular intent of science to replace all mystery with reliable information and to lay open all the secrets of reality in clearly formulated items of knowledge. This intent automatically commits modern science to an unceasing research which (in contrast to the science of ancient times that always presented itself as a finished doctrine) is essentially incomplete. Unlike the Greek cosmos, the world of modern science is open. The second factor is a direct misunderstanding of this last point on the part of some modern philosophers who, while identifying the essence of philosophy with modern science, also wanted to hold on to the old scientific ideal of philosophy as a total knowledge. In other words, they failed to realise that the very scientificity of the new science excludes such totalism of knowledge. 'Modern scientists have understood that an all-embracing world-system, which deduces everything that exists from one or a few principles, is impossible.'[3] Jaspers maintains that the claims of the old and the new science cannot be confused without great harm to the purity of both philosophy and science.[4] The third component of the modern scientific outlook consists in its absolutisation of objective, universally valid, cogent truth as the only acceptable form of truth.

Although isolated manifestations of this scientific spirit can be found in almost any epoch of man's cultural history, it did not become a major historical force until about the sixteenth century. Even then, its initial application was rather modest: it was conceived as a solution to certain limited problems in physics through the use of the experimental and mathematical methods. However, these methods gained rapid acceptance first in the whole domain of physics, then in the realm of inorganic matter in general, and finally in the study of living organisms and even in the psychological and sociological fields. By the nineteenth century science in this modern sense became a 'new possibility', a new way of looking at the world and arranging human life, so that the present epoch can truly be called the age of science and technology.

This prodigious development of the new sciences took place 'largely outside philosophy, often in opposition to philosophy, and finally in an atmosphere of indifference to it.'[5] When, between periods of intermittent neglect and hostility, men took a second look at philosophy, they demanded that it should be 'scientific' in a different sense than that in which the ancient *epistemé* or *scientia* was scientific: they now expected it to be cogent and convincing as modern science was. And when each successive attempt on the part of philosophy to comply with this demand proved less and less convincing, slowly the impression grew that philosophy was finished. 'Now that all the possible fields of research have been marked off, the days of philosophy are over.'[6] There was nothing left for philosophy to investigate. It had no proper object, nor a reliable proper method either. Philosophy could furnish nothing comparable to the reliable information and universally compelling statements of science. Measured against the norms of science, philosophy appeared hardly more than a string of unverifiable assertions about anything and everything, idle general chatter about some obscure ultimates.

In view of this overall situation, Jaspers poses the question whether it is possible or not for us today to talk of philosophy as a science. In order to put into relief his own answer to the question, he first indicates a few typical positions on the part of other philosophers whose views he considers either unwarranted or inadequate. He is seldom explicit as to which philosopher he has in mind, and sometimes his characterisations fit a more or less identifiable current rather than any one representative of that current.

PROGRESSIVISM

I am not quite sure this is the best word to characterise the attitude of those who, in view of the conquering prestige of science, have abandoned the philosophical field altogether. According to this view, philosophy is only an intermediary stage in the development of thought, destined to be surpassed by the progress of thought itself. With the advent of modern science, the philosophical stage of thought became antiquated. Philosophy has relevance only for students of cultural history who are interested in the genesis of ideologies, or for philologists and aesthetes who are willing to busy themselves with the philosophic writings of the past on account of the style and 'quaint' atmosphere of these works. 'If philosophy is at an end because the sciences have taken over all its subject matter, there remains nevertheless the knowledge of its history, first as a factor in the history of the sciences themselves, then as a phenomenon in the history of thought, the history of errors, the anticipated insights, the process of liberation by which philosophy made itself superfluous. Finally, the history of philosophy must preserve the knowledge of the philosophical texts, if only for their aesthetic interest. Although these texts do not make any serious contribution to scientific truth, they are nevertheless worth reading for the sake of their style and the intellectual attitude they reflect.'[7]

Although Jaspers does not say so, he is actually describing the attitude of the positivistic school of Auguste Comte (1798–1857). Comte's famous thesis of the 'three stages' was designed precisely in order to explain how the human mind has supposedly evolved from primitive imagination to the height of objective rationality, from myth to positive sciences. In his feeble infancy man could account for the phenomena around him only by myth, by stocking the world with innumerable subjective forces and wills, somewhat like his own, but 'divine' in scope and efficacy. Visible events were regarded as the effects of invisible and unforeseeable divine caprice. This was what Comte called the *theological* stage of mentality, which rested on the divinisation of subjectivity, of the subjective conditions of human life and volition. Subjective and mythical explanation was next replaced by a *metaphysical* one, which was characterised by a greater objectivity. The metaphysical mind explains things not by an appeal to supernatural forces but by natural causes and essences which are supposed to underlie the phenomena of nature. Metaphysics is already a decisive step in the right direction in that it de-personalises the forces of theology, but it is still imperfect in so far as it is still haunted by the invisible. In the last stage of its development, the human mind has finally renounced even this last bit of self-indulgence in imaginary explanation and given up the vain search for causes and essences. Causes and essences are irrelevant for the mind in its *positivistic* stage. Positive science is interested only in the constant relations and necessary laws of phenomena which permit man, without any mixture of subjectivity, to foresee and to account for the facts of reality as they objectively happen. This is all man can know with certainty, and all he needs to know for a rational arrangement of his life.

In sum, according to this view, it is positive science and not philosophy that represents the highest achievement of human thought which is seen as progressive evolution whereby thought has been emancipated from fiction, imagination, and subjectivity, and rewarded with complete objectivity. The progress of thought has left philosophy behind.

'STRENGE WISSENSCHAFT'

There is a second attitude that is closely related to the attitude of progressivism. It is represented by a group of philosophers who did not entirely retire from the scene, but joined forces with modern science and set out to make philosophy respectable in such a way that from now on it could hold its own among modern sciences. In other words, what they have rejected was not philosophy as such but the hitherto existing manifestations of philosophy which they thought ill-founded, debatable, unscientific. Clearly, the task was to establish philosophy on solid and incontestable bases, to found it for the first time as an exact science, just like the other exact sciences. There was, however, a special kind of difficulty attached to this undertaking: nobody seemed to know what philosophy was supposed to be all about, since it lacked a suitable object of study. This fact became more and more noticeable as the diversification of special sciences advanced and each of them claimed its own proper object, until the whole of reality seemed to have been divided among them. Finally, it became clear that the only field of study left open to a possible scientific philosophy was the investigation of the scientific method itself. Thus philosophy was reduced to a general methodology of science, it became logic, theory of knowledge, phenomenology. This, in Jaspers' eyes, meant a degradation for philosophy, for 'in the effort to refurbish its reputation, philosophy became a servile imitator, a handmaiden to the sciences.'[8] In its role as a general methodology of science, the new 'scientific' philosophy established the epistemological grounds for the universal validity of scientific knowledge. In a remark that is more peevish than profound, Jaspers notes how superfluous it was to demonstrate this validity, 'which was not questioned anyhow'.[9] In its clearest form, scientific philosophy became formalised logic, which is just another special science. But because of the universal nature of its object, namely the form of all scientific thought, this special science seemed particularly suited to take over the function of philosophy as a whole. To many it looked like the old dream of *mathesis universalis* come true, and even 'today many thinkers regard symbolic logic as the whole of philosophy'.[10]

The currents that embody this attitude are not difficult to identify. Logical positivism and phenomenology are mentioned by name, and the references to method and *mathesis universalis* make us think of Cartesianism. Jaspers' view on the value of logic is short, severe, and in many respects intolerably unjust. He admits its exactitude, but dismisses its importance. He considers it an empty and inconsequential game of manipulating formal relationships whose philosophical worth is slight.[11] His judgements on Cartesianism and phenomenology are a little more extensive and perhaps also more to the point.

In fact, Jaspers wrote a whole book, *Descartes und die Philosophie* (1937), in order to show that the prevalent science-consciousness of modern philosophy dates back to the influence of Cartesianism, or more precisely to René Descartes himself. He contends that the fascinating novelty of Descartes' thought for his contemporaries as well as for posterity was the fact that he turned his attention to the very method of certain and indubitable knowledge; he made this the main theme of his study, and wanted to build a whole philosophy on it.[12] Disgusted with the unsurveyable variety of principles in scholastic philosophy (as he knew it), which always seemed to have one more self-evident principle in its magic bag when in difficulty, Descartes decided to do two things: to discover a single principle of certitude to which all other principles are reducible, and to find a single clear method by means of which he could deduce the rest of his system from this one principle. The former he believed he discovered in the *cogito*, the latter in the mathematical method.

In Jaspers' estimation it is these two elements, namely the certitude of a special first principle and the deductive development of philosophic knowledge, that constitute the core of Descartes' discovery. The accent is on the words 'special' and 'deductive', for the recourse to just any first principle at all and a non-deductive way of developing philosophy into a systematic body of knowledge would not in itself have constituted a novelty in the history of thought. That was always in practice in one way or another.

Descartes' stroke of originality was to call in question, and thereby to purify, the intuitive certitude of the senses (and of the imagination) which for realism is always the last court of appeal in matters of evidence and certitude. In so doing, he anchored certitude in the indubitable self-certitude of the act of thought itself. For the feasibility of such a passage from sense-intuition to thought-intuition he could point to his own invention of analytical geometry, which eliminates the sensible and imaginative elements of ordinary geometry and concrete arithmetic by expressing its objects—lines, curves, surfaces—in algebraic equations.[13] Analytical geometry is a clear instance of the dematerialisation and formalisation of experience of which science is capable. From this particular example Descartes concluded that sense-intuitions were unnecessary not only for geometry but also for knowledge in general. He maintained that the certitude and clarity of thought did not depend on the sense-intuition to which thought referred, but on the very exercise of thought itself, independently of its content. According to Jaspers, Descartes' ideal was not so much to possess clear and distinct intuitive contents as, precisely by overcoming sense-intuitions as sources of opacity and confusion, to arrive at the clarity and distinctness of thought itself.[14]

Jaspers' observations in this regard are short and to the point. On the one hand, Descartes wanted to transfer certitude from sense-intuition to thought-intuition; on the other, he affirmed that the essential notes of thought-intuition are clarity and distinctness. But certitude, clarity and distinctness can only be spoken of if they belong to a thought *of something*, to a thought with intuitive filling. Descartes, Jaspers charges, did not distinguish between the clarity of thought which is pregnant with intuition and the clarity of empty thought which is simply the rational validity of relations and forms that need not contain any intuition.[15] Furthermore, Descartes seems to have overlooked the fact that certitude by itself does not necessarily include clarity and distinctness. His own *cogito ergo sum* is a striking example of this: even supposing that the very exercise of the *cogito* immediately yields the *sum* with certainty, it only assures me of the fact *that* I am, and not of *what* I am.[16] Indeed, it is the very certitude of the fact of intuition that forfeits the clarity of its content.[17] Descartes himself must have sensed this difficulty because whenever he tried to maintain the *cogito* on the level of self-sufficient and pure thought, he always ended up in an impassable void, and whenever he attempted to describe it concretely, he always lapsed into psychologising. Jaspers presses him on this difficulty. He points out that the human *cogito* cannot be considered self-sufficient since it needs an object, without which thought would go round in a circle in its own emptiness.[18] In other words, the acts of *cogito* refer to objects. This is what Descartes seems to admit implicitly when he describes the subject of the *cogito* as a *res cogitans* that doubts, reasons, affirms, denies, and so on. In that case, however, the being of thought is co-extensive with the sum total of intentional acts and states of consciousness which include the correlates of these acts and constitute the object of phenomenology or descriptive psychology.[19] In any case, Descartes' original certitude either ends up in an impasse or in psychologising.

The idea of cogent certitude demanded, furthermore, that Descartes should find not only a unique and certain starting point but also a unique and universal method of development, a procedure that could lead in an unbroken line from certitude to certitude, from evidence to evidence, until at last it would embrace the whole of knowledge. This, he believed, could only be the mathematical method which, instead of progressing by the juxtaposition of countless intuitive grasps, is entirely deductive.

The idea underlying this project was a monistic conception of thought and knowledge and ultimately of reason. Thought, knowledge, reasoning, he thought, constituted an activity which worked the same way everywhere: *sit ratiocinatio ubique una et eadem*.[20] If all knowledge is the same, then all knowledge must have the same method also; then, philosophy and the different sciences may be occupied with different objects, but they must all apply this same universal method. They must proceed mathematically, that is, deductively, in order to maintain the certainty of their first principles undiminished at every point of their progress.

Jaspers' critique of this extension of the deductive *mathesis* to the entire field of knowledge comprises essentially two points:

He admits the significant contribution of Descartes to mathematics, but as far as its application to the other sciences is concerned, he maintains that Descartes had missed the real scientific importance of mathematical method when he thought that the real value of it lay in its deductivity. In reality, the force of the mathematical method derives from the fact that in the scientific investigation of nature it is easily associable with experimental verification, or more exactly, that it lends itself to verification, in so far as mathematical models alone make exact experimental control possible.[21] The true scientific procedure, after some experimentation, first sets up an anticipatory plan by constructing a model of hypothesis, which it then subjects to the test of second experience or experiment. In absolute fidelity to the object in question, it will measure and verify the hypothesis down to its last detail, ready to modify it whenever some of its implications are not borne out by observable proof. In other words, true science does not find any hypothesis or any of the consequences deducible from this hypothesis relevant until such time as these have been verified empirically. 'That is why this method, admitting only such models as can by nature be verified, restricts itself to quantitative mathematical constructions, because measurements alone can be verified with exactitude.'[22] Compared with this meticulous adherence to experimentation, Descartes cuts the figure of a fantast. His contributions to natural sciences, based on allegedly clear and distinct insights, seem worse than scholastic science at its worst. Within a short time of his death practising scientists simply discarded Cartesian science as entirely fruitless.[23] Nevertheless, something of the Cartesian mentality stuck in their minds: the idea of a universal method which should be the touchstone of universal certitude. The general tendency of reckoning the value of all sciences by the mathematical notion of certitude—or if these sciences prove inadequate to this norm, to depreciate them as inexact—can be traced back to this residue of methodological prejudices. They originate in Descartes, because 'Descartes himself had very little sympathy for "inexact sciences" (such as history, for instance). He did not, like Aristotle, try to justify them by saying that each subject matter has its appropriate mode of knowledge, but rejected them.'[24]

As far as philosophy is concerned, Jaspers thinks that the effects of the Cartesian fascination with a universal method were equally fatal. What Jaspers criticises in Descartes' attempt is not the aspiration for the unity of knowledge, which is a legitimate and perennial driving force of philosophy on its way to the One, but the manner in which Descartes has tried to reach this unity. 'The difference lies in *how* this unity is sought. Will it claim to teach the principles from which "everything" can be deduced? In other words, is it held to be a universal method that constitutes the whole of science? Or will it be regarded only as a guiding ideal, which can never be possessed as an object or planned as a programme, but which, by illuminating all the possibilities of thought, knowledge, and science, can lead us to an intuition of the Enveloping in which we gain knowledge?'[25] In the first case a universal method will impose itself on the whole knowledge, in the second, there will be only particular methods. In the first case unity is artificially and dogmatically established, in the second, 'the quest of unity remains a forever urgent problem of Reason,'[26] a task, and an unceasing discovery. Descartes everywhere followed the first way. In full consciousness he admitted only one kind of certitude and one method, and extended them over the field of philosophy also. But an absolutely universal method aims at what is knowable in general, and for this reason it must first detach itself from all particular content which it cannot afterwards recuperate. 'The explicit purpose of Descartes' thought is limited to the knowledge of such existentially indifferent truths as can be grasped in the exact same way by everyone, by every intellectual being.'[27] This is perhaps Jaspers' most damning accusation: Cartesianism and the philosophical scientism that is heir to it only yield a kind of knowledge that is existentially indifferent.

To sum up with James Collins:

In Jaspers' view, then, Descartes was the main source of the typically modern over-evaluation of science. Jaspers refers to this scientism as the 'superstition of science'. It consists in a theoretical absolutising of some area of scientific knowledge, which is confused with philosophy, and in a practical tendency to expect everything from science. . . . On this basis, science is asked to ascertain all values, to decide what ought to be done in moral conduct, and to set the ultimate goals for human life. Within this scientific perspective, philosophy has no distinctive office of determining the norms and ends of our existence.... The only role allotted to philosophy is to supply the general logic of scientific method and of valuational judgements. Individual interpretation and free choice are no longer to be centrally important in either ethical theory or moral practice. Impersonal scientific inquiry and public evidence are to be the sole determinants of the hierarchy of values and actual conduct.[28]

Jaspers' appreciation of phenomenology, and more particularly of the work of Edmund Husserl, leaves much to be desired.[29] His scattered references (mostly biographical) make it clear that he rejects phenomenology as a philosophy, but the reasons for this rejection can only be guessed. Upon reading these references, one has the secret suspicion that Jaspers never really had the patience to inquire into the nature and goal of the Husserlian undertaking, and, consequently, was unable to appreciate its positive results or to show its failures.

These summary references should, therefore, be supplemented with a great deal of interpretation, both psychological and doctrinal, which would in some way clarify Jaspers' position. While I recognise the need for such interpretation, I feel that I too must limit myself to a few summary indications of Jaspers' attitude towards phenomenology as a scientific philosophy, hoping that later on, once we have seen Jaspers' own views on science and philosophy, his attitude will become more understandable, though perhaps not entirely justified.

Jaspers came into contact with phenomenology as a young doctor in 1909 through reading some of the earlier works of Husserl. He took an immediate liking to Husserl's method. He found it uncommonly useful for the description of certain psycho-pathological phenomena whose study occupied him at that time. But more profoundly, he was impressed by Husserl's singularly disciplined way of thinking, and by his tenacity in ferreting out hidden presuppositions everywhere. 'In a world which at that time was full of prejudices, schematisms, and conventions, this felt like being liberated,' writes Jaspers.[30]

Then came the great deception, the traumatic experience, which resulted in Jaspers' alienation from phenomenology. It came in the form of Husserl's article, 'Philosophie als strenge Wissenschaft', in the first issue (1910–11) of *Logos*. Jaspers had to learn from this article that phenomenology, which he admired so much as an 'illustrative re-presentation of individual psychic experience' (*anschauliche Vergegenwärtigung individuellen seelischen Erlebens*),[31] one of the several indirect methods of comprehending personal mental states, now demanded exclusivity not only in psychology but also in the whole realm of knowledge, and called itself philosophy. What he thought to be a useful hermeneutic tool of psychological research whose conceptual constructs must, nevertheless, be constantly tested by observations and orientated towards demonstrable facts, had now been declared a radical science, to which all other sciences must turn for final corroboration.[32] Phenomenology claimed this privileged position because of a supposedly unique and radical method which enabled it to uncover the obscure foundations of other sciences, to make them aware of their hidden presuppositions, and at the same time to penetrate completely its own foundations.[33] It was asserted that, whereas other particular sciences can tell us how things work and can furnish exact information on this point, there is a radical science which can fully dominate its objects by showing what things are. This science can see the *essences* of things and tell their *meanings*, because it has found a way of setting aside the non-essential in things and bringing their pure *eidos* under the equally pure gaze of the intellect. If, then, some of the sciences can be called exact, even though they cannot get at the essence of anything, the eidetic science has the right to be called rigorous. Such a science. because it corresponds to the 'inalienable need of human kind for pure and absolute knowledge',[34] must also be honoured by the name of philosophy.

Jaspers was indignant about what he thought a masterful perversion of philosophy into science and science into philosophy.[35] He saw in it a repitition of the Cartesian attempt to reduce all knowledge to one method and all certitude to one certitude, except that the reduction had been done with more finesse this time. He saw that the same dogmatism animated Husserl as was in evidence in the case of Descartes. *Mutatis mutandis*, Descartes' disavowal of all previously existing philosophies as unfounded finds its parallel in Husserl's charge that up to his time philosophy had to do without objectively founded basic insights and proper methodology.[36] Both philosophers were confident that they at last had found a way to fill this lack. They had found a method which eliminated uncertainty from philosophy and thus resolved 'the spiritual distress' of their age.[37] There are also strong resemblances between the Cartesian doubt and the phenomenological technique of bracketing.

Had Jaspers produced a comprehensive critique of Husserl, it would most likely run along the same lines of thought as the one he directed against Descartes. He would probably have accused Husserl of having no appreciation for inexact sciences, notably, no sense of history. He would have challenged him on the boast that the phenomenological technique is capable of taking complete possession of experience by reducing it to its simplest elements, namely, a pure *eidos* and a pure transcendental subject.[38] And even allowing for the possibility of such a reduction, the philosophic interest of experience thus neutralised and divested of all personal characteristics would be minimal for Jaspers. He would find the result indifferent again.[39] The same reasons that made him reject the enthroning of science in place of philosophy would also make him repudiate phenomenology. He would not accept that the essence of philosophy consists in a mere gazing at phenomena, in a pure spectatorship. Philosophy must, at the same time, engage in an interior praxis (*inneres Handeln*) which has consequences for life and conduct.[40] In general, to the Husserlian *ohne mitzumachen* Jaspers would everywhere oppose an *immer dabeisein*.[41]

In closing this section, I may note with James Collins that these differences between Jaspers and Husserl show that 'there is not an essential connection in every case between existentialism and phenomenology',[42] as is generally presupposed. The opposition of Jaspers is directed to that aspect of phenomenology which ministers to scientific monism and idealism.

ANTI-SCIENCE

There is yet a third attitude that Jaspers rejects. For want of a better expression, I call it anti-science. In contrast to both progressivism, which replaces philosophy with science, and 'scientific' philosophy, which accommodates itself to science, this third attitude is characterised by a sharp mistrust of science. Anti-science is the defence reaction of some philosophers who want to save philosophy by attacking not only scientism but science itself. Hence the somewhat artificial name I have chosen to designate its essence. Philosophers of anti-science try to counter the onslaught of science by renouncing all scientific claim for philosophy, and at the same time claiming a 'superior' validity for it. 'Philosophy—according to this view—is not a science at all. It is based on feeling and intuition, on imagination and genius. It is conceptual magic, not knowledge. It is *élan vital* or resolute acceptance of death.'[43] Representatives of this attitude find it somewhat undignified that philosophy should bother about science at all. From its superior position, philosophy can see through the questionable character of scientific truths anyway. What are modern sciences on the whole but an aberration of the human spirit? Their ruinous effects are all around us. They are directly responsible for all the major evils and the inhumanity of our age. Ultimately, they may dry up the human soul in mechanised mass-culture and destroy human life in technological warfare.

Anti-science is not a definite or definable school of thought, but rather an ever-present dimension of irrationalism, which always accompanies thought. It can appear in various guises and cater for different powers-that-be. Totalitarian governments may invoke it in order to discredit and discourage the free inquiry of science that will not be pressed into the service of political propaganda. 'Science is a whore, said Lenin, for it sells itself to any class interest.'[44] There is a dose of the same anti-science attitude in misguided piety also, which sees in science a rival to its faith, a demoniac power that desacralises all spiritual values. A similar charge is voiced by the poet who laments that science 'leads to bewilder, and dazzles to blind'.

Against these positions, Jaspers will maintain a stand that is distinctively his own. While the full description of this position must wait until a later chapter (Chapter VII), its essential arguments may be briefly indicated here. Contrary to progressivism, Jaspers will assert that 'mythical thinking is not a thing of the past, but characterises man in any epoch,'[45] and that philosophy is not an archaic form of positive science but 'a perennial possibility of transcending the positive'.[46] In face of scientism, he will explode the false idea that total philosophical knowledge is scientific knowledge. In the first place, he will try to distinguish the methodological origins of science from those of philosophy in order to make both of them pure. 'A pure science requires a pure philosophy.'[47] Secondly, he will show that the crucial feature of modern science is that it does not provide a total world-view, because it recognises that it is impossible.'[48] There is, according to him, a built-in awareness in true science which is conscious of the regionality of scientific insights and knows their boundaries. Science is scientific because it can distinguish between what it knows and what it does not know. Against irrationalism, he will maintain the rights of reason which are not only the faculty of scientific understanding but also the medium of philosophical insights. He will grant that there is, and remains, an element of the 'unconquerable non-rational' in reality, but he will also affirm that 'it is appropriate for philosophising to strive to absorb the non-rational and counter-rational and to form it through Reason.'[49]

In order to gradually bring out all these points, I shall gather in the following chapter the most important elements of a Jaspersian theory of science, if such be the word for his loosely-knit reflections that drift in and out of extremely varied contexts, leaving behind not so much an ordered doctrine as a general impression concerning his views on science.

VI   A Description of Science

JASPERS' theory of science is a direct continuation of his theory on objectivity, which has been discussed in Part I. The general conditions of objective knowledge described there apply in varying degrees to science alone. In other words, science is for Jaspers the only domain of strictly objective knowledge, i.e. of knowledge that can exhibit the notes of impersonal validity, stability, univocity, and universality. These qualities derive from the nature of general consciousness, which is the cognitive subject of scientific knowledge. Science is thus the clearest expression and the highest achievement of general consciousness. Nevertheless, science is not strictly synonymous with the activity of general consciousness. Science adds something to the ordinary performance of consciousness in general: it introduces order and method into it. For, as James Collins remarks, although every sort of consciousness is faced with its object or counterpart, 'the scientific mind also lays down certain standards for reliable knowledge. The scientific interest is to secure the maximum clarity, logical necessity, universality and communicability' in the objects it determines and investigates. Science is methodical, and 'the scientific inquiry is guided by the ideal of rational objectivity, guaranteed by evidence that is universally valid and compelling in an impersonal way.'[1]

Although all the qualities discussed in Part I are jointly required for the determination of objectivity, when it comes to assessing scientific knowledge, Jaspers selects necessity or cogency as the central feature in terms of which he determines the domains and methods of objective world-orientation or science. There might be good reasons for this, for, indeed, science has cogency to the precise extent that its performance is impersonally valid, stable, univocally clear and communicable. Cogency seems to be a summary way of including or implying all the other requisite features of scientific knowledge.

DOMAINS AND METHODS OF SCIENCE

Jaspers distinguishes three major areas in science, determined by the three basic forms of cogency:

(*a*) cogent *thoughts* of mathematics and formal logic;
(*b*) cogent *reality* of the empirical (natural and moral) sciences;
(*c*) cogent *intuitions* of the categories of objectivity in general.[2]

According to him, these three areas are heterogeneous both as regards the source of their cogency and the proper method of ascertaining them. Nevertheless, he maintains that in the actual working of science all three of them are involved. He considers, for instance, that the cogent knowledge of empirical reality is 'factually (*sachlich*) impossible' without the other two forms of cogency, while they, in turn, are 'psychologically impossible' without empirical knowledge.[3]

Within *mathematics* itself, Jaspers distinguishes between what we would call pure mathematics and intuitive mathematics. Both these forms derive their cogency from some ultimate *axioms*, which are no longer questioned but serve as indubitable starting points to certain consistent *rules of deduction*. In other words, mathematics is hypothetico-deductive and, not unlike formal logic, only furnishes the *forms* of objective certitude.[4] The only difference between the two forms of mathematics lies in the way they posit their axioms, or rather, in the kinds of axioms they posit at the beginning. If the axioms are posited by a simple act of decision of the mind, without being evident in themselves, we are dealing with pure mathematics. It is pure because it rests entirely on its own position, construction, and operation. As such, it is the model and archetype of all cogent knowledge, but it pays for this exalted status by complete lack of content. As a purely formal science it is both transparent and, as Whitehead would say, 'luminously vacuous'. Jaspers values it as one values a game or pastime.[5] Intuitive mathematics, on the other hand, is based on *a priori* concepts of general object-forms, notably those of quantity and relation. It not only claims consistency in its ulterior development but also claims the evidence of intuition for its starting point. By virtue of this claim, it belongs partially (i.e. foundationally) to the third region of cogency mentioned above.[6]

The *empirical sciences* are divided into two large areas: the sciences of nature (*Naturwissenschaften*) and the intellectual sciences

(*Geistewissenschaften*). In contrast to mathematics and logic which study mere forms, the empirical sciences deal with reality. For this reason Jaspers calls them real sciences. Because they deal with reality, they must introduce additional steps of procedure into their methods over and above the purely deductive and combinatory steps of mathematics and logic. First of all, the empirical sciences must *observe* the facts. But observation already implies a more subtle procedure than simply stating everything about a given phenomenon; it implies the *selection* of relevant factors in the event under observation. This selection takes place according to some *hypothesis* which promises to *explain* the phenomenon in question. If a sufficient number of observations are *verified* by repeated experiment, science may begin to *generalise* by a complex way of *induction* and set up a *model* or *theory*, which will be valid for all similar phenomena in such a way that science will be able to make reliable *predictions* of phenomena as yet unobserved. There is, of course, a curious circularity and endlessness in this procedure, which Jaspers does not fail to note in his critique of sciences. It seems that the finding of facts depends on an anticipatory theory, called hypothesis, while the verification of the theory or hypothesis depends on the facts thus found.[7] In other words, a particular observation has no significance save within a theory, while the adoption of a theory is not justified save through the observational and experimental facts that led up to it. But this way the cogency of empirical research is gravely relativised, because as a fact it is bound to theory and as a theory to fact.[8] There is, moreover, a major difference between the theories of natural sciences and those of the intellectual sciences. The former are more readily expressible in exact mathematical formulae than the latter. The theories of intellectual sciences consist largely of *Verstehen*. Consequently, the methods of verification or falsification of these theories are not entirely reducible to exact measurements. They are rather matter for intuitive sense-reconstruction.

The third field of cogency concerns the intuitions of the categories of objectivity in general. The objects of these intuitions are, therefore, not real but possible objects which constitute the material for an intuitive phenomenology.[9] This phenomenology 'describes, explicates, brings to consciousness certain identical and unmistakable elements and structures of world-orientation as that network in which the objective world exists for us. These structures cannot be defined but must be brought to light in an actively performed intuition.'[10] Dufrenne and Ricoeur remark that this is an allusion to Husserl's *Wesenschau*.[11] This is substantially correct. Jaspers seems to admit here a kind of eidetic insight into the structures of objects in general which, ideally speaking, are identical for consciousness in general. These structures uncovered by phenomenology are the fundamental ones of conscious experience and constitute the very conditions of possibility for having a conscious contact with the objective world. Nevertheless, with all the reserve and qualification that Jaspers brings to the possibilities of phenomenology as a strict science, his conclusions have very little real similarity to the Husserlian doctrine in this respect. Unlike Husserl, Jaspers does not believe that any single method of explicating the content of a phenomenological insight can be regarded as *the* method of phenomenology. The sense-structures whose clear and immediate presence (*Gegenwärtighaben*) constitutes the cogency of phenomenological insight cannot be brought to light except by an actively exercised (*vollzogener*) intuition.

LIMITS OF SCIENTIFIC KNOWLEDGE

Science, it has been said, is never more scientific than when it knows what it is that it knows. It lies in the very aspiration of science to separate knowledge from non-knowledge. 'When we enter into its sphere, we have the sensation of breathing clean air, of leaving behind us all vague talk, all plausible opinions, all stubborn prejudice and blind belief.'[12] It is, therefore, imperative for science to know its own limits and to decide which among these limits are occasional and which are definitive. Given the fact that science is a particular form of thinking, the situation must be investigated from the larger perspective of thought in general.

Before entering into particulars, the limits of scientific knowledge on the whole can be formulated in the following general way:

Scientific knowledge of subject-matter is not knowledge of Being. For all science is particular, directed at specific objects and aspects, and not at Being itself.

Science is unable to provide goals for life. The clearer it becomes with regard to itself, the more decisively it points to another origin inaccessible to itself, to our freedom.

Science is unable to provide an answer to the question with respect to its own meaning. That science shall exist depends on an original will-to-know whose right cannot be proven scientifically.[13]

Science must work on the assumption that all knowledge is knowledge of objects, and that the subject of experience itself is nothing else than a special kind of object among objects. Science strives for pure objectivity and so must disregard subjectivity as something that distorts the pure perspectives of science and introduces arbitrary value-judgements.[14] The best science can do with the subject is to study it objectively. But made in this way the object of scientific research, the subject is deprived of its very subjectivity, 'it is robbed of its soul'.[15]

Scientific knowledge is in principle forever unfinished and incomplete. It is affected by what Jaspers calls endlessness, *Endlosigkeit*. Endlessness in this connection means that scientific exploration can never achieve a rounded and unified view of reality. Every attainable result immediately points to a further limit yet to be questioned and explored. Endlessness signifies the fact that on the phenomenal level—the only level on which science operates—reality is indefinitely open in regard to both space and time.[16] At the lower limit, empirical investigation runs up against the mysterious plasticity of matter, at the other end against the free indetermination of the spirit, neither of which can be surveyed in a final or completed act of comprehension.

Science deals in cogent knowledge, but this cogency is never quite absolute, because both at the beginning and at the end something remains to be questioned, something indefinite yet to be mastered, some presupposition yet to be cleared. This amounts again to saying that science can reach *some* unity and order in the knowledge of the world, but it cannot reach *the* unity of the world.[17] It produces a certainty whose relativity, i.e. dependence on presuppositions and methods of investigation, is the crucial characteristic of scientific knowledge.

However, Jaspers discusses at greater length the limitations of cogency and endlessness. He finds definitive limits to scientific exploration n both areas.

Mathematico-logical knowledge can boast of the highest degree of cogency and certitude, but only because of its pure formalism. It owes this rigorousness to its near complete lack of content. It commits the thinker to one thing and one thing alone: to be consistent with the original axioms that he has posited; to carry the conclusions which flow from his first principles to any end, whether they apply or not. For this reason, mathematics is the least existentially relevant among the sciences, and as such Jaspers considers it the very counterpole of philosophy.[18] In the last analysis, however, even mathematical cogency is limited, because it depends on the cogency of the initial axioms. If these are arbitrary, they can be questioned precisely because they are arbitrary. If, on the other hand, they are intuitively evident, then they meet their limitation in the limitation of language, the ordinary tool whereby intuitions are communicated. The whole marvellous transparency, cogency, certitude of the world of mathematics is supported on something which is yet opaque, questionable and uncertain.

Empirical cogency, as has already been indicated, is somewhat diminished by the reciprocal dependence of fact and theory whereby each limits the other. 'The cogency of facts contains a factor of uncertainty which varies according to the kind of facts we are dealing with, but which always remains in the theorising consciousness of the critical scientist. He must constantly appraise the meaning and measure of facts.'[19] In each theory and interpretation there remains a residue that does not quite harmonise with the facts, and in each fact there is something opaque that is incomprehensible through the theory. The empirical exploration of reality ultimately runs aground on the incomprehensibility of matter.[20] In sum, this means that cogent knowledge cannot cover reality in its totality. Cogency proves only the undeniable existence of object-being, but its relativity proves that everything is not an object.[21] The reason why empirical science cannot penetrate reality completely and with absolute exactitude is that reality is not a perfect mechanism. But inasmuch as reality *is* a mechanism, in a limited and relative sense, empirical science is able to survey it accurately, calculate it, and make reliable predictions about it. Theoretically, however, even these calculations and predictions are only probabilities that border on certitude.[22] Then if empirical science wants to lessen the uncertainty inherent in probabilities, it must progressively detach itself from content and gravitate towards greater and greater mathematisation, only to meet the limitations which affect mathematics.

Intuitive cogency, the cogency of phenomenological *Wesenschau*, is not subject to limitation in itself, because an intuition is by definition the full and immediate presence of something to consciousness. 'An intuition is either present or not present. . . . As such, it does not point over and beyond itself; it claims to be neither real nor cogent as a thought process, but only to be lucid in and about itself.'[23] The limits of intuition lie rather in its communication. Communication is built on the assumption that we can somehow transmit our intuitions and experiences to one another. This assumption is well-founded because exchange is possible. The crucial question is: to what degree? To the degree that language, our ordinary tool of communication, allows it.

Without entering into the very rich and interesting philosophy of language that Jaspers unfolds in *Von der Wahrheit* (pp. 395–449), it will be sufficient to mention the following essential points that are relevant to the question at hand:

(1) Language consists of words. It is customary to distinguish the sound of a word from its meaning, or, if it is written, the visible form of a word from its intelligible content.

(2) The basic phenomenon of human language is the fact that the sound of our words transmits not only a signal which triggers a reflex reaction in the hearer but also an intention which results in intellection. Through language, we are able to hold our experiences and intuitions at arm's length by putting them into words which translate them into meaning.[24]

(3) It is also classical to distinguish the proper meaning of a word from its metaphorical meaning, or more exactly, to distinguish words used in the proper sense from words used as metaphors. For Jaspers, however, this distinction is relative, even though legitimate. He maintains that words with so-called proper meanings are words which by long usage merely lost their original metaphorical character,[25] so that the distinction between the proper and the metaphorical is something like the distinction between clichés and fresh words. It could be argued, then, that fundamentally all words are metaphors and that proper words arise only through the forgetting of the original metaphor.[26]

(4) This forgetting of the metaphorical and tending towards the fixed and univocal meaning is the psychological basis for

abstraction.[27] The process of abstraction makes use of this psychological predisposition by consciously and methodically eliminating the metaphorical elements of words in order to reach the essential element in things, because it is believed that the essential can only be something stable which must be fixed in a univocal meaning. Against this conception Jaspers maintains that the metaphorical is just as much a means of getting at the essential as is the univocal. In the mobile interplay of metaphors, where expressions mutually reflect and interpret each other, a step-by-step sequence of essences can reveal itself to us.[28]

(5) The scientific mind in its desire for maximum clarity and definition prefers univocity to plurivocity, and tries to reduce the metaphorical element of words by transforming them into univocal signs. But as long as language remains language, a living expression that has atmosphere, background, and as yet hidden possibilities of meaning, words can never be entirely reduced to such signs.[29] Although the scientific use of language tends towards replacing word-language (*Wortsprache*) with sign-language (*Zeichensprache*) or with professional language (*Fachsprache*), as long as people continue to experience their being in the world in terms of ordinary language, the complete elimination of the metaphorical elements of words is unimaginable. Word-language remains the ordinary tool of communication and with it the original metaphorical overtones of words remain also.

Given these metaphorical overtones in the communication of intuitions, 'I can never be quite certain of having understood the same thing as the other person.'[30] In describing our common experiences to each other, we must combine every possible means of showing, telling, defining, evoking, without being quite certain that we understand each other. The test of whether we have experienced the same thing or understood it the same way, only comes in the subsequent use we make of our communication. Only further use will prove the true concordance of our intuitions or show up their real differences. It may be that we refer to the essential elements of our common experience by the same words; nevertheless, the recall of this experience may reveal that they affected us differently and had a different meaning for us in the first place. There is no telling beforehand.[31]

In regard to the problem of endlessness, Jaspers put forward the following considerations:

Faced with the undetermined and multiple realm of reality, reason is moved by a threefold impulse: first, it wants to introduce determination into reality; secondly, it tries to extend this determination to the whole of reality; and thirdly, it endeavours to gather the multiple into a unity of knowledge. It is by striving to attain this threefold ideal of determination, totality, and unity of knowledge that reason tries to overcome what Jaspers calls the endlessness of reality. In other words, reason wants to grasp reality completely. It wants to know not only this or that object but also reality as a whole. For it is important to note in this regard that determining single objects in an indefinite multitude of other objects would not be sufficient to satisfy the appetite of reason. Even the registering of an unending series of facts, the amassing of correct but endless information, would not yet attain that which is sought by reason. Reason wants unified knowledge and knowledge that is completed (*vollendet*). Dispersion and unfinishedness do not, of course, militate against the accuracy of knowledge, but they do detract from its relevance.[32]

Now it is Jaspers' contention that science has devised certain methodical steps whereby it can partially overcome endlessness. It has formulated certain rules which permit the determination of the indeterminate within certain limits. Nevertheless, even these methods are incapable of making the whole of reality surveyable.

Mathematics, for instance, was very successful in formulating certain rules that make it possible to localise and determine the properties and relationships of any member of an indefinite series of numerical values without necessarily determining the series itself.[33] That is precisely its paradox: it can master everything within the series, but it cannot encompass the series itself. It can make everything a determined object inside the series and furnish the means of correlating any possible member of the series with every other one, but the series itself extends indefinitely beyond the scope of methodical determination; the series itself is not an object.[34]

With the aid of these methodical rules formulated by mathematics, endlessness can be partially overcome in empirical research also. In so far as empirical reality obeys quantitative rules, science can anticipate and predict particular events within the world, but it cannot determine the world itself as a total process because the world as a total process is not a definite or definable object. Every time we make the world into an object of research, our thought must end up in antinomies. Jaspers refers explicitly to the first Kantian antinomy which in two conflicting theses both asserts and denies the temporal and spatial finitude of the world as a whole. According to him, the very presence of this conflict proves that the world as a whole can no longer be an object, for 'when an object has the feature of giving rise to contradictory statements about itself, then it ceases to be an object. In self-contradiction the object disappears.'[35] Scientific thought finds itself in the impossibility of reasoning meaningfully about the world as a closed totality, as a finite object.

This impossibility can easily be seen in the light of the most fundamental operation of scientific or discursive reason, which is to arrive at the simplest differentiation of objects within a whole. 'By means of a complete disjunction', explains Gerhard Knauss, 'it must be possible to assign an unequivocable place to every conceivable object: the object must be able to be confirmed or denied.'[36] An object, let us recall, demands to be thought of in a univocal way. Without this fundamental univocity the object would remain in a fluid state and, as such, it would escape the grasp of logical thought, 'the first function of which is always determinateness in the direction of unequivocality. If one were to attempt to overstep this boundary an object would encompass both sides of the disjunction; both affirmation and denial would be applicable to it. If, then, logic is concerned with possibilities, we would here confront the presence of an impossibility. Such an object would logically be an impossible object.'[37]

But the world *as a whole* is precisely such an impossible object. We can with equal plausibility both affirm and deny that the cosmos has determined spatial and temporal dimensions. It is logically inconceivable to think of the world as having no definite limits, but it is equally inconceivable that there be something outside it whereby it is limited. The world as a whole is an impossible object for scientific logic because it is not an object at all. It is rather the encompassing horizon *in* which our experiences of objects occur. It is not a goal of research to be determined, but a guiding idea. As such, it cannot become the matter of a closed and complete experience. As Gerhard Knauss puts it, 'the world is not *what* we investigate but *that* we investigate.'[38] The world is the reason that we can know objects. We can know them, because they belong to a totality which permits us to bring them into relationship with other objects. This totality is what we call the world. In this sense, the world is an idea, the idea of the totality of unity of our possible experiences. By virtue of this idea, we are able to situate objects within the world, but we cannot situate the world itself.

In face of this totality, the movements of scientific reason 'must suddenly give way to an unstable condition of suspension. Thrown back upon itself, it senses its own limits in that which lies beyond all determinateness.'[39]

This suspension is a decisive moment for the further fate of thought in general. Will reason recognise its limitations in respect to the whole, or will it try to side-step them? Will it continue to speculate about the world as a whole 'scientifically', or will it try to transform itself into a different kind of Reason? Will scientific thought acknowledge the agonising incomprehensibility of the whole as whole, or will it absolutise itself and carry its method into forbidden realms? Will it re-apply the mathematical method, or will it look for new methods of concentrating upon the totality?[40] On the answers to these questions hangs the fate of philosophy either as an ersatz-science or as a distinct and autonomous discipline.

One thing remains certain: science cannot hope for an exhaustive and complete knowledge of reality. While it constantly gains on endlessness, it also always succumbs to it. It is suspended over vast spaces of the indefinite, as it were.[41]

SCIENCE IN CONTEXT

Endlessness and restricted cogency constitute the formal limitations of scientific knowledge. They flow from the specific structure of scientific endeavour as a methodical effort to assess reality in terms of determined objects.

However, science is subject to conditions not only in its formal aspects but also in its dynamic aspects. Science forms a part of a larger dynamism of thought in general, which, in turn, is inscribed in the context of life itself. Consequently, in pursuing the investigation of the nature and scope of scientific knowledge, sooner or later we must advert to some extracognitional factors, which, though not formally part of science, will nonetheless qualify it in some sense.

Jaspers is especially sensitive to the possible influence these factors may have on the evaluation of science. Among other things, he pays a great deal of attention to the dynamism of thought in general, of which scientific knowledge is only a particular manifestation. He believes that a purely formal analysis of knowledge is insufficient for a true understanding of the deeper roots of science. He considers that by far the most important task of a theory of knowledge is to penetrate into the dynamism of thinking and to comprehend it from within its movement. It is in this dynamism of thinking that Jaspers sees the efficacious reality of knowledge. According to him, it is the movement of thought that lends purpose and meaning to knowledge, and also imposes some limits on it.[42] To be sure, he does not deny all value to a formal analysis of knowledge, which tries to determine the stable logical elements of rational thought, but on the whole he considers such an analysis far less important than a genetic study, which surveys the progressive maturation of reason, as reason gradually transforms its own structures in order to meet the demands placed upon it by the manifold and moving reality it encounters in experience.

1. *Thought and Temporality.* Thought, then, is dynamic. For Jaspers, this means first of all that thought is *temporal*. This temporality of thought is obvious as far as the psychological unfolding of it is concerned. Human knowledge is not infused knowledge, but the fruit of a long psychological process of learning. However, Jaspers means much more than this unfolding when he refers to the temporality of thought. He means temporality which enters into the very sense-structure of thinking.[43] For him, the temporal character of thought is not a mere accidental quality, but constitutive of the very essence of thought.[44] Thought is possible, because our consciousness includes several temporal dimensions and is not restricted to momentary flashes of awareness, but endures through time.

The temporal structure of our consciousness is decisive for our acts of thinking. Such acts do not consist in a mere juxtaposition of instantaneous grasps of timeless meanings, but in the active transformation, in the present, of past meanings into future intentions. In other words, a concrete act of thought is really the synthesis of two dynamisms: *recall and projection.* Consequently, the content of such an act, far from being an a-temporal meaning, is one that stretches over both past and future; or as Jaspers puts it, a present act of thought allows us to live by looking forwards and to understand by looking backwards.[45] Of course, this 'looking' should not be understood as a simple contemplation of the past and future, but as the active shaping of both through a present act of understanding.

By this essential temporality of thought Jaspers does not mean to deny the fact that there is also something timeless about thought, but he maintains that the distinction between what is temporal and what is trans-temporal in it is not simply the matter of the 'how' and the 'what'. In other words, all is not settled by asserting, for instance, that what is grasped in thought is a timeless meaning, while the mode of grasping this meaning is temporal; i.e., progressive. Nor is there any use in inverting the formula, saying that what we know is temporal, while the mode of knowing is a-temporal. These distinctions, Jaspers feels, do not quite touch the essential point in question. According to him, it is neither the content nor the mode of thought that is timeless. The only timeless factor of thought is its *a priori* formal structure: 'What is this timeless element? Timeless are the structures of consciousness in general; the forms of identity and contradiction; the categories.'[46] In other words, the timeless element of thought is not a 'what' but only the form of a 'what'. As such, it is undoubtedly exempt from time. But what gives body to this form is an intuitive filling, and that is not timeless. In short, Jaspers believes that the content of thought is grounded in the temporal element and changes with it.[47] Consequently, even the truth-content of thought is rooted in time: 'Truth is ushered into thinking by time.'[48] Without time, he argues, there could not be any truth, but only the timeless validity of formal relationships.

Nor is the 'how' of our thinking a purely trans-temporal factor. Our thinking is conceptual thinking, but concepts are not entirely static. They are rather like moving signs that mark the trajectory of thought's movement through time; they are at most points of stop-over in the march of thought, where the mind takes a short respite and catches its breath for further thinking.[49] Each concept has its proper place in a *time-chain* of concepts;

stands in relative temporal proximity to, or distance from, the experience whose meaning it tries to interpret; is at once the depository of past meanings and the carrier of future intentions.[50] This position of any given concept in the time-chain is not irrelevant to the point under discussion. Greater or lesser temporal distance from experience; greater or lesser historical residue; proximate or remote intentions: all these factors will modify also the 'how' of thinking and give it a more fluid contour. The full import of these factors cannot be grasped in a single, instantaneous glance, just as a symphony cannot be heard all at once: I must accompany it through time; I must 'hear it out'. A grasp that could cancel out time from the understanding of this moving ensemble would be a radically different kind of grasp than what we know to be ours.

On reading these considerations, one would only wish that Jaspers had given us a more technical description of the manner in which time enters into the content of thought. There are a number of issues that are left unclarified. For instance, if truth is essentially temporal, as Jaspers maintains, then we are faced with the question of deciding the truth-value of the vast body of apparently timeless scientific truths. Do these truths amount to nothing more than a set of logical laws with formal validity (*Gültigkeit*), but unrelated to the real state of things? Somehow this would be hard to believe. Are we, then, to conclude that the timeless quality of scientific knowledge is only apparent, and that latently even scientific knowledge is temporal? If so, then Jaspers should have shown in a few detailed analyses how temporality affects even scientific concepts, since it is not immediately evident that such concepts have a temporal character. As we saw, he clearly maintains that the conceptual articulation of thought both springs from a temporal movement of thought and serves a further aim of this movement,[51] but does this necessarily imply that either the meaning, or the content, or even the goal of thought is affected by temporality? He owes us at least a psychological explanation of the fact that sometimes we have the impression of making trans-temporal statements; statements which, we feel, hold always and everywhere.

2. *The Active Will-to-know.* Thought is said to be dynamic because it is temporal, but more profoundly because it is an *activity*. The dynamism of thought is still inadequately stated by

a simple reference to temporality. Temporality, according to Jaspers, brings thought into relation with reality and thus introduces the question of truth. Temporality puts real content into thought; it saves thought from being an empty cogitation and makes it into a knowledge *of* something (*Erkennen, Erkenntnis*). Knowledge is thought with real content. However, this still does not settle the question of the reality of thought itself. Is thought real just because it is related to real things? Does the simple fact of reflecting real contents suffice to make thought real in itself? The answer given by Jaspers to these questions is negative. He implies the following points:

(*a*) The passive mirroring of reality does not constitute the reality of thought. Knowledge cannot be called real on account of its being related to real contents.[52]

(*b*) The reality of thought lies rather in the fact that it is an activity. This activity is the actual exercise of a certain appetite or will, which seeks its satisfaction in Being. In short, the reality of thought is this active will-to-know. Thought is real as a dynamism.[53]

(*c*) Finally, Jaspers implies, and later explicitly affirms, that this active will-to-know which constitutes the reality of thought is originally identical with Being itself. In other words, the dynamism of thought is really an expression of Being itself. What makes thought real is the fact that thought is the very self-manifesting impulse of Being. This is so because, basically, Being is self-revealing; Being is inhabited by a fundamental conation towards self-disclosure. It is this active appetite for self-disclosure that we ordinarily call thought.

In a moment we shall see some texts that will bear out these points, but first we must note the articulations of this will-to-know by Jaspers. In an ascending order he lists four different levels, we might say four different finalities, to which this will-to-know may be directed. He is again talking from the larger context of thought in general.[54]

I want to make something: 'Thought becomes reality as a power to make things' (*Machenkönnen*).[55] The first impulse of thought is to be a measure of reality. It wants to be creative. Thought proves its efficacity and gathers its self-confidence best when it can show that it is not entirely passive in face of reality. But that reality itself is responsive to the predictions and calculations of thought and lets itself be shaped by thought. Jaspers often quotes the Kantian phrase: 'I can really know only that which I can make.' In a global way, we could say that this is the pragmatic ethos of thought, as it shows itself in civilisation.

I want to live in a human world: The efficacity of thought leaves its imprint next on intersubjective reality, by shaping common ideals and working out common destinies. Here thought is the expression of the creative will of a community.[56] This is the social ethos of thought, as it shows itself in culture.

I want to become myself: The central dynamism of thought is reached in the existential ethos of thought. This shows that the object or purpose of thought is not to get lost either in pragmatism or in ideologies, but to help us grow in personal stature; to realise greater humanity within ourselves; to come to self-possession by thinking.[57] The existential ethos redirects our will-to-know towards self-clarification, self-realisation. These are the impulses of freedom.

I want to ascertain authentic Being: The existential ethos of thought, the bid for self-realisation by means of thinking, if it is seriously followed up, reveals another dynamism of thought which leads to the ultimate source of all being: Transcendence. 'Through knowledge a certain metaphysical certitude of the efficacious reality of Transcendence is realised.'[58] The existential orientation of thought would soon lose itself in solipsism, defiant freedom, and finally in nihilism, if it were not seconded by the deeper desire for Transcendence, for God. All the other impulses of thought and knowledge lead up to this one, and receive their particular impetus from here. We may call this the metaphysical ethos of thought.

It is interesting to note in passing that the identification of the reality of thought with the will-to-know permits Jaspers to avoid the basic attitudes of both idealism and realism. While idealism identifies the order of thought and the order of reality, realism says that the order of thought and the order of reality are different. For Jaspers, thought and reality are neither identical nor different: they are 'be-longing'.[59] They coincide in the primordial ethos of thought, which is also the ethos of Being. Between idealism and realism, Jaspers opts for a kind of voluntarism. 'If the reality of thought is the will in it, then the real content of what is thought reveals itself only to the will of the thinker.'[60] If we still want to speak about the identity of thought and reality, this identity should be sought in the primordial coincidence of the rational appetite, the will-to-know, with Being itself. That which in the split of thought and reality now stands divided and strives to reunite, was originally one.[61] Needless to say, the unity of thought and reality in the will-to-know is nowhere given as an empirical fact and is never reached by knowledge. It is merely the constant object of our searching knowledge. Our knowledge is inspired by a certain trusting belief in this unity, and is guided by it as by an ideal.[62] In fact, knowledge, as an ongoing and dynamic activity, is the very effort to reach this unifying ideal.

3. *Science and Praxis*. It might be objected that all this talk about dynamism and activity, though instructive in itself, is largely beside the point in deciding the nature and scope of scientific knowledge. Undoubtedly we *do* something before we can come to possess science, but science itself is not a doing. Science is *theoria*, vision, spectacle. All the activity of getting to know is merely a preparation, which is to lead to this vision. Activity is only the means towards this end.

This is just the thesis that Jaspers questions. Considering the matter from the broader context of thought, he takes an almost completely reverse stand. For him, it is not the knowing activity that serves as a means towards the theoretic end of science, but the 'seeing' of science that constitutes a subordinate phase in the knowing activity. Again, his conception tends to absorb the stable aspects almost entirely into the dynamism of knowledge. Theory and contemplation are not considered the end of know-ledge. *Theoria* is not desired for its own sake but is integrated into a larger flow, which Jaspers calls *praxis*. By praxis, he simply means an original totality of thoughtful doing, *denkendes Tun*.

This is a delicate point. It should not be construed to mean that science has a right to existence only if it can point to practical applicability, or that the immediate concern of science is directly pragmatic. The chief concern of science is, in fact, theoretical, but Jaspers' point is that theory itself is only a necessary means to an end, and not an end in itself. The end is thoughtful doing or praxis. Praxis contains both theorising and doing. 'These are not two possibilities of equal worth side by side;' writes Jaspers, 'rather, pure theorising is only a phase or else the break-down of the original whole, which is knowing as thoughtful doing.'[63]

Here are some other texts, saying more or less the same thing: 'The distinction between speculation and doing is too simple, for even in detached speculation there is a residue of doing, and in simple pottering a leftover of speculation.'[64] 'Thinking, as a Being-centred reality, is thoughtful doing.'[65] 'All genuine science consists in praxis.'[66]

It should be noted, therefore, that Jaspers does not deny the formal possibility or even necessity of theory: he only denies that theory is the ultimate end of knowledge. He has no use for knowledge that would be an inefficacious mental play.[67] In true knowledge and genuine science each act of seeing is also an act of realisation, and each act of realisation a better insight. Viewed from the larger horizon of thought as a whole, science can be seen as both theoretical and practical. To be sure, for reasons of method we must distinguish between these two aspects as two separate moments of a dialectical progression, where looking and doing alternate, but we must realise that in reality they constitute an uninterrupted movement of the same underlying ethos of thought. Both are manifestations of the same rational appetite, the same active will-to-know, whose ultimate object is Being.

We have already made reference to the ideals towards which sciences must tend. Confronted with the endless flow of multiple experiences, reason as it is operative in the sciences must strive towards the ideals of determinateness, totality, and unity of knowledge. Having considered the question from a broader context, we can now see that these three ideals converge towards one single goal: the progressive identification of thought and reality. We now realise that the end of all knowing activity, including that of the sciences, is somehow to recapture the unity of the rational appetite in which thought and reality originally coincide. Particular sciences are all manifestations of this unifying endeavour. Each in its own particular and partial way explores some empirical domain of object-being, thus preparing the way for a metempirical or philosophical exploration of Being itself. As such, sciences are 'the necessary ground and first stage of philosophy, but are not capable of achieving the unity and totality which reason cannot renounce.'[68] The sciences initiate a movement of thought which points and finds fulfilment beyond them. Thus they begin an exploration of Being, but stop short in object-being. Philosophy's task is to continue this exploration.[69]

VII   The Relationship of Science and Philosophy

HAVING briefly indicated Jaspers' thinking on the nature, goal, and limitations of scientific knowledge, we are now in a better position to summarise his views regarding the relationship between science and philosophy. His position is basically a very simple and balanced one. Against scientism, which confuses the two, Jaspers maintains a sharp distinction between science and philosophy. Against anti-science, which dismisses objective knowledge, he insists on the necessity of a mutual alliance between science and philosophy.

For the proper understanding of his views, we must recall his ideas concerning objective knowledge, which were treated in Part I. There we saw the qualifications Jaspers placed on objective knowledge. Here we must note that, in fact, for Jaspers *knowledge is either objective, or it is no knowledge at all.* Perhaps the most consistent thing about Jaspers is that he does not apply the term to any and every kind of mental act. For him, knowledge is an intentional grasp of a particular object which is apprehended in an objective and univocal way. As far as he is concerned, there might be all sorts of thought, intuition, awareness, and total vision, but there is only one kind of knowledge: objective, univocal, scientific knowledge.[1] '"Knowledge",' notes James Collins, 'is not an indeterminate general term, covering every relation between the mind and things. Instead it connotes one definite sort of thought; that in which a polar relation is set up between the subject and the phenomenal object.'[2] But, of course, this sort of thought obtains only in science; science alone is knowledge. And if science alone is knowledge, then it follows that philosophy must be some sort of non-knowledge, *Nichtwissen*. It is clear from the beginning that philosophy is nourished by other sources than science. It is non-knowledge, because its relation to reality is not the same objective relation that science has to its objects.

DISTINCTION IN KIND

From this designation of philosophy as non-knowledge, the distinctions that Jaspers makes between science and philosophy flow more or less logically. These distinctions are manifold, but I shall try to condense them into two major points:

1. *Philosophy is not a cogent science.* One of the chief characteristics of science, as we saw, is intellectual cogency. Science is cogent knowledge. It is cogent precisely because it proceeds from the impersonal intentionality of general consciousness, and deals with determined object-beings according to universally accepted and controllable methods.

The same cannot be said of philosophy. 'If we call science that which is cogently knowable for every understanding, and which for that very reason has actually gained universal recognition, then neither philosophy not theology can be called sciences.'[3] It is important to note that this restricted use of the term 'science' is not entirely arbitrary. It is not simply the question of terminology, for there is something about the existing state of science and philosophy that makes them different from each other. For instance, we cannot ignore the fact that while scientific cognition is identical throughout the world, philosophy, in spite of its perennial claim to being the universal science, has never in its history gained universal acceptance. In view of this fact, Jaspers considers 'as right and desirable, especially today, to use the term "science" in the narrow sense'.[4]

Measured against the cogency of science, philosophy is less than science, 'for it does not gain any tangible results, nor any intellectually binding insight.'[5] This is because philosophy is not the act of an anonymous consciousness, but the act of a concrete Existence. It does not determine itself by logical rules and impersonally valid methods, but by the necessity of personal faith. Philosophy is not objective knowledge, but a passionate quest of Existence for true and genuine Being. In it, the individual seeks a more intimate relationship with reality than the disinterested search of science can afford. Consequently, the truth of philosophy may be unconditionally valid for the individual who wagers his life and dignity on such a truth, but certainly not for universal predication. 'Scientific truth is one and the same for all—philosophical truth wears multiple historical cloaks; each of these is the manifestation of a unique reality, each has its justification, but they are not identically transmissible.'6

But philosophy is not only less, but also more than science, in so far as it is the source of a truth that is inaccessible to scientifically compelling knowledge. It is this plus which is usually referred to by the various 'definitions' of philosophy. In these, philosophy is presented either as a supreme science, or as the knowledge of all being as being, or as the way to the good life. According to Jaspers, the meaning of such definitions is that 'philosophical thought is inward action; that it appeals to freedom, that it is a summons to transcendence.'7

To sum up: the sciences do not contain the whole of truth, but only the truth of exact knowledge that is cogent and universally valid for all intellect. But since truth has a greater scope, part of which can reveal itself only to philosophical reason, there is need for philosophy.

These distinctions between science and philosophy are distinctions in kind. The two differ from each other on all essential points: they proceed from different intentions; deal with different subject matters; aim at different results; use different methods of approach. Consequently, there can be no question of reducing either one to the other: science is science and philosophy is philosophy. Their meeting or synthesis can take place only within the life of a concrete, individual human being, who desires both to know scientifically and also to ascertain Being in philosophical reflection. He is perfectly entitled to engage in either or both activities, as long as he is constantly aware of what he is doing, and does not mistakenly attach scientific claims to his philosophical activity, or philosophical claims to his scientific research.

2. *Philosophy has no object, but only an encompassing ground.* The domain of objective knowledge, as we saw earlier, is coextensive with the domain of intentional knowledge, which is wholly defined by the dualism of subject and object. Objective knowledge or science has some particular object to which it is directed and which it investigates. Philosophy, on the contrary, has no particular object.8 This lack of object, however, does not constitute an obstacle to philosophy; it merely shows that philosophy is not objective knowledge; that it is not a science. To know objects is different—and according to Jaspers, much less—than to grasp Being, which philosophy is trying to do.

This is so because Being is precisely that which envelops the subject-object duality and which makes the emergence of objects possible. In order to know this encompassing ground, to have it as an object, we should have at our disposal a kind of global awareness which would embrace both object and subject, and thus include itself in its own act of intending. While admitting that the notion of a global awareness is by no means an impossibility, we know for certain that it is not the kind of awareness we, humans, operate with in ordinary objective awareness, which always stands in the dichotomy of subject and object. Therefore, if we ever come to have a grasp of Being, we may be sure that that grasp is not an instance of intentional knowledge. We only know objects. Intentional knowledge, or science, cannot attain the unity and totality of Being to which Reason aspires. That will be left to the efforts of philosophy.

Thus, while science is constituted through the intentional knowledge of objects, philosophy consists in the non-knowing, non-objective awareness of the Enveloping. Unlike scientific consciousness, philosophical consciousness is not intentional, not subject to the opposition of the self and the object. Jaspers maintains that in a philosophical act of awareness the self is contained in the object itself, in the sense that what is sought in such an act is self-revelation through the object. A philosophical act is an interior act of self-realisation or self-assertion through thinking of objects.[9]

To sum up with James Collins:

Scientific thought remains wholly objective and finite, it cannot attain to the encompassing whole of Being. This accounts for the distinction in kind between science and philosophy, a distinction which scientific progress is incapable of removing or attenuating. Philosophy draws its vital strength and truth from inner awareness rather than from any sort of knowledge. Hence philosophy has an origin that is intrinsically independent of science. For philosophy to return to its origins does not mean to return to scientific thinking as its source. The wellsprings of philosophising lie deep within the individual man, in so far as he is a free existent, straining toward Transcendence.[10]

It may be mentioned in closing that the distinction between science and philosophy, which I am summarising here in terms of knowledge and non-knowledge, is often discussed by Jaspers in terms of knowledge and intuition, *Wissen* and *Innewerden*. The essential points of the two considerations amount to the same thing: whereas science is the province of intentional knowledge of objects, philosophy rests on a non-knowing awareness of the Enveloping which is believed to transcend the intentional split between the subject and the objest.

THE ALLIANCE OF SCIENCE AND PHILOSOPHY

The very sharp and fundamental distinction between science and philosophy is necessary in order that we may clearly see how they are related to one another. It is imperative to avoid confusion and to create clarity as regards their respective essences. Both science and philosophy must be made pure. This can be done only by exposing as false the idea that philosophical thought is scientific knowledge. On the other hand, it must also be shown that scientific knowledge does not exhaust all truth. Only as thus distinguished, can the two be of any assistance to one another. Science can help philosophy, but only if the latter abjures its scientific pretensions; and inversely, philosophy can help science, provided that science abandons its metaphysical claims.

The ties of mutual cooperation between purified science and purified philosophy are manifold, but again I shall try to reduce them to two important points:

1. *Philosophy needs science*. Although philosophy is aware of its distinct character, it is inseparable from science. In fact, 'philosophy could be called science in so far as it presupposes the sciences.'[11] In the words of H. J. Blackham, 'philosophy begins with science and cannot do without it, because there is no other world independent of the objective world which science explores.'[12] In this he echoes Jaspers correctly, for whom 'there are no two worlds, side by side,' one which science explores and another which philosophy deals with: 'there is only the one world.'[13] Both science and philosophy explore the same world, but they explore it differently. Science investigates it under the aspect of objectivity, philosophy illuminates it under the light of Being.

Jaspers insists that anyone who wishes to philosophise must also keep account of the sciences, and must be skilled in scientific ways. In an age where science and technology have left such

9

profound marks on the mentality of people in general that one could rightly characterise our epoch as an 'age of science', to ignore the impact of science as inconsequential for philosophic reflection would be extremely unrealistic. Science-consciousness is today part and parcel of the way we experience the world around us; and if it is true that philosophy must take the world as it finds it, that it must reflect on experience as we live it, then no aspect of the given world, no aspect of lived experience should be left out. This is why Jaspers demands a solid scientific formation and constant contact with science: 'Any philosopher', he says, 'who is not trained in a scientific discipline and who fails to keep his scientific interests alive, will inevitably bungle and stumble, and mistake uncritical rough drafts for definitive knowledge.'[14]

More fundamentally, philosophy needs scientific knowledge also because science is the indispensable way to genuine non-knowledge. Jaspers writes: 'It is as though the most magnificent insights could be achieved only through man's quest for the limit at which cognition runs aground, not just seemingly and temporarily, but genuinely and definitively. . . . Only definitive knowledge can make definitive non-knowledge possible.'[15] In other words, science helps philosophy by precipitating an awareness of non-knowledge, which is all the more pronounced, the more resolutely science pursues its rigorous exploration of empirical being. The farther this investigation is pushed, the clearer its limits will appear; the more evident it will become that its principles and axioms apply only to the phenomenal world, the world of objects. The realisation of these limitations may hasten the advent of philosophical awareness which will transform the world of objects into a language of Being.[16]

2. *Science needs philosophy.* The assistance that philosophy can render to science consists basically in the clarification of the sense and meaning of science. 'Science left to itself', say Jaspers, 'becomes homeless as mere science.'[17] It is the business of philosophical reflection to provide the scientist with guidance as to the animating principle and purpose of his work.

Scientific inquiry, as we saw earlier, is already a truncated manifestation of a transcending, philosophical impulse. The very tendency of particular sciences to proclaim themselves, each in its turn, to be the supreme explanation of everything is a sign of this transcending impulse gone astray.[18] The paradoxical fate of the sciences consists precisely in the fact that in practice they may not follow up this impulse which alone gives them existential relevance. In order to remain pure, in order to become metaphysically relevant, they must refuse metaphysics.[19] It is thus that Jaspers can assert in two seemingly contradictory propositions that 'science is meaningful only through metaphysics,' and 'science is genuine without metaphysics.'[20] What is operative in the sciences is a philosophical quest for the transcendental unity of Being. But they must exercise this search in a domain where Being only shows itself in partial aspects, the objects.[21] Their methodological commitment to clarity, determinateness, and univocity, prevents them from attaining what their impulse directs them to attain: Being in its unity and plenitude. Dufrenne and Ricoeur summarise this dilemma of science very well: 'Even though science must always return to empirical being which is enclosed in the limits of objectivity, it exerts an unceasing effort to transcend itself. It is as if science were torn between an ambiguous vocation to positive facts which it must verify, and a desire for the absolute which, it feels, it cannot grasp without betraying itself.'[22]

By pointing out the profound meaning of science, philosophy revalorises science. On one hand, by showing the dignity and autonomy of science, it defends science against its enemies who would dictate from above what science may or may not proclaim as true.[23] On the other hand, by calling attention to the limits of science, it restrains the natural tendency of science to turn into bad philosophy and to set itself up as the only valid approach to reality. Philosophy keeps science pure, rejecting superstitious belief in science as well as contempt of science.

It may not be without interest to note that this theory of the true relationahip of science and philosophy has its existential roots in Jaspers' career itself. His life may be regarded as an itinerary from science-consciousness to philosophical self-awareness. His gradual 'conversion' from medicine to philosophy reflects, biographically, the natural development of thought as well as the tension between the positivist and the philosophic demands in which this development must take place. He endured this tension in his own person without yielding to the excesses of either demand. All his early positive researches were accompanied by an unsparing methodological critique of his own field, psychiatry.

The fruit of this critique was a double awareness, a double realisation on his part. On the one hand, he became convinced that scientific exactitude is an indispensable factor of thought today, so that no serious thinking can bypass it. On the other hand, he also realised that science had definite limits, of which a good scientist must be aware if he knows the nature and method of his discipline at all. This awareness is, in fact, the result of his scientific exactitude. This double realisation slowly nurtured in Jaspers the conviction that there is another type of thinking which, from the point of view of factual science, is not compelling, not universally valid, but which can rouse the inner resources of each man's personal selfhood and give meaning to all his endeavours, including his scientific pursuits. This type of thinking is philosophical thinking. It is philosophy that places science in context and provides guidance for it.

His 'Philosophical Autobiography' (1957), written specially for the volume of critical essays edited by Professor Paul A. Schilpp in the series of the *Library of Living Philosophers,* gives eloquent testimony to the struggle Jaspers had to fight in order to remain faithful to his double conviction, and in order to keep a balanced position between extremes of scientism and irrational philosophising. 'These two concerns have gone with me through my whole life: a constant interest in science, the insistence upon a basically scientific attitude in a person who claims to be a philosopher, and the assertion of the indispensability of science and of its magnitude; and secondly, an interest in philosophising, the insistence on the seriousness of thought which transforms, without having factually objective results, the assertion of the dependency of the meaning of science (but *not* of its correctness) upon philosophy. The consequence was that I tried to assert myself against the contempt for philosophy on the part of too many representatives of the sciences as well as against the contempt for the sciences on the part of fanatical, irrational modes of philosophising.'[24]

In sum: philosophy is radically different from science, but not brutally opposed to it. Philosophy and science are allies. They become enemies only when they are confused. It is then that misunderstandings and mutual recriminations begin. They must, therefore, be kept distinct and yet placed within the open horizon of human thought, where they can complement each other.

I close this chapter with the words of Dufrenne and Ricoeur, who have been particularly felicitous in formulating this double demand of Jaspers. They recognise that the relationship of science and philosophy must, in the end, be dialectical.

Science owes its dignity to the fact that it is both complementary and opposed to philosophy. On the one hand, science receives its driving force from philosophy; on the other hand, philosophy proceeds from a will-to-know that finds its first realisation in science. For this reason, philosophy cannot afford to misunderstand the results of science or to neglect its tools. The two confront each other not so much in a hostile fight as in a brotherly combat, which serves the interest of both true science and true philosophy. Science assists philosophy by preventing philosophy from mistaking itself for a science, and thereby recalls philosophy to its proper vocation, which is to follow the momentum of existence. Philosophy helps science by disclosing its limits, by preserving it from dogmatism, and keeping it in contact with its proper object.[25]

VIII   Reason in Science

It would be belabouring the obvious to insist that science is a work of reason. With the possible exception of a few fanatics, who look upon science as an aberration of reason, nobody would dispute the fact that science is rational knowledge. In fact, science is quite generally regarded today as the most perfect expression of man's rationality. If there exists a problem in this connection nowadays, it is certainly not how to prove that science is a manifestation of rationality, but rather how to show that it is perhaps not the only manifestation; that scientific rationality is not synonymous with rationality *tout court*, and therefore does not meet all the demands of Reason.

Speaking of scientific rationality in a general way, we must include all the various ways and means by which reason endeavours to organise our experience into a coherent body of objective knowledge. Reason is precisely this power of organisation. It is unnecessary, however, to emphasise the fact that the rational organisation of experience by the various sciences is not a stereotyped operation. The most cursory survey of the range of sciences suffices to convince us of the remarkable flexibility and power of transformation that reason can exhibit in dealing with diverse subject matters. It can be a rigidly formal rule of coherence, but it can also be a supple tool of strategics, which is able to cope to a large extent with the aleatory variables that intervene in human events. Indeed, if there is a characteristic proper to Reason as a whole, it is its adaptability to the shifting, changing contours of reality as it presents itself in our experience. Reason renews and subtilises itself incessantly in order to be able to deal with the oncoming diversity of phenomena and to gather them into its interior unity. This prodigious openness and adaptability of reason in general is already evident in the workings of science.

Nevertheless, this flexibility does not exclude a certain amount of unity or even uniformity (1) of the rational *faculty* that is operative in the sciences; and (2) of the *principles* that govern the use of that faculty. The present chapter will concentrate on these two aspects of scientific rationality according to Jaspers.

THE UNDERSTANDING

'Reason is inseparable from the thinking of the understanding. . . . Although Reason operates through the medium of understanding, it is more than the understanding.'[1] These two statements by Jaspers provide the starting point and set the tone of his whole treatment of reason. They tell us that Reason is both inseparable and different from what is here called the understanding. The German term for understanding is *Verstand,* which I have already translated several times indifferently as 'intellect' or 'understanding', and noted that it is the organ of the encompassing general consciousness.[2] This intellect or understanding is here designated by Jaspers as the indispensable medium through which Reason must operate, but which is nlt identical with Reason. As we shall see much later on, Reason transcends the intellect as that dynamism of thought which dilates the confines of intellectual grasp towards the ideal of an all-embracing unity of thought and reality.

For the moment, however, we must stay with the intellect, for it is the intellect that functions as the organ of scientific rationality. As the faculty of objects, it is the intellect or understanding that constitutes the universal cognitive power of scientific knowledge. A brief characterisation of this power according to Jaspers is now indicated.

(1) The intellect is man's spiritual faculty for knowing and apprehending reality. It designates man's essential openness to being, and as such, it is clearly an aspect of his rational nature. The intellect operates on the basis of several closely related presuppositions, which could be summed up as the presupposition of the *universal intelligibility of reality.* This is usually regarded as the absolute presupposition of thought, without which thought could not even begin to operate. Not quite so for Jaspers. Natural and basic as this presupposition may seem, it is not primary; it rests on other presuppositions which must be spelled out. Among other things, the presupposition implies a metaphysical view according to which any sector as well as the whole of reality could, in principle, be an object for the understanding.

Stated in other words: it is assumed that whatever is, is an object, and therefore objectively knowable. It is taken for granted that being is identical with determined object-being, or that being is the sum total of objects.[3] Consequently, the understanding would recoil from the admission that 'it is thinkable that there be the unthinkable.'[4] By a sort of hidden connaturality, it believes itself adequate not only to particular entities but also to the ground of reality, which it hopes to determine in the same way as it can determine objects. In short, the intellect presumes that Being has the same metaphysical qualifications as object-being.

(2) Chief among these qualifications of object-being is *determinateness,* for the undeterminate is precisely that which cannot be intended as an object. It is this determinateness that the intellect transfers to Being itself. Included in the idea of determinateness is the relation to other determinations; a determined object is thinkable only against other determined objects. Thus, whatever the intellect touches becomes automatically finite and relative. It follows then that the intellect cannot deal with the infinite in any form, except by manipulating it as though it too were finite.[5] For the sake of simplicity, we can therefore say that the intellect is a faculty concerned with finite objects.

(3) In order to attain this determinateness of objects to a maximal degree, the intellect must introduce some *categorical reduction.* In other words, it must try to gather the variety of aspects presented by experience into a few easily manageable categories and correlate them according to a few simple rules. In doing so, it must necessarily neglect certain aspects of experience. We could call this the mathematising and logicising tendency of the intellect. The preferred categories of this tendency are those of quantity, for only quantitative terms can be clearly and rigorously determined, examined, measured, and verified. This effort to reduce all aspects of reality to quantitative terms is evident in most of the modern sciences in so far as most of them tend towards the mathematisation of their basic laws.[6]

Other privileged categories of scientific reason are the categories of relation. Additional clarity and distinctness obtain when the intellect is able to represent its quantitative terms in formal relationships.[7] Clear and distinct knowledge is found only 'where quantity and formal logic prevail. This latter contains an essential moment of quantity under the aspect of extension.'[8]

(4) The same clarity further demands *judicative articulation*. The clear and distinct presence of an object is never given to the understanding in the immediacy of simple apprehension, but must be achieved in a judicative division and composition. In other words, simple intuitive presence is not enough: an act of judgement must be involved before we have a fully constituted object.

What Jaspers means is that intellectual thought is essentially judgemental thought, for it is only through acts of judgement that objects are fully constituted and brought into the presence of consciousness. In the first place, it is through an act of judgement that the object is detached and determined against its background. In other terms, the seemingly first perception of a distinct object (as distinct) is already the result of an implicit or exercised act of judgement. Some philosophies refer to this as the perceptual judgement. Jaspers expresses the same idea by saying that thought is already present in perception as that function which remakes the matter of intuition into an object. For him, the awareness of an object of perception is already the result of a sort of condensed judgement, which dismantles sense-intuition and re-assembles it into an object. Without this activity there would be only stimulus and sensation, but no perception.[9] Secondly, even after the object is delineated by a perceptual judgement, the clear and distinct intellectual presentation of the essence of the object requires further articulation, whereby it is analysed into various aspects which can serve as predicates of the object.[10] This is, of course, explicit conceptual judgement, the chief operation of the intellect proper.

The twofold judicative articulation is required by the intellect's demand for clarity. Clarity obtains when all the distinguishable elements of a whole are sorted out and distinguished. To be sure, the judicative act will also immediately restore the separated predicates to the subject through the copula 'is', but the point that Jaspers wants to put into relief is that the intellect would not have to do so at all were it not for the 'original partition' whereby the predicates were dissociated from the whole.[11]

It seems, therefore, that in contrast to intuition, the basic act of the understanding is analytic, disjunctive, and only secondarily synthetic. For the sake of greater and greater clarity, the understanding must continue this disjunction indefinitely and thereby tend to a sort of atomisation of reality in conceptual thinking. Although by a subsequent synthetic activity the intellect tries to counteract this atomising effect, it cannot altogether remove it.

To summarise: the understanding is the organ of scientific reason. It is our faculty for knowing reality, in so far as reality is knowable to us in terms of discrete, finite, and determined object-beings. These objects are constructed and clearly grasped by the intellect in analytico-synthetic acts of judgement and correlated to one another according to certain definite rules of categorical logic, the principal categories of which are quantity and relation. Even more briefly: the understanding is the faculty of clear and distinct thought. In order to see the further implications of this, we must now turn to the principles that regulate the operations of the understanding.

THE PRINCIPLES OF SCIENTIFIC REASON

The operations of the understanding are governed by two supreme principles of thought: the principle of identity and the principle of non-contradiction. Although Jaspers treats of them separately, it soon becomes clear that he regards identity and non-contradiction as reciprocal, as two aspects of a single principle of knowledge. He maintains that the principle of identity is readily convertible into that of non-contradiction, and vice versa. His idea seems to be that the principle of identity, which primarily refers to the meaning of concepts, prevents contradiction in our judgements; while the principle of non-contradiction, which is primarily a law of judgement, assures the invariability of our concepts. In the end, identity and non-contradiction are only two sides of one single law of thought: consistency.

(1) *Identity*. No matter how one formulates it, the principle of identity seems to be so obvious a truism that one is hesitant to waste much time with it. It is hardly worth insisting that 'whatever exists, exists,' or 'things are what they are, and not something else.' All this is self-evident, not to say trivial.

Yet, it is precisely on such trivialities that the nature of thought turns. They are trivial and tautologous only if we take them at face value, not recognising that what derives from them is the very possibility of consistent thinking. Thus, the principle of identity may be self-evident, and as such may not require any further justification, but that does not mean that it is void of all mystery. On the contrary, through it we can once more come into contact with one of the deepest puzzles of knowledge: the relationship between thought and reality.

Unfortunately, the ordinary schematic expression of the principle of identity, 'A is A,' does more to mask than to reveal the mystery of this relationship. It gives the impression that thought is nothing else than the enunciation of a flat tautology that means little or nothing, because the predicate simply repeats the meaning of the subject. We must therefore recognise that this is not the paradigm of our real and meaningful predication. Real and meaningful predication takes place rather in the form of 'A is B,' where the subject is identified through a predicate whose meaning differs formally from that of the subject. 'The different is posited as identical,' says Jaspers. 'The puzzle lies in the real relation through which the different is said to be the same; it lies in the copula "is".'[12] It is here that we can begin to realise that the two formally different meanings contained in the subject and the predicate are somehow rooted in the mysterious ground of reality, which permits our predication to join the two meanings and to express the one through the other, even though they are formally different. It is astonishing that we should be able to identify a whole, the subject, through one of its particular formalities, the predicate, and to be able to say that one 'is' the other: 'The cow *is* brown.' What is hidden in the 'is'? Evidently more than a simple substitution of meaning, for we could not say that 'such-and-such an animal' means 'such-and-such a colour'.

Jaspers is intent on showing us that the mystery of identity, as contained in the relation of subject and predicate and expressed in the copula, must remain a mystery for the understanding, because this relation cannot be determined both universally and univocally. In other words, the 'is' is analogous.[13] The copula has different particular meanings in different particular judgements, and the understanding is unable to determine what 'is' means in general. For instance, in 'A is A' the copula means the *invariance* of a concept; in '2 × 3 is 6' it means *equivalence*; in 'A is real' it affirms *existence*; in 'A is B' it designates either the substantial or the accidental *belonging* of a predicate to an object. And there is nothing in the copulae of these different propositions to which the understanding could attribute a single universal meaning: equivalence is irreducible either to tautology or to existence; belonging is irreducible either to invariance or to equivalence, and so on. All the various meanings are carried by the indeterminate and analogous ground of Being, of which the intellect cannot take possession by determining, in a supreme judgement of judgement, what 'is' is. Such a judgement is impossible for the understanding, for no judgement can pronounce about itself.[14] Thus, the ultimate meaning of the judgement and of the copula, whereby the identity of the different is affirmed, remains an enigma for the understanding. Consequently, the understanding remains an enigma for itself.[15] It can determine and identify everything, save that in reference to which it determines and identifies everything.

And this is to indicate that the seemingly trivial principle of identity, when sufficiently followed up, introduces us into the mysteries and limits of our knowledge of Being, which limits are often lightly treated. With this principle, our thought moves somewhere between tautology, where it runs into the void, and Being in the transcendental sense, which it cannot attain.[16]

Nevertheless, within these limits the principle of identity is an iron law of coherent thought. Jaspers distinguishes three levels or dimensions in it: the psychological, the logical, and the ontic.

The psychological dimension simply designates the formal invariance of general consciousness, which is the necessary requisite for objective knowledge. Objective knowledge is not a fluid state of consciousness, but every act of objective knowledge must be accompanied by the awareness of a stable and identical self, which remains the same in all the acts of knowledge and to which all these acts are related as their unique and permanent source and reference point.

The principle of identity is not only a psychological law of consciousness, but also a logical law, a law of concepts. 'A concept is identical with itself. This is a logical necessity in the matter of concepts. Only where there is identity, can there be a concept. Where this is missing, only flowing, thoughtless, constantly changing sensation is possible (less than the stuff of dreams), but no intelligibility.'[17] In order to assure this identity and stability of concepts, the understanding has to introduce its own timeless forms and structures into the flow of experience. These structures transform experience by precipitating its permanent elements into timeless concepts or meanings. This process is known as conceptualisation. To think conceptually means to operate with fixed meanings which are not subject to temporal variation, and are therefore indefinitely repeatable in the same sense and with the same stable relationships that link them to one another.[18] 'This cow is brown' is (or can be) a true statement, in which the cow is identified by its brown colour, precisely because in making the statement we shut out the night where, we are told, every cow is unidentifiably black. Negatively, therefore, identity simply means the necessity of achronisation, the exclusion of temporal change from our concepts. Concepts thus stabilised have nothing to do with history, or rather they are removed from history. For the sake of consistent thinking, the understanding lifts the concepts out of their natural time-chain, so that time does not enter as one of the elements of their meaning. 'Cow' does not mean 'cow now' or 'cow later' but simply something like 'domesticated, female bovine ruminant'. In our logical discourse, this same law of consistency obliges us in the name of the principle of identity to persevere in the definition thus adopted and not to change the meaning of a given concept in the middle of an argument.

Moreover, timelessness is not the only feature that the principle of identity as a law of concepts introduces into the objects of our experience. It also introduces generality. Concepts are universal class-designations, from which the individual peculiarities are dropped so completely that the remaining content applies to all the members of the class in identically the same way. Bessie and Elsie may be very different creatures in temperament, breed, colour, and milk-giving capacity, but they are identical as 'domesticated, female bovine ruminants' or simply 'cows'.

The third level of the principle of identity announces an ontic necessity: things are what they are; things are identical with themselves; things have determination. The force of the principle of identity also comes from reality itself.[19] In other words, the principle holds not only for the makeup of our consciousness and the structures of logic, but also for being. Being too is governed by the law of identity.

Here Jaspers is trying to relate the psychological and logical invariance of concepts to reality itself. This does not mean, however, that he is now arguing from the logical to the real order. That would be out of character with the overall Kantian tenor of his philosophy. The key to a more probable interpretation of his meaning is provided by the words 'thing' and 'ontic'. If we look at the last footnote, we can see that Jaspers refers to an *ontisches Gesetz*, and not to a *Seinsgesetz* or *ontologisches Gesetz*. In other words, his reference is to beings, things, *entia*, not to Being as such. As we saw earlier, the difference between beings and Being is precisely that beings are the appearances under which Being becomes objectively knowable for us. Therefore, to say that beings are identical with themselves amounts to pronouncing an ontic law, which is binding on the appearances of Being, but not necessarily on Being itself. It is not an ontological law. The ontic law merely stipulates that beings be self-identical. Its force in reference to Being is only hypothetical: *if* Being is to be known objectively, it must obey the law of identity. Thus formulated with a hypothetical clause, the law says nothing of realism or of Being as such; it merely states the general condition of objective knowability. Such is in fact the meaning of the closing sentence which terminates Jaspers' description of the threefold sense of the principle of identity: 'The threefold meaning of the principle of identity is only a threefold aspect of a single meaning. It applies to our consciousness, to our logic, and to Being, in so far as the *latter becomes thinkable*.'[20] He adds, moreover, that in so far as this identity is affirmed of the essences of things rather than of their temporal reality; in so far as the law is taken for a *principe des essences* (Leibniz) rather than for a *principe des existences*, the ontic dimension of the law tends to repeat what the logical law of concepts has already announced about the necessity of achronisation and stabilisation of experience.

To sum up: the principle of identity is the supreme principle of objective intelligibility and, as such, the highest norm for the use of scientific reason or understanding. Because this principle has a threefold anchorage in the identity of consciousness, in the invariance of concepts, and in the determination of objects, the rule for the scientific use of reason could be stated in three cumulative propositions: an act of scientific reason must proceed from an invariable consciousness; it must operate with trans-temporal meanings; it must refer to determined objects.

2. *Non-contradiction*. Parallel to the threefold dimension of the

principle of identity, Jaspers has a threefold meaning for the principle of non-contradiction also: the psychological, the logical, and the ontic meanings. The first of these is relative to the act of judgement, the second to its content, the third to its object, and taken together they represent the negative side of the principle of identity. Here is a brief survey of them:

'Two acts of judgement, corresponding to two contradictory statements, cannot be performed by the same consciousness at the same time. . . . It is the very nature of understanding that while it judges that something is the case, it cannot also judge that the same is not the case.'[21] To entertain two contradictory propositions at the same time would destroy the unity of consciousness. Jaspers remarks, however, that the consciousness concerning which the impossibility of entertaining two contradictories is affirmed here is the ideal consciousness of clear and distinct thought.[22] In practice, this ideal clarity is seldom reached, and is very seldom coupled with perfect presence of mind or with sufficient will to pursue an issue to the point where some of its internal inconsistencies become apparent. So in practice, in the absence of a clear disjunction between the compatible and incompatible elements of our working consciousness, many of our judgements may in fact contain a hidden contradiction. Nevertheless, to hunt out contradictions and thus to achieve perfect clarity is native to consciousness in general. We must recall that the clarity of consciousness is directly proportionate to the distinctness with which its objects are delineated and opposed to one another. But the greatest distinctness, and hence the greatest clarity of consciousness, obtains when an object is contrasted to its contradictory. In other words, the clear determination of a given object is often attained only through the perfect exclusion of its opposite.[23]

On the logical level, in reference to the content of judgement, the principle of non-contradiction admits several formulations: 'Two contradictory propositions cannot be true together;' or 'A given proposition cannot be both true and false;' or 'Every assertion that implies its own negation is necessarily false;' or 'A predicate cannot be both affirmed and denied of the same subject at the same time.' In these forms the principle mentions the universal logical condition of the truth of propositions. It no longer merely states the psychological impossibility of combining two contradictory acts in the same clear consciousness, but also lays down the norm for any true judgement. A true judgement must perfectly exclude its contradiction. As normative of the very content of judgement, this dimension of the principle is more basic and originary than the one relative to the acts of judgement, which is only a result of this, as it were.[24] The psychological impossibility of performing two contradictory acts of judgement at the same time only comes about when, in virtue of the logical necessity for perfect disjunction between two contradictories, our inquiry reaches the point where the alternatives arise of either rejecting both sides of the distinction or else opting for one of them, since both of them cannot be true together. Although Jaspers never says so explicitly, many of his formulae imply that he considers the principle of excluded middle as a derivative form of the principle of non-contradiction which admits no third possibility between true and false, between being and non-being.

In reference to the object of judgement, the principle legislates about what the object can or cannot be: 'Nothing can be and not be at the same time;' 'A thing cannot be A and non-A at the same time.' Here the principle affirms the absolute distinction between being and non-being, and proscribes objects affected with contradictory qualities and properties.

At first glance, this dimension of the principle of non-contradiction appears to have a larger application than the corresponding level of the principle of identity. It seems to hold not only for the content of every true judgement, not only for reality in so far as it becomes a thought-object for us, but also for reality as it is in itself. In other terms, the force of the principle seems to extend beyond the mere logical and ontic domains to include also the ontological domain. In fact, many of Jaspers' statements confirm this impression. Contradition, he says, is not only incompatible with the lucidity of consciousness, not only inadmissible from the point of view of logic, but 'it is the basic feature of reality itself not to be able to exist as contradictory. The law of non-contradiction in this sense is absolutely universal. It is an ontological law.'[25]

Nevertheless, Jaspers also maintains that this ontological claim, absolutely universal as it may be, still does not amount to a necessary law of Being. Rather, it is rooted in an act of *faith* that our thought cannot refrain from making in reference to reality as a whole. As the expression of this act of faith, the principle implies a particular consciousness of reality, a law of thought, rather than a necessary law of Being. It implies a basic presupposition, a fundamental trust on the part of thought, that reality somehow obeys the same laws as thought; that what is unthinkable is also impossible. All that Jaspers wants is that we recognise that this trust, natural as it may be, is in no way a necessary or demonstrable certitude.[26]

For instance, the proposition that two truths cannot contradict each other is undoubtedly correct in the sense that, in the case of contradiction, they are simply unthinkable together, and that by complete disjunction at least one of the 'truths' will prove false. 'However,' he adds, 'when both truths result from reality, both proved and verified, then the proposition, "Two truths cannot contradict each other," is the expression of an implicit trust that truth, because it originates in reality, cannot in the end lead to unresolvable contradictions. It is a trust that both Being and its knowability are fundamentally "in order", and in principle can be accomplished without contradiction.'[27]

It is precisely here that Jaspers introduces a rather important distinction. This trust in the universal intelligibility or non-contradictoriness of reality underlies two entirely different types of thinking: scientific thinking, which consists in a progressive investigation of particular objects; and philosophical thinking, which consists in an anticipatory insight into reality as a whole. Jaspers believes that the principle of non-contradiction expressing this trust is valid for the advancing movement of scientific thought, but not as an anticipatory philosophic assertion about Being as a whole.[28] The chief task of advancing science consists precisely in the progressive elimination of the temporary paradoxes and contradictions which may occasionally arise in the course of its endeavours to represent reality in terms of perfectly discrete and unambiguous objects. The presence of contradiction merely serves as a temporary irritant, which the scientific mind must neutralise by acting upon a trust in the final non-contradictoriness of positive object-beings. By contrast, philosophical thinking is much less secure in its trust. Its history is full of instances of doubt concerning the absolute intelligibility of its object: Being as a whole. The trust in the final non-contradictoriness of reality, and thereby the anticipatory meaning of the principle of non-contradiction, has repeatedly been called into question or altogether abandoned by philosophical thinking.[29] It is this wavering confidence that prompted the thinkers of all ages to search out the final and unresolvable antinomies of Being.

But even this search may be conducted in two different mental attitudes, with two different expectations. We may hope that through these antinomies we will eventually reach the deepest ground of Being, the grasp of which will resolve even these antinomies. This, Jaspers maintains, was what Kant expected to achieve by his investigations of the antinomies of pure reason. But we may also accept the antinomies as final, hoping that their unresolvable opposition will in the end precipitate for us a radically new awareness of reality, a new relationship with Transcendence, which will put into sharp relief the limits of all knowledge and of all intellectual approach to Being as a whole. This expectation is precisely the principal hope of Jaspers' philosophical faith.

To summarise: together with the principle of identity, non-contradiction is the supreme principle of positive knowledge; of 'knowledge that succeeds', as Jaspers would say. Its applicability, far from being absolute, is restricted to the scientific use of reason. It regulates the knowledge of the ontic region of particular things, but not necessarily the ontological region of Being as such. The very possibility of doubting the ontological meaning of the principle shows that non-contradictoriness is only an undemonstrable presupposition, or at least a sign for the success of scientific knowledge, but not 'a pillar of Being'.[30]

Conclusions to Part II

JASPERS' treatment of scientific reason contains several valuable insights, and opens up a number of ways, that could eventually lead to a radical reappraisal of the generally accepted notions of reason and rationality. The idea of reason is very often construed in too narrow a sense signifying the faculty of scientific logic, or at best the power of conceptualisation. This impoverished conception is actually at the root of several aberrations in contemporary philosophy. To mention just two: both logical positivism and existentialism labour under the disadvantage of this narrow view of reason. Even though they react to it differently, both of them take reason to be no more than a simple faculty of intellectual thought. Positivism is entirely satisfied with such a view. Consequently, it regards science as the only strictly rational activity worth pursuing, and at the same time it relegates philosophy to the status of an auxiliary discipline to science, whose sole function should be to elaborate the logic of sciences. Existentialism, on the other hand, recognising the insufficiency of conceptual thought to cope with some of the vital issues of human existence, repudiates scientific rationality altogether, and gives itself over to an irrational cultivation of feeling and affectivity. As a reaction to narrow intellectualism, existential philosophy often falls into the other extreme. It is precisely such extremes that Jaspers, the scientist turned philosopher, wants to avoid by integrating the positive elements of both tendencies into a larger view of reason. He does not deny the place and value of scientific knowledge, but neither does he try to extend it to cover certain domains which, by necessity of the methodological restrictions required by the sciences themselves, lie beyond the competence of scientific thought. Rather, he tries to transcend science by a more comprehensive thought which, though no longer strictly conceptual, would still be rational. Needless to say, his doctrine is far from being an exhaustive solution to the problem. Nevertheless, it represents a significant beginning. Further reflection is needed to fill out the many lacunae and to elaborate a fuller and more systematic presentation of the matter. But even so, the principal outlines of his general doctrine are clearly traceable already.

The first interesting item of this doctrine is the rather unorthodox view that Jaspers entertains of the relationship between science and philosophy. Although his expressions lack the necessary precision and his general manner of dealing with the problem is more rhapsodic than methodical, it soon becomes clear that he advocates a sharp distinction in kind between science and philosophy, and correspondingly between scientific and philosophic rationality. This distinction hinges on the fact that, contrary to the usual traditional views which regard philosophy as a kind of knowledge, Jaspers insists that only scientific knowledge is knowledge in the proper sense of the term, because science alone deals with determined and particular objects. He calls philosophy non-knowledge, because philosophy does not deal with univocal concepts of determined objects but refers to the undertermined and analogous ground of objects.

Under these circumstances one would expect Jaspers to have some definite views on analogy, but he has none. His teachings in this regard are extremely incomplete, to say the least. He does not even try to elaborate a doctrine on analogy or to give at least a principle from which the question might be approached. His idea seems to be that in analogy, where beings are thought of as different and yet 'somehow the same', the disjunctive determination required by clear and distinct understanding is no longer practicable. In other terms, reason cannot determine both universally and univocally *how* beings are the same. It seems that they are the same differently.

One of the ways to attenuate this paradox is to explain the sameness of things by their dependence on a common cause. However, Jaspers thinks that the principle of causality only complicates the problem, without really solving it. First of all, the appeal to causality merely pushes back the problem of analogy from the things themselves to their relation to a common cause, but it cannot determine univocally and universally the *how* of this causal dependence. How do the manifestly different sorts of things as effects depend on the same common cause? If their common cause is only a partial cause, there is no problem, because then we can always invoke some other causes beside it which would account for the differences in the effects. But the relationship becomes undeterminable when it is a question of a unique and total cause of beings, because then one and the same cause must serve to explain both the sameness and difference in things. Moreover, causal inquiry and explanation always leads to endlessness. If to understand a phenomenon means that one has to understand it through its cause, then to understand the cause one would have to look for the cause of that, and so on indefinitely. Of course, in order to cut short this endlessness of inquiry and explanation, the mind simply stops at one point. *Non est procedendum ad infinitum* is a decree of a more or less tired mind which declares at least one of the causes as first. This first cause is posited as an absolute beginning, an uncaused cause. The only great difficulty with absolute beginnings and uncaused causes is that they are by definition incomprehensible, because there is no further cause to explain them by. In the long run, then, this amounts to explaining a causally linked series of phenomena by an unknown: *ignotum per ignotius*. Jaspers' conclusion is that an absolute beginning and an uncaused cause is a circle, a contradiction, which may be a tremendously rich figure of speech, a basic metaphor, but has no objective standing in itself.[1] In short, analogy remains undeterminable, and never becomes an item of univocal, objective knowledge.

If we were to ask Jaspers by what right he restricts knowledge to univocal knowledge, he would point to the laws of identity and non-contradiction. Knowledge, he would claim, is coextensive with the realms governed by these laws. But in analogy, where we have to mix the same with the different; in absolute beginnings and uncaused causes, where we cannot separate the condition from the conditioned, the cause from the effect: there these first principles of knowledge break down, and the famous self-reference sets in. Therefore, analogy is no longer a sign of a strictly intellectual relationship to clearly determined objects, but a sign of a symbolical or intuitive relation to the encompassing horizon of things, namely Being.

The scientific form of reason is the strict understanding or intellect. In this form, reason has for function the ordering of experience. This ordering function involves, above all, a stabilisation and generalisation of experience. Change and individuality are banished, and experience is transposed into a network of timeless concepts and relationships, which, once constituted, can be extended beyond experience. This permits us to anticipate experience yet to come, so that we do not have to face the future with complete ignorance: we can, in a schematic sort of way, foresee what reality will be in the future, because we see what it is and what it was. Thanks to this uniform pattern which reason imposes on experience, reality becomes manageable for us to a large extent. It is to the credit of reason that it fills a kind of large pragmatic purpose in furnishing us with reliable general information about reality, which allows us to calculate the future and to arrange our lives and projects accordingly. Reason in this sense is the light that permits us to find our way in the world. That is why Jaspers says that the first performance of reason is world-orientation, *Weltorientierung*.

On the debit side stands a certain artificiality that this schematising function of reason introduces into experience. This can be especially crippling if it is coupled with a hidden value-judgement that the general aspects shown in our concepts are the more genuine features of reality; that the 'really' real is that which is reflected in our understanding, rather than that which is given in experience. 'On that hypothesis,' as George Boas puts it, 'any woman will do to marry and any god to worship. There is no self-evident reason why the general is more inherently valuable than the particular, the formal than the material, in spite of tradition to the contrary.'[2] This is somewhat the sentiment of Jaspers also who, as we saw, refuses the primacy of the universal. For him, 'real' reality is neither the universal nor the particular, but the matrix of both. From this it follows that scientific reason or understanding does not entirely satisfy the native appetite of thought, because it reveals reality only in so far as the latter fits into a network of universals.

Nor is Jaspers particularly clear on the relationship between the theoretical and practical aspects of science. On the one hand, his idea seems to be that thought is, originally and essentially, praxis, or thoughtful doing. It is only science that has split this original whole into two separate parts, doing and knowing as a means to an end. This, he thinks, takes away the existential and moral interest of thought, and makes it irrelevant for life. On the other hand, he admits that the immediate concern of science should be with speculation. It should aim at knowing whatever is knowable, regardless of utility, applicability, or ethical relevance. In order to keep its purity, science must keep the subjective interests and value judgements of the scientist in check. In order to state in all objectivity what the facts are, it must set aside any other consideration. 'The scientific duty to see the truth of facts and the practical one of sticking up for one's ideals constitute two different obligations.'[3]

Perhaps Jaspers' point is that the artificial separation between doing and knowing is the necessary price modern science must pay for its increasing objectivity. In order to be more and more exact, science has to become less and less human. Disinterested research tends to replace passionate involvement, and while we possess more and more correct information, we know less and less what is worth living and working for.

Nevertheless, in the words of Gerhard Knauss, 'man does not have to overthrow science in order to save his being human. If some quarters desire a new 'saving knowledge' alongside the pure 'ordering knowledge' of science, we must reply that no truth can bypass the truth of science. For the evil consists precisely in the division of our modern consciousness and in the co-existence of truths. The task is rather to transform the scientific consciousness by a new awareness of Being.'[4] In Jaspers' terms this would mean to transcend the object-bound orientation of science by philosophising.

I believe that a very simple initial distinction on Jaspers' part would have helped to avoid much of the uncertainty and confusion on this matter. I am thinking of the distinction between the *finis operis* and the *finis operantis*. Knowledge simply as such does not have to be a doing. It does not have to be effective in order to be graced by the name of real knowledge, because as an immanent activity it has no other demand to satisfy than the speculative one of seeing. It is up to man, the thinker, the *operans*, to turn his speculation to worthwhile account and not to be satisfied with mere contemplation. The separation between speculation and action is, of course, always possible, but that is not the fault of knowledge. Rather, it is the fault of the knower who does not let his thought have any bearing on his life. The fault lies with the *finis operantis*. Knowledge can, indeed, become a means to a higher existential end without abandoning its speculative character. It is not very profound to blame one thing for not being another; to berate thought for not being action.

However, Jaspers is quite right on another point. He is right in asserting that scientific consciousness is in need not only of a complement but also of a transformation by philosophical consciousness. This transformation must start with an act of recognising the necessary limits of science. Excellent as it may be, science is limited knowledge. In fact, every one of its features of excellence is also a limitation: its objectivity devalorises the subjective; its clarity demands disjunctive articulation and thus leads to fragmentation; its conceptual character tends to eliminate that which is individual and historical in experience. These limitations must be recognised by the practitioners of science.

Above all, scientists should not be led to think that scientific rationality is the only kind of reason there is. They should not fall into the error of those who take the nature of thought in too narrow a sense, in the sense of the understanding, 'which exhausts itself in mechanical thinking, distinguishing, defining, and ordering.'[5] Above such knowledge is the thought which pertains properly to Reason in the fuller sense. It is a knowledge about knowledge. Philosophy has the task of re-awakening reason to full self-awareness by knowing about knowing. 'How I understand my knowledge', says Jaspers, 'is a basic question of philosophising from its inception on. It is the self-consciousness of reason.'[6] One should not imagine that this additional awareness interferes in any way with the exactitude, clarity, and logic of science; on the contrary, it will challenge science 'to dare the utmost in knowability',[7] for the clearer knowledge becomes, the sharper its limits appear. Beyond these confines lies another kind of awareness, another kind of rationality, which takes into account not only the objectively knowable aspects of reality but also its existential aspects. As Jaspers puts it, 'it is not sufficient to say: be rational! but rather: be rational out of Existence, or better, out of all the modes of the Enveloping.'[8]

We saw that Jaspers' perspective in discussing science was constantly larger than science itself, and his treatment of Reason larger than understanding. He calls Reason the 'pre-eminence of thought in all the modes of the Enveloping.'[9] This pre-eminence means that Reason can bring to light all the modes of the Enveloping, even those that are recalcitrant to the grasp of the understanding, and thus are usually classed as counter-rational or irrational. Reason means the omnipresent demand for thoughtfulness even in those areas where the intellect is helpless. Reason is a patient, binding, recollecting, and progressive power that is not satisfied with mere scientific accuracies. 'With the full rational attitude,' writes Jaspers, 'I desire unlimited clarity; I try to know scientifically, to grasp the empirically real and the compelling validities of the thinkable; but at the same time, I live with an awareness of the limits of scientific penetrability and of clarity in general.'[10] This full rational attitude belongs to philosophy. It is the task of philosophy to achieve Reason, to restore Reason, to bring Reason to full maturity.

Part III
Reason and Philosophy

Introduction

THE problems of Part II must now give place to a new set of considerations which will deal with philosophical rationality. There have already been numerous indications that Jaspers distinguishes sharply between the ideal of scientific reason and reason as it operates in human existence and in philosophical reflection. Now it is time to investigate more systematically and in greater detail how philosophical reason differs from, and in a sense is larger than, scientific reason. We must extract from Jaspers' writings some sort of composite description of the way in which philosophy is reputed to transcend science. As we have seen, he held that reason somehow transforms the objective works of the scientific intellect into an intuitive grasp of Being as such. Therefore, the important task here is to find out whether this transcending is merely an amorphous feeling, without method or order, or whether transcending has a method of its own, its own internal logic. Is philosophising a rational activity or not? If it is, how does reason guide the course of philosophical reflection? Is it through formal logic or through some other means?

In his numerous writings, Jaspers has drafted many answers to these questions. Depending on the particular context, these answers may vary considerably in tone and accent, but they all share the same underlying idea. For our purposes, I have selected two such answers, each from a different period of his career, in order to show their convergence. The first is taken from *Philosophie* (1933), where Jaspers was more interested in clarifying the existential conditions of philosophising than in giving a doctrinal exposé of its logical possibility.[1] The second, taken from both *Vernunft und Existenz* (1935) and *Von der Wahrheit* (1947), dates from a later period during which Jaspers began to elaborate and perfect his ideas on the Enveloping and started to reflect more explicitly on the correlation of the rational and existential elements that jointly condition the nature of philosophy. It must be kept in mind, however, that the two descriptions constitute a single whole not only because their underlying view is the same but also because what is said about the human conditions of philosophising in the first description is irrevocably decisive for philosophical rationality in the second. From the elucidation of

the existential consciousness of Being, which is the general theme
of the first description, to the clarification of philosophical self-
awareness, which is the theme of philosophical logic, there is no
radical break but only a shift of emphasis.[2] I agree completely
with Fr Xavier Tilliette who judiciously points out that Jaspers'
philosophy 'is not alternately a philosophy of existence and,
through a kind of internal violence, a philosophy of reason: it is
both at once by virtue of a single act of will.'[3] The result is that
the elucidation of existence already shows in *actu exercito* how
reason guides knowledge towards self-transcending thought
while philosophical logic shows how existence directs and inspires
the works of reason. These two elements, the existential and the
rational, are dialectically intertwined in Jaspers' philosophy.

IX   Elucidation of Existence

WE may recall that the three principal dimensions of reality which were said to be inaccessible to objective science and its methods were the totality of the World, the originality of Existence, and the inseity of Transcendence. These are the Jaspersian equivalents of Kant's noumenal entities: the world, the soul, and God. In Part II, we saw Jaspers trying to supplement the objective world-orientation of the sciences by a philosophical one, consisting essentially in a certain critique of the sciences. This was to show that the world is not a closed totality, let alone the whole of Being as such. Consequently, it was pointed out that the sciences are incapable of covering the whole of Being and thus of satisfying the deepest impulses of thought. On the whole, his method of philosophical world-orientation was a negative one: it amounted to a systematic search for the various definitive limits of objective or scientific knowledge. However, one of the positive results of this search was a growing awareness that perhaps, over and beyond the objective world and outside the reach of science, there might exist other aspects of reality which, though by nature non-objective, could nevertheless be thinkable by reason.[1] In other words, philosophical world-orientation took us to the verge of discovering some new realms in Being that do not fit into the idea of the world and yet, we feel, belong to the integral concept of reality.

The difficulty, of course, is in naming and describing these a-mundane modes of reality. Would not any designation immediately objectify them and thus make them a part of the world? Jaspers begins to help himself out of the difficulty by saying that a change in terminology at this point might be of some initial advantage. If, due to the mythical and reifying force, the traditional terms 'soul' and 'God' bring to mind some sort of spiritual objects, then a more philosophical set of terms, such as 'Existence' and 'Transcendence', could perhaps lessen this suggestion and not make us think of objects immediately.

I have already indicated earlier in what sense Jaspers speaks about Existence and Transcendence. Here I would like to take them up again with the special aim of seeing by what methods Jaspers thinks he can approach them, for we know already that they will be inaccessible to direct and objective investigations.

THE UNKNOWABLE EXISTENCE

'What is there', Jaspers asks himself, 'that stands outside and confronts the entire objective being of the World?' And his answer is: 'There is a reality which, under the appearance of empirical being, *is not*, but *can be and ought to be* and thus decides in time whether it will be eternal or not. This being is myself as Existence. I am this Existence in so far as I do not objectify myself.'[2]

Such is a first description of Existence. By a single leap we are in the very thick of all the difficulties that beset our grasp of Existence. First of all, we are given to understand that Existence is not something of which we simply affirm that it is, if by 'is' we mean the actuality of something that is there, given, present, and positive.[3] Existence is rather the source of yet unrealised future possibilities. In the words of Dufrenne and Ricoeur, existence is both 'an affirmation and a conquest. It is a being that I *am not* by nature, but which I *make* through a series of decisions about myself.'[4] All this should warn us that *Existence is not to be confused with Dasein*, that is, with our empirical individuality. This empirical individuality is actually there as a something, and is conceivable as the particular product of causally interacting impersonal forces. On the basis of its actuality and according to the criteria of general laws, the objective possibilities of empirical individuality can also be calculated and predicted. But it is not these objective possibilities that Jaspers refers to when he says that Existence is the sort of being that is not but can be, or that 'man is possible Existence in empirical individuality'.[5] He refers rather to that indetermination proper to human reality which is liberty. The possibilities of Existence he has in mind are not based on objective reality alone but also depend on free choice and decision.[6] They are not calculable or observable empirically; they are free and contingent possibilities. To be sure, every existential decision takes flesh in objective reality and makes use of the determinations of the objective world as the field in which it manifests itself, but it does not have its origin there; the world is not its source.[7] Existence, in so far as it is synonymous with freedom, is its own source. To say that Existence is its own source and origin simply means that it is essentially the possibility of autonomous selfhood. Only a self depends on itself for its own constitution, or according to another expression of Jaspers, selfhood is constituted by the active rapport whereby an individual comes to realise himself.[8] Or again, Existence is 'that which creates itself'.[9] It is this singularly incomprehensible *Sichzusichselbstverhalten* and auto-creation, whereby Existence both *is* what it makes itself and *makes* itself what it is, that poses the first major difficulty for our understanding. How can we think of something that is its own cause and effect, donor, gift, and beneficiary at the same time?[10]

In the second place, if Existence is that irreducible free individuality that Jaspers claims it is, then it should be fairly clear that Existence is entirely ineffable on account of its complete lack of universality. In this, Existence is totally dissimilar to things in the world. The individuality of things in the world, their *Weltdasein* as Jaspers calls it, consists in their each being a member of a class of things, and it can be known through class concepts. Existence, on the contrary, cannot be known but only elucidated, because it is not affected by any degree of universality. It is never just an illustrative case of a class.[11]

Jaspers himself sees the knot of this difficulty: 'If Existence is thus set off against empirical being, against the world and all that is universal, then there seems to be nothing left. If it cannot become an object, then it seems hopeless to want to grasp it in thought.'[12] There is no use trying to talk about Existence if all that we can ever say in objective language refers only to our empirical individuality.[13] In that case the very being of Existence is subject to an invincible doubt, and it would be far better not to think about it at all, but to hold on to what is objectively graspable by good, healthy intelligence.[14] Obviously, we can only *be* Existence, but we cannot *know* it.

Logical as this conclusion may appear, Jaspers would not find it altogether acceptable, especially the phrasing of the last statement. Even though he insists on the unknowability of Existence, he maintains that we can achieve authentic Existence only if

11

we try to elucidate it through reflection.[15] It is part and parcel of human reality to be reflective. In fact, we have already seen that the whole quest of thought for Being which constitutes the heart of the philosophical endeavour is never the enterprise of our empirical being but of Existence which wants to clarify itself in the light of total reality. This effort of clarification is essential to human selfhood, because 'Existence is immanent to the movement which discovers it.'[16] Sheer Existence that would rest entirely on feeling, blind impulse, or whim, would end up as violence and so fall under the empirical laws of biology and psychology which govern these forces. In other words, unreflective Existence would not be Existence at all, but a form of animal Dasein.

Acknowledging his own difficulties, Jaspers nevertheless forges ahead in order to show that perhaps there are ways of rescuing Existence from absolute muteness and inexpressibility. He tries to indicate by what methods language and thought can be pressed into the service of elucidating Existence. Since even philosophy cannot dispense with objective thought and language altogether, some changes must be introduced into their use in order to make them apt tools of existential expression. Somehow or other, the precision of thought must throw some light on the dark depths of Existence; the universality of language must express the uniqueness of selfhood without, however, making Existence into an object.

As we shall see presently, Jaspers employs three closely related techniques for this purpose: two of them rather negative, and the third one more or less positive. The first two are supposed to make us aware of the inadequacy of the objective categories of language in coping with the richness of Existence; the third is an attempt to elaborate a special set of existential 'categories', better fitted to existential discourse.

METHODICAL STEPS OF ELUCIDATION

The problem of clarifying Existence could have been stated in different ways. I have chosen to attach it to the disparity which exists between the irreducible subjectivity and uniqueness of Existence, on the one hand, and the essential objectivity and universality of thought and language, on the other. This way, the problem can be posed squarely in terms of the rapport between the subjective and the objective; the particular and the universal. The problem of these relationships has both ontological and epistemological implications. One could treat these implications separately, but Jaspers does not do so because, as we noted above, he considers that in the case of Existence the two problems fall into one, so that he regards the dicibility of selfhood as essential to its very being. He would reject the idea of a 'speechless Existence' as impossible.[17] Genuine Existence is possible only through genuine reflection. The ascertainment of Existence is neither prior to, nor independent of, the universal medium of thought in which it emerges for itself.[18] Therefore, the final form of the problem is to see whether and how the emergence of selfhood could be promoted by the means of universal language.

(1) *The negative method*

The first employment of language in the service of Existence-elucidation is aimed at a negative goal, namely, to express what Existence is not.[19] In this phase, language is subjected to an unsparing self-examination, put on trial, as it were. As judge, jury, defendant and prosecutor all in one, language must confess to the insufficiency of its own objective concepts and categories in defining Existence. The motive force of this cross-examination derives from an initial doubt that I entertain in regard to the unlimited competence of language to designate what I am. I feel that the real transcendence of my personhood can surface only if I succeed in breaking through the limitations of object-language, language designed for speaking about things in the world.[20] In order for this breakthrough to be authentic, I must pursue this scrutiny of thought and language to the point where 'no more object emerges, and only the void is left.'[21]

We have already seen an accelerated version of this scrutinising process in Part I. We noted how our selfhood seemed to elude all positive designation. In spite of the deep solidarity and even partial identity with my body, I am not my body. Even though my body is the necessary openness, the point of contact I must have with the world, I am not completely identifiable as my body. Rather, my body belongs to me. Whether it serves or tyrannises me, I can retain a certain ultimate power over it. Nor, as we saw, am I identical with my social significance. Though I owe much to society and am deeply grateful to it for having provided the space and means for my growth, I can, and at times I must, refuse to be regarded as a creature of society. Even if society should cast me out, something of my self would survive for a while to prove that I am more than what society conferred upon me. I am also more than the sum total of my past achievements. I am more than my character, my entrenched or nascent dispositions. In spite of their pressure and constant urge, I retain a certain degree of freedom. It remains in my power to take myself back from their facticity. Nor am I the complexus of all this, a formal ego. To speak of *the* ego is an artificial way of making a noun out of a personal pronoun that tricks us into imagining the self as an object-being.[22]

The same could be repeated about the other existential concepts, such as *freedom, historicity, situation, death, guilt.* Perhaps I shall have occasion to speak of them in other contexts. Here it is more important to evaluate how such a scrutiny of language contributes to the clarification of Existence.

As stated earlier, the first result of the negative method is that it helps us to state what Existence is not. For purposes of clarification, this in itself would be a very slim result. We must remember, however, that the negative phase is only a first step in the process of elucidation and, as such, important for two reasons. Methodologically, it is important for the further orientation of our search to know from the beginning what Existence is not. Thus we are permanently disabused of any attempt to discover Existence in the realms of objectivity or positivity. The transformation of General Consciousness into absolute consciousness, to which we have alluded previously, is impossible as long as we still entertain the hope that, underneath the multiple empirical aspects which adhere to the appearance of Existence, we will somehow be able to uncover a metempirical object that would be Existence itself. Existence is not an object, not even a metempirical one, and the negative method prompts us to break with objects and objective knowledge if we want to undertake a non-illusory elucidation of Existence.[23] Secondly, if this break with objectivity and objective knowledge is salutary in the order of method, it is still more so in the existential order of self-awareness. The fact that we can seriously question and doubt the absolute empire of objectivity is a sign that already there is something in us that is not entirely empirical being, something that is not satisfied with objectivity alone. It is a sign that we are awakened to Existence from the spell of empirical being. The act which liberates our selfhood from this spell and from the fascination with objective knowledge is the same act through which the self, once awakened, begins to clarify itself: it is the active doubt. This doubt has, therefore, a double function: it helps us to re-enact on the level of thought the same leap (*Sprung*) from empirical being to Existence that it first helped to execute on the level of being. 'Thus the negative method is not a simple artifice,' remark Dufrenne and Ricoeur. 'Just as the rational doubt of Descartes engenders the *cogito* and constitutes the transcendental consciousness, so here the existential doubt constitutes the movement through which Existence conquers itself by putting into question all objectivity.'[24] This is the meaning of the expression that Existence is immanent to the movement which discloses it.

The second effect with which Jaspers credits the negative method is a little more constructive. He claims that the radical experience of the insufficiency of objective thought and language to grasp what I am myself can lead to an indirect clarity about Existence. First, the strange feeling of incompleteness and dissatisfaction which I experience every time I am tempted to identify myself with any one of the objective aspects of my selfhood, and which prompts me to say every time that I am still otherwise, throws a certain light on the inexhaustible richness of me as a possible Existence. Secondly, the realisation of the fact that I have the power to take myself back from every aspect of facticity that besets the embodiment of my Existence in the world gives me an indirect knowledge *about* me, even though this knowledge is not a direct knowledge *of* me.[25]

Jaspers seems to attach great importance to this distinction between the *knowledge of*, and the *knowledge about*, something. In the light of all that I have said before, it is not difficult to guess the meaning of this distinction. We have to do with knowledge of something when the thing to be known is laid out before us in its full actuality so that our knowledge can envelop it completely. Let us explain. To say that the object to be known is present to us in its 'full actuality' is not to imply that the thing is pure actuality or determination. What is meant is that, together with its present determinations, its future actuality—which as yet is only in the state of potentiality—is also given. In other words, both the genesis and the future development of the thing in question are predictable in principle. It suffices to know the objective causes that have made it what it is and the future causes that will actuate its present virtualities and make it what it will be. By contrast, we have to do with knowledge *about* something when the thing to be known is not given at all because it is only a free possibility, or, in the words of Jaspers, 'a being that is not, but can be and ought to be.' Such a being cannot be known directly, because it cannot be determined either in itself or in its causes.

For the sake of precision, it should be noted briefly that free existential possibility should not be confused with the mere absence of objective causal determination, with the fashionable 'freedom of the electron'. Jaspers vigorously rejects any 'latter-day physics of freedom', and maintains that there is no relationship between mere causal indetermination and existential freedom.[26] Merely to show that Existence cannot be determined either in itself or in its causes would not yet constitute a proof of existential freedom for him. The same indetermination could be asserted in the case of certain microphysical phenomena also, yet few thinkers would deduce the freedom of subatomic particles from this inde-termination.[27] Existential freedom does not consist merely in being exempt from causal necessity, but in the creative possibility of investing causal necessity (to which Existence is subject in its embodiment) with human meaning and value which, as such, are not given in the causal order. What we cannot comprehend directly in all this is, first of all, the very creativity by which Existence brings forth these meanings and values and, secondly, the interior distance and autonomy a person is able to retain in regard to these values even while he is engaged in their realisation.

(2) *Surpassing objective logic*

The second methodical step continues in a direct line the scrutiny of objective language, the only language we have at our disposal. But this time, instead of emphasising the incompetence of language, we begin to inquire into its possibilities for Existence-elucidation. This second step will comprise three more or less distinct phases: the inversion of objective concepts and categories; the presentation of logical circles; the affirmation of logical paradoxes. The joint impact of these procedures is going to be a growing realisation that something more than straight logic is operative in existential discourse. We will begin to observe how philosophical reason gradually modifies the ordinary acts of thought in order to press them into service for Existence-elucidation. Only thus modified will thought be able to reveal its non-objective existential ground and give us an indirect knowledge of the nature of Existence. Naturally, the price thought will have to pay for this revelation is going to be a certain disruption of its logical order, the emergence of ambiguities, circles and paradoxes.

(a) *Inversion of the universal and the particular.* It is Jaspers' conviction that objectivity, pushed to its limits by philosophical reason that seeks to clarify human existence, is more than objective: it can become the vehicle of deep existential possibilities.[28] Sufficiently pressed, language will yield up some positive information about its source, namely, Existence. However, the fulfilment of this new demand cannot be accomplished without some torsion, some shift of accent, some destruction of the logical features of language. Above all, the existential use of language will affect those qualities of language which have to do with universality and abstractness. For example, in so far as a statement of a given language is bound to the objective form of that language (and every statement is), it has a universally applicable sense. When, however, the same statement is intended as a vehicle of Existence-elucidation, its sense will surpass the universal and will not be generally applicable.[29] Even language that is intended for Existence-elucidation cannot do away with the universal form of language, but in that form it must express a personal, inimitable, and unrepeatable content. In other words, existential language must be universal in form, but particular in content.

This does not mean, of course, that the existential use of language is altogether different from its ordinary use, so that universal validity is entirely banished from its content, while the universal itself is kept only begrudgingly as an inevitable but useless form. That is not the point being made. Jaspers maintains explicitly that even existential language must have universal validity, because the truth expressed in existential discourse would not be true if it were true only for me.[30] Rather, the point is that in existential discourse pride of place goes to the personal appropriation of the truth content, because without it the universal (*allgemeingültig*) statement would remain indifferent (*gleichgültig*) for the listener. Unlike the hearer of an objective statement, the hearer of an existential statement cannot stand apart from the spoken truth, merely registering its impersonal cogency, but must become an active participant in it. Although it is not this participation that makes the particular statement true, it is participation that makes it existential and living truth for him who commits himself to it. On the other hand, it would also be mistaken to think that existential language does not differ at all from ordinary language, that the function of universality and universal validity is the same in both cases. In order, then, to reduce the danger of misunderstanding what existential discourse is, it is useful to touch upon a few pertinent aspects of Jaspers' grand theme: existential communication. Through it we may be able to suggest that, in the case of elucidation, the functions of the particular and the universal are inverted.

Existential communication is both the setting and the aim of elucidation. In other words, elucidation of Existence takes place in the framework of, and happens for the sake of, an existential dialogue. We have already noted that, according to Jaspers, what constitutes the very possibility of Existence is the active rapport of the self with itself. We have also noted that the dicibility of selfhood is an integral ingredient of being a self. Now we can join these two formulae and make of two things one by saying that authentic selfhood can be realised only in existential communication, which is a reciprocal relationship of two free beings each of whom in a loving confrontation recognises and promotes the other as another self; and thereby both of them recognise and promote their own selfhood also.[31] Texts and references to explain the elements of this quasi-definition will follow later. For the moment there are other points to hold our attention. I would like to point out, for instance, that the theme of communication tempers the apparent isolation and self-sufficiency of Existence, hitherto described only under the aspect of autonomy and self-determination. Communication enlarges the initial *Sichzusichselbstverhalten* of personhood to a communicative *Zueinandersein* of coexistence. Secondly, noting that existential communication is the means of both self-discovery and self-realisation by way of exchange between individual selves, we can see that through the idea of communication the initial concept of the auto-creation of the individual self is widened into a 'reciprocal creation' of two selves.[32] Being an authentic person no longer appears the single-handed labour of a lonely individual standing against the world, but a gracious gift and bestowal at the hand of a friend who kindles the spark of selfhood in me while receiving his selfhood through me.

Existential communication, unlike impersonal communication, fosters self-expression. The relationship in which two people are engaged when they communicate existentially is a veritable I-Thou relationship, rather than a functional I-It relationship. This rapport protects the partners against being objectified or impersonalised at each other's hands. Instead of employing every possible effort to keep the other an object and oneself impersonal, communicative Existence challenges the other person 'to be himself in *his* truth'.[33] Instead of passing back and forth some general information, both partners speak in their own name, both express their own selves. Authentic existential communication is not a mere commerce in public information, but a revelation and a sharing (*Mit-teilung*) of the selves involved; a gift of selves. Consequently, the language that serves such an existential dialogue cannot be a neutral meeting ground, a linguistic no-man's-land where nameless opponents discuss some abstract issue, but rather must it be the very battlefield of a 'loving strife' where two persons meet face-to-face not to vanquish but to liberate each other.[34] What is encouraged is that each partner express himself, not everybody or anybody in general. Whereas ordinary communication tends to induce a certain levelling of differences between the interlocutors and tends to create a certain anonymity in the use of language, existential communication shows a marked preference for the unique, the personal, the particular aspects of communication, and puts a premium on self-expression. Existential communication is the delicate hyphen which both links and separates the selves who meet there. That is why loving strife is the permanent situation of existential communication: love tends to unite, while strife separates, and loving strife maintains this unity in separation.

The rapport between the particular and the universal is altered in existential communication. The fact, then, that the elucidation of selfhood is set in existential communication (where the aim sought for is not the sharing of general information, but self-expression and self-realisation) makes us understand, at least partially, that in speaking of Existence the value of the particular and of the universal should not remain the same as in ordinary communication. 'The particular becomes more than the universal,' says Jaspers.[35] What is this 'more' he has in mind? Dufrenne and Ricoeur express it well: 'Whereas for science the individual is only a sample of the species or the concrete figure of a concept, the singularity of Existence has an unfathomable depth; and it is richer when it is simply and resolutely itself than when it is attached to the universal, such as the race, the state, or humanity, in whose favour it risks being alienated from itself.'[36] A statement that expresses a particular person *qua* particular becomes more important for the elucidation of Existence than a general statement which shows what a person is in virtue of his belonging to a universal pattern or profession, race, or nation. More significantly, a statement whose content needs the added supplement of personal authentication to be valid for the hearer is more important existentially than a statement that is valid by itself. If a given statement fails to evoke this personal supplement, its existential validity remains debatable. Only he who receives it as the expression for which his silent inner self was searching all along will consent to it. As a result, existential communication speaks only to *others*, not to *all*.[37]

In sum, we could rephrase our initial formula by saying that, paradoxically, an existential proposition is universally valid, but only for those who fill it out from their own Existence with their own particular truth. This, of course, amounts to saying that the proposition is only particularly valid, though perhaps universally comprehensible.

(b) *The presentation of logical circles*. The negative method has taught us what Existence is not and given us a certain indirect insight into it. Then, in the first phase of the second methodical step, we have learned that the application of objective discourses to the grasp of Existence necessitates an inversion of their habitual sense and value. The result is supposed to be revelatory of their hidden existential import, but also highly disruptive in respect to the logical order of thought. It is, however, Jaspers' claim that Existence-elucidation can draw profit from this havoc. He believes that the logical circles necessarily involved in statements about Existence do permit us to think about the origin and originality of Existence, not logically, to be sure, but paradoxically. The result of such circularity is again both negative and positive: in them the objective content breaks down, loses its foundation and disappears, and precisely through its disappearance remains what it is supposed to be for Existence-clarification.[38] It reveals selfhood as a 'vanishing object'.[39]

Let us take an example. We may recall the expression 'self-production', used earlier as designating the very constitution of selfhood. Later, by introducing the theme of communication, this expression was enlarged to that of 'reciprocal creation' of two selves in an act of existential polemics. But we can see that in both cases these expressions contain a logical circle. Whether I produce myself, or whether I am created by the other while I also create him through our act of communication, in either case we are dealing with something which both precedes and follows the act whereby it is constituted. In order to enter into an active rapport with myself or into a communicative relationship with the other, I must already be myself; on the other hand, I am not myself until so constituted through this relationship. Even if we disregard strict auto-creation of selfhood and restrict our consideration to the interaction whereby two individuals 'create' each other reciprocally in their act of communication, the logical circle remains unresolved. If I am myself only through the other, and the other is himself only through me, then it is impossible to sort out the cause and effect, or rather, we are obliged to think of the self now as the cause, now as the effect of the other. We are really going round in circles.

Of course, one could attempt to resolve this circularity of *Durch-einandersein*, as Jaspers calls it, and make it more digestible for our intellect by introducing some distinction between, say, what Existence is in itself and what it becomes under the influence of another Existence. Or from another point of view one could say that before communication I am myself virtually, but through the act of communication I become myself formally. However, all such attempts are cut short by Jaspers as irrelevant because they all refer to my empirical being, not to my selfhood. He flatly affirms that 'the proposition, "I am an Existence", is without meaning.'[40] To study the two poles of the communicative I-Thou relationship as two independent beings, each existing by itself, would only refer to the observable, psychological side of their Dasein. Such a study is, of course perfectly possible and legitimate, and can furnish valuable information about the objective process of interaction between individuals, but it cannot deal with their existential beings because their existential being as such is simply never there apart from their communion.[41] But if there is nothing of Existence on either side before the communication, then the objective condition of their interaction as actual Existences also falls away, and it becomes meaningless to think of their mutual interrelation in mere objective terms because, objectively speaking, the effect of two nothings, even interacting, is still nothing.[42]

Evidently much depends on how literally one should take Jaspers' assertion that there is 'nothing of Existence' apart from the communicative situation. The difficulty is that every sign, every turn of phrase of Jaspers seems to point to the fact that he means just what he says: Existence is simply absent before communication.[43] That Existence as such is not formally present in the reality of Dasein before communication would not pose an insurmountable problem in itself and would not necessitate a recourse to logical circles to think of its emergence. It could be conceived as one of the potentialities of human Dasein, given together with our empirical individuality, but remaining in a virtual state until such time as an existential dialogue should come to activate it. In that case the origin of selfhood would not have to be regarded paradoxically as an entirely spontaneous act of self-creation or as a mutual creation in dialogue but rather as a passage from virtuality to actuality under the dual influence of interior gravitation and exterior appeal. According to this theory, human Dasein would not be considered as mere Dasein which has 'nothing of Existence', for it would contain precisely the potentiality of Existence. It could be readily admitted that this potentiality is not like the other potencies of Dasein in that the realisation of this potency lifts Dasein over and beyond itself onto the level of Existence. In other words, Existence could be regarded as the very potency of Dasein for self-transcendence. In his later works where, according to some commentators, Jaspers is a little more 'scholastic', he seems to admit just such an interpretation of human Dasein. In *Von der Wahrheit*, for instance, he affirms that the empirical being of man harbours in itself a gravitation over and beyond itself; that there is something in man that can carry him above his empirical reality.[44] Is not this hidden gravitation which can surpass man's empirical being the very possibility of selfhood whereby he is able to transcend himself and become a free individual?

One can sympathise with Jaspers' eagerness to keep empirical selfhood and Existence distinct, discontinuous, and irreducible, but would it necessarily mean that we are reducing Existence to Dasein if we claimed that the possibility of Existence is virtually given in human Dasein?[45] One can understand Jaspers' fear of givenness and facticity when it comes to the problem of self-transcendence, because self-transcendence is always also a dynamic self-transcending, but should this lead us to the assertion that transcendence is in no way given? Is it not given precisely as a possibility of freely transcending the facticity of empirical reality? Granted that freedom, the heart-piece of Existence, is not something which I have by nature, automatically, as it were, does this mean that the power or possibility to be free is not mine by nature either? All in all, one has the impression that Jaspers goes too far in his emphasis here. In order to preserve the incomparable originality of selfhood and the spontaneity of freedom, he seems bent on breaking all its ties with the givenness and facticity of Dasein. A strict phenomenological analysis of Dasein that would show the point of insertion of selfhood into facticity would have been more clarifying to our mind than the insistence on logical circles.

Still, one must admit that this treatment of the origin of selfhood is perfectly consistent with the rest of Jaspers' philosophy. The distinctions I have suggested above in order to eliminate the logical circle are practicable only in a philosophy of substance, which is alien to Jaspers' line of thinking. For him, empirical reality is not the soil out of which selfhood grows, nor the immanent ground that carries the possibility and aspiration of Existence.[46] In short, Existence is not an inherent virtuality of Dasein. He sees Existence rather as an irruption into Dasein, an occupation from without, so to speak. 'Existence settles into Dasein,' he says quite Platonically.[47] Selfhood is not given, rather 'it takes over what is inevitably given.'[48] Selfhood is not a natural outgrowth of facticity, not a result of the natural process of maturation, not the combined effect of heredity, environment, and sociological influences.[49] Existence is of another lineage than Dasein, and Dasein is only the embodiment, the appearance, the phenomenon of Existence. Like all appearance, all incarnation, Dasein hides as much as it reveals the reality it embodies, because it has the tendency of arresting our attention and preventing it from penetrating to the *noumenon*. Although a phenomenological analysis might discern the presence of the transcendent reality there, it cannot really light up its origin.

Thus, according to Jaspers, the origin of selfhood can only be hinted at in circles: my selfhood is elicited by the other whose selfhood is elicited by me. The circle is only an attempt at explanation, not an explanation in itself that would yield an item of objective knowledge. Through the circle the objective content of knowledge collapses, and by its very ruin sheds some indirect light on the incomprehensible origin of selfhood. While the shell of its appearance is shattered, we catch sight of selfhood for a moment as a receding, vanishing object.

(c) *The affirmation of paradoxes.* Another way of approximating selfhood through ordinary categories is to affirm it in logically contrary statements. Such statements are the kind in which the same attribute is both affirmed and denied of Existence, or, in which two intellectually incompatible attributes are predicated of it simultaneously. These two conflicting attributes form a concept-pair in such a way that only jointly—that is, in their undivided totality—do they express the transcendent reality of selfhood. The unresolved tension of this concept-pair fulfils its function of elucidation in that it prevents the objectifiation of selfhood by rendering the fixation or unequivocal determination of Existence impossible.[50]

Before I go any further in discussing this question, let me show briefly some of the examples Jaspers puts forward to illustrate his point. He claims, for instance, that in speaking of Existence we must use 'temporality' and 'eternity' together. Why? Because the consciousness through which Existence becomes aware of itself is at once the consciousness of being in time and thereby of being above it. Jaspers calls this form of consciousness 'historical'. Historical consciousness, then, is the site where the experiences of time and of eternity take place together and are jointly attributed to Existence. In other words, in one and the same act of consciousness I am aware of my limitation in time as well as of my depth in eternity, of my transitory existence as well as of my abiding being.[51] However, in order to express and to communicate this simple item of existential certitude, I must use either two contradictory statements: 'Existence is temporal' and 'Existence is eternal', or a single statement with an incompatible concept-pair as predicate: 'Existence is eterno-temporal'. In the words of Kurt Hoffman, 'Existence is on the one hand a record of changing circumstances, hopes and fears, while on the other hand, it reaches beyond the limits of the empirical world and of time. Its historicity is eternity embodied in time or history at the limits of eternity.'[52]

Similarly, 'solitude' and 'communication' belong together to selfhood and belong by equal right. I learn solitude only when I confront the other in communication, and I can enter into communication only as a solitary self. Here we touch upon the mystery of the human individual, the person, who is absolutely incommunicable and yet the only being that can communicate of himself. Here we meet also our fundamental loneliness which no amount of superficial 'togetherness' can efface and yet which unites us as much as it separates. Human individuality is the curious coincidence of loneliness and communion, a union in separation and separation in union. Taken by themselves, singly, these terms do not designate existential reality; communication by itself means the psychological rapport between random subjects, solitude alone means the mere physical or psychological isolation of individuals. On the level of objective knowledge, we think of selfhood sometimes in terms of solitariness, sometimes in terms of communion, but in Existence-elucidation we must think of both in one, we must think their unity.[53]

In like manner, 'freedom' and 'dependence' must be fused when applying to selfhood. I am free, but only through another who wants me to encounter him as a self. I am dependent on him for my very freedom. Neither unbounded freedom nor easy dependence can characterise my true self adequately. Genuine existential freedom is rather the paradoxical union of freedom and dependence.[54]

But by far the best examples of the paradoxicalness of existential predication are the statements concerning the reality of the 'I'. Let us first consider it under the aspect of consciousness, for if there is something that characterises the 'I' in a major way and sets it off from objects, it is its active intentionality which we generally call consciousness. Consciousness is that directional mode of being whereby the subject 'I' is aware of its counterparts, the objects.

Among the problems connected with consciousness the question of self-awareness is particularly ambiguous. Self-awareness means that I am capable of envisaging not only the other but also myself. And it is here that the relatively simple problem of intentionality is exchanged for the greater mystery of the self-reflexivity of consciousness. Whereas an intentional object is only a 'being-for-the-other' (i.e. for the subject), the self-conscious 'I' is also a 'being-for-itself'. In other words, self-reflexive consciousness implies a sort of duality in unity and unity in duality. It expresses a kind of mediated immediacy, and designates a logically impossible being which is two-in-one and one-in-two.[55] Inasmuch as it is relational, this being implies the duality of a *terminus a quo* and a *terminus ad quem*; inasmuch as it is self-conscious, it implies the unity and identity of these poles. Differently put: in self-awareness the 'I' as a conscious subject is both the active source of its intention and also the passive term of it, its object. As consciousness, the self is both exterior and interior to itself. This is ungraspable logically. If we want to save logic, we must either abandon the unity of self-awareness by saying that the 'I' as the subject and the 'I' as the object of self-awareness are really distinct, or we must give up trying to understand consciousness in terms of the intentional split between subject and object which, nevertheless, seems to be the basic phenomenon of consciousness.[56] In the first case we would be incapable of accounting for the unity of the conscious self, in the second, for the duality of consciousness. There remains, therefore, no other way than to hold on to the a-logical position that in self-awareness the conscious self remains one in spite of its scission into two.

All this concerns the 'I' as consciousness, but evidently the 'I' is much more than just consciousness. It has numerous other existential aspects, such as concern, anxiety, love and hate, but the grasp of all of them necessitates the same dual affirmation of unity in duality: neither unity nor duality, but the two in one. All these signify once more that the being of selfhood is essentially and irremediably ambiguous for a logic of the understanding.

Both on the level of consciousness and in its concrete rapports, Existence is precariously poised between interiority and exteriority; it is suspended between unity and multiplicity; it is indistinguishably a self-being (*Selbstsein*) and a self-becoming (*Selbstwerden*); it is shared between myself and the other, yet possessed by neither of us without the concurrence of the other. Selfhood risks losing itself in Dasein, yet it must appear in Dasein in order to find its true identity. We think of it only in paradoxes, in which it manifests itself as a vanishing object.

At this point some comparison between Hegel and Jaspers would be in order, all the more so since many of Jaspers' ideas and expressions show an unmistakable Hegelian parentage. However, since such a comparison would make the present chapter too long, let me just point out one Hegelian feature of Jaspers' dialectical approach. Just as the affirmation of 'contradictions' and paradoxes is an integral part of the methodical process through which the philosophy of Hegel tries to trace the various stages of the development and self-realisation of the Spirit, so also Jaspers' existential dialectic is a necessary methodical step towards the elucidation and realisation of Existence. In this dialectic we reach the point of the greatest possible torsion that intellectual thought can ever reach. In spite of the many disturbances caused by the previous steps, the intellect was still not fundamentally shaken, for it could still retain its most basic operation, namely, disjunctive determination. Even in the case of logical circles, our understanding was still allowed to oscillate between two alternative views and was not obliged to settle down in either. In the affirmation of paradoxes, however, that is no longer the case. After having made the last set of disjunctions, the intellect is now called upon to render them all but useless in that it is forced to a joint affirmation of the two disjuncts. In the affirmation of temporal eternity, solitary communion, free necessity, and undivided duality, the intellect turns against itself, it alienates itself. By a single twist, it goes against its basic nature by obliterating the distinctions it carefully maintained before. It is as if the very last act of logical thought were an a-logical one in which the mind turns away from its habitual activity of differentiation and turns back towards a sort of intuitive global grasp. It seems that the final act the intellect is ever able to perform is a gesture of abdication, an act of self-sacrifice even. The last word of logic is an invitation to be silent.

12

But this silence can be telling. It can be a sign that we are entering the realm of mystery, that we are encountering for the first time the 'ground' of all thought, our incomprehensible Existence. The very failure of the intellect and the silence to which it is reduced on these sacred grounds may become a language through which this profound reality will speak and reveal itself.

(3) *Existential signs*

Failure and silence may be the end of our understanding as it grapples with Existence, but perhaps not the end of reason. The a-logic on which the intellect comes to grief at the limits of conceptual knowledge can become, according to Jaspers, a 'rational a-logic'.[57] Reason will not resign even here but will try to initiate a new language by means of a new set of categories—categories that do not belong to the language and logic of world-orientation.

The categories of this new language will be such, therefore, that they will be powerless to determine new objects in the world. Their intended meaning will not be a statement of fact about something that exists objectively, but an evocation of free possibilities in myself and in others. Strictly speaking, they are not even categories but mere indicators, *signa*, as Jaspers calls them. As signs, they will have a certain degree of universality and thereby lend themselves to philosophical discourse, but what is signified in them must find an echo in the life experience of others, without which they will not only be empty but, indeed, nothing.[58] For instance, the new language will speak of *the Self* in a general way and will even show its structure, but it will refer to *myself* in particular. 'I seek *the* Self, but only in order to find *my*self,' says Jaspers.[59] Similarly, the new discourse will treat of many selves, but 'many' here will signify something different from 'several of the same class'. In short, the categories of existential discourse will not be generic concepts.

This, of course, poses a specific problem. If that which is envisaged by the sign is neither a concrete individual Existence (since that is ineffable), nor the meaning of a generic concept that would be called 'Existence' (since that is empty), then the sign must signify something intermediary. This intermediary in the given case can only be the *formal schema of an Existence*. This schema, instead of performing the generic function of subsuming, will merely act as an exemplar for the other selves.[60] That is why Jaspers next takes up the question of existential schematisms.

'In thinking of Existence through signs a formal schema of Existence is constructed. This relates to Existence not as the schema of an object-group relates to these objects, but altogether inadequately. Since an Existence is not to be subsumed, the schema can serve only as an approach to addressing an individual Existence. This is the only purpose the schema has.'[61] The mention of schematisms here is an obvious reference to Kant's doctrine on the Schemata of Pure Understanding. In fact, we shall see presently that Jaspers compares his existential schemata with the Kantian schemata. There we shall be able to observe in greater detail the differences between the two doctrines. But already we can discern some fundamental differences. Unlike Kant's doctrine in which the schemata play a mediating role between sense intuition and pure understanding, Jaspers' schemata are meant only as means of addressing (*mitansprechen*) an individual self, so that through them the individual self may achieve some degree of clarification. Whereas the problem which preoccupied Kant in elaborating his doctrine on schematism was the problem of how to mediate the subsumption of sense phenomena under pure concepts, there is no question of subsumption for Jaspers. And because there can be no question of subsumption, Jaspers sees that the relation of the existential schema to its 'object' (i.e. to Existence) will be inadequate, meaning that the schema will be insufficient by itself to mediate the intellectual grasp of the existential reality under an eventual category, called 'Existence'. Existential terms, as I have just noted, are neither categories nor generic concepts but only signs.

However, the root difference between the two philosophers on this point is that Kant's use of schematisms is strictly limited to the grasp of phenomenal reality, reality which is first given in sense intuition, whereas Jaspers tries to force a cognitive intuition of the noumenal reality of selfhood through them, an intuition which he knows is never given and never attainable directly.[62] All in all, the schemata of Kant and the schemata of Jaspers will be different both in nature and function: the former refer to objective reality, the latter to existential reality. The sole basis of their comparison lies in the fact that both objective reality and existential reality must appear in time, and therefore both schematisms are based on some kind of consciousness of time.[63] But this is as far as the similarity goes because the rest is almost pure contrast.

In the following, I shall reproduce Jaspers' comparison of his existential schemata with some of the Kantian ones. Because his comparison is extremely sketchy and mixed, I shall have to rearrange and amplify it a little.[64] Paragraphs (*a*) will refer to the Kantian schemata; paragraphs (*b*) to the corresponding existential schemata of Jaspers.

(*a*) The schema of Quantity in general is *number*, i.e. 'the unity of the synthesis of the manifold of a homogeneous intuition in general, a unity due to my generating time itself in the apprehension of the intuition.'[65]

(*b*) The schema corresponding to objective quantity is the intensity, level, or *rank* of a particular existential phase of life. This rank cannot be determined objectively, however, nor can the existential moments be counted according to some unit because they do not form a continuous and homogeneous time-series.

(*a*) The schema of Quality in general (reality, negation, limitation) is the continuous production of experience as an inner *sense-quantum*. 'The schema of reality as the quantity of something in so far as it fills time is just this production of that reality in time as we successively descend from a sensation which has a certain degree to its vanishing point, or progressively ascend from its negation to some magnitude of it.'[66]

(*b*) The existential schema is a *leap*, an abrupt leap, from Dasein to Existence in the moment of decision. Against the degree of sensation stands the loftiness and vigour of decision which is discontinuous with its causal antecedents or psychological determinants. Consequently, the Existence that manifests itself in decisions is not gradual or continuous but intermittent and fluctuating.

(*a*) The schema of Substance is *endurance* in time. 'The schema of substance is permanence of the real in time, that is, the real as a substratum of empirical determination of time in general . . . while all else changes.'[67]

(*b*) The schema of the existential substance or self is abiding (*Bewährung*) in *fidelity*. The substantiality of selfhood consists in fidelity. Existence vanishes and reappears, but beneath its fluctuations there stretches a faithfulness to the memory of a past existential moment.

(*a*) The schema of Cause is *succession* in time according to rule. 'The schema of cause and of causality of a thing in general is the real upon which, whenever posited, something else always follows.'[68]

(*b*) Existential casuality is freedom and its schema is *spontaniety* of origin. Instead of being the regularly recurring consequence of objective causes, freedom is the manifestation of Existence in so far as Existence is self-determining.

(*a*) The schema of Community is simultaneous *interacting* between substances. 'The schema of community or reciprocity, the reciprocal causality of substances in respect of their accidents, is the co-existence of the determinations of the one substance with those of the other.'[69]

(*b*) The existential category is communication and its schema is reciprocal *creation* through dialogue. The communicative partners promote each other's being not only in the accidental order but in the very order of Existence. Their relationship is a veritable co-Existence.

(*a*) The schema of Possibility is *compatibility* with the conditions of objective time, or 'the agreement of the synthesis of different representations with the conditions of time in general.'[70]

(*b*) Existential possibility consists in a radical *openness* of the future, which makes further free choices possible. The futurity and contingency of time permits the appearance of novelty in history.

(*a*) The schema of Actuality is the existence of something in some *determinate time*. This time is measured as to its scope by determined time-units.

(*b*) Existential actuality occurs in its *proper time*. 'Existence has its own time, not time as such.' The scope of existential time is not measurable because it is intermittent and because the events it contains have unequal existential importance.

(*a*) The schema of Necessity is existence at *all times*, or duration without beginning, end, or change. This is time conceived as infinitely long.

(*b*) Existential necessity is figured as an *abiding present*, or eternity as concentrated in the depth of a historical moment.

This is a moment of destiny in which freedom and necessity are fused.

As one can readily see, the Kantian schemata are all *a priori* determinations of objective time according to rules. 'These rules relate in the order of categories to the time-series, the time-content, the time-order, and lastly to the scope of time in respect of all possible objects.'[71] By contrast, the existential schemata are analogous determinations of subjective time according to free associations. These analogies refer to the intensity, authenticity, originality, and historicity of possible selfhood as it appears in its time. Both kinds of schemata serve a mediating role, but they do so in different ways. In Kant's system they stand between the sensation and the understanding of an object. Without their mediating help the sensation of an object would lack the consciousness that only understanding can impart to it, so that sensation could never rise to the knowledge of an object. The existential schemata stand between the mute self-certitude of an individual Existence and its elucidation through reason. Without their mediation the self-certitude would lack the articulation and clarity that come from elucidation, so that the vague experience of selfhood would not result in a knowledge about possible Existence.

Jaspers is very much aware of being at variance with his master, Kant. He notes that Kant has expressly rejected many of the existential signa and schemata, testing them against his own objective categories. Notably, he rejected discontinuity and intermittence in both time and space; denied the existence of hazard; showed that there is no destiny, no necessity not governed by rules; argued that there can be no novelty in the substantial world. Of course, Jaspers agrees: 'Indeed, all these things do not exist in the objective world and do not exist as objects of knowledge. But when an explanation of Existence is attempted, all these words come back.'[72] With their help our ineffable Existence becomes a little more responsive to the demands of reason.

CONCLUDING REMARKS

Here my brief description of Existence-elucidation ends. To summarise, I would like to re-state some of the main points of this description and to throw certain others into relief.

First, as something of general significance, we have to remember that Jaspers considers Existence to be entirely non-objective. From this it follows that he also considers Existence to be entirely unknowable by the ordinary means of objective knowledge. In order to clarify Existence to some extent, thought must modify its habitual way of knowing to the point of radical transformation. It must elaborate some other than objective modes of representing existential reality. In this process, Jaspers resorts to both negative and positive techniques. The former are supposed to cast some indirect light on selfhood by showing what selfhood is not. Confronted with existential reality, the intellect is capable of recognising it as something in favour of which it must humiliate itself or even sacrifice itself. The negative approach implies Existence as a vanishing object. The second, the positive, approach consists in the invention of existential signa and schemata. We have seen that these signs are not to be taken for objective categories but as symbols to be interpreted subjectively by the individual hearers who have to fill them out with personal content. There are one or two new points that have to be emphasised about these signs:

(1) The existential signs and schematisms are the fruit of transcendental imagination. As such, they try to present something that is never given to sense intuition nor can ever be objectified. For this very reason, their power to mediate a general knowledge of selfhood is inadequate: they can only invoke or address the other person. Their structure is too mobile and changing to serve as a basis for a general theory of Existence. Their function is merely exemplary.

(2) Because of their imaginative and symbolical character, existential signs are more original, more basic, more primitive, than objective concepts. As such, they are able to survive to some extent the havoc worked in logic by the presence of circles and paradoxes which inevitably appear in existential discourse.

(3) In this regard, existential discourse has a certain analogy with myth. In view of the fact that the existential schemata are placed in an imaginary time ('Existence has its own time'), we could call them mythical instead of merely symbolical. It is customary to remark that mythical time is not a homogeneous flow, measurable in time-units, but a qualitatively differentiated duration.[73] I believe that some of these traits of mythical time

can be discerned in the existential schemata of 'rank', 'fidelity', 'abiding present'. It is also said that mythical time is 'the time of origins, the stupendous instant in which reality was created'.[74] Whoever enters into this time becomes contemporary with the reality that is emerging there. This quality of originality is present, I believe, in the existential schema of 'spontaneity'. With the help of this schema, the thinking subject can become aware of his selfhood as an origin, a radically new possibility in the world. Moreover, mythical time is said to be original in another sense too. It is original in the sense 'that it came into existence all at once and that it was not preceded by another time, because no time could exist before the appearance of the reality narrated in the myth.'[75] This means that each thing in question has its appointed time in myth. Similarly, it may be recalled that existential time does not precede the sudden rise of Existence, or conversely, Existence does not exist before its time: Existence and its time are contemporary with each other. They appear and disappear together. The inseparable union of mythical time and its content may be an image of the inseparable union of existential time and its content. In other words, Existence is essentially historical. Just as in mythical thinking the reality is incomprehensible without the time that contains it, so also in existential thinking.

These similarities suggest that existential clarification is a kind of reprise of myth's original mode of thinking. Having failed within its own limits, logical thought tries to re-enact with adult consciousness the stages of its spontaneous childhood from its very origins.

Although both myth and existential thinking make use of the power of imaginative presentation, they differ vastly in their manner of self-awareness. The naïve imagination of myth takes its representations objectively: *et ita est in re*. It projects its images upon reality, and thereby carries out a materialisation of its own language. Here, imagination mistakes itself for information. Regarding myth from this point of view, Jaspers sides with those who take up the cause of demythologisation.[76] Philosophically critical imagination, on the contrary, takes its images and representations for just what they are: symbols and ciphers of the otherwise ineffable. What is meant by critical imagination is mature, self-conscious imagination directed by reason. As such, it has a cultivated awareness of its own symbolical nature, and it is precisely this awareness that sets it apart from mythical mentality, which is unaware of its cipher character and mistakes its evocative language for factual knowledge. False as knowledge, mythology is true 'as a carrier of meanings that can be expressed only in symbolical language.'[77] It cannot be translated into another language. Only a narrowly rationalistic reason would want to translate and replace it. If demythologisation is to be understood in this rationalistic manner, Jaspers is against it. Even to speak of demythologisation in the name of this narrow reason seems almost blasphemous to him, because such an act 'would extinguish one of the most basic virtualities (*Grundvermögen*) of our reason.'[78]

These faint analogies between certain qualities of mythical and existential comprehension allow us to understand to some extent why a philosophical study of selfhood cannot result in an explanation proper, a generally valid theory of Existence, but only in a shifting, changing elucidation addressed from the historical depth of one person to that of another. The comprehension of what is said in this elucidation is never guaranteed by a uniform existential structure which would somehow unite the interlocutors in a durable way. Jaspers' belief is that, on rare occasions, a momentary common bond of comprehension *might* establish itself between one Existence and another. If my words light up in my interlocutor a possibility more or less similar to mine, then comprehension will follow. Otherwise not. This is so because men are radically individual not only in their existential reality but also in their existential possibilities, in short, they are unique. For this reason, each can only hope that *his* communication will find an echo with others and help them to find *their* possibilities.

In wanting to fathom the strictly individual dimensions of human existence, Jaspers at times seems to be trying to take over the task of art and poetry. But, of course, no thinker can do so consistently and still claim to remain a philosopher. In fact, as we shall gradually see, Jaspers himself soon realised that philosophy cannot be grounded on Existence and uniqueness alone. Philosophy must have other sources for otherwise it would remain inadequate to the whole of human experience and perhaps even untrue to authentic Existence itself. Without abandoning what he had discovered as valid about the uniqueness of selfhood, Jaspers tried later to search out those other, more universal, sources of philosophy.[79] In other words, he gradually turned towards a more communicable form of philosophising and a more encompassing and universal view of Existence. He realised that the resoluteness of Existence must go hand-in-hand with the larger scope of reason. In *Vernunft und Existenz*, which forms the link of transition between the earlier and later Jaspers, he has already outlined his future philosophy in this spirit. In contrast to the lack of communication exemplified for him by the extreme positions of Kierkegaard and Nietzsche, Jaspers wanted his further philosophy to be a more communicative one. 'Since it is not to be a philosophy of the exception but of the universal, I will regard it as true only if it is capable of being translated into the reality of the many, that is, if the possibility of reason in its widest possible range is methodically brought to self-consciousness.'[80]

The next phase of this awakening of reason to a wider range of self-awareness begins when we attempt to articulate the relationship of Existence to God. How finite reason can come to grips with the Infinite is going to be the subject matter of our next chapter.

X   Cipher-Reading

THE central reference point of Jaspers' philosophy lies in possible Existence, but its gravitation is metaphysical. His whole reflection hastens towards Transcendence, where even Existence will be overshadowed by the plenitude of God.[1] At the core of his passionate affirmation of freedom stands the awareness that freedom itself is a gift of Transcendence.[2] In the experience of freedom there comes a moment of recognising that the proudest self-reliance places man wholly in the hand of his God. 'The most extreme insistence on freedom', notes Paul Ricoeur, 'is only a stage to be surpassed by an exigency which remains always unsatisfied. The very meaning of a philosophy of freedom . . . is to awaken a double conviction: Existence is not the reality I am ultimately searching for, and Existence comes about only through the Being which Existence is not.'[3] Existence and freedom have their proper time, yet freedom is still something inferior that will cancel itself in the end in favour of an affirmation of God.[4]

It has been remarked that Jaspers' philosophy does not offer any proofs for the existence of God or any kind of analyses that would show how the certitude of Transcendence emerges from that of free Existence or from the objective knowledge of the world.[5] This is substantially correct, but it should not be mis-understood to mean that he takes no care at all to support his affirmations. To be sure, he gives no formal demonstrations in the sense of logically incontrovertible arguments, but he does, nevertheless, show that the certitude of Transcendence is an intrinsic dimension of the existential certitude of my selfhood. It is true he never strictly explains *how* this is so. Jaspers' attitude toward demonstrating God's existence is perfectly in line with his general principles: regarded as proofs, such demonstrations are false and deceptive, but as likenesses and symbols, they are extremely rich and meaningful for philosophical reflection.[6] It is in a symbolical sense (and not demonstratively) that some of Jaspers' expressions which suggest the beginning of a proof should be taken. For instance, expressions such as, 'I have not created myself' (*VdW* p. 110), and 'Transcendence through which I am myself' (*Ibid.*), should not be interpreted as preliminaries to an eventual proof, but as expressions of a primary awareness of the constitutive relativity of Existence to Transcendence. 'Existence is only in relation to Transcendence, or not at all.'[7] All through Jaspers' reflection there remains a margin of belief. Consequently, he sees neither the possibility nor the need for establishing God's existence demonstratively, for he considers it a matter of lived experience. Transcendence is present in our philosophic quest for authentic being all along, and the only problem for Jaspers is to find appropriate ways of expressing this basic belief in speculative language.

<h3 style="text-align:center">PHILOSOPHICAL FAITH</h3>

Jaspers' metaphysics rests on a kind of faith, philosophical faith, to be exact. Philosophical faith is a many-sided affair, but in our present context it signifies the secret assurance of authentic Existence that the world and selfhood are not the whole reality, that neither of them are self-subsisting, but that both are grounded in the being of Transcendence. Faith, in the striking expression of Dufrenne and Ricoeur, is 'the umbilical cord' whereby the individual freedom remains tied to Transcendence, a sort of 'primordial connivance between self and God which precedes all discourse, all argument, all proof.'[8] Needless to say, the intellect, as a discursive faculty, cannot grasp this original certitude and can only oppose faith by intellectual demonstration. Nevertheless, 'faith is not alien to that ultimate demand of thought which we call reason or quest for unity, totality, and peace.'[9]

In fact, faith is the matrix and the completion of thought. Understanding both arises out of faith and turns into faith at the limits of discursive thought. At a certain level of consciousness, Existence must have recourse to faith in order to clarify its relationship to the ground of all reality. In this sense, faith is a second look at things, a new vision, a new and meta-physical mode of thinking proper to Existence. This new mode of thinking carries out a fundamental transformation of thought, in that it gains insight into the universal phenomenality of empirical reality.[10] Whereas for the understanding everything (including Existence) is an object, for faith everything can be the appearance of Another. All reality becomes transparent to the vision of faith. 'Becoming transparent' is a key concept of Jaspers'. It expresses his belief that our minds, properly disposed, can penetrate the otherwise opaque reality of things which prevents their inner transcendence from shining through. Faith effects a luminous transfiguration of the world from within. Faith lets the world fall away as the ultimate reality, but reaffirms it as the appearance of transcendent Being. The word 'appearance' here signifies both 'revealing' and 'rendering present' something which in itself is absent and hidden. In this transparence, or trans-appearance, the objectivity of the world ceases to be 'the tomb of Existence', and becomes compatible with it.[11]

But perhaps faith might be compared to a new faculty of hearing, a 'readiness to keep listening'[12] more properly than to a new kind of sight. To the patient ear of faith the silent objects around us begin to speak 'the language of their ground.'[13] With this readiness we can experience the world as the auditorium where the permanently ambiguous word of God is addressed to us.[14] We have hope of articulating our existential certitude of God because, in manifold guises, God has spoken to us first; through the objects of creation he has revealed his presence.

For the rest, the two sorts of images of sight and hearing are often intermingled by Jaspers. Note the play of light and word in the following text: 'The objects of the world possess a two-fold transparence: they are manifestations or phenomena of the enveloping reality of the World, and also relate to Transcendence. As phenomena, they reveal the encompassing reality of the World through their intelligibility; as ciphers, they speak the polyvalent language of Transcendence, a language that is as penetrating as it is unknowable.'[15] Whether expressed under the image of transparence or that of language, whether stated in terms of sight or of hearing, faith considers the objects of this world as manifestations of the encompassing World, or as ciphers of the all-embracing Transcendence. In either case, however, the objects lose their independent standing for metaphysical thought and become the ambassadors of transcendent reality.

METAPHYSICAL OBJECTIVITY

Thus, the revelation of transcendent reality is achieved by looking beyond the objectivity of objects and grasping the metaphysical ground of their being. It must be understood, however, that this 'beyond' is not 'elsewhere', but in the objects themselves. Metaphysical thought does not go anywhere beyond or beneath, or even inside things. It simply takes hold of the same objects as empirical thought, but it considers them in their transcendent dimension, where objects turn into code entities for Transcendence. Metaphysical intention does not leave the world behind, but raises it and converts it into metaphysical objects. As metaphysical objects, the entities of this world are no longer intended in their own right, but only as ciphers *of* Transcendence *for* free selfhood. In Jaspers' words, 'the reality of the world has a vanishing reality between God and Existence.'[16]

Elsewhere, Jaspers expresses the same idea by saying that 'being-there (*Dasein*) and being-symbol (*Symbolsein*) are like two dimensions of one and the same world: in the former the world reveals itself to general consciousness, in the latter to Existence.'[17] This double life of the world cannot be seen by the intellect which only looks for its facticity: it can be discovered only from the vantage point of existential faith. Unlike the intellect, the vision of faith has the power to loosen up the facticity and determinateness of positive objects, so that they may become more fluid symbols for existential concern, ciphers through which God may trans-appear.

Metaphysical objectivity, then, is the representational power inherent in positive reality to mediate the presence of Transcendence for us; to let it appear in veiled but palpable form. As such, metaphysical objectivity is half-way between absolute reality and subjective reality. It is the vanishing objectivity of the world as symbol. Needless to say, it is extremely difficult to maintain the world in this sort of suspension, to keep it in the state of symbol-being. The precarious character of the world as symbol constitutes the most persistent danger for metaphysical thinking, according to Jaspers. Because of the difficulty of maintaining the world as symbol, metaphysics forever threatens to lapse either into the worldliness (*Weltlichkeit*) of empiricism, or into the other-worldliness of mysticism. These two tendencies, opposed as they may be in other respects, have one common element in that they both represent definitive fixations of metaphysical objectivity. Indeed, Jaspers considers mysticism a kind of other-worldly empiricism. While ordinary empiricism never leaves the facticity of this world, mysticism leaps beyond it into another world and treats that with the same mental attitude as a second positive domain, composed of metempirical objects, laws, and states of affairs. Empiricism knows nothing of Transcendence and thus remains in pure immanence, mysticism pretends to know all about it and claims to be on familiar terms with divinity. What Jaspers thinks of the respective possibilities, merits, and faults of these two tendencies is not the question here. The only point he wants to emphasise is that metaphysics is neither empiricism nor mysticism. Empiricism and mysticism are rather the Scylla and Charybdis of metaphysics. In order to avoid them and save itself, metaphysics has to hold on to its own notion of *immanent Transcendence*, i.e., divinity that reveals itself only through the symbolic reality of this world, never directly. 'Existence can resist these temptations, if it regards Transcendence true only when the latter speaks from within the world. Only immanent Transcendence can lend weight to Existence in the world.'[18]

Metaphysical reality is, then, like a second universe within the objective world. As such, its elements are necessarily of an ephemeral nature. Jaspers indicates this in three sets of considerations.

Metaphysical objects have no consistency in themselves: they are only symbols. Jaspers distinguishes symbolisation from all other means of indirect signification, such as signs, images, similes, comparisons and allegories. The basic difference between symbolisation and these other ways of indirect representation lies for him in the manner in which all of them relate to that which is signified through them. Whereas the latter group more or less *translates* into pictures or gestures something which can itself be grasped intellectually as an objective meaning, a symbol simply *presents* a dimension of reality which is inaccessible to any other mode of apprehension.[19] A symbol is essentially and specifically an 'objectification of the non-objective'.[20] As such, it stands for a reality from which it is radically different yet inseparable. It is inseparable in the sense that the reality symbolised is nowhere given outside the symbol; it is the symbol alone that mediates its presence. In order to fill this mediating role, the self-consistency of the symbol must be entirely erased; the symbol must turn transparent; it must vanish in its own right and become a pure medium. A simile may cast some light on what symbols are: we might compare them to eye-glasses: in order to be efficacious means of seeing, means that facilitate our vision instead of obstructing it, the glasses must be clean, transparent, unnoticed, almost not there at all. Likewise, in order to be a good symbol, an efficacious means of leading our vision beyond the empirical aspects, a symbol must not distract our attention, must not get in our way.

Since a symbol stands for non-objective meaning, it cannot be translated or interpreted, except through other symbols.[21] This idea is like a first principle of Jaspers' interpretation of symbols. It governs the whole of his hermeneutic doctrine. The fact that the interpretation of a symbol is itself symbolic has far-reaching implications for Jaspers' views of Reason and rationality. Among other things, it already suggests that the aim of metaphysics is not to convey objective knowledge about ultimate realities, but to mediate the profoundly human experience of our relatedness to Transcendence.[22] In other words, the primary purpose of metaphysics, and of philosophy in general, is not a cognitive purpose as an experiential or existential one. Metaphysical reflection is the work of reason, but reason understood in its infrangible relationship to Existence.

Metaphysical objects have no logical consistency either. 'A metaphysical object suffers logical collapse when the intellect tries to think it clearly. Its concept appears as a circle, or as a tautology, or as an internal contradiction.'[23] This logical break-down results from the fundamental limitation of categorial thinking, which can grasp logically only determined or determinable objects. The symbol character of a metaphysical object, by contrast, refers to the transcategorial unity of Being which eclipses all determination and particularity, and frustrates all disjunction. If anything, it is the negation of all clear determinability and disjunction that constitutes the basic logic of Transcendence. This negation is absolutely direct and evident in contradiction; more veiled and indirect in circles and tautologies. When we say, for instance, that 'God is self-subsistent and from himself', we are trying to give expression to his logically inexpressible inseity and aseity. Here yet again, we meet the basic dilemma of logical thought: in so far as the categories of logic are determined, they are inapplicable to Transcendence; and in so far as they become indeterminate, they are no longer logically thinkable.[24] Their logicality collapses in metaphysical thought. It has been remarked, however, that this collapse of logic, through which thought turns into an inability to think,[25] is at once the highest homage which the intellect pays to the Absolute and also the highest tribute Jaspers pays to intellectualism.[26]

Metaphysical objectivity is correlative to a special intentionality. Depending on whether we confront them by empirical consciousness or by the intention of authentic Existence, metaphysical objects appear with different reality quotients. For empirical consciousness, the metaphysical aspects of objects are simply unverifiable and unreal; for the absolute consciousness of Existence, they are revelations of the very ground of reality. In short, the reality or unreality of metaphysical objects depends on the level of consciousness that intends them.[27] But since our active life of adaptation to the pragmatic aspects of reality prevents us from maintaining our intentionality on the level of absolute consciousness, the reality of Transcendence appears to us ephemeral and at best occasional.

What these three sets of considerations show in common is the fact that, paradoxically, metaphysical objectification consists in trying to undo the work of intellectual objectification. It is a process of cancelling objects, a kind of disobjectification. Jaspers refers to this process as one in which 'objects become floating (*schwebend*), as it were.'[28] Consequently, the end products of metaphysical objectification are not forms of stability, but on the contrary, forms of evanescence.[29] Transcendence can be thought of only in these evanescent, floating forms. It must be noted, however, that evanescence dissolves only the rigidity and determinateness of objects, not their intrinsic value of mediation between Existence and Transcendence. It is this value that Jaspers designates as the very 'substance' of objectivity.

Thus, metaphysical discourse, like existential discourse, ends everywhere in the failure of logical discourse, and necessitates a recourse to symbolic language. It forces the intellect to acknowledge that God, the radical origin of all reality, cannot be grasped in categories either of objectivity or of subjectivity. Both naturalism and anthropomorphism are excluded. There remains only the ambivalence of symbolical language, mediating no new knowledge of objects, but merely stirring the depths of our existential awareness of God's all-pervading presence in the world.

13

THE NATURE OF CIPHERS

It is Jaspers' unvarying teaching that all metaphysical expressions are symbols rather than concepts. They are not correlates of intentional consciousness; they speak only to absolute consciousness. 'In the disappearance of their objective character, they make authentic Being manifest to Existence.'[30] All affirmations whereby we refer to God as Light, Cause, Knowledge, Being, Love, Logos, Nature, Personality, Wisdom, Power, Goodness, are merely ciphers of his ineffable reality.

There remains a last point of precision to be made with regard to the nature of such symbols. Symbolisation in general is understood to be an indirect mode of signifying something. The reality symbolised is usually something absent, complex, or abstract, so that it can be presented only in this indirect way. In this, symbols already differ from diagrams and models whose reference is open to direct access (at least in principle), but for reasons of style or convenience is presented indirectly. Diagrams and models are abbreviations and *stand for* the reality signified, whereas symbols *incorporate* in themselves the reality symbolised. Within the general class of symbols, Jaspers further distinguishes between symbolism that can be converted through proper steps of interpretation into univocal designations, and symbolism that can be interpreted only through the convergence of other symbols. He calls them interpretable (*deutbar*) and intuitive (*schaubar*) symbols respectively. It is important to note that ciphers belong to this latter group.[31]

The main distinguishing factor between the two kinds of symbols seems to consist in their different relationship to ultimate interpretation. When we ask what a given symbol means ultimately, the first type of symbolism does in fact name such an ultimate. A general theory of myth, for instance, would tell us that a given symbol in the myth re-enacts such and such a nature process, or such and such an agricultural gesture. Psychoanalysis designates the sexual urge as that which appears in various disguised forms in all dreams, fantasies, and behaviour patterns. The common feature of these modes of symbol-interpretation is found in the fact that whatever they designate as the ultimate is no longer considered a symbol of something else, but reality itself.[32] By making the complete tour of all the manifestations of this ultimate, they are able to show by what surveyable processes this ultimate diversifies itself. Whatever its nature may be, the ultimate reality is univocally determined in the end.[33] This kind of symbolism exists for general consciousness and serves the ends of rational knowledge; it is objective and its meaning univocal. Paradoxically though, at the end of the manifold interpretation these symbols remain polyvalent and indefinite, in so far as they signify anything and everything.[34] In such a system of interpretation there is nothing to which the symbol of the ultimate reality would be inapplicable. In Freud's system, for instance, there are no phenomena, including the most conscious ones, that could not somehow be termed libidinal.

By contrast, 'intuitive symbolism knows no ultimate.'[35] The meaning of an intuitive symbol or cipher cannot be resolved into univocal meaning. In a cipher, sign and signified are fused in such a way that their separation is impossible. 'Since a cipher is always the unity of immanent and transcendent dimensions, it ceases to be a cipher whenever it is taken for a univocal symbol of Transcendence. The separation of the symbol from what is symbolised is impossible in cipher-script. It renders Transcendence present, but it is not interpretable.'[36] Unlike ordinary symbolism which ultimately operates a cleavage within the symbol between sign and signified (comparing and relating the two), cipher-reading grasps sign and signified together, and develops vertically through a process of deepening.[37] Instead of looking farther and farther outside the symbol, cipher-reading goes into the progressively greater depths of the cipher itself. Instead of searching for a meaning known from elsewhere and by other means, it clarifies what it already has by disclosing its own interior layers, its own depths.[38] A cipher is like a shaft which traverses objective reality towards a dimension of depth and transcendence, into which one can only descend, but never measure it.[39] Thus, the cipher-script of Transcendence is without any real possibility of interpretation. It is meaningful only for Existence, not for intentional consciousness. The very discourse which seems to interpret these ciphers is itself further symbolisation. Evidently, symbols of this sort do not, and cannot, function in a semantic role: their function is merely evocative. One could ask, of course, what such evocative symbols have to do with philosophy. For Jaspers, they have very much to do with it: they express the deepest aspirations of philosophic thought and answer the need of Existence to establish some reflective contact with Transcendence.

In sum, a cipher is that mode of symbolisation which objects acquire when they become expressions of Transcendence for us. Their symbolic character is such that the phrase 'symbol of . . .' cannot be completed properly by designating an ultimate reality or meaning. The completion of the phrase can be done only by further symbols. Whereas in ordinary symbolisation all the elements of interpretation converge towards a certain univocity, the elements of cipher-reading lead towards an 'unknowable univocity' (*unwissbare Eindeutigkeit*). There comes a historical moment when a particular object, event, or thought becomes totally charged with the presence of God and completely fills the consciousness of a particular Existence in an incomparable way.[40] At that decisive moment, all the elements pull together into an unmistakable meaning and an indubitable certitude. However, this certitude is not allowed to remain fixed: what a moment before looked like a final resting point for our metaphysical quest becomes, a moment later, an occasion for further questioning. 'The cipher can always be read differently.'[41] The reading of ciphers has no final act even for the same person, let alone a universal conclusion for everyone.[42]

THE COMMUNICABILITY OF CIPHERS

With this in mind, the question of communicability becomes particularly urgent. Can the momentary meaning of these elusive ciphers be stabilised at all, so as to serve as the basis for some kind of philosophic discourse? Can the certitude that they engender in a particular person at a particular time be transmitted to others and maintained through some length of time? Is there at least some sort of order or succession of ciphers that corresponds to progressive stages of consciousness on its way to a deeper and deeper grasp of God's presence in the world? If one set of symbols is interpreted by another, does the interpreting set represent a clearer awareness of Transcendence than the interpreted set? What are we to think of the value of past ontologies and theodicies that traditionally claimed to give us an objective understanding of the ultimate nature of Being and of God?

It is in an attempt to answer such questions that Jaspers has elaborated a hierarchical arrangement of ciphers. He realised that without some universality and order, the personal experience of Transcendence would soon fall into darkness and be subject to lasting doubt. He tried to show how consciousness ascends from a silent contemplation of primitive ciphers to an articulate speculative awareness of Transcendence without ever leaving the realm of symbolism. This ascending process begins with the intuitive experiences of Being. Such experiences take place during certain privileged moments of repose when we are freed from our customary preoccupation with the pragmatic and exploitable aspects of reality and become attuned to the overwhelming presence of Transcendence permeating all things. The general mood of this first phase is one of calm listening. That is why Jaspers calls the set of experiences that constitute the content of this phase the 'immediate language of Being'. Hearing this language is an experience of intimacy between an individual and his God. This experience is entirely silent at first, but almost immediately it begins to gravitate towards communication. The silent listener begins to recast what he experiences into his own language. In other words, the communication of the immediate language of Being initiates a certain process of universalisation. Even the original listener can understand his experience as language only after he has entered on the way of this process of universalisation.[43] Thus a second stage begins, which is like man's answer to the first language of Transcendence. It is the language of mythical communication in general. In this phase, man dissociates himself from the immediacy of lived experience and, in the form of a story or picture, creates a transferable content. What was originally a language of Transcendence now becomes part of the common culture. By making use of the original ciphers, mythical language both preserves and transforms the original experience. Finally, man's critical thought focuses on this picturesque language itself and, in dialogue with it, writes a new language for reflection. It traces the myth back to its source and 'in the form of metaphysical speculation constructs a third language for philosophical communication.'[44] Thus, our awareness starts with the contemplation of the primordial ciphers; it traverses the domain of mediation in myth and speculation; and finally, enriched by all this, it returns to the contemplation of the original symbols. The whole process is manifestly circular, but the circle is not vicious. Between the beginning and the end of this circular movement there is a growth from innocent wonder to a critical self-awareness.

1. *The language of Being*

Jaspers believes that ordinary things and events can have a metaphysical dimension. Sometimes in the midst of an ordinary experience of empirical reality we are struck with a heavy sense of dissatisfaction. All the familiar objects, sights, sounds, and enjoyments become of a sudden distressingly flat and tasteless. Or it might happen that just as unexpectedly we experience an overwhelming sense of joy and fulfilment, as if something from beyond the realm of daily living had visited us. According to Jaspers, it is in moments of such distress or visitation that Transcendence announces itself to us in the outer framework of ordinary experience.[45] Unfortunately, because we cannot voluntarily induce these states, when they come we tend to dismiss them as entirely subjective and regard them as momentary malfunctions of our physical or psychic powers. But if we do accept them without prejudice as unexpected gifts, they can bring us an extraordinary revelation for a fleeting instant.

Fleeting and insubstantial as they may be, such moments can mediate an experience of Transcendence, an experience marked with a sense of unity and completeness seldom found in direct, non-symbolical experience.[46] In fact the experience of Transcendence grows paler and paler as it gains on universality; it is forceful only when it feeds on a *hic et nunc* particular. A landscape or a humble flower, when concretely seen, can suddenly present the whole of its world.[47] Being affirms itself wholly in each concrete thing, and the metaphysically open mind engaged in cipher-reading focuses on this wholeness. Unlike scientific orientation that isolates and divides its objects, metaphysical cipher-reading keeps its awareness for the totality.[48] In this, cipher-reading resembles the study of physiognomy: it gives a total impression. Not unlike the silent appeal that flows out to us from a human face, where the whole of a man's life is tellingly written, the physiognomy of things can solicit our wonder and love for their inner Transcendence.

Thus, each of the thousand faces of Nature may become a silent cipher for us. In each of them we encounter an Other, but also a totality that includes us. Philosophies of nature have always tried to translate this experience of totality into universal terms by telling us what the ultimate objective reality of Nature was: cosmic life and growth, ecstasy of becoming, static or evolving hierarchy of forms, alienations of the Spirit, and so on endlessly. These interpretations, according to Jaspers, are both true and false: true as temporary insights, false as definitive fixations which pretend to pass for science. In other words, they are true as ciphers which interpret the experience of wholeness (in turn re-interpreted by other ciphers), false as a knowledge of totality. Nature is inexhaustible in giving rise to metaphysical symbols.

During a short moment of contemplative immersion, Nature offers herself to our love, but can also seduce us to aestheticism. Our contemplation of Nature can sometimes make us oblivious to our duty to communicate with men. It may turn into an *ersatz* for human relationships.[49] The lack of human accent is the great shortcoming of Nature. She speaks to me in her own terms, but when I question her in my language, she remains dumb. 'The speechlessness of Nature is the realm of non-communication.'[50]

History can be another cipher in the silent language of Being. But just as the philosophies of Nature are wrong in trying to immobilise the ultimate meaning of Nature, the philosophies of History are wrong also when they speak of a final sense of History. History is merely a cipher of the essentially ambiguous human condition. It is the symbol of man's fundamental sameness through time, but also of his inexorable evolution which makes and shapes the course of events. History stands for the ordered design of man's destiny from Creation to Fall, from Fall to Redemption, from Redemption to the Last Judgement, but also for his life engulfed at both ends by darkness. History is the image of human time that has given birth to the Seven Wonders of the World, and of cosmic time that crumbles them to dust. The reading of History can be a transcendental event. Read as a cipher, History is indeed a kind of divine revelation. 'It is as if Transcendence announced itself while an old god stands unveiled and dies, and a new god is born.'[51] Placed between an inscrutable beginning and an unknown end, History appears as an endless process of success and failure: the divinities of one age are unmasked as the idols of the next. Man's works and achievements are transitory and destined to be superseded by the march of time, and yet their enduring human value lies in their very transitoriness. 'The cipher of History is the general shipwreck of all that is authentic. That which is authentic must exist between a beginning and an end, for only the trivial endures. . . . Real truth always ends in failure (*scheitert*), but it can also be revived and repeated in a fresh grasp.'[52] History is a cipher of the individual's pathetic struggle against time and oblivion, but also of his victorious solidarity with others before and after him, a solidarity which overcomes time. History is like the immortal '*corpus mysticum* of free and creative spirits'.[53]

The phenomena of consciousness and knowledge are also primordial ciphers. The inexplicable split between the conscious subject and its object (as well as their inseparable correlatedness) symbolises the mysterious be-longing of thought and reality. Regarded as a cipher, consciousness appears as the prime expression of that basic striving for self-revelation which inhabits Being. But the cipher of consciousness is ambiguous: it appears as both an approach and a trap for our coming into contact with Being as such. Intentional consciousness, as Dufrenne and Ricoeur put it, 'is the result of both defiance and supreme obedience to the call of some hidden divinity. It is as if the will-to-know were at once the forbidden fruit and the divine vocation of man.'[54]

By far the greatest cipher of Transcendence, however, is man himself. Man is a whole world in himself. Widely divergent aspects of reality meet in him. But he not only recapitulates the whole of reality, he also transcends it. His selfhood is, in fact, a perpetual self-transcendence. 'World and Transcendence are intertwined in man, and his Existence unfolds between their common frontier.'[55] Yet, nobody can say unequivocally what man is. He is a cipher even for himself:

> Created half to rise and half to fall;
> Great lord of all things, yet a prey to all;
> Sole judge of truth, in endless error hurled:
> The glory, jest, and riddle of the world.[56]

He is an animal that gropes for the Absolute. Locked in limited vistas, he yearns for the unlimited vision of metaphysical reality. 'He comes closest to catching sight of Transcendence when he contemplates his own being as a cipher. This is expressed mythically when we say that man was created in the image and likeness of God.'[57] By the help of this image man can at times catch a glimpse of the incomprehensible unity of God. Man's freedom and nobility can reflect the autonomy and goodness of God, from whom both of these gifts derive.

2. *Man's first reply in myth*

'Echoing the language of Transcendence, which is audible only in the immediacy of a fleeting moment, man produces other languages. In the form of pictures and images, these languages try to communicate what has been heard. Next to the language of Being comes the language of man.'[58] The immediate experience of Being now passes into mythical transmission in a cipher form. Man expresses his experience of Being in terms of the sublime and the sacred. This expression, according to Jaspers, takes place on three successive levels, corresponding roughly to the three cycles of mythology, religion and art.

The first of these is the language of myth in the ordinary sense, as in Greek mythology, for instance. What characterises myth is the fact that in myth the transcendent and natural elements are not yet radically separated. The Greek gods, for instance, are still part of this world. Nevertheless, as special figures alongside the natural reality, they supplement and personify natural reality in order to indicate its transcendent dimension for man. They add a human accent to the language of nature: thus Poseidon stands for the life, movement, and grandeur of the sea.

In the second kind of human language, the language of religion, the transcendent and natural aspects of reality are strictly distinguished, set apart, and the latter is entirely overshadowed by the former. For the religious mind, the natural takes second place to the supernatural. True reality, it is believed, is above the natural; it exists in another world. From this other dimension the supernatural or divine reality enters into this world in the form of visible signs and wonders or as invisible grace. The attitude accompanying all religious consciousness is seen by Jaspers as a flight from the world. Instead of trusting the reality of this world as divine in its essence, religion tries to listen to an other-worldly reality which, so the claim goes, has disclosed itself in direct revelation.[59] Whether revelation is regarded as accomplished or as a continuous process, the world drama is assumed to derive its real meaning not from within itself, but from this 'other' world.

The third highest type of mythical expression is found, according to Jaspers, in art. Art transfigures ordinary reality by bringing out the transcendence within things. Unlike religion, art does not depreciate the visible face of things, and unlike ordinary myth, it does not personify natural reality. The revelations of art are both worldly and transcendent at the same time: they are transcendent in their worldliness. The language and expression of art is said to be the highest form of mythical communication because, by an almost complete circle, it returns to the original language of Being, to be all but re-absorbed in it.

In contrast to the immediate cipher-language of Being, myth in general is a mediated language, a language of tradition and shared inheritance. As such, it possesses a greater degree of internal unity and universality than the first language. Nevertheless, this universality is not absolute. According to Jaspers, there are no universal myths, no prime religious patterns (*religiöse Urformen*), no uniform vision in art. The multiplicity of intuitive ciphers is replaced here by a multiplicity of traditions: the first reply of man to the appeal of Transcendence is already broken up into several languages.

Myths and religions are integral elements in the life of a cultural community. Each myth and religion is lodged in its own language and tradition. Inside each language there reigns a certain relative universality of belief which permits its adherents to comprehend the myth in more or less the same way. Belonging to that community of belief is essential for the understanding of its myths. That is why Jaspers warns us that myths cannot be comprehended from the outside: 'The sense of myths unveils itself only for those who still believe in the truth which acquired its specific (and therefore, vanishing) expression in those myths.'[60]

These remarks are important for the philosophical interpretation of myths and for the status of philosophical rationality in general. At first sight it would seem that by their communicability within the limits of a given tradition, myths initiate a progressive universalisation of the ineffable original experience of ciphers and begin to extract some common meaning from that experience. Ill-defined as this common element may be, one expects that the process of universalisation, once begun, will continue and find its fulfilment in philosophical reflection. One expects that the relative universality of common belief will expand into the absolute universality of speculation. One is led to think that the philosopher, by virtue of rationally founded insights, will be able to recover all the traditions, integrating them into a higher unity according to a criterion that embraces more than the common faith of a given group. However, the surprising turn in Jaspers' thought on this point is that, according to him, the rational appropriation of myth by philosophic reflection depends on the personal faith of the philosopher, and not on universal insight. It is this personal faith that prompts the philosopher to accept and to maintain what he considers the truth-content of the myth in question. To be sure, he does not return to the speechless contemplation of the original cipher, but neither does he pass to the objective universality of science. He proceeds to what Jaspers calls the unique-universal (*Einzigallgemeines*). The unique-universal, as far as I can see, is the multiple presence of Transcendence discernible in all things when they are approached from the perspective of philosophic faith. Unlike individual intuition which is strictly unique, and unlike scientific knowledge which is strictly objective and universal, the awareness of Transcendence in speculative terms is unique-universal. God's presence in things is 'the unthinkable unity of the universal and the particular'.[61]

It might be relevant to note a certain similarity and contrast between Jaspers and Comte on this point. Both thinkers agree on the fact that myth, philosophy, and science constitute three distinguishable levels of human thought. But unlike Comte who taught that these levels resulted from a historical maturation of human intelligence, Jaspers maintains that myth, philosophy, and science are permanent possibilities of the human mind. They constitute not so much three successive stages of thought in history as three initial directions in which thought might opt to explore reality at any time. These directions correspond to the three degrees of universality which Jaspers designates as relative universality; objective universality; unique universality. The first is the universality of belief shared by a historical community; the second is the universality proper to metaphysical appropriation; the third is the universality of objective knowledge of science.

The parting of the ways for these three directions occurs in the relative universality of myth:

(*a*) if thought remains in the relative universal but develops it, the result will be religion and art;

(*b*) if thought turns to the unique-universal, we have metaphysics, or simply philosophical speculation in general;

(*c*) if thought turns to the objective universal, we have science in all its forms.

The following diagram indicates that the first and second orientations of thought are circular, while the third is linear:

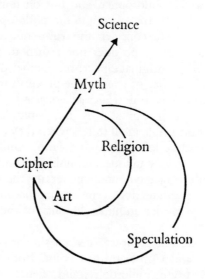

As one can see, both philosophical speculation and science reach beyond the primitive grasp of myths, but do so differently. Whereas science simply eliminates myth, philosophy returns to the origin of myths and tries to decipher the ineffable message of Transcendence that prompted the telling of myths in the first place. In short, myth is rejected as dogma, but preserved as a mediating expression of an original experience of reality. Although the mythical approach is necessary for all of us at a certain stage of our mental development (and is for many the only sure way of ever coming into contact with Transcendence), myths are destined to be superseded in all their forms by philosophical speculation. 'Philosophy repels the myth from which it took its origin. It opposes rational insight to the telling of tales, which are its dream and deception. But one day, having become autonomous, philosophy turns its gaze backwards and tries to grasp myth as truth.'[62] This reprise of myth by philosophy, this re-writing of stories in a speculative language, is necessary for the evolution of thought, because myth is not completely aware of its own truth. It is still mixed with error. Philosophy is supposed to clarify this truth and show the true vocation of myth.

The ensuing polemics between myth and philosophy is one of the most difficult points to understand in Jaspers' thought. This difficulty is disconcerting because, according to some commentators, the relationship between myth and philosophy may be the key to Jaspers' whole work.[63] If it is, then the only clear message of his philosophy is that philosophy as a whole constitutes an immense, self-conscious metaphor. There are several crucial statements in Jaspers' interpretation of myths which, taken jointly, allow no other conclusion. On the one hand, he considers myth 'an expression of a certain truth' which remains forever inaccessible to any other mode of thought. This truth must be comprehended *in* the myth itself.[64] On the other hand, he states that the grasp of mythical truth 'demands philosophical reflection on the myth'.[65] I fail to see how this solves anything; particularly, how it clarifies the relationship or determines the status of myth and philosophy. Jaspers says that the truth peculiar to myth is to be grasped *in* myth itself. Perhaps! However, it would be more instructive to know whether mythical truth is grasped *by* myth or *by* philosophical thought. If the ultimate truth proper to myth is really extra-philosophical in the sense that whatever philosophical reflection is able to grasp of it is *not* the truth of myth, then philosophy is hopelessly beside the point as far as the comprehension of myth is concerned. On the other hand, if this truth, though mythical in origin, is progressively accessible to philosophical inquiry, then to the extent that philosophy comprehends the myth it will transform it into a rationally founded truth, and thereby eliminate it as a myth. Even if we 'live' with the myth—as Jaspers often recommends—but live with it in the clear recognition that myth is a 'dream and a deception', we shall have unmasked it already in the name of some extra-mythical insight. Even our acceptance of myth as an initial and truncated form of truth presupposes that we are comparing it with a more complete truth, which we no longer consider merely meta-phorical, but objective. Is there any other possibility than to regard myth either as error, pure and simple, or as a partial truth? In either case, we already pass judgement on it in the name of non-mythical truth.

For reasons of his own, Jaspers refuses to accept these alter-natives and considers even philosophical truth to be symbolic. For him, then, the difference between myth and philosophy does not seem to lie in the difference between symbolical and non-symbolic thought (both are more or less symbolical for him), but rather in the degree of self-awareness that these two modes of thought are said to possess. Myth lacks the awareness of its own symbolical character, whereas philosophy has this awareness. This means that philosophy knows itself to be a myth, that is, a merely symbolical adumbration of truth. Myth believes that it possesses the truth; philosophy knows that it can only work towards it. Jaspers would fully espouse Brunschvicg's statement: 'L'humanité désormais va méditer en vue de la vérité, non plus à partir de la vérité'.

Puzzling and incomplete as such a view may be, at least it avoids most of the classical mistakes made in dealing with myths. The lack of self-reflection characteristic of mythical mentality constitutes the first danger, the danger of exaggerated realism, which accepts the myth tautegorically. All the dogma, magic and superstition of the world owe their existence to such tautegorism. Tautegorism takes the symbolic communication intended by the myth to be a description of some positive fact of event. This extreme realism is most strikingly demonstrated in the case of magic, which goes so far as to attempt to produce some positive empirical effect by manipulating the symbolic act or word of the myth, because it believes that there exists a positive causal relationship between symbol and the desired real effect. Dogma is simply myth gone authoritative: it demands intellectual assent and practical compliance to the myth by moral or physical pressure. But if these forms of naïve realism give too much credit to the communicative form of myths, critical rationalism tends to accord them none at all. Reacting massively to the tautegorical acceptance of fables, rationalism denies all truth content to mythical communication, and explains the existence of myths by sheer ignorance on the part of the primitive mind. At best, rationalism regards myth as some kind of allegory, the meaning of which is more adequately stated in rational terms by psychology, sociology, or anthropology. This interpretation regards myth as a pedagogical device that aims to entertain while it instructs by disguising its objective message in a picturesque language. All the philosophical interpreter has to do to discover the real message of myth is to strip away the symbol character that hides this signification. It is worth noting that both exaggerated realism and rationalism treat the content of myth as if it were an objective universal. In so doing, they both destroy the metaphysical objectivity of myth, that is, its language character. The only conversion of myth into objective discourse which Jaspers admits as legitimate is outright demythologisation by science proper which, however, 'is always aware of its own limitations, understands the particularity of its insights, and knows that it can never explore Being but merely objects in the world.'[66] But if Jaspers admits this demythologisation by science as legitimate, he also remarks its utter poverty, precisely because the methods of science do away with the transcendent aspects of mythical expression. 'How wretched, how lacking in expressiveness (*spracharm*) our life would be if the language of myth were no longer valid; and how untrue, when the irreplaceable mythical form is filled with banal content! . . . Does the splendour of sunrise cease to be an ever novel and inspiring reality, a mythical presence, just because we know that we are revolving with the Earth around the Sun, so that, scientifically speaking, we cannot talk of sunrise?'[67]

The task of undertaking a more respectful sort of demythologisation will, therefore, devolve not upon the scientist but upon the philosopher, who knows how to respect the language character of the myth. He will 'translate' the myth into another language without destroying the presence of Transcendence that is manifested in it.

3. *Man's second reply in speculative ciphers*

The last phase of advancing towards Transcendence and the highest degree of awareness of the ground of beings is reached in philosophical reflection. Still responding to the original appeal of Being, but no longer satisfied with mythical expression, philosophy resorts to rational discourse in order to express its awareness of what is transcendent in reality. How is this done? Jaspers replies with a deceptively simple formula: philosophy 'interprets the original cipher-script by writing a new one. It thinks of Transcendence *in analogy* with the intuitively and logically knowable being of mundane reality.' Thus far the formula is quite orthodox: Jaspers is calling for ontological reflection based on the analogical mode of thought. But then he adds immediately: 'What is thus thought is only a symbol, another form of language, which now has become communicable.'[68] This part of the formula is considerably less orthodox. What we are told in fact is that even ontology is merely a symbol, the highest, most communicable perhaps, but a symbol nevertheless. We are warned not to think of analogy as a form of knowledge, *Wissen* (knowledge being understood as a univocal representation of an objective reality), because analogy too is merely a symbol to be further contemplated: 'In wonder or hate, in shudder or despair, in love or poignancy I see: *thus it is*.'[69] It seems that the wonder and admiration which started our exploration of Being must also terminate it. Speculation merely exchanges one set of symbols for another.

There is a difference, however. During speculation, thought and reality are supposed to rejoin each other in that ineffable unity of which I spoke earlier as 'be-longing'. Ontology, which is speculation at its best, is called by Jaspers a kind of thinking that is 'aglow with Being', *seinsdurchglühtes Denken*. In it, the customary disjunctions of ordinary thinking are dissolved in the unity of thought and reality.

Unfortunately, Jaspers' further description of this speculative mode of thinking is scanty and mostly negative: speculation is not a knowledge of objects; nor merely an appeal to freedom; nor categorical thinking; nor simply an expression of our desire for Transcendence. Jaspers refers to it as 'a contemplative self-immersion that touches on Transcendence by means of a meticulously articulated cipher-script invented by the thinker himself and which brings Transcendence before the mind as a metaphysical object.'[70] This is supposed to make speculation essentially different from all the other modes of thinking which are presupposed, made use of, and then dissolved by speculation. Speculation 'lets them evaporate in its own thought movement and does not hold fast to any object.'[71] All this is rather obscure and gratuitous, but perhaps this is to be expected in the case of a 'thought which by thinking pushes beyond the thinkable.'[72]

(*a*) *Grandeur and poverty of ontologies.* Speculation is true as symbol, but false as knowledge. This double judgement is the key to Jaspers' attitude towards the ontologies of the past. He praises and assimilates them as the cipher-language in which the philosophical faith of bygone ages speaks to us, but condemns them as school subjects. He appropriates them as food for contemplation, but refuses them as doctrines of Being. On a larger scale, this is also the key to his attitude towards tradition in general. He always stresses the fact that man is still a child of tradition, even when he is most singularly and resolutely himself. The correct attitude towards this tradition is neither acceptance nor simple refusal. Our duty should rather be to reflect on the objective elements of tradition, not for their own sake, but for the sake of rediscovering through them the inspiration that nurtured them.

Paradoxically, Jaspers thinks that the very quality that makes past ontological systems great also makes them inacceptable for us today. What is it that makes them great? To quote him: 'In an undivided burst of thought they give us *cogent knowledge* of positive being, they *transcend* the world towards its ground, and they *appeal* to the hearer who in his freedom can accept or refuse them. So they produce a cipher which becomes the disclosure of transcendent Being. The tremendous force of great philosophies is to have touched all these aspects (and thereby the whole being of man) in their fundamental thought, enabling man to know, to see, and to will in one.'[73] It is this impressive striving for unity and totality that makes these philosophies an eloquent cipher for Transcendence. Each such philosophic system is a powerful witness to an authentic selfhood whose whole being was animated by a desire for the One. The gathering of knowledge, will, and contemplation into an undivided impulse of thought makes these systems the expression of a kind of thought which, 'instead of being the thought of some object, was incandescent with Being.' This kind of thinking is precisely the thinking of Reason that aims at Being in its undivided unity. The great systems really express the presence of transcendent reality that is not separable from the process that discovers it.[74] In short, great speculation unites thought and Being in a cipher of be-longing.

14

Of course, the idea that thought and reality should be the same makes no sense to intentional consciousness, because the thinking of intentional consciousness is always turned upon the 'other'. But it makes sense when thinking itself becomes a cipher of the metaphysical unity of thought and Being.'[75] To call something a cipher is to indicate that it expresses something else; that it itself is not an ultimate, but has its *raison d' être* and explanation in something ulterior. Now, to call thinking itself a cipher is to raise the 'why' of thinking and to indicate the reality that tries to find expression in thinking. This reality is, first of all, the profound ontological unity of Being and consciousness. Secondly, it is the profound continuity and oneness of the self, namely, the self of those great system builders who have left us their thought constructions in witness of lives spent in committed relatedness to Being. As Dufrenne and Ricoeur remark, 'a cipher is not only this or that thing, nature, freedom, history, but also the totality of witnesses who rise to the call of the privileged witness, namely, *my* thoughtful existence.'[76] Briefly, the ontological systems of the past are *ciphers of* their makers' selfhood and, at the same time, *ciphers for* my selfhood.

However, the formidable unity and totality of former ontologies also constitute their weakness and limitation. It is no longer possible for us to accomplish knowledge, appeal, and contemplation in one single train of thought, according to Jaspers. 'Our force is in separation, for we have lost our naïvety.'[77] 'We', of course, means everybody who accepts Jaspers' general plan of philosophy. According to this plan, philosophy has three distinct phases: knowledge, which refers to the categorial grasp of objects; appeal, which deals with the elucidation of subjective existence; contemplation, which is self-immersion into the cipher-script of Transcendence. Once we realise the separateness of these phases, this 'torn state of Being for us,' our desire for an all-inclusive grasp ceases and ontology falls apart.

This realisation bears upon two closely related points. First, if we think for a moment, we are bound to realise that these ontological systems were failures even as used by the original thinkers themselves. The thought structures they managed to put together reflected their penetrating insights into Being in a crippled sort of way. Expressed as general doctrine, their thought strikes us sometimes as an esoteric parody of their basic intuition.[78]

Still, for them, the system was true because it was nourished and sustained by their personal experience. For this reason, each ontology has something to command our respect, but also something that signals its fundamental limitation, namely, that 'it can be true only once.'[79] Secondly, we must realise that every ontology becomes false when we try to repeat it as an act of the intellect alone. It becomes a bloodless ghost when, instead of being taken up into the resonance of a personal destiny, it is treated as hand-me-down knowledge. Our real appreciation of past ontologies must, therefore, begin with a critical appraisal of their fundamental intention. We must see that their unitary structure contains many disparate elements, such as 'psychological analysis, categorial definition, positive world-orientation, elucidation of Existence, and reading of cipher-scripts. Not until such separations will we be able to rediscover the unity of their symbolic character in all clarity. . . . Only then shall we hear distinctly the voice of a historical self telling us how he knew his Transcendence.'[80] Our assimilation of the past must be a communicative battle which, in order to be a genuine dialogue, can neither simply repeat nor lightly reject the past. We must find our own voice while listening to what is personal in the voices of bygone great philosophers.

Thus the road of retreat to past systems is definitely blocked off by Jaspers, but the lines of communication are not cut. He believes in the irrepressible relationship that unites free personalities anywhere, any time. This relationship, in order to be really free, cannot be a slavish acceptance of ready-made truth. The *philosophia perennis* that many thinkers like to appeal to is not found in this or that particular system, not even as the common residue of all systems (a sort of *Urphilosophie*), but in the perennial philosophic impetus which, like the fabulous Phoenix, is forever reborn of its own ashes. It is each time fresh, but each time itself, because it rises out of an enduring human élan towards Transcendence. 'Perennial philosophy', says Fr Tilliette, 'exhausts itself in every one of its manifestations, and there is nothing regrettable about this.'[81]

Let us note in passing that one of the important reasons for Jaspers' rejection of certain aspects of ontology is attributable to the enlightenment that modern science has brought us. The methodic labours of science have led us to realise more accurately what we can or cannot 'know' in the proper sense of the word. It is this critical awareness that prompted Jaspers to combat the scientific and objective claims of ontology. However, this opposition may be beneficial both for science and philosophy. Philosophy must reckon with the critical findings of world-orientation or science in order to become aware of its own task so as to concentrate on those aspects of reality which do not fall within the limits of scientific investigation.[82] On the other hand, the metaphysical search for the transcendent aspects of reality may exert a salutary pressure on the sciences and may incite the will-to-know to a relentless discrimination between fact and symbol, knowledge and cipher-reading. This separation between factual knowledge and symbolism is necessary in order to deprive philosophy, from the start, of any claim to scientific objectivity and to force it to recognise its own intuitive, analogous, symbolical character.[83]

(b) *An example of speculative cipher-reading.* In order to illustrate how a thoughtful approach to ancient problems can prepare us for a personal metaphysical experience of Being, Jaspers discusses four classic ontological themes: the proofs for the existence of God; the origin of the world; the nature of knowledge; and doctrines about the unity of reality. In order to show how Jaspers interprets these questions I shall briefly consider the first of them: does Transcendence exist?

'Neither empirical observation nor cogent reasoning can demonstrate that there is a Transcendence at all.'[84]   With this bold statement Jaspers sweeps away all the classical proofs for the existence of God. But then he adds: 'For all that, the proofs are not simple errors, since a certain existential awareness of Being can be clarified through them.'[85] Considered in this light, the proofs are useful as 'ciphers in which the thought and being of the thinker who constructs the proofs achieve a certain state of unity.'[86] Their force in proving Transcendence is, therefore, indirect. They express directly the existential indwelling (*Innesein*) of the thinker in any of his genuine acts of thinking about reality. This indwelling is intuitive and, as such, more primordial than any demonstration and more certain than logical cogency. The unity between subject and act in this kind of intuition next 'demonstrates' the indwelling of the object thought of in the act of thinking. What this object or content is finds various verbal formulations—such as the Infinite, the Greatest-Thinkable, Transcendence, the Supreme Person, God—but in each case the heart of the proof consists in that certitude which comes from the very indwelling of the reality thought of in the reality of the act of thinking itself. It is for this reason that Jaspers is able to reduce the argumentative form of all the proofs to the following formula: 'That which is present as Being in existential intuition must be real, for otherwise that intuition itself could not exist.'[87] What does this rather dense formula mean?

As Jaspers proceeds to explain it, it becomes clear that the formula represents the rock-bottom structure of what is known in philosophy as the ontological proof for the existence of God. Generally, the proponents of this proof argue that the concept of God as the most perfect and infinite being, greater than which cannot be thought of, implies his existence or actuality. For if the concept referred to something merely possible, if God did not actually exist, one could think of something greater than the Greatest-Thinkable, namely a reality which is not only possible but also actual. But to think of something greater than the Greatest-Thinkable is a contradiction in terms. Therefore, the thought of the most perfect and infinite Being includes his existence and actuality.

This mode of argumentation, Jaspers thinks, is both too much and too little. It is too much for logic: 'Just as I cannot think of the greatest possible number, neither can I think of any other greatest thing. . . . The greatest, as something actual, cannot be made into a thought-contest.'[88] Whatever I might think of, must be either actual or the greatest, but it cannot be both at the same time and still be logical. In other words, the Greatest-Thinkable is a logically impossible object: in so far as it is subject to thought, it is something determined and finite, but in so far as it is termed the greatest, it is supposed to be without limits. Moreover, the proof is without demonstrative force also because it concludes from the mere cogitation (*sich-etwas-ausdenken*) to the reality of a thing, which is not allowed. Only the possibility of reality can be ascertained by cogitation: reality itself must be experienced.

It would be quite a different matter if thought itself ceased to be mere cogitation about reality and were to become the sort of metaphysical experience in which intentionality is surpassed in such a way that the reality thought of would be inherent in the activity thinking it. In other words, thinking would be able to ascertain Being only if it ceased to be intentional and returned to its pre-reflective and transcendental unity with Being. And this is precisely what Jaspers maintains as the extreme possibility of thinking under the impulsion of that primordial appetite for reality that is the mainspring of all thinking activity. One may recall that it is the reality of this basic will-to-know that constitutes also the reality of the kind of thought through which thinking is originally identical with Being itself. Whereas for intentional thought reality is always 'other' than the act of thinking, in this transcendental relation object and act are the 'same'.

Here, in explanation of the above formula of the ontological proof, Jaspers repeats basically the same thesis in three slightly different forms, the difference being that he marks the gradual identification first between the thinker and his thinking and then between thinking and its metaphysical object, which is Transcendence. This is what he says: 'The thinking mode of being (*Denkendsein*) which constitutes intuition (*Innesein*) is that being which in existential unity is identical with his thinking, and by this fact also shows forth the reality of its thought object.' Secondly, 'if the thinking of this existential being were not united with the reality of its thought content, i.e., with the reality of Transcendence, then itself would not exist as a thinking mode of being. But it exists, therefore, Transcendence exists also.' Thirdly, 'The being of Existence exists only in union with the thought of Transcendence. This union is first the existential union of thinking and being in the thinker, and then it is a cipher of the union of thought and Transcendence.'[89]

But the ontological proofs are also too little, too poor, because for the most part they ignore this ultimate possibility of thought, that of harbouring Transcendence, even though this is what constitutes the nucleus of their certitude. Their greatest shortcoming consists in having mistaken the original identity of subject, act, and object (Existence, thought, and Transcendence), which here is expressed in a speculative form, for an intentional passage from thought to reality. But here thought has no need for passing to reality, for the latter is already united to it. Whereas on the level of intentional consciousness thought requires the external confirmation of experience to assure the reality of its object, here, and only here, thought is already inhabited by the reality of its object, so that a separation and opposition of thought and reality would mean the very elimination of this kind of thought which is a *Denkendsein* or *denkendes Innesein*.[90]

Thus, for Jaspers, the ontological proof is one of the strongest, most genuine ways of ascertaining the reality of Transcendence by speculative means. This ascertainment is not a demonstration, to be sure, but a certitude that comes from cipher-reading.

We should like to clarify and explain this a little, showing why for Jaspers the ontological proof is not a demonstration. From what has been said on the last few pages one might think that all Jaspers did to the ontological proof was to point out where its real demonstrative force lies. This would certainly be a wrong impression. His claim about the primordial union of thought and reality as the source and goal of all certitude can in no way be taken for a first evidence. This union is certainly not evident to the intellect (*Verstand*) whose first evidence is rather the opposite, namely, that thought and reality are really distinct.[91] Nor is it evident to ordinary experience. Let us remember that the metaphysical experience in which this identity presents itself with certitude is not an ordinary experience, but an experience *sui generis*. Without repeating all that has already been said on this subject, let us simply recall that metaphysical experience is not an experience of the positivity of an object which would impose itself on the mind, but precisely of the relativity of any given object which points beyond itself to a plus-being or transcendence. For this reason, this experience engenders no lasting evidence, and can be doubted by the intellect almost as soon as the experience is over. Differently put, metaphysical experience is not so much an ascertaining of facts as an opening of the mind upon the depth, unity, and totality of reality, which are the proper concern of Reason. It is not so much an occurrence as a quest. In particular, the experience of the unity of thought and being is more like a pledge than a fact, more like an act of faith than an evidence. In short, using Jaspers' expression, the unity of thought and being is a cipher.

If the doubt which surrounds the cipher on every side is nevertheless overcome, this occurs not through invincible evidence or counter-argument, but through a sort of action:

'Against my doubt there can be no refutation, only a doing. One does not demonstrate Transcendence, one can only bear witness to it. The cipher in which it reveals itself to me cannot become real without my doing. From dissatisfaction and from love an activity springs forth which actively realises the cipher which as yet does not exist. . . . The Transcendence that concerns the philosophic thinker is no more demonstrated than the God of religion, who also must be encountered in ritual celebration.'[92]

There is yet another closely related reason why the ontological proof is not regarded as a demonstration by Jaspers. We may recall that he attributed reality to thought not on account of the latter's reflecting real contents, but ultimately on account of thought's active prospecting for real objects, that is, because of an activity that is the exercise of a certain *will*. Then he concluded that if the reality of thought is derived from this will operative in it, then the reality content (*Seinsinhalt*) of what is thought of reveals itself only to the will of the thinker. This indicates again that he considered the ultimate certainty of speculation not so much as an evidence for the intellect, but as a dynamic project for the will informed by Reason.

As a last remark, I wish to advert to yet another point which will prove of capital importance for our purposes later on. We have heard Jaspers repeat on several occasions that Existence exists in liaison with Transcendence or not at all. The nature of this liaison, however, was left either unexplained or defined almost exclusively in terms of freedom, which cast the shadow of utter irrationalism over the entire philosophy of Existence. It is therefore doubly reassuring to read here that the primary bond between selfhood and Transcendence is thought: 'The being of Existence exists in union with the thought of Transcendence.' This suggests that the rational activity of thinking is at least as important for selfhood as freedom since it is required for the very 'being' of it. Of course, the texts quoted earlier go much deeper than that and indicate that this thinking is not something added to selfhood, but is in a certain sense identical with it; so much so that Jaspers does not hesitate to give Existence a new name: *Denkendsein*. But even that is not the end. Next Jaspers identifies *Denkendsein* (which is already a union between selfhood and thinking) with a 'thinking indwelling' which now annexes even the reality of the object thought of. The result is a more complete unity which now envelops not only the distinction between subject and act, but also the opposition between thinking and being. This intrepid unification permits us to surmise that the prime mover behind the whole operation is Reason, whose 'basic propensity is precisely a limitless will-to-unity.'[93] We know already that ciphers exist only for Existence, but now we suspect that it is Reason that causes Existence to turn everything into a cipher. Even the subject-object dichotomy, the *Grundfaktum* of the intellect, is made into a symbol of the ineffable unity of thought and reality by Reason, because Reason cannot tolerate any separation. It goes along with freedom, but when freedom threatens to be disruptive, Reason is there to fill the breach with law and order.

CONCLUDING REMARKS

'Jaspers talks much and often about God but never really says anything about him; he ends up by reducing him to a nonentity.'[94] This criticism by an eminent contemporary thinker is typical of the dissatisfaction Jaspers' enigmatic doctrine on God leaves behind in the mind of anyone who is even a little familiar with his writings. Both philosophers and believers are bound to feel let down by the idea of a Transcendence that reveals itself only in inscrutable and ambiguous ciphers that do not allow any positive interpretation. 'Thus, if the cipher is, as Jaspers claims, the language of transcendence, this language can, by definition, never communicate anything whatever to the human mind; therefore it has no meaning except that of a cipher or symbol to which man has not and can never have the key.'[95] The transcendence man can attain by reading the ciphers is the absolutely hidden God, the totally alien and incomparable Other, to whom all cognitive access by way of analogy is barred forever. The only certain truth we can know about him is that he is entirely unknowable. He is certainly not a personal presence to whom one could pray in trust and who would answer with his grace. He is not a redeemer. In rare and fleeting moments he seems to draw near to our existence, only to recede into a distance greater than before. Each of his visitations seems to make him more and more remote, until, at last, only his absence is left to us.

One cannot help wondering about the usefulness of such a divinity and about the nature of the 'philosophical faith' that is supposedly called upon to affirm his existence. Philosophers and believers alike suspect that the whole God-problem of Jaspers results from the unhealthy position Jaspers tried to assume between faith and unbelief. Lacking the humility needed for the former and the courage needed for the latter, he allowed his thought to build up into a vast system of contraries: 'under the appearance of a drastic assertion of transcendence there is accomplished the most integral immanentism; under the appearance of an all-encompassing faith there is hidden the most radical unbelief; under the appearance of a continual reference to God there is hidden a radical denial of the possibility of any real approach by man to God and any attempt by man to enter into personal relationship with God.'[96] It is this unresolved dialectic that induced many confirmed atheists like Sartre to interpret Jaspers' system as a *théologie manquée* and also caused believers like Ricoeur to read it as an *athéisme manqué*.[97]

Inevitable and merited as such criticisms may be, they all seem to labour under two common difficulties. In the first place, they all imply a rather clear and unambiguous God-concept in comparison with which Jaspers' idea of Transcendence appears either too mystical or too secular. One could not indict him for theologism or atheism unless one had a positive idea of what the 'proper' concept of God should be. This in turn implies that, for both kinds of critics, the Infinite can really become immanent to finite thinking not only as the movement that constitutes its transcending dynamism, as Jaspers maintains, but also as content that can be comprehended and retained by the intellect in a permanent form. Secondly, both kinds of criticism suggest that neither the denial nor the affirmation of God should be so flimsy and timid as to allow a lasting doubt. They secretly demand that ultimately both faith and its opposite, unbelief, resolve themselves into cognitive certitude based on the demonstrable existence or non-existence of God. Both faith and unbelief are seen by them as a species of knowledge, or at least as introductory phases, *praeambula*, that lead directly to a cognitive grasp.

Jaspers' idea of faith is, of course, diametrically opposed to this. An act of faith, according to him, can never lead to an indubitable certitude because it is not an act of knowledge but an act of freedom. Doubt, fear of opposite, risk, are not merely accidental but essential elements of the certitude engendered by such a faith. In this context, affirmation of God means precisely overcoming the continual temptation in his denial; transcendence means a continuous movement out of immanence; certitude means an active detachment from phenomenal appearances in order to seek the fulfilment of freedom in the vast embrace of the Infinite.

The faith that gives rise to these ventures is indeed philosophical since it does not rest on a special revelation but on the natural trust and confidence Reason has in itself to open out beyond the domain of positive knowledge. Philosophic faith cannot be much more specific than that. It can express itself only in the fluid language of symbols. Revealed faith, which can say more definite things about God than the evanescent expressions of ciphers can, is a gratuitous gift not granted to all, consequently it cannot provide the impetus of reflection for someone to whom this gift is denied. Thus, if a philosopher like Jaspers does reflect on the religious faith of others, he can do no more than acknowledge it as one more cipher among others through which God speaks to the particular historical consciousness of these believers. Jaspers may regret not having this faith (or the opposite but equally comforting unbelief), but he certainly cannot give it to himself: he has to master its secular version through the efforts of philosophic Reason.

XI Transcendental Logic

It may be helpful to recall at this point the general trend we have been pursuing in the last couple of chapters. At the outset of this section we decided to inquire into the possibility of a non-objective philosophy. Is it true, we asked, that philosophic thought can penetrate beyond the limits of objective knowledge without running aground in amorphous feeling or undisciplined mysticism? Can Reason transform our ordinary understanding in such a way that our reflection is able to come into contact with Being itself? We saw that Jaspers seems to claim an affirmative answer to these questions. We also saw that his answer takes in both the existential and the rational aspects of the question, and that these aspects complement each other, making his philosophy a dialectical balance between Existence and Reason. Chapters IX and X dealt with the existential aspects of the question, and tried to show that philosophy is rooted in the concrete possibilities and attitudes of Existence. Now we shall turn to the rational aspect and try to see what rational form this philosophy will take. Thinking, which in the existential part of our meditation only showed itself *in actu exercito*, will now become the explicit theme of our reflection. This reflection will endeavour to render an account of some further possibilities of thought, thereby promoting a greater philosophical self-awareness. Reason, which up to now operated behind the scenes, will step into the spot-light. Instead of the different existential contents of thought our attention will now concentrate upon the very conditions of the thinking activity whereby these contents are revealed to us. Briefly, the accent will now swing from *reality* to the manifestation of reality, which is truth.[1]

The framework of this new presentation will be the Enveloping and all its modalities. A very brief and schematic description in Part I has indicated what considerations brought Jaspers to the concept of the Enveloping. We may recall that he arrived at the idea from the basic philosophical insight that all particular distinctions made by intentional consciousness take place within certain horizons which envelop these distinctions and make them possible. Any distinction is a distinction only against a larger background. Even the very fundamental dichotomy of subject and object is carried by such an encompassing ground from which subject and object emerge when they confront each other in intentional thought. From this Jaspers concluded that Being as a whole cannot rightly be thought of in either objective or subjective terms, but must be seen as the Enveloping which manifests itself to us in the diverse polarities between subject and object that constitute intentional thought. The Enveloping and its modes are, therefore, the various trans-objective possibilities of Being for us. We become aware of these modes when we try to go beyond the subject-object-dichotomy and reach the ground that makes this dichotomy possible.

I have called these modes trans-objective in order to indicate that one achieves some apprehension of them by piercing 'through the objects'. A more current locution would be to call them 'transcendental'. This latter term has the advantage of suggesting that the Enveloping is the fruit of a transcendental consideration and that it is tributary to the making of a sort of transcendental logic, that is, a logic which is concerned not so much with the content, order, and connection of intentional representations as with the ontological conditions that make such representations possible for us. In fact, at one point Jaspers defines the Enveloping as 'the condition under which Being becomes actually Being-for-us.'[2] Elsewhere, he describes the philosophy of the Enveloping as 'a non-objective mode of reflection' which, unlike symbolism, concentrates on 'the transcendental possibilities of Being-for-us', rather than on the existential content of ciphers.[3] Mr Thomas Räber judiciously points out that the expression 'possibility of Being for us' must be taken quite literally here. 'This becomes evident', he says, 'when we consider that for Jaspers Being as such is already "for us", and that sheer Being in itself does not exist for him.'[4] Then he goes on to explain that Jaspers' existential elucidations already bear on *Being which* is for us, but that the philosophy of the Enveloping does more: it explicitly envisages this *Being in so far* as it is Being for us.[5] On closer scrutiny, this is the difference between the approach of *Philosophie*, which I have treated in the last two chapters, and that of the *Philosophische*

Logik, which I now propose to examine briefly. This latter work thematises the various modes of the Enveloping as the very conditions that make it possible for Being to become *Für-uns-sein*, Being revealed to us. As such, it constitutes a kind of transcendental logic. The subject will be truth.

As we shall see, however, this logic will not altogether neglect the reality content in favour of formal truth, Existence in favour of Reason.[6] The genius of this logic is precisely that it maintains a dialectical balance and tension between the two aspects of philosophy, namely reality and truth, Existence and Reason, in all the modes of the Enveloping. This tension 'will allow neither a synthesis nor a complete separation' of these two aspects.[7] The search for truth will be, by the same impetus, also a reaching for reality. Here we shall see again the balance in Jaspers' thinking: he is trying honestly to bridge over the separation between reflection and realisation created by the Kantian *Critique* without ending up in a triumphant Hegelian synthesis. Between the Pure Reason of Kant and the Absolute Idea of Hegel stands Jaspers' existential Reason, which cannot settle either in separation or in a deceptive reconciliation. It can do no more than explore incessantly all the modes of the Enveloping in order to gather and bind together whatever intelligibility can be found in each. This is why the truth of this logic is 'neither a norm, nor an adequation, nor a value, nor a system of totality,' remarks Fr Tilliette. Rather, he notes, 'it coincides with the Enveloping and the movement that develops in it.'[8]

Since the extremely detailed table of contents at the beginning of *Von der Wahrheit* gives a fairly complete idea of the scope and articulation of this enveloping logic and makes the treatment of particular structural questions unnecessary, we may turn to a set of more fundamental questions about it. We might, for instance, try to discover Jaspers' beliefs concerning the relationship of thought and reality. How does thinking reflect reality? Does transcendental thinking have a logical form at all? What are the basic characteristics and purposes of transcendental logic? These inquiries could yield us some valuable information towards an eventual definition of philosophical Reason. They might also indicate again (this time from the expressly rational side) how Jaspers proposes to transcend mere knowledge through thought, mere understanding through Reason.

THE PRIMACY OF THOUGHT

We know the modes of the Enveloping, we have seen their main divisions. We have noted also that their number and articulation present some grave difficulties. For example, the very plurality of the modes seems to be shocking since the very idea of transcending to the Enveloping suggests leaving behind the subject-object-dichtomy and penetrating to Being which embraces both subject and object. To transcend seems to mean to advance towards unity which excludes multiplicity and variation. Jaspers is aware of this difficulty and answers it by saying that the one and only Enveloping splinters immediately into several modes as soon as we try to clarify its content.[9] This fact is for Jaspers an expression of our finite approach to the Enveloping which, for us, must take on finite perspectives again and again. Even the transcending reflection on Being must always and again pass through the Envelopings that we are, that is to say, it must become Being-for-us. Although absolute Being surpasses the relative Envelopings that we are, its clarification is, nevertheless, conditioned by the latter.[10] This means practically that the unity of Being, even in transcendental thinking, can only be experienced through an uninterrupted dialectical movement to and from the different modes of the Enveloping.[11]

I shall come back to this question later on. Here I must bypass the objections that could be brought against Jaspers' thesis. Instead of dealing with these, I would simply like to ask him to tell us about the relative importance of these various modes, for, in spite of the unresolved difficulties, I have the distinct impression that these modes are not thrown together haphazardly, but that they form a sort of hierarchy, a sort of internally articulated structure. Although we know that they are not derived either from a common principle or from each other, there seems to be a difference of rank or value or priority among them. Indeed, Jaspers' text bears out this impression: 'Among all the Envelopings there is one mode which, for logical presentation, enjoys priority: thinking.'[12] 'Thinking has a formal priority, not a priority of being or value. The priority of thought signifies that no mode of the Enveloping can be present to us or become effective in us unless its content takes shape in the medium of thinking.'[13] Thought enjoys this formal priority on account of its all-pervading presence and its unifying effect on the various dimensions of reality. Thought is the activity that relates everything, and everything else is in some way related to thinking. Jaspers almost says that everything else exists for the sake of thinking: 'Thought has its formal priority, firstly, because it penetrates everywhere, because nothing can withdraw itself from its contact. Everything else becomes matter, impulse, meaning and goal, content and fulfilment of thought.'[14] It should be needless to remark that thinking is an activity specific to man's essence. It is in man and through man's thinking that reality emerges into light and is invested with meaning. It is man alone who can relate to reality, who can experience it, penetrate it, assimilate it, bring it into his presence through his thinking. Even though the sheer actuality of some of the other modes has real priority over thinking, yet this priority itself can only be brought to light by thinking. It is thought that formally confers this priority on reality by acknowledging the irreducibility of being to thinking. Secondly, thinking creates order and cohesion among the various levels of reality. 'There is nowhere the single, true, and finally correct form of the Enveloping in time. Thinking is the thorn (*Stachel*) which forces the multiple modes into correlation with one another; thinking is the medium of movement in the Whole.'[15]

Nevertheless, we are warned by Jaspers that in this privileged position of thinking there lurks a great danger. Thought, after having laid open and shaped into order the multiple layers of reality, can become empty thinking, endlessly revolving in abstractions and formalisms. This happens when thought is detached from being and becomes its own end. 'The originally positive aspect of opening up possibilities becomes in formalisation something negative, which destroys everything serious in reality.'[16] This danger is all but inevitable and is linked with the general risks of human destiny itself. Our human condition is such that reality is not immediately open or accessible to us. We must first disclose it, bring it out of its original hiddenness. This we do by endless inquiry of thought, because only thought can open up and liberate the possibilities of reality for us.[17] It is possible for us to lose ourselves in this endless questioning. 'This fate of thinking is our destiny which is not quite in our power to control.'[18] As a destiny, thinking is both our vocation and our downfall. So is the accompanying formalisation to which thinking is attracted by a near fatal gravitation. To know reality, to think, to disclose Being, inevitably involves the creation of forms and thought patterns which tend to become the *a priori* rules of Being in the sense that we measure reality by intelligibility, thereby reducing the real to the thinkable. However, in spite of this danger we cannot, and must not, give up thinking, since it is also our vocation. 'This destiny of our humanity must have its origin in the ground of Being itself. There lies the reason why everything that exists, everything that we are or can be, rushes to be disclosed through us.'[19] This idea is becoming quite familiar to us; we have met it repeatedly. According to this idea, an ancient desire for self-disclosure runs through the ground of Being and finds its outlet in man's rational being. This means that in a certain sense Being is synonymous with truth. Truth, we must recall, was defined by Jaspers as the unconcealment of Being. The various modes of reality are nothing else than the multiple ways in which Being opens itself and reveals itself to us, and the various ways of this unconcealment constitute the manifold forms of truth.[20] Originally, thinking derives its truth from these modes; its truth is ontologically based. Later, however, it can formally detach itself from the multiple manifestations of reality and arrogate all truth to itself. That is when formalisation and logicism sets in, and that is the danger we must avoid.

To counteract this formalisation, we must realise that there is truth in all the modes of Being's unconcealment, in all the modes of the Enveloping. There is truth in action, in feeling, in a gesture or a look, in art, in poetry and music, because something of Being is disclosed in each of them. Formal thinking cannot replace what is revealed or communicated to us in all these modes.

Nevertheless, this poses a difficult problem which Jaspers never answers in a satisfactory manner. The problem is this: what is philosophical logic to do if, on the one hand, it must concern itself with *all* truth, while, on the other hand, its professional tool inevitably tends to run into formalisation and to convert all other truth into formal-logical truth? Jaspers can only answer, rather obscurely, that this logic will present truths *in* thinking which are the truths *of* thinking. So doing, it will integrate these other truths into an *organon* of philosophical life.[21] But he is not clear on how this is to ward off the dangers of formalisation.

15

Another puzzling thing at this point is the fact that Jaspers is discussing the primacy of an Enveloping which, as such, did not figure in the previously outlined scheme of the Envelopings. Which of the seven modes does he identify with 'thinking'? To which of them does he attribute formal priority? Is it General Consciousness? It would seem so. 'In fact,' says Jaspers, 'the form of thought has its origin there.' But then he adds that the kind of thinking he has in mind is different. The thought that has priority for transcendental logic is not simply the product of General Consciousness, but the effect of this Consciousness 'transcending itself'.[22]

But is it possible to transcend General Consciousness? In reply, Jaspers submits the following line of thought: we can never step over the confines of General Consciousness. Go as far as we like, we remained enclosed in it. However, there is a great difference between being actually confined within Consciousness and yet unaware of it, and being equally confined but knowing about our confinement. It is precisely this difference that accounts for the possibility of transcending. In the first case, we tend to imagine that we can have all reality in our cognitive grasp; in the second, we can at least 'have our ears against the wall' and listen for the beyond.[23] One can compare this with what has been said about philosophical faith as a new faculty of listening to the voice of Transcendence. In short, our awareness of the limitedness of General Consciousness liberates our thought and makes it transcend what it cannot overstep. Transcending thought, then, seems to be the thought that is aware of its own limits. To know about limits is to transcend them.[24]

As to the agent of this transcending, Jaspers has the following to say: 'That this transcending takes place, that universality is willed radically, arises not from General Consciousness, but from the ensemble of the modes of the Enveloping that we are. All of them rush towards the light through which they first genuinely come into being; they are all Reason in this sense.'[25] What Jaspers is describing here is a mode of thinking that has come to be known as existential thought. Advocates of existential thought claim that genuine human thinking, thinking which traditionally came to be recognised as the principal attribute of our essential humanity, involves more than a disembodies cogitation of a Cartesian thinking substance. They insist that thought expresses the concerted thrust of the total human substance towards clarity and being. Reason and rationality, far from being limited to the operations of the *cogito*, include, and contribute to, all the other dimensions of human existence. Only in this enveloping sense can Reason break the confines of the immanence of consciousness and contact concrete reality in its transcendence. Transcending, then, is the operation of Reason.

However, Jaspers tries to indicate that the goal of this operation is not reached all at once, but in two successive stages; that it is possible to talk about incomplete transcendence and partial rationality, depending on which modes of the Enveloping we include in the unifying operations of Reason. Noting that all the modes of the Enveloping strive towards a rational end, he tries to discern what this end is. He sees that, in fact, this end is a four-fold one: logical clarity, totality, universality, and law-likeness. But then he remarks immediately that this is not yet the full aim of transcending. Although, in a first effort, Reason also drives the modes of the Enveloping in this direction, it 'aims beyond these goals, not only because it cannot find satisfaction in any clarity, totality, or order, but also because it is open to the essentially unclear, the genuinely fragmentary, and to the anti-rational itself.'[26] In other words, the rationality to which the modes of the Enveloping are first driven by Reason is only a minimum: 'That which is logically graspable, non-contradictory, univocally known by General Consciousness, is rational in the narrowest sense, the understandable.'[27] This degree of rationality, while necessary as a first approximation, is not yet the final goal of transcending thought and does not yet constitute the foundation of its primacy. The reason for this is easily discernible from Jaspers' diagram of the modes of the Enveloping. The modes which here are gathered by Reason and which tend towards this minimum of rationality are only the immanent modes (Empirical Being, General Consciousness, Spirit) and do not include Existence which is designated precisely as the 'trans-cendent mode of the Enveloping that we are'. And if we recall that Existence is also the ground (*Boden*) of all the Envelopings, we might say that the rationality realised in this first phase is still 'groundless' or 'ungrounded'. The incompleteness of this phase can be seen also from the fact that the unity of thought, the highest goal of full-blown Reason, is not yet reached in the four-fold aim mentioned above. 'Reason seeks unity,' says Jaspers, 'but not just any sort of unity for its own sake. It seeks the oneness that embraces all.'[28] The partial unity proper to the operations of the intellect (*Verstandeseinheit*) itself calls for an ultimate oneness 'in which nothing is lost and everything is dissolved and preserved (*aufgehoben*).'[29] Reason always enters the scene in the form of understanding. Understanding, since it is the activity of General Consciousness, already enlarges this Consciousness. Reason, however, as the *organon* of the total existential reality of man, has the further capacity of also transcending Consciousness.

This brings us to a final point of Jaspers' view on the goal of transcending thought. 'The communicability of thought which passes beyond the understanding of General Consciousness comes to forms, which eventually run counter to the understanding (*verstandeswidrig sind*). Through Reason I catch sight of something which is communicable only in the form of contradiction and paradox. Here a rational a-logic arises, a true Reason which reaches its goal in the shattering of the logic of the intellect.'[30] The statement is clear in itself: the final goal of transcending is to run counter to the thinking of the intellect, thereby to inaugurate the full reign of Reason which is the source of philosophical logic, in the form of a rational a-logic. Paradox and contradiction, ultimately inadmissible and senseless for the intellect, are the necessary forms of communication of this a-logic.

Transcendental logic, then, is this a-logic that grows out of the totality of the modes of Enveloping. Under the joint impulse of Reason and Existence, thought is able to explore its own transcendental possibilities, possibilities that lie beyond the limits of ordinary logic. Once these limits are transcended, logic is replaced by a-logic.

We must now briefly examine this a-logic, briefly because its principal elements of paradox and contradiction are already known to us from Existence-elucidation. However, we must be prepared to meet some insurmountable difficulties in trying to show the rapport between ordinary logic and rational a-logic. All of these difficulties originate in the fact that the relationship between these two modes of thought is actually transcendental and enveloping. A-logic constantly envelops logic, without really absorbing it, so that their relationship cannot be described logically.

RATIONAL A-LOGIC

For a first illustration of rational a-logic, Jaspers takes the case of Kant's transcendental analytics. In this part of the *Critique*, Kant has tried to derive the categories of understanding (e.g. 'unity', 'plurality', 'substance', 'causality') from the primordial unity of the thinking consciousness, the unity of transcendental apperception, as it is called. Ultimately, it is this unity that binds all that we ever encounter into the unity of an object. It is also this unity from which the lesser unities of concepts and categories are derived. Kant noted that this unity of consciousness, since it is *a priori* to all concepts as acts of synthesis, is not at all identical with the category 'unity', the first category of Quantity. 'Thus', Jaspers comments, 'Kant requires us in thinking through categories—and, according to him, we cannot think otherwise— to grasp something which does not come under the categories. This he had to do since he wanted to touch upon the origin of all objectivity which itself could not be objective. Thus, I must think something non-objective objectively, something which grounds the categories (including that of unity) under the category of unity.'[31] This, Jaspers claims, results either in a circle: unity is explained through unity, or in a contradiction: unity is not unity.

It is doubtful whether Kant would have accepted such an exegesis. For one thing, it is not at all certain that Kant had ever regarded transcendental apperception as non-objective just because he held it to be the condition of objectivity. The fact that Kant proposed it as the transcendental ground, justification, and condition of possibility for all ulterior objectivity seems to argue, on the contrary, that he considered it the only sure objectivity that ultimately there is. That this condition is found in consciousness rather than in the objects of consciousness (the specifically Kantian point lies here) does not necessarily make it non-objective. It is non-objective only from the point of view of Jaspers' special definition of objectivity which, for all practical purposes, is equivalent to univocal determinateness. Evidently, in that sense, the original apperception is not objective, not univocally determined, but precisely transcendental and analogous. Similarly, the unity of this apperception is circular or contradictory only if we take unity in the univocal sense, which Kant does not. He distinguishes between the synthetic unity of the categories and the noumenal unity of consciousness. Although, like any other noumenal aspect of reality, this unity can only be grasped phenomenally through one of the categories, the unity proper to consciousness is not the same as the unity proper to the categories. The former explains, grounds, and makes the latter possible, because the former is a simple unity, whereas the latter is always the result of an active synthesis of the multiple.

But perhaps the real crux of the matter is not whether Jaspers is right or wrong in interpreting the intention of Kant, but whether he is right or wrong *sans plus*. Perhaps there *is* a circle and a contradiction which Kant did not intend or notice, but which in practice he had no way of avoiding because it goes with the very nature of his reflection. Perhaps transcendental reflection does involve these logical breakdowns. Can the ultimate and total condition of all objectivity be itself objective, regardless of whether Kant thought so or not? Can we extend the claims of objectivity so far as to make it applicable even to analogous notions without contradicting ourselves at some point? Is it or is it not really circular to derive the multiplicity of categories from transcendental unity which, in turn, we can grasp only in terms of one of these categories?

It is as if to anticipate questions such as these that Jaspers next takes a look at the process by which these alleged circles and contradictions arise. He is convinced that 'in all genuine philosophies we find such circles and contradictions at decisive points, whether it is a question of metaphysics, transcendental reflection, or Existence elucidation. And everywhere one sees the critics at work, triumphantly exposing these shortcomings and imagining that thereby the criticised philosophy is demolished.'[32]

In order to indicate, therefore, that these circles and contradictions are unavoidable by the very nature of transcendental reflection, he again has recourse to the concept of self-reference or self-reflexivity, which we have already seen in a similar context elsewhere. He shows that the heart of all philosophical statement involves precisely this self-reference on which strict objectivity must come to grief. His reasoning is simple and can be reduced in substance to the following: unlike science which inquires about distinct and determined things in the world, one alongside the other, genuine philosophical speculation sets out to penetrate the totality and unity of all things by going back or descending into their fundamental origin. Consequently, its object 'is something which, if it is to be touched upon, can permit nothing outside itself when we think of it since it is the fundamental origin, be it Being itself, or the condition of all objectivity, as in Kantian philosophy, or it may be Existence.'[33] Under any one of these aspects, a philosophical 'object' is enveloping, infinite, absolute. Enveloping means precisely that it is not something alongside other objects, but that it 'penetrates, rules and governs' the others. The others depend on it (here only their logical dependence is considered) while it does not depend on them. Now, thoughts and statements about such an object necessarily provoke self-reflexivity, that is, while we explain everything by reference to this object, we must explain it by itself. We say it is self-explanatory; it is its own point of reference.

There are two remarks to be made here, First, we must recall Gerhard Knauss' observation, quoted in Part II, that an enveloping object always turns out to be a logically impossible object, because in regard to it the fundamental logical operation of disjunctive determination breaks down. The object of philosophy (inasmuch as it is the Whole, the Enveloping, the One, the First, the Ultimate, or whatever name it goes by) satisfies both sides of any possible disjunction; both an affirmation and a denial of the same predicate becomes applicable to it. Thus, for instance, Being can be said to be both similar and dissimilar, the same and different, in every being. Here logic contradicts itself, because it must use the same reference point twice: once for the affirmation and then for the negation of the same quality. Differently put, it must invoke the same subject as the total reason for two opposing predicates. At this level, it is of very little use to introduce aspects and co-principles in order to doctor up our tottering logic. They may provide a temporary relief by bandaging over the contradiction, but eventually they may do more harm than good. We may save logic for a while by saying, for instance, that beings are different in so far as they are each this or that limited being, but the same in so far as they all partake in the perfection of being. They are *simpliciter diversum, sed secundum quid unum*. They are composed of essence and existence which respectively explain their differentiation and their sameness. But we can speak in this way only because we are talking about beings, individually or collectively ('a heap of things'), but when we come to their Origin, their Ground, to Being itself, we must invoke *that* as the explanation of both their limitation and their perfection. Being itself must account for both the difference and the sameness of things. Being is the ground of both essence and existence. In regard to the ultimate, therefore, we must affirm that in it either the two aspects are absent or else they coincide, without knowing how that is possible. Thus, in the end, the logic of the ultimate is necessarily an antinomic one. The harm lies in the fact—and that is my second point—that just because we are able to side-step the antinomies on the ontic level, we imagine that we can do the same on the metaphysical level also, and begin to treat metaphysical statements as if they were logical ones. Wanting it or not, we thereby make their content relative and no longer transcendental. 'If we treat the content of philosophical ideas as one reference point next to another (which we inevitably do when we make logical assertions about it), then, as so expressed, it is no longer the philosophical content. Therefore, such assertions must be reversed.'[34]

And how are such assertions to be reversed? They are reversed by the contradictions of a-logic. 'The thinking of that which is inaccessible to the intellect takes on the appearance of a logical impossibility or insolubility, where what is asserted as an alleged cognition of something cancels itself out. Only thus can we reach the point where the essential sense of philosophical thinking is not displaced by a false insight of mere understanding.'[35] By contrast, every philosophy that wants to improve itself into an unambiguous and logical system by removing or denying its circles and contradictions 'falls flat on its face, as it were, and becomes totally empty.'[36]

If the main lines of this reasoning are correct, then it would seem that it is logic itself that demands this final leap of thought into Being where, instead of enveloping its object, itself is enveloped by it. It appears that this last exertion of thinking is made on logical grounds, so that the resulting a-logic is really a rational one. A-logic is not the abdication of Reason, rather the expansion of it. Reason in all its forms is indispensable even for a-logic. This may explain, at least partially, one of Jaspers' often quoted cryptic phrases, 'I have non-knowledge itself only through knowledge, and perfect non-knowledge through a maximum of understanding.'[37] Even though they cannot be extended indefinitely in their objective form, logic and understanding play an important role in the development of philosophical consciousness that transcends the boundaries of logic and understanding. With regard to the enveloping origin of thought, understanding breaks down and logic turns into circles and contradictions. However, this does not mean that once the turning-point of transcending is reached logic is abandoned altogether in favour of a-logic, understanding discarded in favour of Reason. One should not forget that understanding *is* already reason, reason under an inchoate aspect, but reason just the same. Knowledge, science and logic are retained to serve as dialectical counterpoints to non-knowledge, philosophy, and a-logic. Jaspers never tires of repeating that the result of transcendental thought is not a new and improved sort of knowledge that would somehow replace the old and imperfect ways of understanding, but a change in our attitude towards Being, a change which 'silently brings forth an unconcealment and transformation in the inmost being of man.'[38] This new attitude is that of open Reason which rejects the arbitrary option between logic or a-logic, because such an option would either restrict Reason to the narrow confines of logicism or drown it in undisciplined mysticism. There is thoughtlessness in both. Reason, on the contrary, must keep itself open for all the modes of reality and for all the possibilities of thinking and try to bind and recollect them all. Open Reason desires both *clarity*, the glory of logical understanding, and *unity*, the transcendent aim of rational a-logic. 'In the rational attitude I desire clarity without limits. I try to know scientifically in order to grasp the empirically real and the compelling validities of the thinkable, but at the same time, I also live with the awareness of the limits of scientific penetrability and of clarity in general. Still, I push forward from all the sources of the enveloping modes towards a universal unfolding of thinking, and reject thoughtlessness everywhere.'[39]

The difference between Jaspers and his immediate spiritual ancestors is best seen at this point. He is certainly a Kantian in the main lines of his thought, but his version of the *Critique* does not stop with the division of Reason into two separate faculties:

theoretical and practical reason. The two are joined by Jaspers in the dialectical tension of existential Reason. This tension is permanent and is never slackened in favour of a triumphant resolution or reconciliation. In this regard, Jaspers differs from Hegel. Hegel also recognised an initial tension between *Verstand* and *Vernunft*, only to reconcile them in the dialectic of absolute Reason. For Jaspers, 'Reason is always too little when enclosed, once and for all, in determinate forms; and always too much when it appears as its own substance.'[40] He cannot admit either to definitive separation or to final reconciliation. He is midway between Kant's transcendental logic and Hegel's absolute logic in so far as he affirms the unity of Reason in tension.

The difference between Jaspers' and Hegel's thought could also be expressed in the following way: Hegel started with contradiction which he claimed to surmount in a final synthesis of non-contradictory knowledge, Jaspers, on the other hand, recognised that it is precisely on the level of transcendental reflection that contradiction is unavoidable. By contradiction he means the logical impossibility of resolving the opposition of contrary concept pairs by means of which Being must ultimately be thought of. He does not see his way beyond recognising and affirming the opposites.

However, his acceptance of contradiction is not a simple one, because he feels that a tired sort of resignation to contradiction would be a false posture in philosophy. He recognises the fact that the first movement of Reason is towards understanding, which is animated by an ineradicable will to clarity, coherence, and non-contradiction. But he also knows that, beyond these goals, Reason also strives for comprehensive unity. It is double awareness that lends a distinctly dialectical and polemic character to Jaspers' philosophy. On one hand, he insists that perfect coherence of thought cannot be maintained once we rise to the level of transcendental reflection. On the other hand, he struggles with contradiction, and refuses to succumb to it without a fight. 'It is impossible to accept contradiction, to negate the condition of knowledge through knowledge, so to speak.'[41] Finally, the idea matures in his mind that perhaps the best way to deal with contradiction is to 'radically consummate it' (*radikal vollziehen*). 'This means that I think something which in thought dissolves itself into nothing, but in such a way that in the very process of this dissolution Being itself is revealed to me indirectly. This is the immemorial way of speculative thinking which apprehends Transcendence through contradictories. Now, all statements which assert a *coincidentia oppositorum* are contradictory. But Being, which is not a mere finite entity (*Seiendes*), not a determined thing next to another, demands to be thought of in this way in order that it may be distinguished from finite being which is accessible to our knowing. The dissolution of thinkability is the form (*Gestalt*) through which we overcome finitude and touch upon the Infinite.'[42]

Transcendental a-logic is at times designated by Jaspers as a 'knowing of knowing', *Wissen des Wissens, Wissen vom Wissen.*[43] The expression suggests either a sort of meta-logic or some kind of absolute knowledge. Actually, it is neither of these. Knowing of knowing is not a particular science, but simply the possibility of explicating the implicit awareness that accompanies factual knowledge in all its modes and on all levels. By virtue of this awareness we know that we know, and the explication of it assures the critical quality of our knowledge, because it sorts out what we know from what we do not and cannot know, but merely assume that we know. Therefore, knowing of knowing or knowing about knowing is fundamental to philosophical reflection. Jaspers calls it the very 'self-awareness of Reason'.[44] At the same time, knowing about knowing also denotes a deep existential dimension of knowledge, in so far as it refers to the presence of the thinking self in all of its particular acts of knowing. Although the awareness of this presence is occasioned by particular acts of knowledge, it really transcends them all. That is why Jaspers calls it 'absolute consciousness', which is not the consciousness of an object but of the subjective Existence itself who has this object-consciousness. Absolute consciousness, it should be recalled, is Jaspers' term for Kant's 'transcendental apperception'. Any act of knowledge could, then, be regarded as the result of an encounter between two noumenal presences: Existence and Being itself. And since Being itself can be present in many ways, one could translate the expression 'knowing of knowing' as 'the manifold appearances of Being to the self-presence of Existence'.

Thus, transcendental logic is not only the fruit of critical Reason, but also the work of self-conscious Existence. Existence

Reason Revisited

has this infinite appetite for all the modes of reality. This is why Jaspers remarks: 'It is not enough to say: be rational! but rather: be rational out of Existence, or better still, out of all the modes of the Enveloping.'[45]

THE PRINCIPAL QUALITIES OF PHILOSOPHICAL LOGIC

According to Jaspers, philosophical logic must be characterised by three main qualities. The following is a summary of these distinguishing characteristics:

(1) *Comprehensiveness:* To be truly a knowing about knowing, philosophical logic must embrace *all* the possible modes and ways in which Being can be present to us, all manner of certitude, knowledge, awareness. It may exclude or forget nothing. Even though logic concerns itself mainly with the sciences since these are the clearest forms of objective knowledge, it may not neglect the other forms of everyday thought and experience. Logic must be anchored in, and relate to, the precategorial and transcategorial range of experience, even though its communication must, by necessity, take place in logical categories. This quality of inclusiveness explains the vast scope of Jaspers' *Philosophische Logik*, which treats of such far-ranging topics as 'working thought', 'managerial thinking', 'playful thinking', 'art', 'drama and poetry', because all of these, and many more, are ways in which Being presents itself to us. According to James Collins, Jaspers' logic 'does not pretend to be an independent and closed system, but it does undertake a systematic inspection of all the ways of "being for us", of being as it is made available in the cognition, experience, and pursuits of man.'[46] Perhaps one could call this the phenomenological or descriptive aspect of philosophical logic.

(2) *Discernment:* According to Jaspers, ordinary logic, the logic of the intellect, operates with the presupposition that everything knowable is of the same type of intelligibility, 'is situated on the same level', as he puts it. The intellect naturally assumes that all knowability is 'essentially the same' and universally evident. By contrast, 'philosophical logic recognises discontinuities (*Sprünge*) in the modes of Being and in the modes of knowing them. It distinguishes and sees the limits of each mode.'[47] The philosophical knowing of knowing consists, therefore, in discerning how these various modes of knowledge are articulated by degrees,

spheres, and leaps into an organic network of truth-relations. Philosophical logic examines the peculiar character of each mode of knowing and relates it to the rest. One could perhaps call this aspect of philosophical logic its critical quality.

(3) *Unity:* In order to counteract the splintering effect of constant distinguishing which tends to break up Being and thought into an endless multiplicity of modes, philosophical logic also looks to the whole. 'Resolute as it is in recognising the limits of each mode of Being and thinking (rejecting their muddy mixture and averting their allegedly facile transitions), it is no less resolute in seeking their unity in such a way that it permits nothing to stand isolated, but rather endeavours to relate everything to everything.'[48] In this search, logic is guided by the ideals of unity and totality of Being and thought, without pretending, however, that any of the achievements it has reached so far constitute the ultimate realisation of these ideals. The unity it seeks is subject to progressive realisation. The shape it will take cannot be outlined in advance. As a result, philosophy has a more or less clear past and perhaps a general direction towards the future, but that is all: its final form is not in sight yet. In other words, its unity and totality is in becoming, not yet determined. Because we do not possess the end, the task of philosophical logic is so to organise the acquired truths of its past that it does not obstruct, but rather keeps open, the ways of unpredictable future possibilities of truth. According to Jaspers, our epoch is indeed witnessing the emergence of a new and encompassing logic. We are participants in an awesome and thrilling change in the very nature of man, a change largely due to the transformation of his knowledge. Nobody knows and nobody can predict the results of this transformation. This third quality might be called the eschatological dimension of philosophical logic.

As has been noted, the light through which logic becomes conscious of its own scope is the light of Reason; or better still, the very self-awareness of logic is identical with the self-awareness of Reason. The width and breadth of this logic allows the omnipresence of rationality to appear. The openness of this logic shows the openness of Reason. On this account, it would be more correct to speak of logic as a *process* of Reason, rather than a *system* of Reason. Logic is Reason becoming-conscious-of-itself (*Selbstbewusstwerden*). The clarity of this consciousness grows to the extent that we explore the various modes of Being for us, without ever reaching a stage that would be its full measure.

This process of Reason becoming conscious of itself should not be understood as a simple psychological self-reflection. It requires an act of transcendental reflection. Transcendental reflection forces knowledge to return upon itself, away from its objects.[49] This is not as natural and easy as it may sound, because what Reason finds in returning upon itself is not an object, but a source (*Ursprung*). Transcendental reflection requires a veritable about-face, inversion (*Umkehrung*), or conversion (*Bekehrung*) of our object-bound natural attitude. This conversion demands a great deal of exertion of the part of Reason. The new logic is a matter of struggle. 'Reason is not easy but difficult to realise,' says Jaspers.[50]

It can be realised only if individuals make it part of their personal formative process. They must become 'wholly involved and interested in it, if this logic is to succeed.'[51] In other words, it cannot be learned or taught from a detached and safe distance. Philosophical logic, as we already know, is an act of Existence.

Logic, understood in this way as an *organon* of Reason, belongs to philosophy from its immemorial beginnings. Jaspers claims even more: 'It is itself the *prima philosophia*, the foundation of true thinking, feeling, experiencing in general,' because it is by means of this logic that rationality is perfected in all its amplitude.[52]

XII Philosophical Reason

LET us now summarise the principal stages of thought examined in the last chapter. We have seen that the field of inquiry for philosophical logic is the Enveloping and all its modes. Among these modes, formal priority belongs to thinking because it is thinking that brings the other modes to light. The universal organ of thinking is Consciousness in general, but the ground from which it rises is found in all the modes of the Enveloping that we are.

Rationality is achieved at a first level, when we produce logical clarity, universality, and order in our thinking. But this minimum of rationality of the understanding is transcended when Existence, the transcendent mode of the Enveloping that we are, joins the other immanent modes, and by means of Reason drives our thinking to a rational a-logic.

Jaspers has tried to show that this transcending process, leading from intellectual logic to rational a-logic, is part and parcel of all truly philosophical thinking which wants to render a comprehensive account of all the aspects of reality. All statements dealing with Being as such inevitably take the form of logical circles and contradictions, which constitute the basic figures of this a-logic. Of course, the presence of these contradictions causes upheavals in our thinking and forces it to reflect on its own nature and limits: contradictions make thinking aware of itself. This self-awareness is the work of Reason itself, rationality at a second level.

Ultimately, then, the priority of thinking belongs to self-conscious Reason whose work philosophical logic is. This logic is not a special knowledge, but simply knowing about knowing, an act of awareness which accompanies knowledge of facts or contents in all its modes and on all levels. 'Knowing of knowing' signifies more than knowledge: it signifies a critical consciousness of all the modalities in which Being becomes present to us. Since the different ways in which Being becomes present to us are the modes of the Enveloping, philosophical logic consists in the unceasing exploration of these enveloping modes. The driving force of this exploration, as has been noted, is Reason.

In order to see what Reason is, how it operates in philosophy, we must place it in the context of the modes of the Enveloping. From the mass of knotty problems surrounding Reason I would like to pick out three leading threads: the relationship of Reason and Existence; the question of unity through Reason; and Reason in connection with the nature of truth.

EXISTENCE AND REASON

The close alliance of Existence and Reason can already be seen from the foregoing considerations. They are always mentioned together by Jaspers. We saw, for instance, that Reason in the full-blown sense always comes into play in logic when Existence is joined to the immanent modes of the Enveloping. At one point, Reason is called an activity of Existence itself.

The correlatedness of the two is explicitly underscored everywhere in Jaspers' logical works. The importance of these underscorings lies in the fact that they emphasise repeatedly the inseparable unity between the two aspects of Jaspers' philosophy: the existential and the rational. That Reason is not permitted to drift apart from the rest of man's existential pursuits shows that there is no real break between *Philosophie* and *Philosophische Logik*. To recall an earlier remark made by Fr Tilliette, Jaspers' thought 'is not alternately a philosophy of Existence and, through a kind of internal violence, a philosophy of Reason.' To evaluate Jaspers' philosophy under a purely existential light would be inadequate.

This close relationship between Existence and Reason is variously stated by Jaspers. Here are some representative texts. All of them say more or less the same thing, namely, that neither Existence nor Reason can be authentic without the other:

The great poles of our being which encounter each other in every mode of the Enveloping are, therefore, Reason and Existence. They are inseparable. Each of them disappears when the other gets lost.[1]

Existence becomes *clear* only through Reason; Reason has *content* only through Existence.[2]

Reason is in need of something else: of the substance of selfhood which supports it, which clarifies itself by Reason, and which gives

decisive impulses to Reason. Reason without this support would be
mere understanding, and as Reason groundless. Just as the concepts
of understanding are empty without intuition, so also Reason is
hollow without Existence. . . . Existence (depending as it does on
Reason, through whose clarity it first experiences the unrest and
beckoning of Transcendence) comes into real motion under the goad
of Reason's questioning. Without Reason, Existence is inactive,
sleeping, and as though not there.[3]

Reason without Existence, for all its possible wealth, finally passes into
indifferent thinking, a merely intellectual movement of General
Consciousness, or into a dialectic of the Spirit. As it slips away into
intellectual universality, without the binding root of its historicity, it
ceases to be Reason.[4]

Existence without Reason, which rests on feeling, experiencing, un-
questioning impulse, instinct, or whim, ends up as blind violence, and
thereby comes under the general laws which govern these forces of
empirical reality. Without historicity, lost in the particularity of contingent empirical existence with its self-assertion that is unrelated to
Transcendence, Existence ceases to be Existence.[5]

These texts need no commentary: they speak for themselves.
They depict the poverty of Reason that is left to itself, and the
brutality of Existence that barricades itself against Reason. In
both cases, it is philosophy itself that suffers by lapsing either into
narrow rationalism or into a fatuous irrationalism. Both of these
are disfigurements of the true philosophical ethos. Reason and
Existence are twin supports of philosophy, for philosophy 'is the
interior of discipline of man's total being'.[6] One could almost
agree with Jean Paumen, who maintains that the specific climate
of Jaspers' philosophy is provided by this complementarity of
Reason and Existence.[7] Almost, because in the Jaspersian scheme
of things complementarity (in the sense of *Sichergänzen*) is proper
to the relationship between the immanent modes of the Enveloping, whereas the relationship between Reason and Existence is
called a *polarity*.[8] It is true, of course, that for Jaspers the interplay
between Reason and Existence characterises the specific climate
of philosophy, but this interplay should not be regarded as a
simple complementarity. As the German word suggests, in
complementarity the separate complements come together to
form an integral whole, whereas in polarity the poles never exist
separately at all, but only through each other, through their
reciprocal tension. 'They elicit each other mutually' says Jaspers.[9]

16

These points are fairly obvious and clear from the texts themselves. But it can also be shown that the interrelation of Reason
and Existence is much more profound than the above texts would
make us suspect.

In order to do this, we have to return more to the context of
the Enveloping and all its modes. If we look at the first schema,
as it is set down in Part I, we can see that the modes of the
Enveloping fall into three distinct groupings:

(1) *modes of Being, in so far as Being presents itself from without,*
or modes of Being itself. One could call them the objective
modes, for in fact they reflect the first pole of the great primordial
split of object and subject. But in order to avoid the confusion of
suggesting that they are categories of object-being, it would be
better to designate them negatively and, in contrast with the
second group, call them modes of Being 'that we are not ourselves,' or simply modes of *non-I*;

(2) *modes of Being, in so far as Being presents itself from within,* or
modes of Being that we are ourselves. For reasons similar to the
ones given above, we will not call them subjective modes, but
modes of the *I*;

(3) *Reason and Existence*. The curious thing about these two is
that they are not identified either with Being that we are, or with
Being that we are not. They belong neither to the modes of the
I, nor to those of the *non-I*. They form a third and separate group.
In other words, they do not reflect the fundamental split of
Being, rather they reflect Being in its primordial unity. They are
figures of the unique Enveloping, the One.

This already suggests that the origin (as well as the finality) of
these last two modes is the unity of Being itself which encompasses
both the *I* and the *non-I*. Existence is the figure of man's ultimate
oneness in that it envelops the multitude of subjective and
objective elements and acts of his life in the unity of absolute
consciousness. Reason, on the other hand, is the self-revelatory
presence of Being itself in the depth of Existence that gathers its
multiple manifestations into unity, or, as has been remarked
apropos the question of knowing about knowing, Reason
reflects the multiple indwelling of the One in us. As we shall see,
however, this presence of the One in us must be thought of as
a *goal to be achieved* rather than an already accomplished fact; a
call to be followed rather than a datum to be presupposed. Reason

is said to be a 'ceaseless gathering into the One'.[10] Reason is a
vow towards the One which is fulfilled only by a constant
exploration of the multiple.

The situation appears even clearer in the second schema set
out in Part I. There, Existence is ranged among the modes of
the *I*, or the modes of the Enveloping that we are. To be sure,
it is set apart from the others as the transcendent ground which
makes the other modes of the *I* possible. By contrast, Reason
stands altogether outside of the schema in order to indicate that
it is not a mode of the *I*, but only 'the bond of all the modes of
the Enveloping in us'. One could say that Reason has its origin
neither in the *I*, nor in the *non-I*, but rather in both, in so far as
they belong together in the One. Reason *wills* the belonging of
these modes in the One; it is a will-to-unity. Reason has both its
origin and its centre of gravity beyond itself, and even partly
beyond the Self. It is neither subjective nor objective, rather the
in voto identity of the subjective and the objective in the One.

Something similar to this double eccentricity of Reason is
hinted at by Fr Tilliette in one of his comments.[11] The same
thing is quite explicitly stated and elaborated by Thomas Räber,
who writes: 'Reason does not have its origin in the *I*, but in the
One itself, which envelops the *I* and the *non-I*. Therefore, that
which in turn originates in Reason cannot be regarded as though
it had been produced by the *I* alone.' Then he proceeds to draw
some implications of this fact: 'The transcendental consideration
of Being, i.e., the consideration of Being in its being-for-us, is a
consideration which is conducted by Reason. But since Reason
is not reducible either in its provenance or in its aim to the *I*
(rather it comes from the One and seeks the One), the cognitive
tools and schematisms it produces for conducting its consideration
cannot derive solely from the *I* either. In this way, logic, the
transcendental consideration of Being through Reason, . . . seems
able to grasp a mode of Being which, though not the One itself,
nevertheless unites in itself the *I* and the *non-I*.'[12] This mode of
Being, needless to say, is the being of Reason, since it is Being
in Reason.

These remarks are necessary in order to forestall some possible
simplifications and misunderstandings about the interrelation of
Reason and Existence. They are all the more called for as some of
the very texts quoted above lend themselves to some misunder-

standings. For instance, when it was said that Reason is an activity
of selfhood, or that Existence is the substance of Reason, one
might have thought that Reason is merely an accident of
Existence, or that Existence by itself is a sufficient source of
Reason. Now we can see that the case is not quite that simple.
We see that Existence seeks the One through Reason, because
inside Existence there stirs a will which is already the presence of
the One in Reason. We see that Reason is the votive presence of
Being in the depths of man's being. We see that Reason is Being's
pledge of self-revelation to the transcendental self of man. When
it was said that Existence becomes clear only through Reason,
one might have thought that Reason is like a torch which by its
proper light illuminates the dark depths of selfhood. Now we
see that the light it throws on Existence is the light of Being.

These remarks may prove useful from another point of view
also. Some of them may be retained and stored away for a future
attempt at 'defining' Reason according to Jaspers. The following
points may constitute the elements of such an eventual definition:

that Reason is the medium of philosophical logic, that is to
say, the means of a transcendental consideration of Being;

that Reason is a kind of will or dynamism in which the
singularity of Existence encounters the amplitude of reality;

that Reason owes its origin to the convergence of this double
dynamism emanating from both the *I* and the *non-I*;

that Reason, consequently, is neither entirely subjective, nor
entirely objective, but envelops both subject and object in its
impetus towards the One;

that Reason can attain the unity of the One only by moving
constantly within the multiple manifestations of Being.

Finally, then, the relationship of Reason and Existence is
firmly anchored in Being itself. They elicit each other mutually,
because both of them are driven by the same limitless desire
towards the One:

Reason, by its very essence, is something which pushes on towards
the One in complete openness. It will not allow anything to drift
away unrelated, or let anything stand by itself. But as such a drive
towards the One, *Reason is Existence itself,* bound to the One. Existence,
by its very essence, is the unique, historical concretion of the individual.
It wants its eternity before Transcendence, not in the petrifying isolation of its facticity but rather in a limitless communication with others

through which it first becomes what it can really be. As such an openness in communication, *Existence is Reason itself*.[13]

It might appear that there is something Hegelian about this final identification of Reason and Existence. That they should be polar opposites which 'elicit each other mutually,' so that their mutual tension is constitutive of their very being, would not in itself be alien to Jaspers' thought. But here he seems to follow Hegel to the point of reconciling these opposites in a superior term in which they become identified. Perhaps what saves Jaspers from being an out-and-out Hegelian at this point is the fact that the synthesising superior term in which the polar opposites are identified is itself an essentially unfinished, moving, 'contradictory' entity: a will, an impulse, a drive towards the One.

THE WILL TO UNITY

Reason, as we saw, is characterised primarily by a will to unity. This will is said to be the essence of Reason, and on certain occasions, Jaspers purely and simply identifies this will with Reason itself: 'Reason is the will to unity.'[14] It was also indicated that this will originates in both the *I* and the *non-I*, so that we may now set out the following more complete formula: Reason is the will to unity of Being as a whole manifesting itself in Existence.

Furthermore, this will to unity is limitless and completely open. The implications of this fact are various and far-reaching. I shall try to explicate some of them. First of all, this openness implies quite obviously that the unity sought by Reason is not just any unity, but the one and only unity which is possibly unlimited, namely, 'the One that is all'.[15] The object of Reason is this ἕν καὶ πᾶν, from which it proceeds and which it seeks.

This unlimited openness, however, puts Reason into an equivocal position. In order to ward off the fragmentation of the real into an unrelated, unbelonging multiplicity, Reason must gather the multiple manifestations of Being into the unity of its own universal forms, which, however, it must again discard when it comes face to face with the unruly *exception* that flouts the criteria of universality.[16] When the exceptional breaks through the unity of the universal, Reason must still be at hand to patiently receive it into the unity of the All. In order to remain faithful to its own pledge of boundless receptivity, Reason, the principle of order and unity, must find a place even for that which rebels against order and unity. As the encompassing Logos through which man encounters reality, Reason must endow with speech the strangest, the oddest, the most irrational exception, and bring it into being by giving it meaning. Thus, Reason forever demolishes, as temporary and insufficient, every particular unity that excludes the exceptional, the irrational, the unique. In so doing, it wants to forestall the real, metaphysical fragmentation of the unity of Being.[17]

The point in question is significant. In a certain sense it summarises all the difficulties of Jaspers' philosophy. At least it throws some light on the curious duality which characterises his thought as a whole. In his later work, Jaspers wanted to give his philosophy a definitely logical and universal tone, without at the same time abandoning or absorbing what he had discovered as valid about the unconquerable exceptionality of selfhood in his earlier existential meditations. According to him, Reason is capable of recognising and admitting the exceptional, of addressing it, of letting it be, without absorbing it into a universal form. This lends Reason a non-possessive and altruistic quality. Jaspers sometimes talks about the attitude of Reason in terms of an interested receptivity which is close to the attitude of wooing, of courtship: neither a calculated indifference, nor a grasping possessiveness, but a reverential concern.[18] In this regard, Reason is akin to love.

Reason is fittingly characterised also by its *open will to communication*. This means that Reason wants to unite men not only as impersonal intelligences, but also as irreplaceable and incomparable selves. Such an attitude makes the communicative effort of Reason really unrestricted and non-exclusive. Reason implies a readiness to receive the one communicating with me *as another* who may be altogether different from me, 'with whom I can nonetheless live in the solidarity of limitless self-realisation.'[19] This reverential interestedness in the other as other makes Reason a preparatory schooling for love. 'Reason is not yet love; nevertheless, it is the condition for the freedom, truth, and purity of love.'[20]

Because Reason wants to exclude nothing, not even the universally unpredictable and unjustifiable exception, it can never close down into a *system of Reason*. We saw that unity was already a leading ideal at the level of the sciences. The sciences constantly try to build a unified system. They can do so because they can act on the presupposition that whatever is, and whatever new values and realisations will emerge later on, are or will be of a positive type. It is assumed that everything is a kind of object-being and is accessible to objective inquiry. Existential Reason, conscious of the depths of selfhood and of Transcendence, can no longer make this presupposition. Yet it can no more abandon its search for unity than scientific reason can. Full-blown Reason may have lost its naïve belief in unitary systems, but not its will-to-unity. Hence it must seek this unity in an unceasing movement which goes beyond all systematic unities.

This radical detachment from partial and particular unities is the condition for approaching the source of all unity. 'In order to be able to follow unhampered the completely open will-to-unity which forgets nothing, Reason dares and demands the detachment from everything that has become finite and definite, . . . even if it were the whole world.'[21] Although these unities are necessary and even desirable, they become deceptive and harmful when they usurp the place of the One. Reason knows no rest in any of the determinations of the intellect that strives for rest in the possession of Being as a substance. Reason, on the contrary, wants the One which is beyond all determination. Consequently, Reason is a movement 'that knows no halt or cessation'.[22]

Viewing the subject under these aspects, Kurt Reinhardt is right in calling Jaspers' philosophy 'a philosophy of "becoming" rather than a philosophy of "being"'. He is also right when he calls it 'anti-intellectualistic and voluntaristic'.[23] It is indeed a will, an unlimited one, that drives Reason into absolute mobility and disrupts the tranquillity of intellectual assimilation of Being.

Mr Reinhardt is completely mistaken, however, if he thinks that for Jaspers '"becoming" is better, more perfect, richer in content than the "become".' That is not Jaspers' point at all. He is not against the *become* as such, but against the sclerosis and immobility of thought and action that usually accompany it. The restless stirring of Reason is supposed to prevent this immobility. Jaspers would agree that 'it is self-contradictory and nonsensical to assume that the fulfilment of such a striving leaves man poorer than he was in the state of striving.'[24] But he would question the meaning of the word 'fulfilment'. He would not deny that 'movement and becoming are as such incomplete, deficient realities, . . . aspiring towards fulfilment of being.'[25] But again he would call attention to the words 'aspiring' and 'fulfilment'. All depends on what is understood by these terms. If we consider that the particular and finite aspirations, intentions, and aims of the intellect are fulfilled by the cognitive assimilation of finite objects, then we must admit that any particular fulfilment of advancing knowledge leaves man better off than the mere striving for such knowledge, that the *become* is richer than the *becoming*. Nevertheless, there is something in the intellect itself which usually leaves it unsatisfied with any of its particular results. There is no one answer that could put an end to the intellect's inquiry, no cognitive possession that would fulfil its appetite in such a way that it would not aspire for more than what it already has. In other words, there is something like a *negative power* in the intellect itself. This means that the intellect can regard every one of its particular achievements as incommensurate with its aspirations.[26] However, the tragedy of the intellect lies in the fact that, after having transcended one particular result, it cannot but aspire to another such; that it can look for fulfilment only among object-beings which, as such, are always finite and particular, be they ever so great. This drama is sometimes halted by artificially arresting the movement of the intellect and making it settle down in a particular result, as though that were the fullness of possession, the knowledge of Being.

It is at this point that intellectual possession turns into poverty, because further fulfilment is denied and further aspiration dismissed as unnecessary. This is self-deception pure and simple, which is all the more tragic since man's highest possibilities are at stake. By stopping and obstinately insisting that there is no more to be achieved in the way of truth, man falls from the conquered heights of knowledge and becomes less than what he was at the beginning, says Jaspers.[27]

The drama of the understanding poses a threefold alternative: either to absolutise one of the particular results of intellectual grasp, and thereby to lame its negative power; or to denounce the intellect and its aspirations as futile, and thereby to lapse into radical scepticism and nihilism; or, thirdly, to save the intellect through the self-awareness of Reason. In the first two cases, the intellect becomes less than itself, in the third, more than itself.[28] In the third case Reason takes hold of, reanimates and redirects the negative power of the understanding, and makes it seek its fulfilment in moving towards the One which, as such, is never attainable in object-beings but must be patiently pursued in all its disclosures, in object-being as well as in all its other modalities.

With this in mind, statements such as, 'to see, as Jaspers does, reality exclusively in its aspect of "becoming", means to disregard the highest forms of reality,'[29] seem doubly unfounded. First of all, it is not true that Jaspers considers reality exclusively under the aspect of becoming. Secondly, if he emphasises *becoming*, it is precisely in order not to leave out any form of reality (higher or lower), not even those that have not yet become and have not yet been disclosed.

For the rest, it is not enough to imagine or to anticipate the so-called higher forms of reality, for in many instances the patient disclosure of reality through plodding Reason belongs to the very realisation of reality. It is 'not through intoxication with the thought of perfection,' we are told by Jaspers, 'but by following the ways of suffering,' that the rise of thought towards perfection will be accomplished. To be sure, Reason must have faith in itself, but how far it will succeed at any given time is always a matter of actual experience. 'It would become irrational if it should anticipate itself. Its rationality lies rather in the fact that it does not presuppose itself unquestioningly.'[30]

Nor can the unity of knowledge and reality be anticipated, because 'unity enters into knowledge and reality only through Reason. Reason itself is not the unity, but . . . an impulse towards the One, towards the realisation (*Verwirklichung*) of unity. . . . *Reason is unity only as a task and a way*, and movement is the only effective form of this unity which, even though constantly unfinished in temporal existence, is nevertheless detectable in every activity of Reason as the very source and goal of Reason.'[31] The playful symbols through which we conjure up the unity of reality as it must have been 'in the beginning,' or anticipate the way it would be 'beyond the end of days,' are of use only if they help us to keep alive our striving towards the One. They are great as fuel for our hope and love. We may represent for ourselves that 'in the beginning was the One,' but only if at the same time we also remember that now, in time, that One 'is inapproachable for us' without tireless effort. Now we are in time, and although the 'One is lost to us, it still beckons from the depth of all temporal things.' Although we can never reach the One this side of eternity 'it is always present in the movement that goes towards it.'[32]

THE BOND OF TRUTH

As has earlier been pointed out, the modes of the Enveloping are for Jaspers the various basic modes in which Being becomes Being-for-us. Put in different terms, the modes of the Enveloping are the transcendental conditions under which Being can appear and manifest itself to us. They are like horizons where a meeting and a revelation can take place: thanks to them, man encounters and recognises Being. Apart from his explicit affirmations, Jaspers' whole way of speaking is such as to suggest that this encounter is primarily an initiative on the part of Being itself. In cipher-reading, for instance, the first language to be read was the language of Being itself. Here again he suggests that it is Being that comes to meet us: Being is said to be *entgegenkommend*. Thanks to this initiative, we, on our part, can come to know Being. We make its acquaintance, so that it is no longer the unknown, the hidden 'other' but becomes revealed and familiar to us. This encounter, this having-become-revealed, this uncon-cealment of Being sometimes goes by the name of *truth*.[33]

Thus the modes of the Enveloping can with justification be called modes of truth. At least, one might say that the articulation of truth is based on the modes of Being that are the Envelopings.[34] And since Reason is called the bond of all the modes of the Enveloping in us, it is also the bond of all truth.

Presumably, then, there will be as many basic modes of truth as there are basic ways in which Being stands revealed to us and, within each mode, an unsurveyable variety of lesser ways.[35] To be more exact, Jaspers discusses only six basic modes of truth, resting on the various Envelopings, excepting Reason itself. In turn he describes:

pragmatic truth,	as the truth of Empirical Being
cogent truth,	as the truth of General Consciousness

ethical truth,	as the truth of Spirit
personal truth, (faith)	as the truth of Existence
ontic truth,	as the truth of World
absolute truth,	as the truth of Transcendence[36]

It should be noted that the truth of Reason is not listed, because 'Reason is not a proper source as far as truth content goes' but only a bond which ties the truths of the other modes into a unity.[37] Reason has no truth proper to itself, except the truth of unity which it has the task of bringing about. Reason is the general principle of searching out truth everywhere and holding its findings together in a network of truth. But just as the different modes of the Enveloping lack a common principle from which they could be derived or to which they could ultimately be reduced so as to form a coherent system, so also the modes of truth lack the unity of a system. Reason can hold them together only by continuously moving among them. Its very movement *is* the unity of truth.

In short, Reason cannot lead its work of unification to a triumphal conclusion. Its work is never terminated in a final achievement. It cannot find the truth that would be the final, one and only revelation of reality. Truth too remains a task for philosophical Reason. Very often, Jaspers does not even speak of truth (truth sounds so formal!), he talks about the 'true', *das Wahre, Wahrsein*. For him, all manner of reality is capable of being true, and it is the vocation of Reason to let this truth appear.

Truth is as manifold as Being is, yet also one. There is truth in all the different truths, otherwise they would not be true. Truth is conferred on them by the One that manifests itself in each of them.[38] All of them reveal the truth of Being, but none of them exhaust it. The truth of Being is touched upon by Reason, but never possessed by it. 'Truth exists,' says Fr Tilliette paradoxically, 'because Truth escapes us.'[39]

Philosophy, the search for truth, lives by Reason, but not out of Reason. It nourishes itself on reality which Reason did not posit by itself and therefore cannot entirely absorb or justify either. Reason is the effective movement of philosophy, but not its soil. Its substance comes from elsewhere. 'True philosophising is a convergence to which Reason contributes the space and movement, love the fulfilment, and cipher the content of our consciousness of Being.'[40]

Conclusions to Part III

IN the last two chapters we have been following some of the salient points of Jaspers' concept of philosophic Reason. The insights obtained in these chapters seem to point towards a descriptive definition of Reason. In spite of its artificiality, the following may be regarded as such a definition:

Reason is the expression of Being's unlimited tendency to reveal itself in human Existence and, at the same time, of man's boundless will to communicate with other humans in the amplitude of Being. Reason, therefore, is the universal agent of a philosophical logic that attempts to furnish a communicable account of all the possible modes of Being-for-us in an open dialectic, which transcends the univocal determinations of purely intellectual consciousness. It urges our thinking to gather up the multiple modes of Being-for-us into a dynamic network of truth relations, and move them towards the enveloping oneness of Being itself in its analogous unity and totality. Briefly, Reason is the infinite openness of analogical thinking, the priority and omnipresence of thought in every mode of reality for us.

Without pretending that this definition is in any way exhaustive, I hope it does mention all the essential elements of Jaspers' concept of philosophical Reason. It presents Reason as the inalienable be-longing of thought and Being, the global relatedness of man to reality. In the words of James Collins, 'Reason addresses itself not exclusively to this or that limited sphere, but to all the possibilities of consciousness and being. It seeks insights into man's existence as it moves towards Transcendence.'[1]

The definition also underlines that man's relationship to reality, global as it may be, is articulated by Reason into some sort of logic. Even though this logic lacks the elegant harmony and stability of a perfect system (since it no longer operates on the principles of univocal determination), its progressive development has a manifest direction: it moves towards more and more encompassing unity. Notably, 'it examines the placement of man in a world of limiting and beckoning surroundings precisely as it respects Reason's demands for unity and rest in the divine Transcendence. This ideal is not attainable within time, yet we find support in the philosophical faith that our human achievements converge upon the goal of human freedom and hope.'[2]

By its openness, philosophic Reason transcends scientific reason, which always tends to close down into clear and distinct determinations. While scientific reason seeks clarity, philosophic Reason also wants unity. Clarity and unity are, therefore, the two basic demands of *Reason as a whole*, and because these two demands are irreconcilable, the structure of Reason as a whole is irremediably antinomic. Its operations oscillate back and forth between univocity and analogy in an open dialectic.

Consequently, the thinking of Reason as a whole is only inadequately represented by the concept of a peaceful contemplation or *theoria*.[3] It is rather an unceasing *movement* which makes and unmakes its own achievements in both directions: it unites what it first has kept apart and articulates what it has first experienced in a global way. It touches even on the One only in motion.[4] And because it desires ultimate unity, it becomes, paradoxically, peaceful only in restlessness and 'restless in repose'.[5]

Part IV
General Conclusions

General Conclusions

'EACH philosophy makes its own concept and has no higher standard outside to live up to,' says Jaspers.[1] What he means is that each philosophy must be allowed to create its own atmosphere and its own expression, and that it should be understood on its own terms. There is a great deal of truth in this. External critique, even when it manages to avoid the pitfalls of extrinsicism, tends to judge a given philosophy according to criteria which that philosophy did not intend to satisfy and on terms that are foreign to it. I sincerely hope that my efforts of presenting Jaspers' thought are not guilty of such extrinsicism. I have tried to limit myself to a purely descriptive presentation. I wanted to approach him with sympathy and comprehension, letting him speak for himself. I have few illusions concerning the completeness of my study. Still, I hope it is broad enough to give a panoramic view of Jaspers' thought to the yet uninitiated, but also detailed enough on some points to stimulate further reflection in those who are already acquainted with him in a general way.

Trying to understand Jaspers' philosophy on its own terms does not authorise me, however, to remain altogether non-committal or uncritical towards him. In addition to the occasional questions, appreciations and criticisms scattered in my footnotes and passing remarks, I must now make an attempt to give an overall appreciation of his thought. At least, I must answer some questions for myself. What did Jaspers' thought contribute to philosophy? Did he help to promote philosophical consciousness? Did he provide efficacious means towards realising the ideals commonly held to be the aim of philosophical reflection? Did he contribute something new to tradition? Is he a great philosopher?

POPULARITY OF GREATNESS?

Jaspers is certainly not a popular philosopher, and it is very unlikely that he will ever be one. His thought is too difficult for that. Moreover, as Professor De Waelhens pointed out, 'the genius of Jaspers is as profound as it is chaotic.'[2] A profound but chaotic philosophy is not likely to elicit the enthusiasm of drawing-room thinkers or the attention of professional systema-

17

tisers. Consequently, he has no following and no isms named after him. Walter Kaufmann tells us that 'Jaspers' lack of influence among German philosophers is almost total. Ten years after the war, there was among German university teachers of philosophy one Jaspers-Schüler and one Hartmann-Schüler, and both were unable to obtain a chair, though there were vacancies.'[3]

What Kaufmann says about German philosophical circles holds more or less for the whole Western scene: Jaspers has found very little response in Europe and practically none in America. By contrast, there is a thriving *Jaspers-Gesellschaft* (founded in 1950) in Japan, which publishes its own quarterly, assures a steady flow of monographs about Jaspers, and has undertaken the systematic translation of his works into Japanese. Fumio Hashimoto reports that certain books of Jaspers' are widely read by Japanese students of all faculties and that, 'next to Spranger, Jaspers is about the only living German philosopher whose writings have been published as German reading texts for students in Japan.'[4] He feels that Jaspers' thought represents a 'genuine East-West communication' which is powerful enough 'to penetrate the bone and marrow of orientals, and to summon them to a flow of ancient and genuinely Eastern thought.'[5]

The causes of Jaspers' unpopularity in the West are manifold. Some commentators seem to suggest that it may simply be a question of arbitrariness on the part of the devotees of philosophy. Others see it as a historical accident of a few years that it is Heidegger, and not Jaspers, who is celebrated as the father of twentieth-century existential philosophy.[6] While these may be partial explanations, I think the deeper reasons for his unpopularity are to be sought in his efforts to go beyond not only all manner of scientism in philosophy, but also beyond every kind of ontologising. In doing so, he antagonised not only the whole camp of positivists, idealists, rationalists, but also separated himself from the strongest Western stream of philosophising which runs from Aristotle to Hegel, and, as Jaspers sees it, even to Heidegger and Sartre. He has cast his lot rather with the exceptional figures of philosophy: Heraclitus, St Augustine, Nicholas of Cusa, Giordano Bruno, Kierkegaard and Nietzsche.

We should not, however, measure greatness with the yardstick of success and popularity. Worth is not decided by a referendum, nor yet by *referieren*. Its criteria must be more intrinsic than those of fashion or tradition. In the following pages I would like to show that his obscurity, unpopularity, and sometimes regrettable incoherence notwithstanding, Jaspers is a great philosopher, whom one can ignore only at the price of forgoing some valuable philosophical insights. He is also undoubtedly one of the most difficult philosophers, but again, that should not militate against his worth.

I shall not insist on his obvious merit in having tried to reintroduce or at least revalorise the idea of Transcendence in philosophy, which other important philosophers of this century all but left aside. This has been sufficiently emphasised by almost all the other commentators. I shall concentrate rather on his merit in having contributed something valuable to philosophical awareness in general through his concepts of Being and Reason.

AWAKENING A NEW AWARENESS OF BEING

To start on the broadest possible basis, let us agree to call philosophy a methodical reflection on our sense of reality as a whole. Any further definition of what one should understand by 'method', 'reflection', 'sense', or 'reality' is here omitted, because the only point I want to make is that philosophy is always undertaken as the outcome of an original awareness of 'everything that is'. When we are first touched by this awareness, it is vague and confused, but we hope to clarify it by reflecting upon it. This reflection, when carried out consistently and with some method, is philosophising. Briefly, philosophy could be called the clarification of an original awareness of Being (*Seinsbewusstsein*). Anything that promotes this awareness automatically promotes also the cause of philosophy. It is my contention that Jaspers' thought can and does help to promote this consciousness, even if at times only negatively, by disabusing it of a few illusions or by bringing it back from the state of forgetfulness into which it has lapsed during the course of history.

We must ask, therefore, what precisely it is that Jaspers has contributed to this consciousness of Being. Hans Mader outlines the question and suggests an answer in the following way: 'The ancient mode of thinking which, in the logic of Parmenides, conceived of Being as identity, in the dialectic of Heraclitus as polarity, in the analogy of Aristotle as totality, no longer holds

valid for Jaspers, for in these senses Being cannot be the One and
the Whole. . . . The above concepts are unitary constructions of
objective thinking within the subject-object split. They do not
correspond to Being as the encompassing whole which is at the
basis of the subject-object dichotomy. Therefore, Being can no
longer be conceived of through the sort of thinking that remains
within this split, i.e., through objective thinking. Consequently,
in the problem of an appropriate access to Being, Jaspers was
faced with the question of overcoming the subject-object
dichotomy of consciousness through a non-objective mode of
thinking which transcends the object-bound mode of thought.'[7]

This is correct as far as it goes. Although Mader's text suggests
more than it says, it is incomplete on the question of what
constitutes the new *Seinsbewusstsein* that has emerged from
Jaspers' attempts to transcend objective thinking. Let us, nevertheless, retain some of the important suggestions of this text.
We know that Jaspers began his philosophy with the double
question, What is Being? and How must I think of it? According
to the text at hand the answer should be: Being is the ground in
which the subject-object duality of consciousness is rooted. In
order to encompass this ground by our thought, we need a mode
of thinking that transcends this duality. Jaspers' expression for
the ground of Being is the Enveloping. The idea of Enveloping,
therefore, forbids us to seek Being on either side of the duality,
to conceive of it either as an object or as a subject. We are
supposed to think of it rather as an encompassing Whole, the
One of Plotinus.

In other words, the thought of Being requires a transcendental
sort of consideration of this Enveloping, and the fundamental
task of philosophy is to institute an inquiry into the various
modes in which this Enveloping appears to us in order to seek
out the multiple relationships whereby these modes are ordered
towards a transcendental unity. I suggest in passing that Jaspers'
logic traces the foundations and extreme horizons of just such
an inquiry. I say, the foundations, for we must recall in this
connection that Jaspers' *Von der Wahrheit* is only the beginning
of a four-volume work on logic. It only 'makes room' for more
detailed presentations of a concrete methodology, theory of
categories, and theory of science, which have not been worked
out by Jaspers.[8]

What is primarily excluded by the idea of Being as the Enveloping is reductionism. Mader's text suggests as much. The inquiry into Being demands not just any mode of thinking that transcends the duality of subject and object, but a thinking which transcends it precisely towards the unity that makes their duality possible in the first place. For there could be another way of 'transcending' their duality, namely one that reduces either side of it to the other. Such a transcending would identify Being *either* wholly with the subjective *or* with the objective manifestations of Being.

Instead of this, Jaspers' idea of Being is that Being is *neither* subjective *nor* objective, but rather the unqualified Enveloping that makes these fundamental modalities originally possible. This Enveloping, Jaspers maintains, is no longer representable objectively. The Enveloping is unqualified reality (neither subjective nor objective), and, as such, does not lend itself to ontologising, because ontology can survey only the objectively determinable appearances of reality. In fact, the ultimate incomprehensibility of the Enveloping by the mind is taken by Jaspers as the surest sign of its reality. The mind, far from being able to envelop Being, is enveloped by it. For Jaspers, a thoroughly intelligible reality would be secondary and accidental, and at the most, a pure *ens rationis*, whose whole reality would consist in its intelligibility.[9]

After this thoroughly Kantian start, where he accepts that knowability is limited to the objective appearances of Being, Jaspers nevertheless turns towards a certain realism, and, instead of searching merely for the conditions of objectivity in the transcendental subjectivity of Consciousness, wants to explore the unknowable reality of Being itself, which envelops and conditions Consciousness itself. This mild realism does not mean, however, that he abandons the lesson of his critical Kantian starting-point and re-introduces the presupposition of ontology as regards the knowability of Being itself. On the contrary, the aim of his further philosophical efforts is to highlight the sense of impenetrability of Being by pointing to the shipwreck that thought must ultimately endure when faced with authentic reality.[10] Knowledge is always finite and cannot dominate reality. But when we experience the shock which awaits our efforts to grasp the trans-categorial reality of Being in categories, we can acquire an extraordinarily keen awareness of reality, which is like a conjuring (*Beschwören*) of reality.[11] Less dramatically put: we cannot know reality itself, but we can have an indirect awareness of it when its overwhelming presence touches our own thinking reality. This is the meaning of *Betroffenheit*.

There is, of course, a terrible ambiguity here. How can Jaspers, once he has accepted that Being is accessible to us only as phenomenon, go on to search for Being-in-itself? How does he connect such a démarche with such a starting point? How can his Kantianism and realism be reconciled? Jaspers never gives an answer. He never tries to effect such a reconciliation. That is why his philosophy is a philosophy of contradictions. These contradictions are not solved in any intellectual synthesis, but only in the concrete act of his thinking (within his own Existence), whereby he tries both to *know* being-for-us and to *ascertain* Being-in-itself. He wants to transcend to reality by means of knowledge. He exploits knowledge and, at the threshold of reality, discards it, replacing it with a transcendent awareness of Being.

All this comes from Jaspers' realisation that philosophy cannot be satisfied with the objectively knowable formal aspects of Being if it wants to come into contact with true reality. It must transcend that which is conceptualisable by pure understanding and confront the ground, which is constantly presupposed but never exhausted by conceptualisation. Still, this would not constitute an unsurmountable difficulty if this ground itself were confrontable, i.e., objective. Unfortunately it is not, for it envelops the subject and object, as well as the act, of confrontation. In other words, thought is completely surrounded: on the one hand, it is enveloped by Being as a whole; on the other, it is preceded not only by the reality of its object but also by the reality of the thinker.[12] In order to grasp the whole of reality, thinking would have to outstrip itself in both directions: it should outdistance its object as well as precede the reality of the thinker. This, obviously, is impossible.

Saying that this is impossible implies that ontology as a *scientia entis ut ens est* is also impossible. The science of the reality of Being is impossible. At best, ontology can aspire to being a *scientia entis ut objectum*, either as general noematics or as a theory of categories.

In face of this impossibility, the question must be asked: what next? Shall we be resigned to a complete philosophical agnosticism? 'Shall we be satisfied with the knowledge of tangible objects and reject all thinking that goes beyond this as "empty chatter", "romantic fancy", as "metaphysics"? In other words, shall we practise science only and not philosophy?'[13] The same question can be put differently: 'Shall we give up the basic operation of transcending just because we are not immediately successful, and in so doing, remain under the spell of objects taken for absolute reality or of the propositions which claim absolute validity?'[14]

There is no doubt in Jaspers' mind that a resignation in face of this impossibility would betray man's noblest philosophical impulses. Man must choose philosophy, he must attempt the impossible. He must try to bring about a conversion, a rebirth, of thinking that will enable him to penetrate beyond the limits of knowledge. Man must try to acquire an awareness of reality that will transform his intentional consciousness. 'The part of thinking in this transformation may be formulated something like this: to carry out the basic philosophical operation, to think about objects in non-objective terms, to jump over one's shadow in thinking, to think by methods which in using the intellect go beyond the intellect. . . . When we say, going beyond the intellect, we must add at once: without losing one's head.'[15]

I think the suggestion is fairly clear: the impossibility of attaining true reality by means of thinking exists for intentional consciousness alone. Only the intellect cannot jump over its own shadow. Things stand differently when we manage to acquire a new sort of thinking, a new awareness, which raises the mind to a higher level without demanding new objects. Such is, in fact, the puissance of transformation Jaspers claims for the age-old philosophic insight that 'by knowledge we do not merely increase the range of our information about things, but we can also rise step by step in the ways of thinking itself. If this succeeds, we do not merely add to the endless learning about things, but, by our ability to engage in a new type of thinking, increase our insight into the whole and gain thereby a new consciousness of Being.'[16]

By virtue of this new awareness, which, needless to say, does not issue from General Consciousness but from Existence, we can be conscious of Being in its impenetrable yet penetrating reality. We are both overwhelmed and lifted by it. It sheds a new light on all our knowledge and action, making them 'glow' with Being (*seinsdurchglüht*) without dissolving their mystery and wonder.

According to one commentator, in this awareness 'the concept of Being has once more been accorded its universal breadth by Jaspers. It has become the horizonless horizon, the last Enveloping, the Absolute, the Transcendent par excellence. Also the concept of thinking has regained its universal scope in the concept of Reason, in which *ratio* and *irratio* are joined together.'[17] I agree with this judgement. Jaspers' concept of Being is really universal in scope, so much so that it ceases to be a concept at all and turns into an open receptacle.

As the horizonless horizon, Jaspers' idea of Being is really open to the infinite. It admits with equal receptivity being which is identical with itself, and also becoming which at each moment is already more and other than itself. It is open to that which 'is', but also to that which 'ought to be'. It acknowledges that which is justifiable by rational rules, but also that which rebels against such rules. Neither the firmness of substance nor the evanescence of freedom is alien to it. It respects reality which is given (*gegeben*), but also the nameless source which is never given but always gives (*es gibt*). Surrounding all this is the constant awareness of Being as a self-engendering act, by virtue of which all real things exist and keep on being even before and beyond the reaches of knowledge.

In all its aspects, Jaspers' idea of Being is without a value judgement, *wertfrei*. He does not consider being absolutely better than becoming (or vice-versa), the 'is' necessarily more important than the 'ought to be', the universal more evidently primary than the particular, that which is stable in every way more basic than the evanescent. The identical, the positive, the similar, the permanent enjoy primacy over the non-identical, the negative, the dissimilar, the fleeting under the aspect of ready intelligibility and logicality, but not as reality. Under the aspect of reality, all of them belong to Being, all are equally important, all are equally real. This refusal of bias in favour of any one aspect of Being gives Jaspers a 'position of positionlessness'. From this it follows that the thought of this 'concept' of Being by Reason is equally inclusive. Even the ineffable and irrational aspects of reality can become material for Reason and, in a certain sense, for philosophical discourse. It would not be rational for Reason to deny the irrationally real, or to admit it only provisionally on the condition that its 'real' reality be demonstrated and made intelligible later on. 'I am rational only if my whole Reason factually and for my knowing is grounded upon unreason,' says Jaspers.[18]

CHALLENGE TO PHILOSOPHY

This new awareness of the infinite and enveloping character of reality, together with the awareness of the limitation of knowledge, could benefit philosophy in many ways. Principally, it could help to clarify the very status of philosophy, because it presents a serious challenge to philosophy to reflect on whether it can really make good its age-old claims. Can philosophy claim to be a scientific knowledge of Being and its divisions, or is it merely a symbolical approach to the manifold mysteries of reality? Can it deduce or construct a systematic and logically coherent doctrine of Being from objectively formulable principles, or is it simply a multiple hermeneutics of the original ciphers of Being? If it is Being that stands at the centre of philosophical concern, and if it is impossible to determine unequivocally (and without bias) what Being means, then the statements of philosophy which converge upon this undeterminable centre form an 'unknowable unity', *unwissbare Einheit*, as Jaspers maintains.

The idea of this unknowable unity puts the traditional doctrine of analogy of Being into a new light. It means that the *ordo ad unum* of analogy is really not a system, but only a network of fluid metaphors, precisely because their common reference point, the *unum*, no longer has a single definable meaning and, consequently, cannot be stated, but merely symbolised.[19]

On this basis, philosophy can no longer be regarded as an extension of logical knowledge, but must be considered as a multiple metaphor of the unknowable unity of Being. Every philosophical statement can serve as such a metaphor alongside others. Each of them contains *some* truth and is capable of symbolising Being, but none of them contains *the* truth about Being, and none can claim to be an unequivocal and universal expression of Being. In fact, philosophy must be determined 'not to seek reassurance in a satisfying *Seinswissen*, but to listen to anything that speaks to us in the open and horizonless space that encloses all horizons, to perceive the signal lights that point somewhere, warn and entice, and, perhaps, also announce that which really is.'[20]

Needless to say, such a theory of Being and of philosophy puts Jaspers' own thought into a curious perspective. Kurt Hoffman has an enlightening comment to make on this point: 'Whereas other thinkers in the great philosophical tradition of the West, in propounding their ideas, believed somehow in their universal validity and, in spite of an awareness of the limitation imposed on human knowledge, in their truth; and whereas they refuted other, contradictory systems in order to establish their own, Jaspers at once accepts the core of truth, the "cipher", in all of the great philosophies with an unequalled openness and critical penetration, while at the same time rejecting their claim to universality. Jaspers' philosophy is, if we may say so, a philosophy of philosophy. With Jaspers, philosophy has reached its self-consciousness. That Jaspers would consistently regard his own thought as *one* philosophical metaphor among others is both his weakness and his strength.'[21] It would seem, then, that Jaspers applies his views on philosophy to his own thought and relativises even his own philosophy. He carries the attitude of positionlessness to such an extreme that he does not even take up a position in regard to the truth of his own system of thought. Is such an attitude really tenable? Is it genuine humility?

METAPHOR OF METAPHORS

Perhaps it is rather too much to say, as Kurt Hoffman does, that with Jaspers philosophy has reached its self-consciousness, as if it had no self-consciousness before. It is true, however, that Jaspers' thought represents a particularly high level of this self-consciousness. His thought is truly a philosophy of philosophy, an attempt to think out what philosophy itself is about. The end results of his reflections are marked by an unusual degree of philosophical humility and lack of pretentiousness. A philosophy that professes the metaphorical character of all philosophy (including its own) and claims no universal validity for itself certainly appears to be a humble one. But perhaps this humility is already excessive and ceases to be an unmixed virtue. For in philosophy, as anywhere else for that matter, the virtue of humility must be coupled with truthfulness. Self-effacement should not go so far as to deny the reality of the self, and the humility of philosophy should not result in the negation of philosophy. The attitude of *vermis sum non homo* is open to grave qualifications. For one thing, it was never spoken by a worm.

Similarly, one must ask just how metaphorically one should take the statement that 'all philosophies are metaphorical'. Does Jaspers really believe that his own philosophy of the Enveloping too is only 'one metaphor of Being among others'? This attitude of relativising every philosophical statement was repeatedly questioned by the critics of Jaspers. 'What are the limits of relativism?' Kurt Hoffman wants to know. 'To what extent, if any at all, is it necessary for philosophy to take a definite position in order to be meaningful? Is it possible, in other words, to see all philosophies as ciphers, including the philosophy of ciphers?'[22] Suspecting that all this tolerance and humility is merely a disguised form of dogmatism, Joseph De Tonquédec noted that, after having repudiated every philosophic system, every objectively transmissible doctrine, Jaspers went ahead to write three volumes of philosophy. 'Whether he admits it or not, Jaspers certainly attempted to teach his contemporaries the one and only way of truth, the only correct attitude towards reality.'[23]

Shall we say that we are dealing here with the central contradiction of Jaspers? Do these critical questions touch upon the basic weakness and inconsistency of his thought? To a large extent, yes. They show up an undeniable lack of logical coherence in his philosophy.

This presents an interesting logical problem. Let us take first the statement that 'all philosophies are metaphorical'. We have already asked how metaphorically *this* statement should be taken. In other words, is this a metaphorical statement too? Granting for a moment that philosophy is a metaphor, can the statement that makes this assertion belong to philosophy? The answer should be obvious: no, the statement cannot belong to philosophy. It must belong to a philosophy of philosophy, just as the statement, 'all propositions of language L are true or false,' does not belong to language L, but to a meta-language. We could say, therefore, that the statement asserting the metaphorical character of all philosophy is a non-metaphorical and objective statement made by Jaspers in virtue of his meta-philosophical perspective of the Enveloping.

Unfortunately, in the very next step this meta-philosophy includes itself in its own judgement, and considers itself as merely one metaphor among others. This self-inclusion in the content of its own judgement is logically inadmissible, just as it would be logically inadmissible for a Cretan to assert that 'all Cretans lie whenever they say something,' because that assertion nullifies itself. There is no doubt about it: this relativising of philosophy by means of one of its own statements is absurd and inadmissible from the point of view of formal logic, because it suspends the basic movement of logic itself, and makes all judgement of truth or falsity impossible.

We have seen, of course, that Jaspers consciously accepted this illogicality because he thought that it was inevitable in the case of transcendent, philosophical thought. He even tried to show that the suspension of logic is the very means of transcending the immanence of logical reason. Therefore, as Kurt Hoffman points out, 'if the ultimate justification of philosophy is seen to lie in the establishment of logical unity, then Jaspers' philosophy founders. But it founders consciously and purposely by humbling itself through the humiliation of logical reason, which must give way to a "philosophical faith" or trust in the ground of Being.'[24] What motivated Jaspers' disregard for logic was his firm belief that it is not logical reason but Existence that is the ultimate witness of Being.

Indeed, the fundamental role played by Existence in transcendent thinking is decisive: it is Existence that in its desire for the Absolute relativises logical thought. Could this lead to an indiscriminate relativism? 'No,' says André Marc, 'for Existence does not relativise except what is relative.'[25] Jaspers himself is a little more circumspect. He admits that the existential truth and certitude by virtue of which logic is relativised could lead to arbitrariness and scepticism. He sees that the problem of the absolute and the relative is that they are inseparable: it is impossible to relativise something without putting something absolute in its place. He who makes objective truth absolute relativises Existence, and he who makes Existence absolute must relativise objective truth. How to get out of this vicious circle, then? How to prevent the absolutisation of either side and the consequent relativising of the other? How to avoid falling into scientism or into a completely subjectivistic philosophy? Jaspers does not know and never gives a clear answer. He merely hopes that his acts of relativising are not entirely negative, since they are carried out in the name of a positive insight he firmly believes he has into the transcendent reality of Being through Reason. 'The relativising by means of which philosophical reflection frees itself from its own objectified results is endless. It can degenerate into arbitrariness and take on the emptiness of a purely negating relativism. Therefore, relativising that has intrinsic value must be accomplished in the name of something positive, in the name of the one truth. . . . The one truth is the truth of Existence that moves in the ideas of Reason and finds its ground in Transcendence.'[26]

DISTINGUENDUM EST

The difficulties of Jaspers' philosophy are numerous. He appears to take delight in posing questions which he cannot answer, or in making assertions which he immediately has to deny. For instance, in the context quoted above, in which he rejects the endless relativity of truth, he also rejects the possibility or even desirability of reaching a firm ground from which the absolute truth of Existence could be stated. 'To make the truth of Existence philosophically objective is not a meaningful aim. Philosophy seeks enlightenment in thoughts which are always further relativisable.'[27] Here is where the fundamental parting of the ways between Jaspers and me takes place. In the first place, I cannot see how this avoids the endless relativity of truth he objects to. Secondly, I *do* think that to explicate our existential awareness of reality, 'to make philosophically objective the truth of Existence,' as he puts it, *is* a meaningful aim of philosophising, because that is the very impulse of Existence itself, the very orientation Being takes in disclosing itself to us, and, therefore, the very destiny of our thinking.

Let us reflect for a moment. Cutting through most of Jaspers' unusual terminology, we may notice that what he is saying is basically very simple. He insists, and rightly so, that thinking issues from experience, or more explicitly, that reality enters into philosophical reflection among the contents of experience. This is indicated by several factors. The very amplitude and receptivity of his concept of Being as the Enveloping shows that Jaspers is anxious to neglect nothing that could occur in experience, no matter how tenuous or ungraspable. The seven modes of the Enveloping also refer to experience; they are results of a 'conscious inner perception' (*Erfahrung*) of the variety of ways in which reality can present itself to us. Even his thesis about the multiplicity of truth is based on the idea that truth is contentual, that is to say, there are as many modes of truth as there are ways in which reality becomes the content of our experience. It is on account of this contentuality of truth grounded in experience that Jaspers opposes the reduction of truth to the concept of cogent, formal truth.

Philosophy, then, is grounded in, and refers to, experience, but itself is not this experience. It is rather a *reflection on experience*, a thoughtful reprise of the reality originally disclosed to us in experience. The purpose of this reprise is clear: it is undertaken by man in order that he may comprehend better what the reality thus presented to him in experience really is. I say, comprehend *better*, because experience already contains a certain mute comprehension of itself, but this comprehension is lived and exercised rather than signified. We saw Jaspers discoursing at length about the priority of thought and reflection, because he himself realised that it is through thinking that reality comes into focus in all its originality, that it is reflection that is capable of surveying the different modes of experience and making them clear and 'eloquent' for us.[28]

In order to effect this thoughtful reprise of experience, the philosopher must, in a certain sense, cease to be immersed in it, and has to convert it into a theme or problem. This is the process of *objectification* whereby the thinker retreats from his experience, puts it at arm's length, in order to see what it means. Without the ability to do so, without this possibility of setting his life at a distance from him, man would remain the prisoner of an empirical sort of consciousness that would condemn his existence to a less than rational level.

Objectification, then, is nothing else than a kind of *rationalisation* of experience by thought, in the sense of making experience meaningful, clear, and transparent, rather than leaving it mute and obscure. He who wants rationality wants objectification. It is the very vocation and destiny of our thoughtful existence to engage in such a process. One must, therefore, considerably qualify Jaspers' thesis that the objectification of existential truth is not a meaningful aim of philosophising.

This process of objectification is admittedly heir to a multitude of fatal limitations and imperfections. First of all, it is perspectival. This means that it grasps experience each time only under a certain aspect and never totally, that it presents the reality content of experience as a series of silhouettes and never in its density. It may be salutary to be reminded of this inadequacy of objectification, but, once it is stated, we have nonetheless to proceed with it because we have no other means of clarifying experience. True, it is poor and incomplete, but to say that it discloses nothing about reality is to overshoot the mark. There may be much more to reality than what objectification can reveal, but there cannot be less. What we obtain through it is a genuine grasp of reality, and not just of a shadowy kind of entity called object-being. The same could be said of the other concomitant shortcomings of objectification, such as abstractness, formalism, generality: it is not abstractions or generalities that we know through objectification, but the concrete reality content of experience grasped abstractly, formally, universally. After all, one should not forget to distinguish between *what* we know and *how* we know.

These limitations placed on objectification imply that the process of making explicitly rational the content of experience can never be completed, but this does not mean that we should, therefore, never undertake it. We can go far in this way of taking possession of experience, even though we know in advance that we can never reach completeness.

I am not suggesting that Jaspers is altogether unaware of these facts, or that he never urges us to engage in objective thought in order to clarify certain aspects of reality. Occasionally, however, he seems to forget certain things which, at other times, he affirms without reserve. Thus, for instance, he admits that the first operation of Reason is an intellectual one, with all the objectification and generalisation that that entails. It may be true that this form of rationality must ultimately be surpassed because the final goal of Reason is higher, but it certainly cannot be bypassed. Jaspers may be right in saying that objectification is not the end of philosophy, provided he affirms with equal emphasis that it is the necessary means of it.

On the whole, his fear of objectification seems unfounded to me. There is no reason why objectification should necessarily lose the reality content of experience. If experience constitutes a first comprehension of reality, objectification constitutes a second one. In a somewhat similar context, Professor Georges Van Riet asks Jaspers the same question: 'If a first structuration of the world is useful, why should a second one be less so?'[29] It *is* useful because it creates further clarity in experience, which in itself is obscure, confused, and haphazard.

For the rest, we know already why Jaspers is dissatisfied with objective thinking as the goal of philosophising. He is dissatisfied because he wants a sort of thinking which, in one and the same movement, fulfils both the *finis operis* and the *finis operantis* of philosophy. Philosophical thinking, for him, is thinking in which the purposes of thought and thinker coincide. He wants a sort of thinking which is both theoretical and practical in the ethical sense. He wants a thinking which does not leave the thinker untouched in his existential concerns. In other words, he demands a kind of thinking which issues not merely from General Consciousness but also from Existence. Not knowing, however, how to reconcile these two demands, he leaves the two sorts of thinking in dialectical opposition. He emphasises very strongly that objective thinking is existentially indifferent, while existential thinking is theoretically indefensible.

I am not convinced that this is really the case. If it were, it would be necessary to establish that there is an unbridgeable gap between Existence and General Consciousness. This would mean that Consciousness can in no way objectify personal selfhood, and that the self can in no way influence the workings of General Consciousness. The two would be entirely discontinuous. Certainly, Jaspers often affirms such a radical split and discontinuity, but he cannot consistently maintain this position. Far from being cut off from each other, both Existence and Consciousness are aspects of the Enveloping that we are. They are united in our subjective reality, even though we may not exactly know how. Even if we admit that 'subjective reality' is not a genus which subsumes both the general ego and the personal self, it does envelop them somehow. Even if General Consciousness cannot objectify the self entirely (since the self is the ultimate source even of the objectifying acts of General Consciousness), it can objectify it partially. It can do so to the extent that the hidden spontaneity of selfhood always manifests itself in concrete acts and situations. Existence always seeks concretisation and embodiment in being-there. Again, Existence may be more and richer than what we can thus know of it through objective thought, but it cannot be less. And what we thus gather is valid, objectively valid, of Existence itself, and not merely of Dasein. To sum up, Existence may not be adequately knowable, but this does not mean that it is entirely unknowable. If it were entirely unknowable, if it could not communicate even with itself by means of knowledge, then Existence as such could not even be, for, as Jaspers himself pointed out, 'a speechless Existence is impossible'. It is, therefore, not irrelevant for the truth of Existence to be explored objectively.

At times, he goes very far in acknowledging the necessity of objective thinking even in the case of Existence without quite admitting that objective thought can grasp Existence itself. 'I cannot think without objectivity. What I think and what I know move necessarily in some form of objectivity. This latter is either the matter at hand or else refers to it. If it refers only, that which is meant is something else and is in so far—even though not adequately objective—nevertheless an *intended objective as something which is not I*.'[30]

I suspect that Jaspers' whole thesis that Existence cannot be objectified meaningfully is based on a tautology: we shall call Existence only that dimension of personal selfhood which is inaccessible to the grasp of objective knowledge, because it is the very source of objectification. Ergo, Existence is objectively unknowable. Unfortunately, this tautology is an integral part of the Jaspersian economy of thought. It shows a basic flaw in his system of thought, but also a desperate determination on his part to speak somehow even of the allegedly ineffable aspects of reality. Whether one respects such an effort or rejects it as nonsense ('Worüber man nicht sprechen kann, darüber muss man schweigen'), one must acknowledge it as part and parcel of Jaspers' philosophic ethos.

OBJECTS AND OBJECTIVITY

The understanding of many of Jaspers' doctrines hinges on the meaning of his concepts of 'object', 'objective', 'non-objective'.

It may be a just criticism to say that, in contrast to his generously open concept of Being, his idea of 'object' and 'objectivity' is extremely narrow. In spite of the distracting variety of things included in it, such as centaurs and $\sqrt{-1}$, his concept is almost univocal. Object is whatever serves as the term of an act of intentional consciousness. The rest is non-objective.

It is the great merit of Ludwig Armbruster's study, *Objekt und Transzendenz bei Karl Jaspers*, to have analysed the different hidden levels of Jaspers' object concept and the corresponding meanings of non-objectivity. He was able to show in what sense the term 'non-objective' should be taken in each particular case. He pointed out, very justly, that non-objectivity is not always and necessarily a negation of objectivity as such.[31] Yet even he had to acknowledge that, when all is said and done, when we come to the 'first step of philosophising' which is transcending, the concept 'non-objective' must be taken in absolute contrast to objectivity in general, because transcending signifies the very critique of intentional thought as such.[32] In opposition to this, Armbruster demanded that a logical continuity be established between the various regions of object-being, including even the so-called non-objective realms of metaphysics. Using the principle of *analogia entis*, he tried to show that the logical foundations of Jaspers' object concept were large and deep enough to allow a factual and objective development of Jaspers' cipher-metaphysics. He tried to indicate that the concept could be put to greater use than Jaspers himself made of it.[33]

Though such a development would be in every way desirable, it would no longer be a logical prolongation of Jaspers' concept. It would be a simple addition to it. The reason for this is clear: objectivity, as Jaspers uses the term, is co-extensive with the concept of intentionality. But it is beyond that, as Armbruster himself has noted, that the operation of transcending and the first step of philosophy begin for Jaspers. Jaspers insisted repeatedly that the sort of transcending which in the end results again in a 'something', an object, is a false transcending. Armbruster knew that,[34] and yet he wanted to build an analogical system of the different realms of Being (objects in the world, Existence, Transcendence) on the general meaning of objectivity, since, according to him, all objects are on the same level in so far as they all fit into the same intentional framework of consciousness.[35]

Such an enterprise, praiseworthy in itself, is, nevertheless, based on the utterly unJaspersian principle of seeking the clarification of even transcendent realities within the schema of intentional consciousness. In this, Armbruster may have been led astray by Jaspers' references to 'existential objectivity' and 'metaphysical objectivity'. But as we saw earlier, neither the existential *signa* nor the ciphers of metaphysics can satisfy the requirements Jaspers has set for object-beings and objective knowability; on the contrary, their interpretation calls for circles and contradictions in which their objectivity disappears.

It is not a good practice to make Jaspers sound more logical than he actually is, or to try to disguise his inconsistencies. Jaspers without his inconsistencies and contradictions, which he willingly accepted because he thought they were necessary for transcending, would not be Jaspers at all, but a harmless sort of system that would fall flat on its face. One can take him or leave him, but one cannot domesticate or thomisticate him. Jaspers himself showed very little enthusiasm for this sort of improvement upon his thought. I remember a personal interview with him, during which I asked his opinion about several of his commentators. Among others, I wanted to know what he thought of the classic work of Dufrenne and Ricoeur. Jaspers' reply was: 'Their work is excellent, but, you know, they are much too clear. They have tried to do away with many of my ambiguities.'

My personal preferences lie with Armbruster's intentions, inasmuch as I too refuse the a-logical ruptures of thinking. I too would want to show that intentionality does not imprison our consciousness in mere object-being, but I would never claim to do so on the logical bases of Jaspers' doctrines, for there are no such bases. I too would insist that 'objectivity' is a larger concept than the use Jaspers made of it, but that would not be according to Jaspers, but in opposition to him. I too would like to suggest that there is perhaps a *tertium quid* between straight logical thinking and unmitigated a-logic, but I would not take Jaspers as my witness, for whom there is no middle ground between logic and a-logic.

THE BOND OF UNITY IN THINKING

Jaspers believed he could relativise and transcend intentional consciousness and logic, because at the same time he also believed in absolute consciousness and Reason. He thought he could compensate for the unity and coherence which he had to forgo on the intellectual level by the higher unity of thinking which, like Kant, Jaspers called Reason.

However, in spite of this Kantian inspiration, Jaspers' concept of Reason differs from Kant's idea of it. To begin with, Jaspers' idea of Reason is not that of a subjective faculty of man, not entirely, that is. Reason is regarded by him rather as the meeting point of two movements: the descent of Being into Existence and the ascent of Existence to Being. In this sense, Reason bears a greater resemblance to the Plotinian *Logos* than to the Kantian *Vernunft*. Moreover, the unity sought by Reason in Jaspers' sense is not only the unity of knowledge (furnished and elaborated by the understanding), but the unity of man's total relatedness to all the possible modes in which Being is disclosed to us.

In this sense, Reason's scope is really boundless, it is coextensive with the unlimitedness of Being itself. Reason, we saw, is nothing else than the omnipresence of our thinking-being (*Denkendsein*) in the whole of reality, or, conversely, the presence of Being (*Sein*) in our thinking (*Denken*). 'Thought and reality are originally one,' we have heard Jaspers say. They coincide precisely in a reciprocal *will* which, considered from the side of reality, is a rush towards unlimited self-disclosure (*aletheia*), and, considered from the side of thinking, is man's limitless drive towards Being. Naturally, this coincidence of thinking and Being makes no sense for intentional consciousness, because for intentional consciousness reality is precisely the object of thinking, the 'other' of thinking, and not identical with it. Consequently, this coincidence cannot be proved or demonstrated for the intellect. It must be experienced in the very performance of an act of transcendent thinking.

One would think that Jaspers was moving fatally towards a Hegelian sort of rationalism where the real becomes rational and the rational real. Without affirming this explicitly, he appeared to come near to saying that the Absolute is Reason. When he posited the identity of thought and reality in a reciprocal dynamism, he all but repeated the Hegelian thesis, according to which the same purpose animates the movement of thought as directs the genesis of reality. When he asserted that Reason was the expression of Being's self-disclosure in Existence, he could have been taken to mean that thinking, which in Nature is unconscious, becomes conscious in man.

The fact that he did not give way to the temptation of such a radical rationalism, that he did not end up in a logically compact system (as he would have if he had carried his affirmations to their logical conclusion), shows that we are dealing with an a-logic that breaks with panlogism by running counter to it. Jaspers' statement about Reason as the identity of thought and reality is a transcendent expression, and not a univocal postulate of logic. Therefore, it cannot be handled deductively or exploited in its objective literalness for the purpose of an intellectual logic. That would result in a 'false logic'.[36] Moreover, the suggested identity of the rational and the real is not the same as the identity of the logical and the real. The rationality that Jaspers had in mind is much wider than rationality in the ordinary sense of logical coherence, and includes the acceptance of the a-logically real also.

His statements should be understood symbolically as ciphers. They express a *recognition* of the universal appetite of thought for reality in all its manifoldness. They do not constitute a scientific *cognition* of reality in a single system. This recognition gives rise not to a single logical system but to a multiplicity of hermeneutical explanations which converge upon the unknown and fabulous unity of Being, the One. Jaspers' theory of knowledge is not an affirmation of panintellectualism, but a plea for universal receptivity on the part of Reason.

Universal receptivity constitutes in fact the very atmosphere of Reason. This atmosphere compels Reason not to sit in judgement upon reality, not to embellish or disguise it, not to simplify it or improve it, but to recognise its rights and to let it be in all candour.[37] Only through this atmosphere of reverence, wooing, and altruism, can Reason preserve the original sense of wonder which alone unlocks reality in all its splendour. Reason, then, is the impulse whereby thought gathers all things real into its own movement and carries them towards unity and light. This means that the unity of Reason lies in the *recollection* of thinking, rather than in a *collection* of thoughts. The true universality of Reason consists precisely in turning our awareness of the manifold towards the One—*versio ad unum*—rather than turning the differences of reality into a conceptual sameness—*versio in unum*.

The real relatedness of Reason and reality, the *Seinsverbundenheit* of thought, signifies that Reason seeks reality itself, rather than its own supposedly immutable image in things.

Yet Jaspers never allows this open attitude of Reason to degenerate into that indifferentism of speculation where 'anything goes' because nothing matters much. We have heard Jaspers characterise Reason as a *Sichangehenlassen*. This untranslatable word is charged with meaning. It means, first of all, that through Reason we allow reality to 'affect us'. It means that Reason is 'concerned with' reality. It also means that this concern with reality makes us 'concerned for' reality. Through Reason, we are really helping to liberate reality from the darkness of concealment. By gathering all the scattered manifestations into the encompassing unity of Being, we help each thing to regain its rightful place.[38]

Such a concept of Reason strikes us by its freshness and openness. In reading Jaspers, one is gradually touched by a sense of freedom, which is a welcome contrast to the oppressive rationalism and *Alleswisserei* of some other philosophical authors. Because of its respect for the existential roots of thought, his philosophy may at times appear irrationalistic, but it is not. In contesting the primacy of reason in the narrow sense, Jaspers expresses his belief that 'philosophy lives *by* Reason, but not *out of* Reason.' His thought is constantly nourished by other secret sources which, though awakened by Reason, do not have their origin in Reason. They are found in faith and love. 'Love reaches out beyond beings to Being itself. It works from deep within us and fills us with yearning and hope. We trust that it will speak to us whenever we need it, and put us in contact with Being that already was before Creation, the fathomless Transcendence.'[39]

There is much in this philosophy that should be supplemented by detailed study, much that is problematic. Notably, the rapport between the two phases of Reason, the scientific and the philosophical, should be worked out in greater clarity before it can become serviceable for a truly fruitful philosophising. With the clarification of this issue, Reason as a whole would perhaps appear less antinomic than Jaspers thinks it is. At the same time, the relation between the 'similar' and the 'exceptional', the 'universal' and the 'singular', the 'theoretical' and the 'existential', would also become more comprehensible and less mysterious. On the whole, Jaspers' work seems to be only a beginning. It opens up new perspectives, but does not settle the question of Reason at all satisfactorily. For the rest, Jaspers himself admitted that, after a half a century of experience and careful reflection, he was 'still not finished with learning what Reason really is'.[40] It is now our turn to try to find an answer. Perhaps he has shown a way that may lead to a greater awareness of Reason and of reality. And that is already much.

Bibliography

Works of Jaspers

THE number of books and articles by Jaspers runs into hundreds. To give a complete list of his works is rendered superfluous by three extant bibliographies of Jaspers, each of them up to date to the year of their publication:

(1) Kurt Rossmann, 'Bibliographie der Werke und Schriften von Karl Jaspers', in *Offener Horizont, Festschrift für Karl Jaspers*, Munich: Piper-Verlag, 1953, pp. 449–61.

(2) This has been brought up to date by Rossmann himself for the 1957 publication of critical essays about Jaspers, edited by Paul A. Schilpp, *Philosophen des zwanzigsten Jahrhunderts: Karl Jaspers*, Stuttgart: W. Kohlhammer-Verlag, 1957, pp. 855–70. The adaptation of this bibliography for the English edition, *The Library of Living Philosophers*, vol. 9: *The Philosophy of Karl Jaspers*, New York: Tudor Publishing Co., 1957, pp. 871–86, was made by Dr Ludwig B. Lefebre.

(3) On the basis of the preceding, and utilising the additional sources found in Hans W. Bentz, 'Karl Jaspers in Übersetzungen', *Weltliteratur in Übersetzungen*, Frankfurt am Main, 1961, and Norobu Hosoo's hand-written list of Japanese translations, Hans Saner brought the list up to date in Klaus Piper's (ed.) commemorative volume, *Karl Jaspers: Werk und Wirkung*, Munich: Piper-Verlag, 1963, pp. 175–216.

Secondary Literature

ALLEN, E. L., *The Self and its Hazards: A Guide to the Thought of Karl Jaspers*, London: Hodder & Stoughton, n.d.
——*The Sovereignty of God and the Word of God*, London: Hodder & Stoughton, n.d.
ARMBRUSTER, LUDWIG, *Objekt und Transzendenz bei Jaspers, Sein Gegenstandsbegriff und die Möglichkeit der Metaphysik*, Innsbruck: Felizian Rauch, 1957.
BARRETT, WILLIAM, *Irrational Man*, London: Heinemann, 2nd ed., 1961.
BARTH, HEINRICH, 'Glaube und Vernunft als Existenzproblem,' *Theologische Zeitschrift*, II (1946), pp. 204–20.
BARTH, TIMOTHEUS, 'Philosophie, Wissenschaft, und Religion. Ein Gespräch mit K. Jaspers,' *Wissenschaft und Weisheit*, XLIX (1958), pp. 379–95.

BATAILLE, G., 'Nietzsche et Jésus selon Gide et Jaspers', *Critique*, VI (1950), pp. 94–114.

BECK, MAXIMILIAN, 'Kritik der Schelling-Jaspers-Heidegger'schen Ontologie', *Philosophische Hefte*, IV (1934), pp. 97–164.

BLACKHAM, H. J., *Six Existentialist Thinkers*, London: Routledge & Kegan Paul, 1961.

BLAHA, OTTOKAR, *Logische Wirklichkeitsstruktur und personaler Seinsgrund.* Graz: Stiasny-Verlag, 1955.

——*Das unmittelbare Wissen*, Vienna: Herder-Verlag, 1959.

BOAS, GEORGE, *The Limits of Reason*, London: Routledge & Kegan Paul, 1961.

BOLLNOW, OTTO F., 'Existenzphilosophie und Geschichte', *Blätter für Deutsche Philosophie*, XI (1938), pp. 337–78.

——'Existenzerhellung und philosophische Anthropologie', *Blätter für Deutsche Philosophie*, XII (1939), pp. 133–74.

BRACK, PAUL J., 'Karl Jaspers und die Christliche Religion', *Schweizer Rundschau*, LVIII (1958–59), pp. 547–57.

BRECHT, FRANZ JOSEPH, *Heidegger und Jaspers*. Die beiden Grundformen der Existenzphilosophie. Wuppertal: Marées-Verlag, 1948.

BURI, FRITZ, *Albert Schweizer und Karl Jaspers*, Zürich: Artemis-Verlag, 1950.

——*Theologie der Existenz*, Berne and Stuttgart: P. Haupt-Verlag, 1954.

CAMPENHAUSEN, HANS (VON), 'Die philosophische Kritik des Christentums bei Karl Jaspers', *Zeitschrift für Theologie und Kirche*, LVIII (1951), pp. 230–48.

ČAPEK, MILIČ, *The Philosophical Impact of Contemporary Physics*, Princeton: Van Nostrand, 1961.

COCHRANE, ARTHUR, *The Existentialists and God*, Philadelphia, Westminster Press, 1956.

COLLINS, JAMES, 'An Approach to Karl Jaspers', *Thought*, XX (1945), pp. 657–91.

——'Karl Jaspers' Philosophical Logic', *The New Scholasticism*, XXIII (1949), pp. 414–20.

——*The Existentialists. A Critical Study*, Chicago: Henry Regnery Co., 1952.

——'Wissenschaft und Philosophie bei Jaspers', see SCHILPP, pp. 101–29.

DELESALLE, JACQUES, 'Cet étrange secret', *Études Carmélitaines*, XXXVI (1957), pp. 295–301.

DE WAELHENS, ALPHONSE, 'Descartes et la pensée phénoménologique', *Revue néoscolastique de philosophie*, XLI (1938), pp. 571–89.

——*La philosophie de Martin Heidegger*, Louvain: Publications Universitaires, 4th ed., 1955.

DE WAELHENS, ALPHONSE, 'Un véritable existentialisme: la philosophie de Karl Jaspers', *Orbe*, II (1946), pp. 11–25.

——'The Outlook for Existential Phenomenology', *International Philosophical Quarterly*, II (1962), pp. 458–73.

DIAZ, GONZALO, *Begriff und Problem der Situation*, Freiburg i/Br. 1961.

DOPP, JOSEPH, *Leçons de logique formelle*, Louvain: Publications Universitaires de Louvain, 1950, 3 vols.

DÖRING, W., 'Nietzsche als philosophischer Erzieher. Kritischer Aufsatz zu K. Jaspers', *Erzieher*, XII (1936), pp. 41–5.

DUFRENNE, MIKEL and RICOEUR, PAUL, *Karl Jaspers et la philosophie de l'existence*, Paris: Éditions du Seuil, 1947.

DUFRENNE, MIKEL, 'La philosophie de Karl Jaspers', *Études Germaniques*, III (1948), pp. 64–79.

EARLE, WILLIAM, 'Die Anthropologie in der Philosophie von Karl Jaspers', see SCHILPP, pp. 515–31.

ELIADE, MIRCEA, *The Sacred and the Profane*, New York: Harper & Bros., 1961.

FAHRENBACH, HELMUT, 'Philosophische Existenzerhellung und theologische Existenzmitteilung', Zur Auseinandersetzung zwischen Karl Jaspers und Rudolf Bultmann, *Theologische Rundschau*, XXIV (1956–57), pp. 77–99; 105–35.

FABRO, CORNELIO, 'Jaspers et Kierkegaard', *Revue des sciences philosophiques et théologiques*, XXXVII (1953), pp. 209–52.

——*God in Exile: Modern Atheism*, New York: Newmann Press, 1968.

FEITH, ERNST R., *Psychologismus und Transzendentalismus bei Karl Jaspers*, Berne: Buckdruckerei K. Baumann, 1945.

FEULING, DANIEL, 'Zur Existenzphilosophie', *Theologische Revue*, XXXVII (1938), pp. 473–82.

FISCHER, HANNS, *Karl Jaspers Trilogy*, New York: Russel F. Moore Co., 1951.

FRANK, ERICH, *Wissen, Wollen, Glauben*, Gesammelte Aufsätze zur Philosophiegeschichte und Existenzphilosophie. Zürich-Stuttgart: Artemis-Verlag; Chicago: Henry Regnery Co., 1955.

FRIES, HENRICH, 'Existenz und Transzendenz', Gott und Mensch in der Philosophie von Karl Jaspers. *Der Mensch vor Gott, Festschrift Th. Steinbüchel*, Düsseldorf: Tabmos-Verlag, 1948, pp. 303–20.

——*Ist der Glaube ein Verrat am Menschen?* Eine Begegnung mit Karl Jaspers. Speyer: Pilger-Verlag, 1950.

——'Karl Jaspers und das Christentum', *Theologischer Quartalschrift*, CXXXII (1952), pp. 257–87.

FURGER, FRANZ, *Struktureinheit der Wahrheit*, Ph.D. thesis presented to the Gregorianum (Rome), Salzburg by the author, 1960.

GABRIEL, LEO, *Existenzphilosophie von Kierkegaard bis Sartre*, Vienna: Herold-Verlag, 1951.

GABRIEL, LEO, 'Die Philosophie der Grenzsituation bei Karl Jaspers', *Universitas*, VI (1951), pp. 609–14.

GIGNOUX, VICTOR, *La philosophie existentielle*, Paris: Lefebvre, 2nd ed., 1955.

GRANGER, GILLES-GASTON, *La raison*, Paris: Presses Universitaires de France, Coll. 'Que sais-je?', 1955.

GRÉGOIRE, FRANZ, *Études hégéliennes. Les points capitaux du System*. Louvain: 1958.

GRÜNERT, ERICH. *Objektive Norm, Situation und Entscheidung*. Ein Vergleich zwischen Thomas von Aquino und Karl Jaspers. Bonn: 1953.

——'Der Einfluss Kants auf Karl Jaspers'. Zugang zur Transzendenz bei Kant und Karl Jaspers. *Freiburger Zeitschrift für Philosophie und Theologie*, III (1956), pp. 21–8.

GUSDORF, GEORGES, *La parole*, Paris: Presses Universitaires de France, 1953.

HARTT, J. N., 'God, Transcendence and Freedom in the Philosophy of Jaspers', *Review of Metaphysics*, IV (1951), pp. 247–58.

HASHIMOTO, FUMIO, 'Die Philosophie von Karl Jaspers in Japan', see PIPER, pp. 165–8.

HENDERSON, I., 'Karl Jaspers and Demythologizing', *Expository Times*, LXV (1953–4), pp. 291–3.

HENNIG, HERBERT, 'Die existenzialphilosophie Jaspers''. Eine Grenzerscheinung der Geisteswissenschaft. *Das Goetheanum*, XVII (1938), pp. 131–3.

HERSCH, JEANNE, *L'illusion philosophique*. Paris: Alcan, 1936.

——'Une philosophie de l'existence. Karl Jaspers', *Lettres*, III (1945), pp. 56–63.

——'La caricature de l'existentialisme et son vrai visage', *Suisse Contemporaine*, VI (1946), pp. 339–57.

——'K. Jaspers. Signification et efficacité d'un refus', *Ibid.*, pp. 803–5.

——'Jaspers in Frankreich', see PIPER, pp. 147–51.

HOFFMAN, KURT, 'Die Grundbegriffe der Philosophie Karl Jaspers', see SCHILPP, pp. 81–100.

HOLM, SÖREN, 'Jaspers' Religionsphilosophie. Ist Jaspers Religionsphilosoph?', see SCHILPP, pp. 637–62.

HOMMES, ULRICH, *Die Existenzerhellung und das Recht*, Frankfurt am Main: Klostermann, 1962.

HORKHEIMER, M., 'Bemerkungen zu Jaspers' "Nietzsche"', *Zeitschrift für Sozialforschung*, VI (1937), pp. 407–14.

HORN, HERMANN, *Philosophischer und Christlicher Glaube erläutert an dem Verständnis Jesu in der Philosophie von Karl Jaspers*, Essen: Neue Deutsche Schule Verlagsgesellschaft, 1961.

HOSSFELD, PAUL, 'Karl Jaspers Stellung zur Religion', *Freiburger Zeitschrift für Philosophie und Theologie*, V (1958), pp. 49–54.

HUSSERL, EDMUND, 'Philosophie als strenge Wissenschaft', *Logos I* (1910–11), pp. 310–57.

HYPPOLITE, JEAN, 'Jaspers', *Dieu Vivant*, I (1945), pp. 63–80.

——'Situation de Jaspers', *Esprit*, XVI (1948), pp. 482–96.

IMLE, F., 'Jaspers als Existenzphilosoph', *Philosophisches Jahrbuch*, XLIX (1936), pp. 178–93; L, (1937), pp. 238–51.

JASPERS, LUDGER, *Der Begriff der menschlichen Situation in der Existenzphilosophie von Karl Jaspers*, Würzburg: Becker, 1936.

JOLIVET, RÉGIS, *Les doctrines existentialistes de Kierkegaard à J. P. Sartre*. Abbaye S. Wandrille: Ed. de Fontenelle, 1948.

——(ed.) *La crise de la raison dans la pensée contemporaine*, Coll. 'Recherches de Philosophie', Paris: Desclée De Brouwer, 1960.

LENZ-MEDOC, PAULUS, 'Philosophes d'aujourd'hui', *Les Études Philosophiques*, XIII (1958), pp. 200–203.

LICHTIGFELD, ADOLPH, 'Jaspers' Concept of Transcendence (God) in Recent Literature', *Philosophy*, XXVIII (1953), pp. 255–59.

——*Jaspers' Metaphysics*, London: Colibri Press, 1954.

——'Der Gottesbegriff in Jaspers Philosophie', see SCHILPP, pp. 663–72.

LOHFF, WENZEL, *Glaube und Freiheit. Das theologische Problem der Religionskritik von Karl Jaspers*, Gütersloh: C. Bertelsmann-Verlag, 1957.

LOTZ, JOHANNES B., 'Die Transzendenz bei Jaspers und im Christentum', *Stimmen der Zeit*, CXXXVII (1940), pp. 71–6.

——'Analogie und Chiffre. Zur Transzendenz in der Scholastik und bei Jaspers', *Scholastik*, XV (1940), pp. 39–56.

MADER, HANS, *Problemgeschichtliche Studie zur Periechontologie Karl Jaspers*. Vienna: 1952.

——'Das Seinsdenken bei Karl Jaspers', *Wissenschaft und Weltbild*, X (1957), pp. 50–58.

MCINERNY, RALPH, 'Metaphysics and Subjectivity. An Approach to Karl Jaspers', *Proceedings of the American Catholic Philosophical Association*, XXXII (1858), pp. 172–82.

MAIRE, GILBERT, *Une régression mentale*. Paris: B. Grosset, 1959.

MARC, A., 'L'existence humaine et la raison', *Revue néoscolastique de philosophie*, XXXIX (1936), pp. 518–24.

MARCEL, GABRIEL, *Du refus à l'invocation*, Paris: Gallimard, 1940.

MARCK, S., 'La philosophie de l'existence dans l'oeuvre de K. Jaspers et de M. Heidegger', *Revue philosophique de la France et de l'étranger*, CXXI (1936), pp. 197–219.

MASI, GIUSEPPE, *La ricerca della verità in Karl Jaspers*, Bologna: C. Zuffi, 1953.

MAYER, ANTON, *Karl Jaspers' Erziehungsphilosophie*, Erlangen: unpublished Ph.D. thesis, 1955.

MAYER, ERNST, 'Philosophie und Philosophische Logik bei Karl Jaspers', *Offener Horizont*, Munich: Piper-Verlag, 1952, pp. 63–72.

MERLEAU-PONTY, MAURICE, *Phénomenologie de la perception*, Paris: 2nd ed., 1945.

MIÉVILLE, HENRI, 'Le problème de la transcendence et de la mort dans la philosophie existentielle de Karl Jaspers', *Revue de Théologie et de Philosophie*, XXVIII (1940), pp. 87–111.

NIEL, HENRI, 'Karl Jaspers et le problème de la vérité', *Critique*, IV (1948), pp. 1080–91.

ORTEGAT, PAUL, 'La philosophie religieuse de Karl Jaspers', *Nouvelle revue théologique*, LXX (1948), pp. 257–73.

PAREYSON, LUIGI, *La filosofia dell'existenza e Carlo Jaspers*. Napoli: Loffredo, 1940.

PATRI, A., 'Jaspers et la foi philosophique', *Monde Nouveau*, IX (1953), pp. 62–4.

PAUMEN, JEAN, 'Signification du premier hommage de Karl Jaspers à Max Weber', *Melanges Georges Smets*, Brussels: Ed. de la Librarie Encyclopédique, 1952, pp. 115–33.

——*Raison et existence chez Karl Jaspers*. Brussels: Ed. Parthenon, 1958.

PFEIFFER, JOHANNES, *Existenzphilosophie. Eine Einführung in Heidegger und Jaspers*, Hamburg: Meiner-Verlag, 3rd ed., 1952.

PFISTER, OSKAR, 'Karl Jaspers als Sigmund Freuds Widersacher', *Philosophische Hefte*, VI (1952), pp. 241–75.

PIPER, KLAUS (ed.), *Karl Jaspers: Werk und Wirkung*, Zum 80. Geburtstag von Jaspers, Munich: Piper-Verlag, 1963.

RÄBER, THOMAS, *Das Dasein in der 'Philosophie' von Karl Jaspers*. Berne: Francke-Verlag, 1955.

RAMMING, G., *Karl Jaspers und Heinrich Rickert: Existentialismus und Wertphilosophie*. Berne: Francke-Verlag, 1948.

REDING, MARCEL, *Die Existenzphilosophie. Heidegger, Sartre, Gabriel Marcel und Jaspers in kritischer-systematischer Sicht*. Düsseldorf: Schwann, 1949.

REINHARDT, KURT, *The Existentialist Revolt*. New York: F. Ungar Publishing Co., 1960.

REISNER, ERWIN, 'Die Frage der Philosophie und die Antwort der Theologie', *Zeitschrift für Theologie und Kirche*, LXIII (1956), pp. 251–63.

RIES, J., 'Menschliche Existenz bei Jaspers', *Die Neue Ordnung*, IV (1950), pp. 418–26; 527–31.

——'Transzendenz bei Jaspers', *Die Neue Ordnung*, V (1951), pp. 230–40.

RICHTSCHEID, PAUL, 'Über die Liebe: Versuch einer Aneignung von Karl Jaspers' Philosophie', *Zeitschrift fur philosophische Forschung*, IV (1949–50), pp. 111–19.

RICOEUR, PAUL, *Gabriel Marcel et Karl Jaspers*, Paris: Éditions du Temps Present, 1948.

——'Philosophie und Religion bei Karl Jaspers', see SCHILPP, pp. 604–36.

SCHILPP, PAUL A. (ed.), *Philosophen des zwanzigsten Jahrhunderts: Karl Jaspers*, 24 erklärende und kritische Aufsätze über Jaspers' Philosophie, Stuttgart: W. Kohlhammer-Verlag, 1957.
English edition: *The Library of Living Philosophers*, vol. 9: *The Philosophy of Karl Jaspers*, New York: Tudor Publishing Co., 1957.

SCHMIDHÄUSER, ULRICH, *Allgemeine Wahrheit und existentielle Wahrheit bei Karl Jaspers*, Ph.D. dissertation, Bonn, 1953.

SMITH, RONALD G., 'Karl Jaspers on Theology and Philosophy', *The Hibbert Journal*, XLIX (1951), pp. 62–6.

SPERNA, WEILAND J., *Humanitas, Christianitas*. A Critical Survey of Kierkegaard's and Jaspers' Thoughts in Connection with Christianity, Groningen: 1951.

THIEL, MANFRED, 'Die Weisheit der Komödie. Karl Jaspers in tiefer Verehrung zum 70. Geburtstag', *Studium Generale*, VI (1953), pp. 118–26.

THYSSEN, JOHANNES, 'Jaspers' Buch "Von der Wahrheit"', *Archiv für Philosophie*, V (1954), pp. 170–224.

——'Der Begriff des Scheiterns bei Karl Jaspers', see SCHILPP, pp. 285–322.

TILLIETTE, XAVIER, *Karl Jaspers. Théorie de la vérité, Métaphysique des chiffres, Foi philosophique*. Paris: Coll. 'Théologie', vol. 44, Aubier, 1959.

TONQUÉDEC (DE), JOSEPH, *L'existence d'après Karl Jaspers*, Paris: Beauchesne, 1945.

VAN RIET, GEORGES, *Problèmes d'épistémologie*, Louvain: Publications Universitaires de Louvain, 1960.

WAHL, JEAN, 'Le problème du choix. L'existence et la transcendence dans la philosophie de Jaspers', *Revue métaphysique et morale*, XLI (1934), pp. 405–44.

——'Le Nietzsche de Jaspers', *Recherches philosophiques*, VI (1936–37), pp. 346–62.

——*Existence humaine et transcendence*, Neuchâtel: Éd. de la Baconnière, 1944.

——'Karl Jaspers et la France', *Critique*, IV (1948), pp. 523–30.

——*Études kierkegaardiennes*. Paris: 2nd ed., Vrin, 1949.

WAHL, JEAN, *La pensée de l'existence. Kierkegaard-Jaspers*, Paris: Flammarion, 1951.

——'Ein Beitrag zum Thema Jaspers und Kierkegaard', see SCHILPP, pp. 430–35.

——*La théorie de la vérité dans la philosophie de Jaspers*, Paris: 'Les Cours de Sorbonne', Tournier et Constans, 1953.

WELTE, BERNARD, 'Die philosophische Glaube bei Karl Jaspers und die Möglichkeit seiner Deutung durch tomistische Philosophie', *Symposion*, II (1949), pp. 1–190.

WERNER, MARTIN, 'Existenzphilosophie und Christentum bei Karl Jaspers', *Schweizerische theologische Umschau*, VI (1953), pp. 21–40.

Notes

A WAY OF POSING THE PROBLEM

[1]'Hegel, Husserl, and Reason Today', *The Modern Schoolman*, XXXVII (1960), 172.
[2]*Ibid.* [3]*The Triumph of Subjectivity*, New York 1958, 119.
[4]*Ibid.*, 125. [5]*Ibid.*, 121. [6]*Ibid.*

PART I

INTRODUCTION

[1]*Ph I*, 1. In the light of this question, the charge made by Heidegger, namely that Jaspers had 'sidestepped the problem of Being as such altogether', appears rather unfounded. Cf. *Bulletin de la Société française de philosophie*, XXXVII (1937), 193.
[2]Cf. 'Die Grundfrage wird Ursprung, aber liegt nicht am Anfang.' *VdW*, 36.
[3]Cf. 'Die Frage nach dem Sein ist zugleich die Frage nach dem Fragenden.' *PGI*, 28.
[4]Ludger Jaspers, O.S.B., *Der Begriff der menschlichen Situation in der Existenzphilosophie von Karl Jaspers*, Würzburg 1936, 1 (italics mine).
[5]Such is the fundamental thesis of Gabriel Marcel's essay, 'Situation fondamentale et situations limites chez Karl Jaspers', in *Du refus à l'invocation*, Paris 1940, 284–326.
[6]*ExP*, 31. [7]*VuEx*, 52.
[8]*VdW*, 37; also called *Grundstimmung, Grundhaltung, Grundverfassung*.
[9]*ExP*, 12. [10]*VuEx*, 43.
[11]Mikel Dufrenne and Paul Ricoeur, *Karl Jaspers et la philosophie de l'existence*, Paris 1947, 27.
[12]*VdW*, 37.
[13]Cf. 'En stigmatisant dans la philosophie cartésienne le témoignage d'une raison livrée à elle-même, Jaspers n'entend ainsi plaider que les droits d'une philosophie du refus des primats, en fonction de laquelle les exigences universelles de la raison puissent s'accorder aux sources singulières de l'existence, dans une réciprocité intimement médiatrice de la transparence de celles-ci et la plénitude de celles-là.' Jean Paumen, *Raison et Existence chez Karl Jaspers*, Brussels 1958, 98–9.
[14]James Collins, 'An approach to Karl Jaspers', *Thought*, XX (1945), 673.

CHAPTER I

[1]*Ph I*, 9.
[2]In this, Jaspers agrees with M. Merleau-Ponty who insists that 'no philosophy can afford to be ignorant of the problem of this finitude under pain of failing to understand itself as philosophy.' *Phenomenology of Perception*, E. tr. Colin Smith, London 1962, 38.

271

19

[3]One must not attach any great importance at this point to my translation of 'Dasein'—a difficult and many-shaded word in Jaspers' use—by the word 'Nature'. It should rather be taken as a point of comparison: as pure and positive Dasein, man is *like* Nature. Jaspers himself uses the word for just such a comparison: 'Als Positivität des Daseins kann er ungebrochen wie Natur sein, aus der Fülle seiner fraglosen Selbstverständlichkeit leben.' *VdW*, 62. For a detailed study of the tremendously complex notion of Dasein, I would like to call attention to the work of Thomas Räber, *Das Dasein in der 'Philosophie' von Karl Jaspers*, Berne 1955.

[4]Cf. 'Dasein weiss sich als das nicht selbst über sich Entscheidende; es ist im tiefsten Grunde das Geschehende.' *VdW*, 62.

[5]Cf. 'Dasein will seine Befriedigung und Glück. Es scheint sie zu erringen und kennt den Augenblick der Volkommenheit.' *Ibid.*, 54.

[6]Cf. 'Grundzug des sich bewusstgewordenen Daseins: Dasein is vergängliches Zeitdasein.' *Ibid.*, 63.

[7]*Ph I*, 2.   [8]*Ibid.*   [9]*VdW*, 62.

[10]Cf. '. . . d'abord la question est inséparable de celui qui questionne; ce qui en termes purement intellectuels est une "question" (*Frage*), c'est-à-dire un énoncé appelant une réponse, est d'abord fiché au coeur de l'existence comme un malaise (*Unruhe*) et une impulsion (*Antrieb*); qui ne s'est pas éveillé à ce malaise et à cette impulsion, ne pose pas la question . . .' Dufrenne and Ricoeur, *Karl Jaspers . . .*, 27.

[11]Cf. '. . . l'angoisse ruine précisément le caractère de "chose" de l'existence.' Paul Ricoeur, *Gabriel Marcel et Karl Jaspers*, Paris n. d. (1948), 23, note 1.

[12]Merleau-Ponty, *Phenomenology . . .*, 37.

[13]Cf. 'Die Spaltung in mich als Subjekt und den Gegenstand als Objekt ist Grund-situation, d.h. immer gegeben, sofern Denken und überhaupt etwas gibt.' Ulrich Schmidhäuser, *Allgemeine Wahrheit und existentielle Wahrheit bei Karl Jaspers* (unpublished Ph.D. dissertation, Faculty of Philosophy, University of Bonn, 1953), 17.

[14]*EiP*, 28.   [15]*Ibid.*, 29–30.   [16]*PGl*, 28.   [17]*VdW*, 231–2.
[18]*Ph I*, 4.   [19]*VdW*, 37.   [20]*Ph III*, 2.

[21]Cf. 'Es ist, als ob wir aus der Wirklichkeit gefallen seien . . .' *ExP*, 67.

[22]*EiP*, 30–31.   [23]*Ph I*, 5.

[24]Expressions of Jaspers, such as 'das Sein als Objektsein *nicht aus sich besteht, sondern als solches Sein für ein erkennendes Subjekt ist, wie es diesem erscheint,*' (*Ph I*, 30) seem to assert not only the causal dependence of objects on something else but also their unsubstantiality or mere phenomenality. A closer examination of this phenomenality of objects will follow in Chapter II.

[25]*Ph I*, 5–6.   [26]See *Ph I*, 104–8.

[27]Kurt Hoffman, 'The Basic Concepts of Jaspers' Philosophy', *The Library of Living Philosophers*, vol. 9: *The Philosophy of Karl Jaspers*, ed. Paul Arthur Schilpp, New York 1957, 98.

[28]Jaspers would particularly protest against any Cartesian type of analysis of selfhood in terms of *res*. One can find an excellent summary of Jaspers' attitude towards Descartes on this point in an article by Alphonse De Waelhens, 'Descartes et la pensée phénoménologique', *Revue néoscolastique de philosophie*, XLI (1938), 571–89.

²⁹Cf. 'Denn das Denken als Denken bleibt in der Spaltung. Aber das Erkennen drängt auf die *Rückkehr aus der Spaltung*, . . .' *VdW*, 250. For the characterisation of man's cognitive situation as a 'situation of return from the subject-object-split' see the article by Johannes B. Lotz, S.J., 'Analogie und Chiffre', *Scholastik*, XV (1940), 39–56.

³⁰Cf. 'Eine ontologisch konzipierte *Allgemeinheit* des Seins, gültig für jedermann, ist unmöglich.' *Ph III*, 24.

³¹The word 'use' is premeditated. Jaspers' terminology is very fluid. I tend to agree with William Earle who, in the introduction to his translation, *Reason and Existenz*, New York 1955, points out (in connection with the term Encompassing) that 'such a term, like all the key terms in Jaspers' philosophising, has a clear *use;* but it has no clear, distinct, objective content' (p. 10). But even that seems to be rather optimistically put, especially if we compare it with Jaspers' own attitude towards clear terminology in philosophy. He warns that 'since philosophical thought is true only in motion . . . the primacy of terminology, or even the leaning and clinging to words, is fatal. The pre-occupation with terminology turns philosophy into a schoolboy-traffic, in which philosophy itself disappears.' *VdW*, 428.

CHAPTER II

¹There exists a very fine work on this point by Ludwig Armbruster, S.J.: *Objekt und Transzendenz bei Karl Jaspers*, Innsbruck 1957. Although some of Armbruster's conclusions do not agree with my way of reading Jaspers, his patient and factual analyses can be recommended as an invaluable complement to my summary treatment.

²*Karl Jaspers* . . ., 31.

³A few random examples: 'gegenständliche Wissenschaft' (*VdW*, 35); 'Gegenstand empirischer Beobachtung und Erforschung' (*Ph I*, 9); 'Jede Wissenschaft hat einen Gegenstand" (*Ph I*, 318); 'Was ich weiss, ist also jeweils ein Objektsein im Bewusstsein überhaupt' (*PGl*, 28); 'Wahrheiten, . . . die also kein reines Objekt für das Bewusstsein überhaupt erfassen' (*Ph I*, 93). Nevertheless it is true that one can find instances where Jaspers distinguishes between the meanings of *Objekt* and *Gegenstand*—but only to fuse them the next moment.

⁴*VdW*, 236; *Ph II*, 338.   ⁵*Ph I*, 7.   ⁶*Ph II*, 338.   ⁷*Ph I*, 61.

⁸'. . . gerade diese Entgegensetzung *allein* macht den Objektcharakter aus . . . In purem Oppositionscharakter *erschöpft* sich das Objektsein.' See 'Kritik der Schelling-Jaspers-Heidegger'schen Ontologie', *Philosophische Hefte*, IV (1933), 103.

⁹Cf. 'Kein Ichbewusstsein ist ohne irgendein noch so dürftiges Gegenstands-bewusst-sein.' *Ph I*, 8.

¹⁰*Ph II*, 41.

¹¹Cf. 'Diese Einheit ist nicht die Zahl Eins; sie ist auch nicht das Eine, das dem Anderen gegenübersteht; sondern sie ist das qualitative Einessein, das alles Gegenständlichsein, auch die Zahl Eins und das Eine, gegenüber dem

Anderen, erst begründet. Sie ist vor allem bestimmten Denken die Kategorie überhaupt, ist das alle Bestimmtheit erst Ermöglichende.' *VdW*, 232.

[12]*Ibid.*   [13]*Ibid.*

[14]Cf. '. . . Kategorien, die aus der Einheit der Apperzeption fliessen, welche Einheit aber selbst nicht Kategorie der Einheit, sondern deren Grund sei.' *Ph I*, 41.

[15]*VdW*, 292.

[16]Cf. 'Es ist ein Subjekt überhaupt, vertretbar durch jedes andere Subjekt, das Bewusstsein schlechthin, der Verstand als der Punkt, auf den alles Wissbare bezogen ist . . . Dieses formale Subjekt is überall, wo Sein als Bewusstsein ist . . .' *Ph II*, 26. Although Jaspers shares the interest of Kant in the *a priori* synthetic unity of the *Ich überhaupt*, which for Kant antecedes all determinate thought (*KrV B. 134*), he shows himself on the whole more concerned with the concrete existence of the thinker, which is the common soil of all the perspectives of thought, including that of general consciousness. It would be interesting to see a comparative study on the affinities and divergences of these two thinkers. All the more so since many of the passing remarks on this point made by the commentators of Jaspers contain misrepresentations either of Kant, or of Jaspers, or of the way Jaspers understood Kant. The best available study that I know of is the extremely short article by Erich Grünert, 'Der Einfluss Kants auf Karl Jaspers: Zugang zur Transzendenz bei Kant und Karl Jaspers', *Freiburger Zeitschrift für Philosophie und Theologie*, III (1956), 21–28. For Jaspers' own understanding and interpretation of Kant I would recommend his *Psych Weltansch*, 408–28; *Ph I*, 40ff; *Ph III*, 157ff; *VdW*, 21–22.

[17]*Ph II*, 339.   [18]*Ibid.*

[19]'Gegenständlich ist was dem Gedanken gegenüber in seiner eigenen Bestimmtheit *steht*, und worin deshalb der Gedanke seinerseits zum *Stehen* kommt.' See 'Der philosophische Glaube bei Karl Jaspers und die Möglichkeit seiner Deutung durch die Tomistische Philosophie', *Symposion*, II (1949), 33.

[20]Cf. 'Gegenüber dem Fliessen der Vorstellungen, dem Wandel der Bilder, dem ruhelosen Werden und Vergehen der Dinge, gegenüber allem Schwanken und Entgleiten wird im Begriff eine Bedeutung *fixiert* und unverwechselbar festgehalten. *Der Begriff bringt gleichsam zum Stehen*, indem er seinen Sinn unterscheidet und anderen ausschliesst, dadurch sich *eindeutig bestimmt*. Im *unbewegten Begriff* wird auch die Bewegung gedacht. Auch der Begriff vom Geschehen ist als Begriff kein Geschehen. Auch der Begriff von etwas, das erst in der Zeit wirklich geworden ist, ist als Begriff ein *zeitloser Sinn*.' *VdW*, 276–7 (italics mine).

[21]*Ibid.*, 232.

[22]Cf. 'Die Grenze einer *gegenstandslosen* Anschauung ist psychologisch zu beobachten (etwa im Erwachen: wenn ich in einem fremden Hotel morgens ein unklar erfülltes beängstigendes Bewusstsein erleide und plötzlich in Ruhe gegenständlich denke: es ist ein vorbeifahrender Zug, gestern abends sah ich ja die Schienen neben dem Hause.' *Ibid.*

[23]Cf. '*Vergegenständlichung* ist verknüpft mit einem Auffassen unter der Kategorie irgendeines Allgemeinen . . .' *Ibid.* 'Ohne diese schaffende Subjektivität tritt deine Objektivität ins Dasein.' *Ph II*, 341.

²⁴Cf. '. . . Hervorbringen nur der Form der Erscheinung, nicht dem Dasein nach.' *VdW*, 238.

²⁵*Ibid.*, 48; *Ph II*, 341.   ²⁶*VdW*, 233.

²⁷Cf. 'Das Allgemeine ist aus dem Einzelsein nicht abzuleiten (es ist denkbar das Dasein von endlosen Einzelnen, Unbezogenen, so dass kein Allgemeines für uns entstände). Das Einzelne ist aus dem Allgemeinen nicht abzuleiten (es ist in jedem Einzelnen ein vom Denken Unerreichtes, eine Grenze, ein Rest).' *Ibid.*

²⁸*Ibid.*

²⁹Erich Grünert notes that in Jaspers' terminology the word *Denken* takes the place of the Kantian generic term *Vorstellen*. In Kant *Vorstellung* in the specific sense has an empirical meaning of re-presentational imagination and an *a priori* meaning of presentational or productive imagination. In both senses *Vorstellung* is an intermediary between sense-perception and understanding, a faculty of schematisms. But, according to Mr Grünert, *Vorstellung* for Kant also has a generic sense of representation in general whereby something is presented to man in any way whatever. The species of *Vorstellung* in this sense would be sense-intuition (*sinnliches Anschauen*), intellectual cognition (*Erkennen*), and thinking (*Denken*). Intellectual cognition for Kant consists in the subordination of sense-data to a category of understanding. From this it follows that anything that is not given in sense-intuition is, strictly speaking unknowable for Kant; thinkable perhaps, but unknowable.

For Jaspers the generic term is *Denken*, within which he distinguishes thinking that results in science (*Wissen, Erkennen, Verstandesdenken*), and thinking which is followed by ascertaining (*Vergewisserung, Innewerden*). By the first kind of thinking man attains Being as being-an-object, being as subsumable to the categories of understanding; in the second kind, being that can never become an object.

As far as Jaspers' doctrine is concerned, this distinction of Mr Grünert's is certainly correct. In regard to Kant, one cannot be quite so sure. For reference, see 'Der Einflusse Kants . . .,' *Freiburg, Zeitschr. für Phil. u. Theol.*, III, 21–33.

³⁰*VdW*, 240–41.   ³¹Cf. *Ibid.*, 241.

³²Cf. 'Es gibt nicht etwa ein Material und Formen, die unabhängig voneinander sind, die dann zusammentreten und die objective Welt bilden. Das wäre eine Hypostasierung zweier Seinursprünge, wäre nicht mehr eine Analyse des gegenständlichen Denkens, sondern eine Ontologie des Seins an sich.' *Ibid.*

³³Cf. 'Das Materiale muss nicht als Material überhaupt, sondern ein schon durch Form bestimmtes Material sein, um *gegenstandserfüllend* zu werden. Die Form überhaupt ist *materialbestimmt*, wenn sie bestimmte Form wird, und das Material überhaupt ist schon *formbestimmt*, wenn es bestimmtes Material wird.' *Ibid.*

³⁴Cf. 'Es zeigt sich weiter, dass in dieser Beziehung nichts gibt, was endgültig nur Material oder endgültig nur Form wäre. Was Form ist, kann in anderem Verhältnis Material sein, und was Material ist, kann in anderer Beziehung Form sein. Je nach der Beziehung im Gedachten gewinnt, was eben Form war, die Rolle des Materials und umgekehrt.' *Ibid.*, 241–2.

³⁵Cf. 'Das uns allen Gemeinsame des Bewusstseins überhaupt ish nicht eine blosse Ähnlichkeit unserer Artung und ihrer Organisation. Diese Gemeinsame

ist vielmehr schlechthin identisch. Abweichungen sind nicht Modifikationen der Artung, sondern sind Fehler, die Unwahrheit bedeuten.' *Ibid.*, 65.

[36]In a more specific but not unrelated context, Jaspers expresses this disproportionality between the universal and the particular. Speaking of thought and sense-intention which, we must recall, furnish respectively the universal form and the particular matter of an object, he remarks: 'Nur im idealen Grenzfall käme Denken und Anschauung als Erkennen so zusammen, dass dem Denken volle anschauliche Erfüllung würde. Gemessen an diesem idealen Ziel vollendeter Erkenntnis hat die faktische Erkenntnis an Anschauung *entweder zuviel* in einem überflutenden, nicht aufgefassten Gewühl *oder zuwenig*, weil Denkintentionen unerfüllt bleiben.' *Ibid.*, 256. Cf. also: '. . . es ist in jedem Einzelnen ein vom Denken Unerreichtes, eine Grenze, ein Rest.' *Ibid.*, 233.

[37]Cf. 'Von diesen Ganzen als Ideen kann ich nicht wissen wie von Gegenständen, . . .' *Ph I*, 53. To see how Jaspers combines the Kantian notion of Idea as a regulative principle with the Hegelian one as the highest, most completed form of objectivity, I refer the reader to Dufrenne and Ricoeur, *Karl Jaspers . . .*, 41–6.

[38]Cf. 'Jedoch erweisen sich . . . alle gedachten Einheiten als Einheiten in der Welt, nicht als diejenige der Welt. Diese ist als erkannt in dem einen Weltbild des Ganzen nicht erreichbar.' *Ph I*, 104.

[39]*Ibid.*, 107. [40]*Ibid.* [41]*VdW*, 284.

[42]Cf. 'Wir müssen trennen um zu verbinden, verbinden um von neuem zu trennen.' *Ibid.*, 386.

[43]'The Concept of the "Encompassing" in Jaspers' Philosophy', *Living Philosophers*, 147.

[44]*VuEx*, 58.

CHAPTER III

[1]*Ph I*, 13–15; *Ph II*, 26–35. [2]*Ph II*, 39–40. [3]*Ph II*, 339.

[4]Cf. 'Die Dunkelheit meiner Ursprünglichkeit habe ich verlassen, indem ich nach ihr frage: das Licht, das in ihr als das Aufleuchten des Innerwerdens meiner selbst schien, erlischt, sobald ich mit ihm zusehen will, was es ist. Es wird klar, dass ich nicht nur die Dunkelheit, sondern den Ursprung selbst verlassen habe . . . Dieses gerade, dass ich nach mir *fragen muss*, zeigt mir, dass ich aus dem Ursprung getreten bin.' *Ibid.*, 25.

[5]*Ph I*, 14. [6]*Ibid.*, 5. [7]*Ibid.*, 8–9.

[8]Cf. 'In solchen Gegenständlichkeiten als Aspekten meiner selbst werde ich mir bewusst wie in Spiegeln. In keinem sehe ich mich ganz und gar, sondern in Teilen; ich erblicke Seiten meines Seins, identifiziere mich partiell mit ihnen, aber ohne ganz und gar identisch mit mir in ihnen zu werden.' *Ph II*, 27.

[9]*Ibid.*, 28. [10]*Ibid.* [11]*Ibid.*, 30. [12]*Ibid.*, 31. [13]*Ibid.*

[14]*Ibid.*, 31–2. [15]*Ibid.*, 32. [16]*Ibid.*

[17]Cf. 'Wohl *weiss* ich auf keine unmittelbare Weise, was und wie ich an mir *selbst* bin, aber ich *schliesse* auf mein Sein als dasjenige, das all meiner Erscheinung *zugrunde liegt*.' *Ibid.*, 33.

¹⁸*Ibid.*, 34.   ¹⁹*Ibid.*, 47.   ²⁰*Ibid.*, 35.

²¹Cf. 'Objektives . . . ist gegeben; ich . . . aber bin Ursprung; zwar nicht Ursprung des Seins überhaupt, aber Ursprung für mich im Dasein.' *Ibid.*, 18.

²²*Ph I*, 13.   ²³*Ibid.*, 10.   ²⁴*Ibid.*, 13.   ²⁵*PGl*, 11.   ²⁶*Ph II*, 26.

²⁷*VdW*, 66.

²⁸Cf. 'Dass ich dieses Bewusstsein überhaupt und darin unpersönlich bin, gibt mir eine spezifische Würde.' *Ph II*, 34.

²⁹*VuEx*, 48; see also *VdW*, 66.

³⁰Cf. 'Aus dem Bewusstsein des Daseins ist das Wesen des Bewusstseins überhaupt nicht abzuleiten . . . Es ist ein Sprung, weil ein anderer Ursprung in Erscheinung tritt.' *VdW*, 68.

³¹Cf. 'Das Bewusstsein überhaupt kann ein daseinsunabhängiges Denken verwirklichen.' *Ibid.*

³²*Ibid.*   ³³*VdW*, 69.   ³⁴*Ibid.*   ³⁵*WiderV*, 27.

³⁶In a private conversation with the author, Jaspers admitted that he had not yet found a satisfying formulation that would neatly express all the aspects he intended by this term. It has already been noted earlier that he was undecided between a Kantian and a Hegelian sort of interpretation of the spirit.

³⁷*VuEx*, 49.

³⁸*VdW*, 72. I would like to point out an important difference between the point of view of this passage and that of the parallel text in *VuEx*, 49. In that work, which dates from 1935, Spirit is presented yet as the universal binding force that 'wants to relate everything to everything, and *exclude nothing*' (italics mine). In *VdW*, dating from 1947, this sort of all-inclusive mediation is reserved to Reason alone (cf. pp. 114, 118).

³⁹The term 'comprehension' already makes us think of the methods of *Verstehende Psychologie* and *Verstehende Soziologie*, as advocated by Dielthey and Weber, whom Jaspers as a young psychiatrist admired very much (cf. *PuW*, 293–4; 306–10).

⁴⁰*PGlangOff*, 115.   ⁴¹*VuEx*, 49–50.   ⁴²*VdW*, 72.

⁴³*Geisteswissenschaften* in German.   ⁴⁴*VdW*, 73.

⁴⁵Cf. 'Die Zeitlichkeit des Daseins ist quantitativ fasslich und homogen, die Zeitlichkeit des Gesites ist qualitativ fasslich als eine sich selbst bewegende inhomogene Zeitlichkeit.' *Ibid.*

⁴⁶*Ibid.*, 71.   ⁴⁷*Ibid.*, 74.   ⁴⁸*Karl Jaspers . . .*, 56.   ⁴⁹*Ibid.*, 42.

⁵⁰*Ph I*, 37–8.

⁵¹*ExP*, 70. For a more detailed treatment of immanence see Bernard Welte, 'Der philosophische Glaube bei Karl Jaspers . . .', *Symposion*, II, 32–5; Johannes B. Lotz, S.J., 'Analogie u. Chiffre', *Scholastik*, XV, 41–50.

⁵²Cf. '. . . der "Satz des Bewusstseins" auch ausgesprochen als: "alles ist Bewusstsein", wird "Satz der Immanenz" . . .' *Ph I*, 49.

⁵³*Ibid.*, 38.

⁵⁴Generally speaking, absolute consciousness signifies two things for Jaspers: the consciousness of unconditioned existential choice whereby man is aware of his ultimate liberty, and the consciousness whereby we intuit Being. More of this later. Here I would like merely to point out the parallelism between absolute consciousness in Jaspers' thought and Kant's practical reason. 'Wie es bei Kant einen Primat der praktischen Vernunft vor der theoretischen

Vernunft gibt, lässt sich bei Jaspers ein Primat des absoluten Bewusstseins gegenüber dem Bewusstsein überhaupt feststellen. Das absolute Bewusstsein "übergreift" das Bewusstsein überhaupt. Was Jaspers mit dem "übergreifen" meint, lässt sich vielleicht so kennzeichenen: Im absoluten Bewusstsein ist der Denkende beim Sein selber; im Bewusstsein in überhaupt ist er nur bei einem Ausschnitt des Seins.'—Erich Grünert, 'Der Einfluss Kants . . .', *Freiburg. Zeitschr. für Phil. u. Theol.*, III, 23. It is to be noted, however, that the parallelism between the two notions is not perfect. From the point of view of Jaspers' terminology, an access to transcendence through practical reason, which would be universally valid, necessary, and within the reach of everyone in general, would still fall under the competence of consciousness in general.

[55]Cf. 'Sein heisst, es ursprünglich *entscheiden*.' *Ph I*, 15.

[56]Although most translators of Jaspers leave this term untranslated (e.g. William Earle, *Reason and Existenz*), I shall render it as 'Existence'. I use the upper case spelling in order to distinguish it from the simple ontological co-principle of essence. Perhaps it would be possible to suggest the same difference by using some such qualified expressions as 'human existence', 'personal existence', 'free existence', and so on, but the usefulness of these expressions is greatly diminished by the fact that they would still give the impression that *Existenz* is one of a series of existences, whereas Jaspers' intention is precisely to indicate that it is beyond the series. The most concise description of *Existenz* I have found so far is that of Dufrenne and Ricoeur: '. . . l'existence c'est l'individu au sens le plus élevé du mot: non pas l'individu biologique défini par le souci vital, mais l'individu libre défini par le souci de l'être; non pas l'homme pensant universellement et défini par un faisceau de règles intellectuelles, intemporelles et incorruptibles, . . . mais l'homme qui joue son destin dans le temps, devant la mort, dans l'État et avec ses amis, l'homme qui, par sa décision, peut se perdre ou se gagner, ou, comme dit Jaspers, "venir à soi" ou "se manquer". Ce pouvoir d'être ou de ne pas être, lié à une décision que nul ne peut prendre pour lui, ne peut qu'ébranler profondément l'individu qui soudain le découvre, par-delà l'habitude de vivre, par-delà toutes les garanties sociales et même ecclésiastiques . . .' *Karl Jaspers . . .*, 22.

[57]*VdW*, 49. To show, however, that the freedom of Existence is not the last word, not absolutely absolute, Jaspers adds, '. . . and thereby relates to Transcendence, in which it is grounded and from which it was given to itself.' In other words, Existence discovers itself in liberty, only to realise that this liberty itself is a 'gift' from God.

[58]*Ph I*, 24.

CHAPTER IV

[1]*EiP*, 30.

[2]Cf. '. . . vertretende Gegenständlichkeit des Seins', *Ph I*, 23.

[3]*EiP*, 30.   [4]*Ibid.*, 31.   [5]*Ibid.*   [6]*Ph I*, 12.

[7]Cf. '*Sein als Bestand* und *Sein als Freiheit* bilden nicht den Gegensatz zweier koordinierbarer Seinsarten. Sie sind auf einander bezogen, aber schlechthin unvergleichlich; Sein im Sinne von Objektsein und Sein im Sinne von Freisein schliessen sich aus.' *Ibid.*, 18.

⁸Cf. '. . . *Verwässerung des Seins* zu allem, von dem sich unbestimmt "ist" sagen lässt, . . .' *Ibid.*, 23.

⁹*Ibid.*, 5–6. ¹⁰*Ph III*, 160, 163.

¹¹Actually, the image of horizon does not do justice to what Jaspers means by the Enveloping because horizon implies circumscription, limitation, the very thing Jaspers wants to exclude from the concept of the Enveloping: 'Dieses Umgreifende ist also nie der Horizont, in dem unser jeweiliges Wissen vorkommt, denn das Umgreifende wird nie als Horizont sichtbar.' *VdW*, 38. Hans Mader, in a study called 'Das Seinsdenken bei Karl Jaspers', *Wissenschaft und Weltbild*, X (1957), 58, compares the Enveloping to a 'horizonless horizon' (*horizontloser Horizont*), which is what I am trying to approximate by the expression 'open horizon'.

¹²Were it not for the fact that Jaspers is repudiating ontology, I could have termed this difference the ontic-ontological difference of Heideggerian fame. Gerhard Knauss does not have this scruple and goes ahead with the expression. He even ventures, though very cautiously, to compare the two thinkers on this point: 'What Heidegger designates "ontic-ontological difference" is—as far as the difference is concerned, not the further interpretation of Being, but— the difference between Being-in-itself and the manner in which Being becomes an object to us. In this underlying thought, arising, perhaps, out of a mutual conviction as to the finitude of man, both philosophers find themselves to-gether in opposing the idealistic attempt at an infinite extension of thought. The experience of the difference and the systematic formulation of this ex-perience, however, lead them into different directions . . . In Heidegger we have a philosophy which loses patience and which, counter to its own trend, conjuringly tries to grasp Being. In Jaspers we have a philosophy of the "longer way", as Plato terms it, which utilises knowledge in order to make faith, in the end, believable.' 'The Concept of the "Encompassing"', *Living Philosophers*, *op. cit.*, 146–7.

¹³*Ph III*, 160.

¹⁴*VdW*, 204. Jaspers himself proposed to write such a theory of categories. It would have been the third volume of the projected *Philosophische Logik*, of which only the first volume (*Von der Wahrheit*) appeared. This theory of categories would no longer be an ontology in the traditional sense but a *periechontology*, as Jaspers calls it. The principal difference between ontology and periechontology could be stated thus: ontology claims to tell us *what* Being is, periechontology only tells us *how* Being appears to us. The term is derived from *periecho*= 'to envelop', 'to contain in oneself'. Thus periech-ontology is a part of the philosophy of the Enveloping.

¹⁵*EiP*, 31–2. ¹⁶*PGl*, 28.

¹⁷Cf. 'Da aber alles, was Gegenstand für uns ist, seine Erscheinungshaftigkeit im Unterschied vom Ansichsein einsehen lässt, so weist das Sein als Erscheinung auf das eigentliche Sein, das darin spricht und fühlbar wird.' *Ibid.*, 29.

¹⁸Cf. '. . . denkend über alles Gedachte hinausschwingen.' *EiP*, 31.

¹⁹Cf. 'Ich bleibe ursprünglich philosophierend der Münchhausen, der sich am eigenen Schopf aus dem Sumpfe zieht.' *Ph I*, 327.

²⁰*EiP*, 36.

²¹In a similar mood Ulrich Schmidhäuser remarks: 'Während also *Erkennen*

das einzelne Seiende *gegenständlich* denkend und *partikular* erfahrend aufweisen und beweisen kann, geht *Innewerden* des *Umgreifenden* auf den *ungegenständlichen* Seinssinn selbst, welchen wir im Transzendieren über alles gegenständliche Denken als letzten Gehalt *total* "erfahren", d.h. seiner als Ursprung innewerden.' *Allgemeine Wahrheit u. existentielle Wahrheit bei Karl Jaspers*, Bonn 1953, 9.

[22]Cf. 'This becoming aware (*innewerden*) is a bridge through which something by nature non-objective (*ungegenständlich*) is thought in the form of an objective entity, which, however, acts merely as a catalyst.' Kurt Hoffman, 'The Basic Concepts . . .,' *Living Philosophers, op. cit.,* 106.

[23]*Karl Jaspers . . .,* 360.   [24]*EiP,* 35.   [25]*ExP,* 76.   [26]*EiP,* 36–7.
[27]*PGl,* 31.   [28]*Ph III,* 38.

[29]Gerhard Knauss, 'The Concept of the "Encompassing"', *Living Philosophers, op. cit.,* 152.

[30]Fr Xavier Tilliette, S.J. notes that the explicit term *Umgreifendes* occurs only twice in Jaspers' *Philosophie:* once in *Ph I,* 81 (p. 70 in the 2nd ed. of 1948 in one volume, quoted by Fr Tilliette), designating the world, and the second time in *Ph III,* 96 (p. 757), where it stands for Being. But Tilliette also notes that the verbal forms, *umgreifen* and *übergreifen,* are employed there throughout in the sense of the Enveloping. Cf. *Karl Jaspers,* Collection 'Théologie', No. 44, Paris 1959, p. 26, note 7.

[31]There exist a number of special studies about the Enveloping which treat both of its merits and of its difficulties in greater detail than this summary chapter could ever attempt to do. In addition to the article by Knauss, quoted above, one might mention his book, *Gegenstand und Umgreifendes,* Kollektion 'Philosophische Forschung, Neue Folge', Band III, Basle 1954.

[32]*VdW,* 183.

[33]Note that these terms have already occurred as objectively discernible figures of Being or of selfhood. Here they are no longer objective but encompassing.

[34]*VdW,* 188.

[35]*VdW,* 127. The above compound schema furnishes another example of the distractingly complex and ambiguous nature of Jaspers' use of words. This time the ambiguity centres round the terms 'transcendent' or 'transcendence'. In the second schema alone there are at least three different meanings attached to these terms. There is, first of all, the transcendence of *all* the enveloping modes, including, therefore, the transcendence of the so-called immanent modes. Transcendence in this usage seems to stand for non-objectivity. In fact, Jaspers suggests as much: 'Jene . . . Transzendenz aller Weisen . . . ist fasslich gegenwärtig als ungegenständlicher Sinn . . .' *VdW,* 127. He calls this form a general or universal transcendence. In addition to this general transcendence, there is, secondly, the 'transcendence proper' or the transcendence of all transcendence, which embraces all the other modes: 'Wir nennen Transzendenz im eigentlichen Sinne nur . . . das Umgreifende aller Umgreifenden, . . . die Transzendenz aller Transzendenzen.' *Ibid.,* 109. Thirdly, there is the transcendence of Existence which is a case apart, since it is neither universal in content like the other modes, nor all-embracing like Transcendence proper.

[36]*VdW,* 53–151.

CONCLUSIONS TO PART I

¹Cf. 'Die von uns unterschiedenen Weisen des Umgreifenden sind in ihrem Gedachtsein geschichtlich, das *Resultat unseres abendländischen* Bildungsprozesses: In ihren Räumen haben unsere Ahnen gelebt und gedacht.' *VdW*, 125.

²*Ibid.*, 124.

³Jean Wahl, *Études Kierkegaardiennes*, 2nd ed., Paris 1949, 550.

⁴Kurt Reinhardt, *The Existentialist Revolt*, 197.

⁵Jeanne Hersch, *L'illusion philosophique*, Paris 1936, *passim*.

⁶Jean Wahl, *La pensée de l'existence*, Paris 1951, 84.

⁷*WiderV*, 49–50.   ⁸*Ph III*, 6.   ⁹*Karl Jaspers . . .*, 371.   ¹⁰*VdW*, 120.

¹¹*Ibid.*, 185.   ¹²*Ibid.*   ¹³*VuEx*, 60.

¹⁴Cf. 'Vielmehr ist sie auf dem Wege der Entmythisierung unseres Denkens der bisher weitestgehende Versuch der Befreiung.' *Ibid.*, 184.

PART II

INTRODUCTION

¹Cf. 'Dies Transzendieren vollzieht sich jedoch, da unser Denken stets an Gegenstände gebunden ist, in solchen, die durch den Gang der Denkbewegung aufgehoben werden.' *RuAusbl*, 253–4.

²Cf. 'Transcender n'est donc point abandonner sans retour l'objectivité . . . Par la philosophie, l'objectivité est *mise en question*, . . . mais le but de la philosophie, c'est une possession *nouvelle* de l'objectivité, qui est alors le moyen d'apparaître de l'existence.' Dufrenne and Ricoeur, *Karl Jaspers . . .*, 67–8.

³Cf. *Ph I*, 29.

⁴Cf. 'Philosophische Weltorientierung fasst nicht letzte Ergebnisse der Wissenschaften zu einem einheitlichen Weltbild zusammen, sondern zeigt die Unmöglichkeit eines solchen gültigen Weltbildes als des einen und absoluten; sie sucht die *Fragwürdigkeiten* der faktischen Weltorientierung.' *Ibid.*, 29–30.

⁵Cf. *Ibid.*, 129.

⁶Cf. 'Nur wer leidenschaftlich sich in der faktischen Weltorientierung bewegt hat, kann wahrhaftig die philosophische Weltorientierung darin finden.' *Ibid*, 29.

CHAPTER V

¹'Philosophy and Science', *Partisan Review*, XVI (1949), 871. Henceforth this article is quoted as PS.

²*ExP*, 3.   ³*PS*, 874.

⁴Cf. 'This identification of modern science and modern philosophy with

their old aspiration to total knowledge was catastrophic for both of them.'
Ibid., 875.

[5]*Ibid.*, 871.   [6]*Ibid.*   [7]*Ibid.*, 872.   [8]*Ibid.*   [9]*Ibid.*   [10]*Ibid.*

[11]Cf. 'No one denies that *Logistik* has made correct statements. The question
is: what do these correct statements mean in relation to the whole of human
Existence; that is, are they important, or are they merely correct, but without
consequences? In the latter case, logic would be empty, serving only as a game
to be played by people who happen to like it and are prepared to accept its
rules.' *Desc* 98–9. Other references to Russell and his work are found in *PuW*,
17–18. They contain the same sort of dismissal of formalised logic. The severity
of this cold-shoulder treatment could only be matched by the similar scorn
with which the Anglo-Saxon thinkers would regard a philosophy such as
Jaspers'.

[12]*Desc*, 32.   [13]*Ibid.*, 37.   [14]*Ibid.*, 37–8.   [15]*Ibid.*, 38.

[16]Cf. 'Als das "ich denke" ist sich das Ich im Augenblick des Denkens *seines
Daseins* . . . gewiss. Nicht *was* es ist, weiss es, sondern *dass* es ist . . .' *Ph II*, 26.

[17]For the rest, Jaspers would be in substantial agreement with Maurice
Merleau-Ponty's critique of the Cartesian *cogito*. He would admit, for instance,
that real thought is never more certain than its object.

Nevertheless, later on Jaspers brought out that this is true of thought only in
so far as thought is object-bound. On the transcendental level, all the evidence
of thought does not come from its object; part of it comes from the thinking
subject itself, or more basically, from the presence of Being which manifests
itself in the duality of subject and object. The transcendental aim of thinking
is to arrive at truth which is defined by Jaspers as the evidence of Being
(*Seinsoffenbarkeit*). In this kind of thinking, the object is no longer what is
really intended. For transcendental thought both the object and the act of
thinking become ciphers in which Being is revealed. Transcendental thought
is 'glowing with Being'. Cf. '. . . seinsdurchglühtes Denken ist ein Denken,
in dem das Objekt als solches nicht mehr das eigentlich Gemeinte ist, sondern
in dem durch das Denken und das Gedachte, beide übergreifend, das Sein
selbst gegenwärtig wird, . . . sofern denken selbst Chiffer und damit Sprache
des Seinswirklichkeit sein kann' (*VdW*, 249).

[18]*Desc*, 12.   [19]Cf. *ibid.*

[20]*Ibid.*, 42, quoting the Adam-Tannery edition of the *Oeuvres de Descartes*
(Paris 1891–1913), vol. 5, p. 177.

[21]*Ibid.*, 53.   [22]*Ibid.*, 39.

[23]Among other testimonies, Jaspers quotes the work of Rudolf Wolf,
Geschichte der Astronomie, Munich 1877, 468, which in turn quotes the judgement of Jean-Baptiste Delambre (1749–1822), member of the French Academy
of Sciences and president of the Institute of France: 'Descartes renouvelait la
méthode des anciens grecs, qui dissertaient à perte de vue, sans jamais rien
calculer; mais erreur pour erreur, roman pour roman, j'aimerais encore mieux
les sphères solides d'Aristote que les tourbillons de Descartes. Avec ces sphères
on a du moins fait des planétaires, qui représentent en gros les mouvements
célestes,—on a pu trouver des règles approximatives de calcul; *on n'a jamais
pu tirer aucun parti des tourbillons,* ni pour le calcul, ni pour les machines.'
Desc, 56. Jaspers does not give particulars, but the quotation is taken from

Delambre's *Histoire de l'astronomie:* vol. 4, *Histoire de l'astronomie moderne,* Paris 1821, 154.

[24]*Desc,* 45–6.   [25]*Ibid.,* 45.   [26]*Ibid.*   [27]*Ibid.,* 46.

[28]'Jaspers on Science and Philosophy', *Living Philosophers, op. cit.,* 122.

[29]For Jaspers' attitude towards Hegelian phenomenology, see his critique of idealism in general, *Ph I,* 222–39.

[30]*RuAusbl,* 386.   [31]*AllgemPsych,* 47.

[32]In order to illustrate Jaspers' understanding of phenomenology, I call attention to the masterly exposé by Ludwig Lefebre, 'The Psychology of Karl Jaspers', *Living Philosophers, op. cit.,* 469–97. Here I reproduce some of its salient statements that bear on the point in question:

(1) Around the year 1910, psychologists were casting about for a suitable method for investigating the subjective experiences of the mind, as distinguished from the objective phenomena of the mind. Husserl was among the first to press phenomenology into this service as a 'descriptive psychology of the phenomena of consciousness', but it was Jaspers who by his article, 'Die phänomenologische Forschungsrichtung in der Psychopathologie', *Zeitschrift für die gesamte Neurologie und Psychiatrie,* IX (1912), 391–408, presented the first comprehensive description of the phenomenological method, and introduced it concretely into psychology. He saw it as a method based on empathy, which enables the psychiatrist to comprehend the manifestations of the mind from within, by their intrinsic development, instead of explaining them from without through causal factors.

(2) Jaspers regarded this phenomenological method as a version of another method called *Verstehen.* In fact, for him phenomenology was the static version of *Verstehen.* Unlike the causal relationships sought and recognised as necessary by the method of explanation, the relations uncovered by *Verstehen* are largely free and fortuitous constellations of meaning (*Sinnzusammenhänge*), which the subject confers upon his experiences. In psychology, they represent for Jaspers the ultimate source of experience, analogous to sensory perception in the natural sciences.

(3) As *Verstehen,* phenomenology adds a new dimension to psychological research, but no more. Because of its purely hermeneutic character, phenomenology can never be the only source of psychological research. It must be supplemented by causal explanation. Every limit of *Verstehen* provides a new impulse for causal inquiry, and vice versa. Thus, there are at least these two complementary methods that are necessary for psychology.

(4) The relationship of these two methods is dialectical: causally demonstrable factors must be gathered into a 'comprehension' of meaning, while the hermeneutic constructs should constantly be tested against observable facts.

(5) The unity of the two methods and the unity of psychology is not achieved by radicalising either method, but in the person of the psychologist himself, who makes use of both of them.

[33]Cf. 'Die Wissenschaft vom Radikalen muss auch in ihrem Verfahren radikal sein und das in jeder Hinsicht. Vor allem darf sie nicht ruhen, bis sie ihre absolut klaren Anfänge ... gewonnen hat.' Edmund Husserl, 'Philosophie als strenge Wissenschaft', *Logos,* I (1910–1911), 340–41.

[34]*Ibid.,* 290.

[35]Cf. 'Es war zwar ein Meisterwerk auch in seiner von keiner Absurdität zurückschreckenden Konsequenz. Mir aber wurde durch ihn die Verkehrung der Philosophie in Wissenschaft klar, die mich empörte.' *RuAusbl*, 386.

[36]Cf. 'Philosophie kann man nicht lernen, weil es hier . . . objektiv begriffene und begründete Einsichten nicht gibt, . . . weil es hier noch an begrifflich fest begrenzten und ihrem Sinn nach voll geklärten Problemen, Methoden und Theorien fehlt. Ich sage nicht, Philosophie sei eine unvollkommene Wissenschaft, ich sage schlechthin, sie sei noch keine Wissenschaft, sie habe als Wissenschaft noch keinen Anfang genommen . . .' *Logos*, 290.

[37]*Ibid.*, 336.

[38]He would have done so for the simple reason that the very act of reduction is performed by a concrete and historical 'I' who, in describing this transcendental reduction, must make use of what Alphonse de Waelhens calls a 'mundane language', i.e. 'a language which makes its own and repeats—no matter how creative it may be in other respects—a heritage of meaning which has been deposited in the course of personal and prepersonal experience, whose characteristics are in no way either transcendental or a-mundane. The instrument, then', continues Mr de Waelhens, 'radically contradicts the work it is calculated to perform.' 'The Outlook for Existential Phenomenology', *International Philosophical Quarterly*, II (1962), 469. I enthusiastically recommend this article as a model of penetration and clarity. Over and above its general interest, it has great relevance to the issue at hand.

[39]Cf. 'Husserl als Philosoph enttäuschte mich. Er vollzog die Gebärde des Sehens; was dann gesehen wurde, war meist gleichgültig.' *RuAusbl*, 386.

[40]Cf. 'Die Phänomenologie für Philosophie zu nehmen, schien mir aus dem Ethos der Philosophie verwerflich. Im Philosophieren kommt man nicht voran durch ein Blicken auf Phänomene, als ob man als Zuschauer verhalte wie in den Wissenschaften, sondern nur durch ein Denken, das zugleich ein inneres Handeln ist. Es hat Folgen in meiner Lebenspraxis in zeigt darin, was seine Wahrheit ist.' *Ibid.*, 387.

[41]*VdW*, 311, 359, 505, 507.

[42]*The Existentialists*, Chicago 1963, 96.   [43]*PS*, 872.   [44]*Ibid.*, 879.

[45]*Entmytholog*, 18.   [46]*VdW*, 40.   [47]*PS*, 879.   [48]*Entmytholog*, 10.

[49]*VuEx*, 7–8.

CHAPTER VI

[1]'Jaspers on Science and Philosophy', *Living Philosophers, op. cit.*, 125–6.

[2]Cf. 'Die Arten des Zwingenden sehen wir in den zwingenden *Gedanken* der Mathematik und formalen Logik, im zwinganden *Wirklichsein* des Empirisch-Objektiven der Natur- und Geisteswissenschaften, in der zwingenden *Anschauung* der Kategorien, Wesenheiten, Möglichkeiten des Objektseins.' *Ph I*, 89.

[3]*Ibid.*   [4]*Ibid.*, 90.   [5]*Ibid.*, 89.

[6]*Ibid.*, 90. As for the rest, Jaspers is both fascinated and baffled by the status of mathematics. He calls mathematics the 'unicum and puzzle among the sciences'. Why is it, he seems to ask, that of all the possible categories it is the

category of quantity that furnishes the stuff for a self-sufficient science? And why is it that of all the elements it is carbon that is suited for organic combination and is thereby the basic stuff of life? *Ibid.*, 164.

⁷Cf. 'Der blinde Zwang der Tatsachen als beliebiger Wahrnehmungsinhalte führt ins Endlose. Die Tatsache muss eine Bedeutung gewinnen, um zu interessieren. Die *Theorien* als gedachte Gebilde von Zusammenhängen und Ganzheiten sind Bedingung für die Relevanz der Tatsachen und gemeinhim sogar für ihre Auffindung. Das Zwingende der Theorie erwächst aus ihrer Bestätigung durch Tatsachen.' *Ibid.*, 91.

⁸Cf. 'Das Zwingende in der *empirischen Forschung* ist also als Tatsache gebunden an Theorie, als Theorie an Tatsache.' *Ibid.*

⁹Cf. 'In der *Kategorienlehre* und ihrer Phänomenologie gibt es die Anschauung im Gegenwärtighaben nicht wirklicher, sondern möglicher Objekte.' *Ph I*, 89.

¹⁰*Ibid.*   ¹¹*Karl Jaspers . . .*, p. 81, note 4.   ¹²*PS*, 875.

¹³'Truth and Science', *Graduate Journal*, V (1962), 30.

¹⁴*Ph I*, 87.   ¹⁵*Ibid.*

¹⁶Cf. 'Endlosigkeit . . . ist wirklich als Ausdruck der *Ungeschlossenheit* jeder Weltrealität als *Erscheinung* in einfachster Gestalt als die nur mit Hilfe der Zahlenendlosigkeit gedachte nie vollendete Reihe der Zeit und der Ausbreitung des Raums.' *Ibid.*, 95.

¹⁷Cf. 'Ich gewinne *zwingende Einsicht*, aber das Zwingende wird *nicht absolut;* ich werde der *Endlosigkeit* Herr, aber sie bleibt auch *unüberwunden;* ich erreiche *Einheiten*, aber *nicht die Einheit der Welt*.' *Ibid.*, 87.

¹⁸Cf. 'Wo Philosophie sich in ihrer existentiellen Funktion begriff, wurde sie zum Gegenpol der Mathematik, die unter den Wissenschaften am wenigsten existentiell relevant ist.' *Ibid.*, 164.

¹⁹*Ibid.*, 90–91.   ²⁰*Ibid.*, 91.

²¹Cf. 'Das Zwingende fasst nicht die *ganze* Wirklichkeit. Dass es dieses Zwingende gibt, bedeutet das Dasein des reinen Objekts für uns. Aber dieses Objektsein ist nicht das Sein von allem.' *Ibid.*

²²*Ibid.*   ²³*Ibid.*, 92.   ²⁴*VdW*, 397.

²⁵Cf. 'Man unterscheidet die Worte in ihrer eigentlichen Bedeutung von den Worten als Metapher . . . Diese Unterscheidung ist aber nur eine relative. Worte mit "eigentlicher" Bedeutung sind solche, bei deren Gebrauch das Bewusstsein ihres metaphorischen Charakters verlorengegangen ist.' *Ibid.*, 398.

²⁶Cf. 'So steckt in der Worten jeweils eine eigentliche oder direkte Bedeutung nur durch Vergessen des Ursprungs.' *Ibid.*

²⁷Cf. 'Das Vergessen des metaphorischen Charakters ist im Sprechen . . . der psychologische Grund für die Möglichkeit, mit den Worten durch den Gedanken Eigentliches auch abstrakt meinen zu können.' *Ibid.*

²⁸Cf. 'Aber schon im Metaphorischen ist der Mensch doch auf Eigentliches gerichtet. Zu jedem Gleichniss gehört auch ein Wesen. In der Wechselbewegung gleichnishaften Spiegelns aller Dinge ineinander durch die Sprache ist nicht die Nichtigkeit des Spiegelns von nichts, sondern in der Tat eine Stufenfolge von Wesen uns gegenwärtig.' *Ibid.* This passage is like a prelude to Jaspers' theory of ciphers. Some of its images and expressions are evocative of the exquisite sonnet by Rilke:

RÖMISCHE FONTÄNE

> Zwei Becken, eins das andere übersteigend
> aus einem alten renden Marmorrand,
> und aus dem oberen Wasser leis sich neigend
> zum Wasser, welches unten wartend stand,
>
> > dem leise redenden entgegenschweigend
> > und heimlich, gleichsam in der hohlen Hand,
> > ihm Himmel hinter Grün und Dunkel zeigend
> > wie einen unbekannten Gegenstand;
> >
> > > sich selber ruhig in der schönen Schale
> > > verbreitend ohne Heimweh, Kreis aus Kreis,
> > > nur manchmal träumerisch und tropfenweis
> > >
> > > > sich niederlassend an den Moosbehängen
> > > > zum letzten Spiegel, der sein Becken leis
> > > > von unten lächeln macht mit Übergängen. (1906)

[29]*VdW*, 401.   [30]*Ph I*, 92.   [31]*Ibid.*

[32]Cf. 'Unbezweifelbare Richtigkeiten auf Richtigkeiten zu häufen führt nicht zum Erwerb dessen, was in der Erkenntnis gesucht wird. Abgleiten ins Endlose ist zwar kein Einwand gegen Richtigkeit, aber gegen Wesentlichkeit einer Erkenntnis.' *Ibid.*, 96.

[33]*Ibid.*, 97.

[34]Jaspers' idea seems to be that 'only what is definite can be an object of knowledge' (*VdW*, 97), whereas a mathematical series—and every totality conceived in its image—runs into endlessness either as indefinitely many or as indefinitely manifold. The complete series of numbers, for instance, is neither given nor can it be constructed. Whatever is constructed can be increased by the addition of a unit. A definite mathematical magnitude, on the other hand, must be conceived as a finite series of integers, themselves indefinitely divisible into fractions. An entity, in so far as it is conceived in the image of quantity, is indefinitely augmentable or divisible.

[35]*VdW*, 97.

[36]'The Concept of the "Encompassing"', *Living Philosophers, op. cit.*, 165.

[37]*Ibid.*   [38]*Ibid.*, 162.   [39]*Ibid.*, 166.

[40]Cf. 'Dann kann, im Erschrecken vor dem Abgleiten ins Endlose, *entweder* jeweils das *mathematische Prinzip* angewandt werden, . . . *oder* es kann die das Erkennen auf das Unendliche umsetzende *ideenhafte Konzentration* vollzogen werdenwelche zu einem im Blick auf Vollendung sich steigernden Prozess wird.' *Ph I*, 98.

[41]Cf. 'Ainsi, qu'il se manifeste par le fini ou par l'infini, le réel se déploie toujours sur un fond de l'indéfini, "sans qu'on puisse penser le commencement et la fin", et le savoir ne peut accéder à l'unité.' Dufrenne and Ricoeur, *Karl Jaspers* . . . , 82–3.

[42]Cf. 'Im Wesen des Erkennens—das allein wir als das unsrige kennen—

liegt die Bewegung als *die unumgehbare Form* seiner Wirklichkeit, . . . die den Sinn des Erkennens bestimmt und ihm seine Grenze setzt.' *VdW*, 302.

[43]Cf. 'die zeitlichen Grundcharaktere . . . die nicht nur empirisch-psychologisch sind, sondern in den Sinnstrukturen des Denkens selber liegen.' *Ibid.*, 303–4.

[44]Cf. 'Denken und Erkennen ohne Zeit hat für uns keinen Sinn. Zeit ist nicht zufällig mit hinzukommend, sondern konstituierend für das Wesen unseres Denkens.' *Ibid.*, 307.

[45]Cf. 'Wir leben vorwärts, wir verstehen rückwärts, beides in der Gegenwärtigkeit des Denkens.' *Ibid.*, 306.

[46]*Ibid.*

[47]Cf. 'Inhaltliche Wahrheit dagegen ist selber im Zeitlichen gegründet. Es verwandelt sich, *was* erkannt wird. Die Wahrheit selber verwandelt sich.' *Ibid.* Fr Xavier Tilliette, S.J., puts forth some interesting analyses and remarks on this point in the second chapter ('La vérité scientifique') of his excellent book, *Karl Jaspers.*

[48]*VdW*, 306. The original sentence is 'Im Denken ist Wahrheit durch Zeit.' but I reworded it in my translation in order to avoid the tiresome alliteration of t's and th's in 'There is truth in thought through time.'

[49]Cf. 'Wo immer im mit sich *identischen Begriffsinn* ein fester Punkt erreicht wird, der sogleich den Charakter der Zeit—und Bewegungslosigkeit hat, da ist dieser Punkt doch nur ein *Haltpunkt,* um an ihm die Bewegung fortzusetzen . . .' *Ibid.*, 305.

[50]Cf. 'Ein Gedanke ist das, was er eigentlich sein soll, nur am richtigen Ort in der Zeitkette mit anderen Gedanken . . .' *Ibid.*

[51]*Ibid.*

[52]Cf. 'Erkennen hätte dann zwar Inhalte, selbst aber keine Wirklichkeit. Es wäre zum passiven Spiegel geworden.' *Ibid.*, 308.

[53]Cf. 'Erkenntnis hat Beziehung auf Wirklichkeit und ist selber wirklich allein dadurch, dass ich in ihr etwas *will*. In der Erkenntnis erfüllt sich ein Wille.' *Ibid.*

[54]It may be useful to mention here that in the terminology of Jaspers the term *Denken* is a generic term, while *Erkennen* or *Wissen* is one of the species of thought. Although he is careful not to use *Erkennen* in place of *Denken*, he has no qualms about using the generic term for the specific one. He also wants to show by this terminological distinction that the appetite for being or the will which constitutes the reality of knowledge is attached not to knowing but to thinking. Thinking does not necessarily stop once the direct and immediate appetite of knowing to attain objects is satisfied. Beyond the objective goal of knowing lie the existential and metaphysical goals of thinking.

[55]*VdW*, 308.

[56]Cf. 'Denken ist das verwirklichende Daseinswille der hervorbringenden Gemeinschaft.' *Ibid.*

[57]*Ibid.*, 309. [58]*Ibid.*

[59]I apologise to Jaspers for this pun à la Heidegger. It is entirely my invention. Nevertheless, by its playful ambiguity the expression gives a true insight into Jaspers' idea. Written as 'belonging', it denotes the simple relatedness of thought and reality. Written as 'be-longing', it connotes what is common to both

thought and being, namely, that both are in the state of mutual longing for each other. Being wants to find and reveal itself in thought, while thought wants to ascertain itself in reality. In other words, they coincide in the ethos of the thinker.

[60]*VdW*, 310.

[61]Cf. 'Die Identität von Sein und Denken wäre am Ende in der *Identität der Wirklichkeit des Willens im Denken mit dem Sein* zu suchen. Im Ursprung war eins, was sich in der Spaltung gegenübersteht und in der Koinzidenz der tiefsten Willensantriebe mit dem Sein, das sich ihnen offenbart, wiederfindet.' *Ibid.*, 310–11.

[62]*Ibid.*, 311.   [63]*Ibid.*, 312.   [64]*Ibid.*   [65]*Ibid.*, 328.   [66]*Ibid.*, 344.

[67]Cf. 'Wissen ist, wenn es wirkungslos ist, nicht mehr Wissen, sondern Vorstellungsbewegung ohne Ziel.' *Ibid.*, 346.

[68]H. J. Blackham, *Six Existentialist Thinkers*, London 1961, 47.

[69]In the words of T. S. Eliot's 'Little Gidding' (see *The Complete Poems and Plays of T. S. Eliot*, published by Faber, London 1969):

> We shall not cease from exploration
> And the end of all our exploring
> Will be to arrive where we started
> And know the place for the first time.

CHAPTER VII

[1]In one of his rare references to Thomism, Jaspers charges that in that school 'particular and total knowledge are distinguished, but both are recognised as knowledge'; whereas in the Kantian school (to which he belongs) 'all knowledge is particular and belongs to the world of appearance, and total knowledge is impossible'. *Living Philosophers, op. cit.*, 800.

[2]'Jaspers on Science and Philosophy', *Living Philosophers, op. cit.*, 125.

[3]*Myth and Christianity* (*Entmytholog*), 105–6.   [4]*Ibid.*, 106.   [5]*PS*, 881.

[6]*Ibid.*   [7]*Ibid.*

[8]Cf. 'Philosophieren im Sichunterscheiden wird . . . bewusst, nicht einen Gegenstand zu haben wie Wissenschaften.' *Ph I*, 318.

[9]*PS*, 881–2.

[10]'Jaspers on Science and Philosophy', *Living Philosophers, op. cit.*, 131.

[11]*PS*, 879. Cf. also: 'Die zwingende Wissenschaft ist noch nicht Philosophie, aber Voraussetzung der Philosophie.' *VdW*, 468.

[12]H. J. Blackham, *Six Existentialist Thinkers*, London 1961, 47.

[13]*Ph II*, 18.   [14]*PS*, 879.   [15]*Ibid.*, 879–80.

[16]Cf. 'Der Gegenstand wird . . . im Philosophieren transparent, weil er Erscheinung ist: er wird, statt erkannt zu werden, Sprache. Wo ich ihn selbst meine, stehe ich in der Wissenschaft, aber ich philosophiere, wo ich in ihm den Blick auf das Sein richte.' *Ph I*, 319.

[17]*PS*, 879.   [18]*Ph I*, 161.

[19]Cf. 'Je reiner Weltorientierung als Wissenschaft sich kinstituiert und

Metaphysik gegenständlich ausscheidet, desto klarer wird sie als Wissenschaft und zugleich metaphysisch relevant.' *Ibid.*, 135.

[20]*Ibid.*

[21]Cf. 'En bref, le drame de la science, c'est qu'elle cherche l'être, mais là où elle n'en peut trouver qu'un aspect incomplet: dans l'objectivité.' Dufrenne and Ricoeur, *Karl Jaspers* . . . , 107.

[22]*Ibid.*, 105.   [23]*Ph I*, 329.   [24]*Living Philosophers, op. cit.*, 38.

[25]*Karl Jaspers* . . . , 108.

CHAPTER VIII

[1]*VdW*, 120.

[2]In the technical terminology of German philosophical tradition, *Verstand* and *Vernunft* have been clearly distinguished ever since Kant, but in ordinary usage this distinction has not always been maintained. Jaspers is intent on keeping them as distinct as possible.

[3]Cf. 'Es ist wie eine selbstverständliche Voraussetzung des Verstandes in seiner Weltorientierung, dass das Weltall da ist, . . . das alles, was *sei*, auch *gegenständlich* und *wissbar* sei, dass Sein identisch sei mit Objektsein oder damit, als Objekt gedacht werden zu können.' *Ph I*, 30.

[4]*Ph III*, 38.

[5]Cf. 'Er fasst nur endliche Gegenstände und macht alles absolut endlich. Das Unendliche selber wird ihm Gegenstand, den er wie einen endlichen Gegenstand behandelt.' *VdW*, 390.

[6]Jaspers goes along with the Kantian thesis that science in the strict sense exists only where mathematics applies.

[7]*VdW*, 468.   [8]*Ibid.*, 467.

[9]Cf. 'In der Wahrnehmung ist das Denken schon gegenwärtig als die das Angeschaute zum Gegenstand konstituierende Funktion; ohne diese wäre sie nocht nicht Wahrnehmung, sondern nur Reiz und Empfindung . . . Unser Gegenstandsbewusstsein ist überall Resultat unseres Urteilens, verdichtetes Urteilens, aus dem die Urteile bei Bedarf auch ausdrücklich wieder herausgeholt werden können.' *Ibid.*, 274–5.

[10]Cf. 'In der anschaulichen Erfüllung ist der Bestand des Gegenstandes zu voller Gegenwart zu bringen. Das ist nicht möglich in einem Akt blossen Sehens, vielmehr wird der Gegenstand erst klar auf dem Wege urteilender Gliederung, die ihn artikuliert und bestimmt vor Augen führt . . . Klare Gegenwart einer Sache gibt es nie als gedankenlose Unmittelbarkeit. Nur durch Urteile vermittelte Unmittelbarkeit ist Wissen von einer Sache.' *Ibid.*, 463.

[11]Cf. 'Im Urteilsakt wird ein Einssein durch Beziehung mehrerer aufeinander gedacht. Um dieses Einssein ergreifen zu können, muss etwas vorher getrennt sein.' *Ibid.*, 283. The expression 'original partition' refers to the etymological meaning of the German word for judgement, *ur-teilen*.

[12]*Ibid.*, 287.

[13]Jaspers has no developed treatment on analogy. His scattered remarks

seem to indicate that he repudiates the usual doctrines on analogy. He suspects that, after having acknowledged the *simpliciter diversum,* most of these doctrines unwittingly re-introduce univocity into analogy by means of the *secundum quid idem.* This is done by trying to determine the primary analogate, the 'proper' meaning of an analogous term, to which the other meanings are proportioned according to some definite relationship, such as causality and participation. Jaspers finds that such considerations can be illuminating for a moment, but that they become immediately false when taken objectively. For him, the 'somehow the same' is the expression of an existential *faith* in the ultimate unity of Being, but not an objective certitude which could be pressed into the service of demonstrations. For a more extensive treatment of the question of analogy in Jaspers see J. Lotz, S.J., 'Analogie und Chiffre', *Scholastik,* XV (1940), 39–56.

[14]Because that would again involve the paradox of self-reference, which constitutes the limit of intellectual judgements.

[15]*VdW,* 290.

[16]Cf. 'Der anscheinend so triviale Satz von Identität ... spricht in einfacher Form eine Grenze unseres Seinswissens aus. Mit ihm bewegt sich unser Denken zwischen der Tautologie und dem Sein selbst, in ersterer sich verlierend, letzteres nicht erreichend.' *Ibid.,* 291.

[17]*Ibid.,* 291–2.

[18]Cf. 'Begrifflich denken, das heisst, einen sich gleichbleibenden Sinn denken, ein zeitlos Bestehendes, dem Wandel und Wechsel Enthobenes.' *Ibid.,* 277.

[19]Cf. 'Das Zwingende kommt nicht nur aus dem Bewusstsein und nicht nur aus der Denkbarkeit, sondern aus dem Sein selbst. Jedes Ding ist, was es ist ... *Ens est ens* (Idem-ens=Identität). Der Satz der Identität ist ein ontisches Gesetz.' *Ibid.,* 292.

[20]*Ibid.*   [21]*Ibid.,* 294.   [22]*Ibid.*

[23]Cf. 'Die Klarheit des Gedachten ist an das Widersprechende gebunden ... Erst die Anwesenheit der Gegenvorstellung im Widerspruch bringt die sichere Bestimmtheit des Gegenstandes für das Bewusstsein hervor. Die Notwendigkeit ... wird deutlich, wenn das Gegenteil als unmöglich begriffen werden kann.' *Ibid.,* 295.

[24]Cf. 'Der Satz des Widerspruchs ist nicht ursprüngliches Gesetz der Erkenntnisakte, sondern des erkannten Urteilsinhalts, nicht des Vollzugs, sondern des Sachverhalts ... Er ist Norm für das Gedachte; das Gesetz des Bewusstseinsmöglichen ist nur eine Folge.' *Ibid.*

[25]*Ibid.,* 296.   [26]It is only an original belief.

[27]*Ibid.,* 297. The grammar is even worse in German: 'Es ist ein Zutrauen, dass das Sein und seine Erkennbarkeit im Grunde "in Ordnung" und im Prinzip widerspruchslos vollendbar sei.'

[28]Cf. 'Der Satz gilt für die vorangehende Bewegung des Erkennens, nicht als vorwegnehmende Aussage über das Sein im Ganzen.' *Ibid.*

[29]*Ibid.*   [30]*Ibid.,* 298.

CONCLUSIONS TO PART II

[1]Cf. 'Ein absoluter Anfang . . . wäre die *causa sui*. Aber dieser Gedanke enthält etwas Unmögliches, weil er ein Zirkel ist oder ein Widerspruch in sich selbst. Er ist als Gedanke objektiv ohne Bestand und nur möglich als Ausdrucksmittel für Erhellungen, in denen er micht mehr als Begriff eines objektiven Seins gemeint ist.' *Ph II*, 188.

[2]George Boas, *The Limits of Reason*, London 1961. 33.   [3]*Weber*, 54.

[4]'The Concept of the "Encompassing" in Jaspers' Philosophy', *Living Philosophers, op. cit.*, 170.

[5]*VuEx*, 122.   [6]*Ibid.*, 123.   [7]*Ibid.*   [8]*Ibid.*, 125.   [9]*Ibid.*, 57.

[10]*Ibid.*, 58–9.

PART III

INTRODUCTION

[1]Or, as Dufrenne and Ricoeur put it, Jaspers gives us 'less of a philosophical statement than a portrait of man who philosophises, that is, of man as he poses radically the problem of Being.' *Karl Jaspers . . .* , 100.

[2]For the question of the relationship between the existential and logical elements of Jaspers' philosophy, see the article of Ernst Mayer, 'Philosophie und Philosophische Logik bei Karl Jaspers', *Offener Horizont*, Munich 1953, 63–72.

[3]*Karl Jaspers*, 23.

CHAPTER IX

[1]*Ph II*, 1.   [2]*Ibid.*

[3]Positivity, let us recall, is the distinguishing mark of Dasein.

[4]*Karl Jaspers . . .* , 111.   [5]*Ph II*, 2.   [6]*Ibid.*   [7]*Ibid.*   [8]*Ibid.*, 36.   [9]*Ibid.*, 35.

[10]This difficulty would be greatly attenuated if we could invoke the usual distinction between actuality and virtuality within Existence, saying that I *am* one thing in act, but *can become* something else (substantially or accidentally) in virtue of a real potency in my actual being. Unfortunately Jaspers does not make this distinction. Moreover, this distinction presupposes the act-potency composition of being that is comprehensible only in the framework of a whole set of other structures, such as the substance-accidents structure, nature-faculty structure, primary and secondary acts, etc., which in Jaspers' scheme of things all refer to the structures of Dasein and not of Existence. H. J. Blackham has seen this difficulty very well. He writes: 'The difficulty is this: unless I have an original essence which has some positive content and is not empty liberty, how can I find myself in decisions which are self-determined; how can I know what I am in order to become what I am, unless I have a positive essence, that is to say, a nature.' He is also completely correct when he sums up Jaspers' answer to this difficulty by saying: 'The answer seems to be that the choices I make and sustain, and by which I make myself, constitute

the consistent ground of future spontaneous choice (not my nature, but my history) . . . I who exist in liberty by conscious separation from my empirical self . . . identify myself with myself and face and acknowledge the vital impulses of my body, the brute facts of nature, the obligations of duty, the limitations of my situation and of all chosen ends: these enter into my decisions, but I am not subdued to them, am not the resultant of their determinations.' *Six Existential Thinkers*, 49.

[11]*Ph II*, 4.   [12]*Ibid.*   [13]*Ibid.*, 5.   [14]*Ibid.*   [15]*Ibid.*, 16.

[16]Dufrenne and Ricoeur, *Karl Jaspers* . . . , 121.   [17]*Ph II*, 11.

[18]*Ibid.*, 10.   [19]*Ibid.*   [20]*Ibid.*, 8.   [21]*Ibid.*, 12.   [22]*Ibid.*, 27.

[23]*Ibid.*, 35.   [24]*Karl Jaspers* . . . , 119.   [25]*Ph II*, 34.   [26]*Ibid.*, 189.

[27]Some modern theoreticians tell us that the meaning of 'natural law' is not the same in microphysics as it is in macrophysics. Often the same law, which on the large scale determines what is possible or impossible, will only describe what is probable or improbable on the subatomic level. In other words, laws applying to microphysical phenomena are regarded more and more as statistical descriptions of the normal behaviour of things—that is, of the way they will act for the most part—without being able to determine with absolute certitude whether such and such a particular thing will really follow this description or not. For instance, in the case of normal radioactive decay of certain heavy elements one can calculate the number or quantity of those atoms which in a given period of time will undergo an interior atomic change by emitting nuclear alpha particles (as well as beta electrons), but one cannot determine which of these atoms will effectively decay, because the curious feature of this radioactive phenomenon is the fact that these particles escape even when they do not have a sufficient velocity to climb over the barrier of nucleic cohesion, while, on the other hand, particles with sufficient energy do not necessarily pass through this barrier. What will happen in the individual case, which particle will remain and which will escape, seems to be left to the random 'choice' of the particles themselves.

There were some thinkers who rejoiced that physicists had discovered such lacunae in the natural chain of determinism because, they thought, this proves that there is 'room' for freedom somewhere in the universe. (Cf. Henry Morgenau, *Scientific Indeterminism and Human Freedom*, Wimmer Lecture XX, Latrobe, Pa. 1968.) For Jaspers, these lacunae are 'a bad place for freedom'. Besides being susceptible to other explanations they prove too little or nothing about the consciousness of autonomy and responsibility which we call our freedom.

For a particularly interesting treatment of the contingency of microphysical event I recommend Milič Čapek, *The Philosophical Impact of Contemporary Physics*, Princeton 1961, 307–22. Many of Mr Čapek's philosophical conclusions show a marked similarity with Jaspers' views on this point.

[28]*Ph II*, 12.   [29]*Ibid.*, 10.

[30]Cf. '. . . denn wahr ist, das nicht *nur* mir wahr ist.' *Ibid.*, 56.

[31]A most comprehensive treatment of existential communication can be found in Fritz Kaufmann's 'Karl Jaspers and a Philosophy of Communication', *Living Philosophers, op. cit.*, 210–95.

[32]Cf. 'gegenseitige Schöpfung', *Ph II*, 58.   [33]*Ibid.*, 11.   [34]*Ibid.*, 65.

[35]*Ph I*, 48. [36]*Karl Jaspers* . . . , 120. [37]*Ph II*, 11. [38]*Ibid.*, 13.

[39]Cf. 'der verschwindende Gegenstand', *ibid.*, 37.

[40]*Ibid.*, 22. [41]*Ibid.*, 13.

[42]Cf. 'Fällt also die Voraussetzung der beiden Seienden als Existierender (nicht nur Daseiender), dann würde der Gedanke ihres Durch-einander-seins als ein bloss gegenständlicher sinnlos, da aus nichts an Existenz auch durch Wechselwirkung nichts werden kann.' *Ibid.*

[43]I, for my part, cannot think of a different interpretation for texts such as these: 'Sofern daher Selbstsein erst in der Kommunikation wird, bin werder ich noch der Andere eine *feste Seinssubstanz*, die der Kommunkation vorherginge . . . Das Selbstwerden in Kommunikation erschien darum *wie eine Schöpfung aus nichts.*' *Ibid.*, 70.

[44]Cf. 'Dasein birgt in sich ein Über-sich-hinaus-drängen.' *VdW*, 62.

[45]This question is one that suggests itself quite naturally. It has been asked before and in quite similar words by other commentators. Cf. Hans Kunz, 'Critique of Jaspers' Concept of Transcendence', *Library of Living Philosophers*, 501.

[46]*VdW*, 78. [47]*Ibid.*, 77. [48]*Ibid.*, 78. [49]*Ibid.* [50]*Ph II*, 14.

[51]*Ibid.*, 126.

[52]'Basic Concepts of Jaspers' Philosophy', *Living Philosophers, op. cit.*, 102.

[53]*Ph II*, 14.

[54]Cf. 'Eigentliche Freiheit . . . ist das Einswerden von Abhängigkeit und Freiheit.' *Ibid.*

[55]*Ibid.*

[56]Cf. 'Bewusstsein haben, heisst in der Helle leben, die durch die Spaltung von Ich und Gegenstand ermöglicht wird,' *Entmytholog*, 17.

[57]*VuEx*, 115. [58]*Ph II*, 15–16. [59]*Ibid.* [60]*Ibid.* [61]*Ibid.*

[62]The whole undertaking of Existence-elucidation shows that Jaspers is conscious of going further than Kant who expressly forbade the use of reason beyond the realm of empirical intuition. Jaspers wanted to find an intermediary way between immediate faith (the only way Kant allows for the grasp of noumenal reality) and strict theoretical grasp. His notion of 'philosophical faith' has one of its mainsprings in this effort. This ambition of Jaspers is very well seen by Dufrenne and Ricoeur: 'Jaspers est plus ambitieux que Kant . . . Il parle aussi d'action de foi; mais sa méthode essaie de frayer une voie intermédiaire entre le savoir et la foi, et les signes sont comme un moyen de forcer cette intuition intellectuelle qui n'est jamais donnée, et de penser positivement le noumène en comblant le fossé que Kant avait creusé.' *Karl Jaspers* . . . , p. 126, note 51.

[63]*Ph II*, 17.

[64]The Kant quotations that follow are taken from the English translation, *Critique of Pure Reason*, by Norman Kemp Smith, London 1958. Together with the page number of this translation I shall give also the references of the first (1781) and/or the second (1787) editions (Riga: Johann Friedrich Hartknock) of the German original, indicated by *KrV* (A) and *KrV* (B) respectively and followed by the corresponding page number. I dispense with references to Jaspers' texts, even when quoted directly, for they can be found on pp. 17 and 18 of *Ph II*.

[65]*Critique*, 184; *KrV* (A) 143.   [66]*Ibid.*; *KrV* (B) 183.   [67]*Ibid.*
[68]*Ibid.*, 185; *KrV* (A) 144.   [69]*Ibid.*; *KrV* (B) 184.   [70]*Ibid.*
[71]*Ibid.*; *KrV* (A) 145.   [72]*Ph II*, 18.
[73]Cf. 'Le temps mythique n'est pas, comme le temps astronomique, une durée homogène et mesurable; c'est une durée qualitativement différenciée.' Georges Van Riet, 'Mythe et vérité', *Problèmes d'épistémologie*, Louvain 1960, 373. This study had also appeared in the *Revue Philosophique de Louvain*, LVIII (1960), 15–87.
[74]Mircea Eliade, *The Sacred and the Profane*, New York 1961, 81.
[75]*Ibid.*, 72.
[76]Jaspers' controversy with Bultmann is highly instructive in this regard.
[77]*Entmytholog*, 19.   [78]*Ibid.*
[79]Cf. 'Dans *Philosophie* le caractère décidément existentiel de la philosophie est à tel point souligné qu'il n'est plus possible de revenir en arrière. Dans la *Logique Philosophique*, l'exigence rationelle est passionnément mise en lumière, mais sans que soit abandonnée un seul instant la prétention existentielle.' Xavier Tilliette, *Karl Jaspers*, 85.
[80]*VuEx*, 129–30.

CHAPTER X

[1]*Ph I*, 27.   [2]*PG1*, 63.   [3]*G. Marcel et K. Jaspers*, 32–3.   [4]*Ph II*, 200.
[5]Cf. 'Or il est remarquable que cette philosophie ne propose non seulement aucune preuve—toute preuve restant sur le plan de savoir, c'est-à-dire de l'objet empirique—mais encore aucune dérivation, aucun désenveloppement de quelque nature que ce soit qui ferait surgir la certitude de la Transcendance de celle de la liberté ou de la connaissance objective du monde.' Dufrenne and Ricoeur, *Karl Jaspers . . .* , 238.
[6]*PGl*, 32–4.   [7]*Ph III*, 6.   [8]*Karl Jaspers . . .* , 241.   [9]*Ibid.*, 249.
[10]Cf. 'Die Erscheinungshaftigkeit des Daseins ist eine Grundeinsicht philosophischen Denkens,' *PGl*, 35.
[11]Paul Ricoeur, *G. Marcel et K. Jaspers*, 45.
[12]Cf. 'Bereitschaft unablässigen Hörens,' *PGl*, 35.
[13]*VdW*, 108.   [14]*PGl*, 35–6.   [15]*VdW*, 108.   [16]*PGl*, 35.
[17]*Ph III*, 16.
[18]*Ph I*, 35. This text may also be regarded as one of the basic texts for Jaspers' constant rejection of specific divine revelation. This rejection was directed against what he calls the 'claim to exclusivity' (*Ausschliesslickeitsanspruch*) of specific revelations. As an example, he cites the claim of Jesus to be God-Man. He thinks that the notion of an incarnate God, as maintained by Christians, is an absurd one, because it is unthinkable that the reality of Transcendence should be localised in space and time in such a way that henceforward the entire history of mankind and of the world take its meaning from this one event in history which is the Incarnation.
[19]*Ph III*, 16.   [20]*Ibid.*
[21]Cf. 'Das Symbol ist nicht deutbar, es sei denn wieder durch andere Symbole.' *Ibid.*

22*Ibid.*   23*Ibid.*, 15.   24*Ibid.*, 40.

25Cf. 'Sichüberschlagen des Denkens zum Nichtdenkenkönnen.' *Ibid.*, 39.

26Cf. 'L'échec est à la fois l'hommage que l'entendement rend à l'Absolu et celui que le philosophe rend à l'intellectualisme.' Dufrenne and Ricoeur, *Karl Jaspers* . . . , 262.

27*Ph III*, 18.   28*VdW*, 1031.   29*Ph III*, 18.   30*Ph I*, 33.

31My opinion in this regard is the direct opposite of Franz Fruger's view on the subject, who claims that 'a symbol . . . would be a special case of cipher.' (*Struktureinheit der Wahrheit bei Karl Jaspers*, Salzburg 1960, p. 71, note 14.) My opinion is supported by Jaspers' own division of symbols in general into interpretable symbols and intuitive symbols. It is this latter sub-class that he calls ciphers, see 'Schaubare Symbolik als Chiffreschrift', *Ph III*, 147.

32*Ph III*, 145.   33*Ibid.*, 147.   34*Ibid.*   35*Ibid.*   36*Ibid.*, 141.

37This process is not at all rare in poetic activity where the poet, upon seeing a natural object, immediately descends into the metaphysical depths of that object. Consider the following line of R. M. Rilke from *Die Sonette an Orpheus:*

'Da stieg ein Baum. O reine Übersteigung!'

38*Ph III*, 147.   39*Ibid.*, 137–8.   40*Ibid.*, 148–9.   41*Ibid.*, 149.
42*Ibid.*   43*Ibid.*, 129.   44*Ibid.*, 130.   45*Ibid.*   46*Ibid.*, 138.

47*Ibid.*, 131. Compare this view with the familiar stanza from W. Blake's 'Auguries of Innocence':

To see the world in a grain of sand,
And heaven in a wild flower;
Hold infinity in the palm of your hand
And eternity in an hour.

48*Ph III*, 171.   49*Ibid.*, 180–81.   50*Ibid.*   51*Ibid.*, 182.   52*Ibid.*, 183.
53*Ibid.*   54*Karl Jaspers* . . . , 296.   55*Ph III*, 187.
56Alexander Pope, *An Essay on Man*.   57*Ph III*, 187.
58*Ibid.*, 131–2.   59*Ibid.*, 133.   60*Ibid.*, 132.   61*Ibid.*, 23.
62*Ibid.*, 26.

63Cf.: 'Quant à la relation de la langue mythique et de la langue spéculative, difficile à interpréter, elle commande peut-être toute la signification de l'oeuvre de Jaspers.' Xavier Tilliette, *Karl Jaspers* . . . , 163.

64*Ph III*, 26.   65*Ibid.*, 27.   66*Entmytholog*, 10.   67*Ibid.*, 19.
68*Ph III*, 134.   69*Ibid.*   70*Ibid.*, 135.   71*Ibid.*   72*Ibid.*
73*Ibid.*, 157.

74Cf. 'Wo im Denken der Mensch das eigentliche Sein erfasste, war das Sein dieses Denkens weder Sein an sich nor Subjektivität eines beliebigen und zufälligen Gedankens, aber . . . Gegenwart des darin denkenden und gedachten Seins.' *Ibid.*, 159.

75*Ibid.*   76*Karl Jaspers* . . . , 310.   77*Ph III*, 160.   78*Ibid.*, 159.
79*Ibid.*   80*Ibid.*, 161.   81*Karl Jaspers* . . . , 192.   82*Ph III*, 170.
83*Ibid.*, 171.   84*Ibid.*, 199.   85*Ibid.*, 200.   86*Ibid.*   87*Ibid.*, 201.
88*Ibid.*, 202.   89*Ibid.*, 201.   90*Ibid.*   91*VdW*, 310.   92*Ph III*, 203–4.
93*VdW*, 118.

[94]Cornelio Fabro, *God in Exile; Modern Atheism*, New York 1968, 896.
[95]*Ibid.*, 897.   [96]*Ibid.*, 905–6.
[97]Paul Ricoeur, 'The Relation of Jaspers' Philosophy to Religion', *Living Philosophers*, *op. cit.*, 639.

CHAPTER XI

[1]Cf. 'Wenn aber die Vernunft in den Vordergrund der Darstellung gestellt wird so kreist sie—statt um die Wirklichkeit—um die *Wahrheit* des Seins.' Ernst Mayer, 'Philosophie u. Philosophische logik', *Offener Horizont*, Munich 1952, 63.

[2]*VdW*, 39.   [3]*Ibid.*, 149.

[4]Thomas Räber, *Das Dasein in der 'Philosophie'* . . . , 110.   [5]*Ibid.*, 111.

[6]The reader is reminded that, since we are now in the context of the Enveloping, upper case letters will be used in the spelling of the modes. Thus, *Reason* designates reason in the full, enveloping sense. This applies even to quotations in which the word might originally be written in lower case letters. The word *reason*, on the other hand, designates understanding, a synonym for scientific reason in the non-encompassing sense.

[7]Ernst Mayer, *Offener Horizont*, 65.

[8]Xavier Tilliette, *Karl Jaspers*, 28.   [9]*VdW*, 47.   [10]*Ibid.*

[11]*Ibid.*, 125.   [12]*Ibid.*, 225.   [13]*VuEx*, 105.   [14]*Ibid.*, 105–6.

[15]*Ibid.*   [16]*Ibid.*   [17]*Ibid.*, 107.   [18]*VdW*, 228.   [19]*Ibid.*

[20]Cf. 'Wahrheit ist in allen Weisen der Seinsoffenbarkeit.' *Ibid.*, 226.

[21]Cf. 'Was nicht Wahrheit des Denkens ist, das will sie durch Denken als Wahrheit vergegenwärtigen und zum Organon des philosophischen Lebens werden lassen.' *Ibid.*

[22]*VuEx*, 107.   [23]*VdW*, 228.   [24]*Ibid.*   [25]*VuEx*, 107.   [26]*Ibid.*, 108.

[27]*Ibid.*   [28]*VdW*, 118.   [29]*Ibid.*   [30]*VuEx*, 109.   [31]*Ibid.*, 111.

[32]*Ibid.*   [33]*Ibid.*, 113.   [34]*Ibid.*   [35]*Ibid.*, 113–14.   [36]*Ibid.*

[37]*Ibid.*, 107.

[38]*Ibid.*, 110. Cf. also: 'Das Ziel und damit der Sinn eines philosophischen Gedankens ist statt des Wissens von einem Gegenstand die Veränderung des *Seinsbewusstseins* . . .' *Ibid.*, 68–9.

[39]*Ibid.*, 58–9; *VdW*, 119.   [40]*VuEx*, 58.   [41]*VdW*, 300.

[42]*Ibid.*, 301.   [43]*VuEx*, 123 ff.

[44]Cf. '*Wie ich mein Wissen weiss*, das ist von seinem Anfang her eine der Grundfragen des Philosophierens. Es ist das Selbstbewusstsein der Vernunft.' *VuEx*, 123.

[45]*Ibid.*, 125.

[46]James Collins, 'Karl Jaspers' Philosophical Logic,' *The New Scholasticism*, XXIII, (1959), 416.

[47]*VdW*, 4.   [48]*Ibid.*

[49]Cf. 'Es ist ein Transzendieren notwendig, vermöge dessen diese Umkehrung des natürlicherweise auf den Gegenstand gerichteten Wissens auf sich selbst erforlgt.' *Ibid.*, 10.

[50]*Ibid.*, 969.   [51]*Ibid.*, 10.   [52]*Ibid.*

CHAPTER XII

[1] *VuEx*, 60.   [2] *Ibid.*   [3] *Ibid.*   [4] *Ibid.*, 61.   [5] *Ibid.*

[6] Jean Paumen, *Raison et Existence chez Karl Jaspers*, 71.

[7] Cf. 'En quête du climat spécifique de la philosophie, Jaspers ne le trouve que, dans la complémentarité de la raison et de l'existence . . .' *Ibid.*, 35–6.

[8] Cf. 'Das Ineinandersein von Dasein, Bewusstsein überhaupt, Geist ist . . . ein Sichergänzen. . . . Das Umgreifende das eigentlich wir selbst sind— *Existenz* und *Vernunft*—, steht zueinander wie eine Polarität.' *VdW*, 131.

[9] *Ibid.*   [10] *Ibid.*, 48.

[11] Cf. '. . . l'Englobant est Origine, *Ursprung*. Ce qui veut dire que la quête de la raison a son centre hors de soi . . .' *Karl Jaspers*, 27.

[12] *Der Begriff des Daseins* . . . , 113.   [13] *VdW*, 131–2, italics mine.

[14] *WiderV*, 34.   [15] *Ibid.*

[16] Cf. 'Wenn sie /=Vernunft/ aus ihrem Wesen heraus den Maszstab des Allgemeingültigen aufstellt, scheint sie selbst diesen nicht absolut gelten lassen. Denn, um die Einheit von allen nicht zu verlieren, geht sie alsbald gerade auf das an diesem Maszstab Unbegründete zu, auf die durchbrechende Ausnahme . . .' *Ibid.*

[17] Cf. 'Im Zerbrechen jeder sich dadurch als vorläufig und unzureichend erweisenden Einheit will sie den metaphysischen Bruch, das Zerrissen des Seins selbst, der eigentlichen Einheit, verwehren.' *VdW*, 115.

[18] Cf. 'Vernunft ist Vernehmen, aber das uneingeschränkte von allem, was ist und sein kann. . . . Vernunft ist nicht das gleichgültige Geltenlassen von allem, das vorkommt, sondern das aufgeschlossene *Sichangehenlassen*. Sie erhellt nicht nur, um zu wissen, sondern sie bleibt das Fragen, das wie ein Werben ist. Vernunft wird niemals zum besitzenden Wissen. . . .' *Ibid.*

[19] *Ibid.*, 973.   [20] *Ibid.*, 115.   [21] *Ibid.*, 116.   [22] *Ibid.*, 117.

[23] *The Existentialist Revolt*, 198.   [24] *Ibid.*   [25] *Ibid.*   [26] *VdW*, 116.

[27] Cf. 'Wo der Mensch nach seinen höchsten Möglichkeiten greift, kann er am radikalsten sich betrügen. Er kann—mit blossem Verstand verabsolutierend oder negierend—die schon erklommenen Stufen hinabstürzen und weniger sein, als er im Anfang war.' *Ibid.*, 117.

[28] *Ibid.*   [29] *The Existentialist Revolt*, 199.   [30] *VuEx*, 136.

[31] *VdW*, 701.   [32] *WiderV*, 37.

[33] Cf. 'Die Wahrheit selbst ist die Offenbarkeit des uns entgegenkommenden Anderen. Wahrheit erwächst im Offenbarwerden. Wahrheit ist das Sein selbst in seinem Offenbargewordensein (das griechische Wort für Wahrheit,' ἀλήθεια, heisst wörtlich Unverborgenheit).' *VdW*, 458.

[34] Cf. 'Wahrheit gliedert sich durch die Weisen des Offenbarwerdens, und diese liegen begründet in den Seinsweisen, die offenbar werden können.' *Ibid.*

[35] Jaspers does not claim that there could not be more or fewer basic ways. He writes in this regard: 'I feel by no means certain to have found in my enumeration the definitive number that corresponds to the ground of Being, precisely because the derivation from a single principle is lacking.' 'Reply to My Critics', *Living Philosophers*, op. cit., 801.

[36] These designations are, of course, loose generalisations. My intention here is merely to show that it is Reason's task to recognise and to articulate the

various modes of truth. For special studies on the problem of truth in Jaspers, I recommend the following works: Ulrich Schmidhäuser, *Allgemeine Wahrheit und existentielle Wahrheit bei Karl Jaspers*, Bonn 1953; Xavier Tilliette, *Karl Jaspers, Théorie de la vérité*, Paris 1959; Franz Furger, *Struktureinheit der Wahrheit bei Karl Jaspers*, Salzburg 1960.

[37]*VdW*, 116.

[38]Cf. '"Dass es Eins doch bleibt, macht das Verschiedene wahr." Goethe spricht diese Grundgewissheit aus, dass die Wahrheit Eine sei, und dass alle besondere Wahrheit nur durch das Eine Wahrheit werde.' *Ibid*,. 654.

[39]*Karl Jaspers*, 148.   [40]*VdW*, 962.

CONCLUSIONS TO PART III

[1]'Karl Jaspers' Philosophical Logic', *The New Scholasticism*, XXIII (1949), 418.
[2]*Ibid*.
[3]Cf. 'Das Denken is nicht nur ruhige Kontemplation, sondern Bewegung in Zerfällung und Beziehung.' *VdW*, 235.
[4]*Ibid*., 125.   [5]*Ibid*., 969.

PART IV

GENERAL CONCLUSIONS

[1]*Ph I*, 240.
[2]*La philosophie de Martin Heidegger*, 4th ed., Louvain 1955, 300.
[3]*From Shakespeare to Existentialism*, Garden City, N.Y. 1960, 379.
[4]'Die Philosophie von Karl Jaspers in Japan', in Klaus Piper (ed.), *Karl Jaspers: Werk und Wirkung*, Munich 1963, 166.
[5]*Ibid*., 167.
[6]Cf. 'Si Karl Jaspers avait publié sa "Philosophie" quelques années plus tôt, il eût sans doute occupé la place qui appartient aujourd'hui sans partage à l'auteur de *Sein und Zeit*. Venant après le "coup d'État" de Heidegger, la tentative de Karl Jaspers a pu paraître timide. Aux yeux du "grand publique philosophique"—que l'on veuille bien nous passer cette expression—Karl Jaspers fait figure de disciple, ou au moins de "suiveur idéologique".' André Marc, S.J., 'L'existence humaine et la raison', *Revue néoscolastique de philosophie*, XXXIX (1936), 519.
[7]'Das Seinsdenken bei Karl Jaspers', *Wissenschaft und Weltbild*, X (1957), 54.
[8]Jaspers once projected his programme in the following way: 'Der Weg führt von den äussersten Horizonten und den durch sie erhellten Ursprüngen ("Von der Wahrheit") über die Vergegenwärtigung der methodisch möglichen Bewegungen ("Methodologie") und der Wissensformen ("Kategorienlehre") zur Mannigfaltigkeit des Wissensbestandes ("Wissenschaftslehre"). Am Anfang stehen die radikalen Erhellungen, am Ende sind die konkreten Probleme möglich.' *VdW*, 27.

⁹Cf. 'Das Wirkliche ist daher, was gegen jedes Gedachtwerden Widerstand leistet.' *ExP*, 59. 'Eine durchaus denkbare Wirklichkeit wäre keine Wirlichkeit mehr, sondern nur ein zum Möglichen *Hinzukommendes*, nicht ein Ursprung und damit der Ernst, sondern ein Abgeleitetes und Zweites.' *Ibid.*, 60.

¹⁰Cf. 'Wenn die Wirklichkeit zwar *als gedachte* vor uns *zurückweicht*, aber doch als das allumfassend *Tragende* gegenwärtig ist, und wenn ihre Gegenwart in dem liegt, was durch kein Denken in Möglichkeit verwandelt werden kann, so hat *der philosophische Gedanke* nicht den Sinn, diese *Undenkbarkeit* des Eigentlichen aufzuheben sondern *zu steigern*. Die Wucht des Wirklichen soll durch Denken, das scheitert, fühlbar werden.' *Ibid.*, 61.

¹¹Cf. 'Der Weg des Philosophierens zur Wirklichkeit hin war . . . ein *Denken mit Kategorien über diese Kategorien hinaus* . . . Das Transzendieren über diese Kategorien ist wie ein Beschwören der Wirklichkeit,' *Ibid.*, 67.

¹²Cf. 'Auch die *Wirklichkeit des Denkenden* selbst geht seinem Denken voran.' *Ibid.*, 60.

¹³'Reply to My Critics', *Living Philosophers, op. cit.*, 793.

¹⁴*Ibid.*   ¹⁵*Ibid.*, 794.   ¹⁶*Ibid.*, 795.

¹⁷Hans Mader, 'Das Seinsdenken bei Karl Jaspers', *Wissenschaft und Weltbild*, X (1957), 58.

¹⁸*VuEx*, 117.

¹⁹In other words, Jaspers' theory takes away the possibility of a *primum analogatum*, in reference to which the multiple relationships that converge upon it could be determined objectively. There is, for example, no *ousia* at the centre of his so-called analogy. Here is how Jaspers replies to one of his critics in this connection: 'Baumgarten asserts that my philosophy circles about a hidden, fixed centre. Yes, I hope so; but not around a formulated or formulatable thought . . . but around something which, as centre, is guidance.' *Living Philosophers, op. cit.*, 833.

²⁰*VdW*, 187–8.

²¹'Basic Concepts of Jaspers' Philosophy', *Living Philosophers, op. cit.*, 109.

²²*Ibid.*, 113.

²³*L'existence d'après Karl Jaspers*, Paris 1945, 100.

²⁴*Living Philosophers, op. cit.*, 113.

²⁵*Revue néoscolastique de philosophie*, XXXIX (1936), 522.

²⁶*VdW*, 736–7.   ²⁷*Ibid.*   ²⁸*Ibid.*, 226.

²⁹'Mythe et vérité', *Problèmes d'éspistemologie*, Louvain 1960, 415.

³⁰'Reply to My Critics', *Living Philosophers*, 798. Italics mine.

³¹*Objekt und Transzendenz bei Karl Jaspers*, Innsbruck 1957, 48.

³²Cf. 'Wir können die Jasperssche Interpretation der transzendentalen Logik nicht einfach mit einem Hinweis übergehen, sie sei zwar keine Wissenschaft im Sinne der empirischen Wissenschaften, wohl aber ein Wissen höheren Ranges. Alles das, was Jaspers vom Transzendieren . . . sagt, lässt keinen Zweifel darüber bestehen, dass es sich in diesem Falle um eine Infragestellung des intentionalen Denkens als solchen handelt. . . . Das Ungegenständliche steht hier im Gegensatz nicht nur zum weltimmanenten Gegenstand, sondern auch zum Gegenstand überhaupt.' *Ibid.*, 65.

³³*Ibid.*, 117.

³⁴Cf. 'Transzendiere ich . . . so, dass ich wieder zu irgendeinem Etwas

komme, wieder einen Gegenstand habe, so transzendiere ich falsch, sagt Jaspers wiederholt.' *Ibid.*, 64.

[35]Cf. 'Insofern sie sich als aufzeigbarer Inhalt auf den intentionalen Akt des meinenden Bewusstseins beziehen, liegen alle Gegenstande auf derselben Ebene.' *Ibid.*, 117.

[36]*VuEx*, 109.

[37]Cf. 'Es gibt gleichsam eine Atmosphäre der Vernunft. Sie verbreitet sich, wo ein alloffenes Auge die Wirklichkeit selbst, ihre Möglichkeit und ihre grenzenlose Deutbarkeit erblickt, wo dieses Auge nicht Richter wird und keine absolute Lehre ausspricht, sondern mit Redlichkeit und Gerechtigkeit eindringt in Alles, was ist, es zur Geltung kommen lässt, nich beschönigt und nicht verschleiert, und es nicht leicht macht durch Eindeutigkeit.' *ExP*, 53.

[38]Cf. 'Auf die Einheit des Einen gerichtet, will Vernunft allem, was ist, gleichsam zu seinem Recht verhelfen.' *WiderV*, 35.

[39]*VdW*, 991.   [40]*WiderV*, 9.